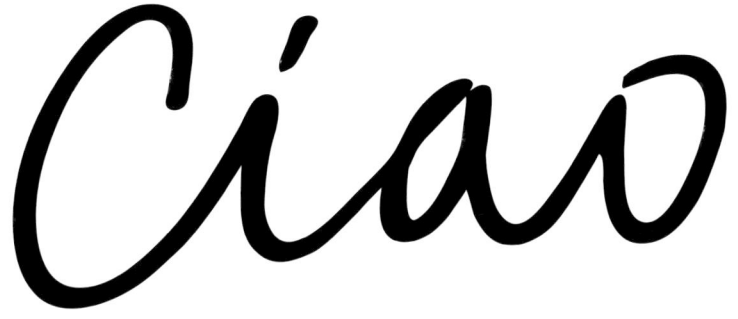

OMAGGIO ALL'ITALIA
MARIO TESTINO

TASCHEN

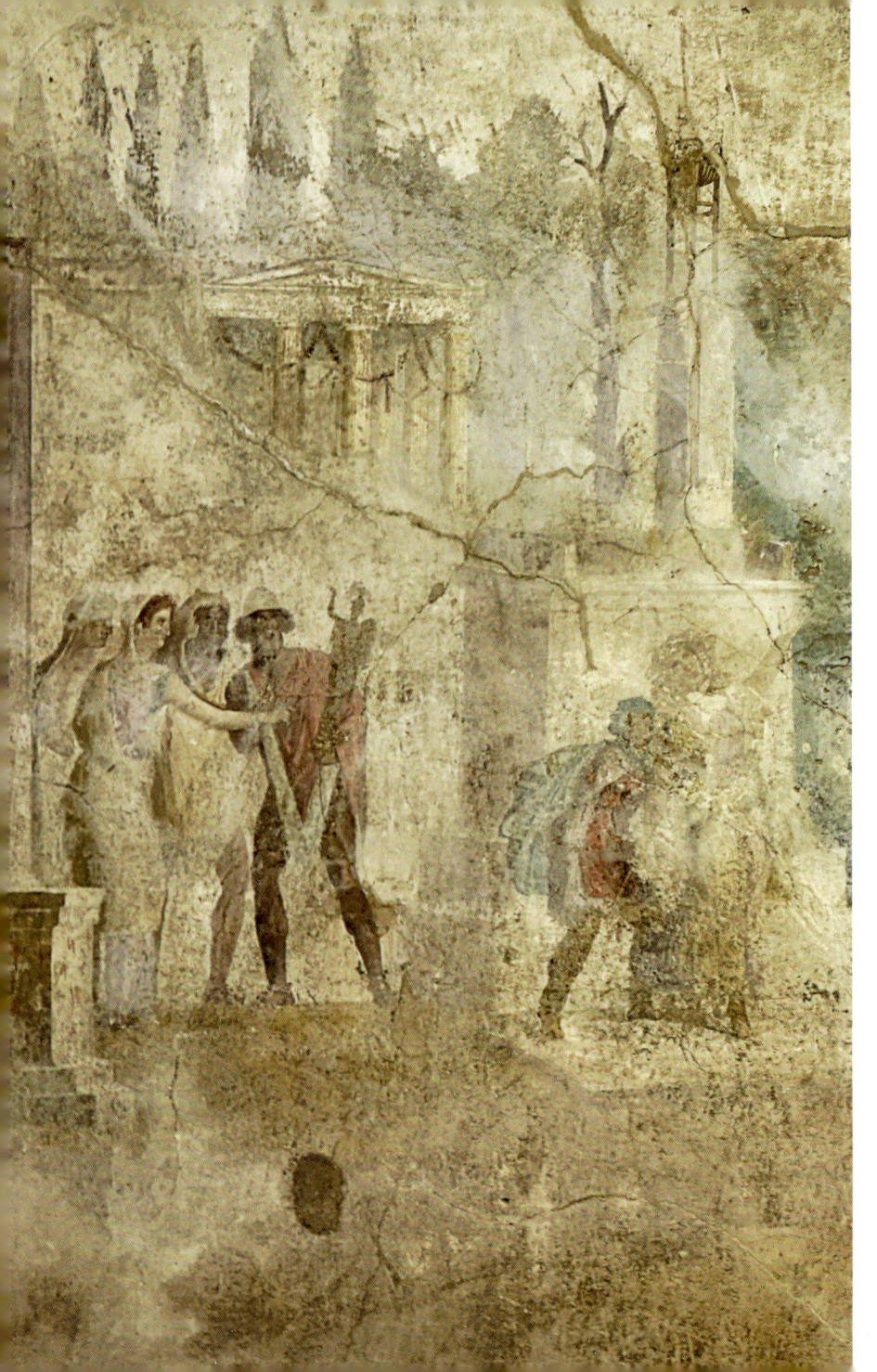

DISCOVERING ITALY
MARIO TESTINO

Even though I grew up in Peru, I always knew that my father's family was Italian. My grandfather, Michele, settled in Peru at the age of 18, following his childhood in Argentina where his family had first migrated to in 1885. It was a time when a lot of Italians were emigrating to Peru, a newfound land, to make their home, influencing Peruvian culture in the process with their inimitable style, their particular ways of seeing, their effortless Italian flair, and, of course, their cuisine. Sadly, I did not get to spend much time interacting with my grandfather, as he passed away when I was very young, but I have always held an indelible image in my mind of this strong, elegant man with a full head of white hair.

In 1976, I decided I wanted to move to London to study, although I had just started to learn Italian at the Instituto Italiano in Lima. My latest performance at university had not encouraged an immediate yes from my father to allow me to go. My typically generous dad always wanted the best for his children, however, so he eventually relented. For now, Italian lessons and Italy itself were put on hold while I began a life in London.

My first trip to Italy was to Rome and Florence, visiting friends from Lima who had moved there at more or less the same time I had moved to London.

Discovering Italy has been a powerful experience that has captured my imagination completely. I felt a profound connection with everything I saw around me. I loved the place and the people, the landscape and the architecture and how its artistic richness and beauty were such a casual, natural part of daily life. I was hooked. Following this first trip, I started visiting on weekends more and more frequently.

Ratto del Palladio (detail) – Courtesy of the Ministero per i Beni e le Attività Culturali – Museo Archeologico Nazionale di Napoli, 2018

Only after a year and a half of living in London did I realize I needed to update my look. I was still wearing the clothes I had brought with me from Peru, so, following advice from friends, I decided to go to Rome for a major change of image. Rome was all about the hottest, latest trends and fresh new styling, and I loved the way Italians could shed the latest look for an even newer thing without ever losing their own identity. Fashion was their playground.

During this period of my life, it was all about discovering the latest looks, then going out in them. A discotheque called Jackie O was the place of the moment in Rome. At that time, I had no idea I would make fashion the bedrock of my career. I had applied to a university in London to study communications, but they had only offered me a place for the following year. I decided to enroll in a photography course that a friend of mine happened to be doing, not because I had any idea of being a photographer, but just so my parents would be satisfied that I was doing something useful while living abroad, as otherwise they might call me home. But I think my growing and deep obsession with clothes was evidence of my emerging fascination with fashion, which in turn led to me to want to express my feelings about it in pictures. Rome was the perfect place for this instinct to emerge and develop into a passion, as it is one of the most consistently stimulating visual cities in the world. That passion then became a drive, and eventually the center of my world, and Rome was for years my most visited city. It was the place I longed for, missed, and went back to—not just for work, but for the comfort, education, and delight of my senses.

When I actually bought a camera and started taking my first fashion photographs, I decided to go to Milan to try and get some work. It was common knowledge in the fashion business that Milan was the best platform for photographers because the magazines and opportunities were many, and allowed photographers and their associated creatives (stylists, hair and makeup, editors and technicians) the most freedom.

Although I went back again and again trying to find my way into the business, aside from partying at the Plastic discotheque, I have to say I didn't get much work. So, to try another strategy, I started taking test shots in London for my portfolio using clothes and accessories designed and made by young, talented Italian designers that I had discovered. The process honed my eye and my craft, but it wasn't until a couple of lean years later that my luck changed when I met Italian magazine editor Franca Sozzani in New York. Ironically, she had just arrived from Milan. It was a life-changing encounter. After she saw my portfolio she immediately asked me to start working for her magazines, which at the time were two influential Italian Condé Nast magazines that were for a

Hierogamia (detail) – Courtesy of the Ministero per i Beni e
le Attività Culturali – Museo Archeologico Nazionale di Napoli, 2018

6

younger audience than *Vogue*: a sort of *Teen Vogue* and a young men's *Vogue* called *Lei* (Her) and *Per Lui* (For Him). Her sister Carla ran literally six other magazines for Condé Nast Italy including *Vogue Sposa* (Vogue Bride) and *Vogue Bambini*, for children's fashion. They were the most incredibly good-looking powerhouse sisters in publishing, with immense visual and business acumen, and originality of vision and taste. I had started on my journey. And it seems no coincidence that two beautiful Italian sisters with amazing waist-length hair were the ones who turned the key in the door and let me in.

I fully embraced discovering fashion as a working photographer in Italy through Franca. She taught me so much, not only about fashion and fashion in photographs, but about the business side of things too. She made her magazines incredible and highly admired in the business not because of high budgets (they were extremely low) but thanks to her wonderful imagination, creativity, human skills, love of life, and an eye for everything interesting, beautiful, and special.

I started working with Franca's editor, Sciascia Gambaccini, who became my collaborator and, by default, my Italian teacher. Finally, through her patience and persistence, I started to learn the language. My school was the endless phone calls I made to Sciascia and Franca in the days before

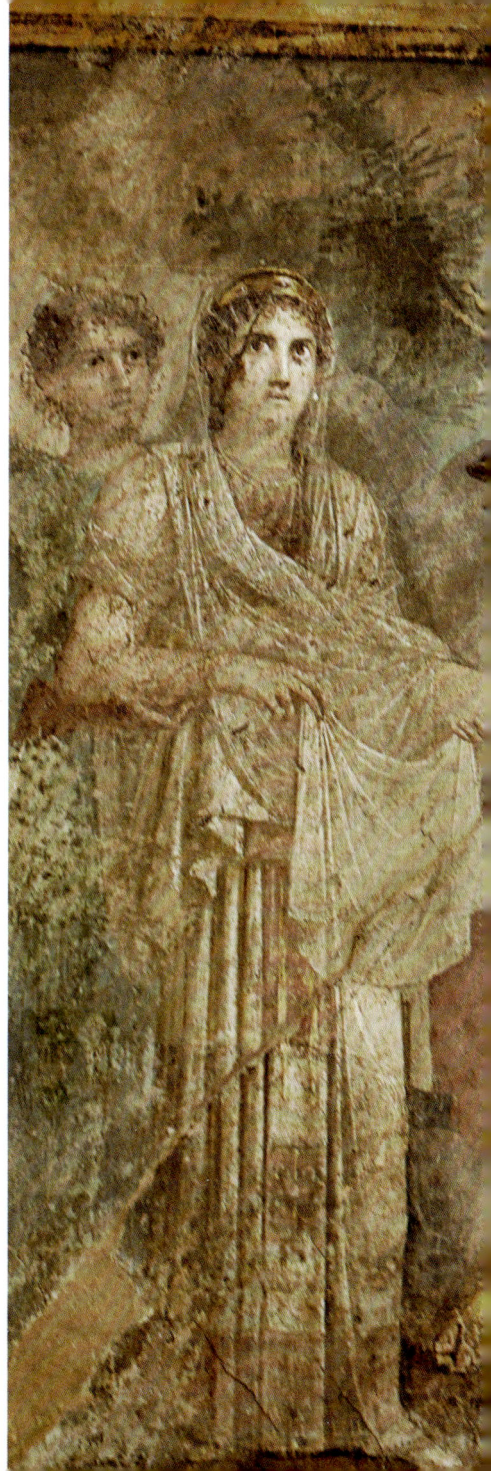

we used mobiles for international calls. She introduced me to Milanese society and opened doors to beautiful people and places, and also to a sense of who I could be. Sciascia was unstoppable, steely, but charming and kind at the same time.

In Italy it's fine to care about colors and shadows, an old painting, or a new one. To care about flavors and qualities. To notice and be moved by how things look. It is the country of education through the senses. Meeting Sciascia's friend Alessandro Belgiojoso, I learned about the idea of correct behavior among Italians, especially elegant ones. I quickly deduced that the young Milanese generation of men I was meeting expressed a new sense of style that was a reflection of my own spirit and ideas, and so I started photographing them for *Per Lui*. For me casting is a crucial part of being a fashion photographer, as the models I choose to work with communicate what I want to say in a poetic, subtle, but direct way, as much if not more than via what they are wearing and how you photograph them wearing it. At the time, I was looking for models to represent my new ideas and aesthetic, and the Italians were the answer: independent, unusual, masculine, and unpredictable.

When I actually started getting work in other parts of the fashion world, the Italians were the first important clients who came back to me for more, and among the first to establish consistent working relationships season after season. Early on, Franca had introduced me to Valentino Garavani and Giancarlo Giammetti and they asked me to photograph his young line. After that I started doing more with Italian designers. Photographing Gucci in the '90s under Tom Ford as designer was a key period and, following him, the Versaces.

I came to the Versaces primarily through Madonna, who had specifically proposed me as photographer for their couture campaign starring her. I could not believe it when I saw how Gianni had chosen to caption it: "VERSACE presents MADONNA photographed by TESTINO." No one had done that for me before. Seeing my surname given equal billing alongside his and hers was an extraordinary moment.

Influenced by Versace's catwalk shows, I started looking toward southern Italy for inspiration. My first visit to Naples came when the artist Philip-Lorca diCorcia told me he was spending a year there and that I should visit and photograph. I loved it at first sight. Soon after arriving, I was fortunate to meet Generoso di Meo and the Raucci/Santamaria gallerists; they all introduced me to contrasting and differing aspects of Naples. It's a fascinating place: elegant and rough, underground and conspicuous, calm and wild, eccentrically sophisticated and utterly everyday, a holiday destination and an art center, ancient and modern, collapsing and regenerating, always in flux. I quickly became obsessed with Naples and started going as often as I possibly could. It was in Naples that I had the first exhibition of my photographs in a gallery space with my prints framed on walls instead of published in a magazine, at the gallery of Raucci/

Santamaria. I shot the 2001 Pirelli calendar there and did more editorials than I can count. I discovered the joy of the Italian coast and the sea by going to Capri and then sailing boats along its coasts all the way to Sicily. The Aeolian Islands became a magnetic destination each August, and I realized that Italian cuisine enhanced by sun and sea gave the incredible food of Peru, which I missed so much in London, a run for its money.

Dolce & Gabbana were responsible for commissioning my first television commercial and Capri was the location, so it became an annual destination as we continued to make films and stills for their ongoing Light Blue fragrance campaign. Working with movement in film changed my perception of photography's possibilities. Time and especially sound became key elements and together they allowed influential new dimensions to flourish. My experiences on this campaign really sealed my love of Italy, and I saw the country as a destination that was unmatched by any other.

I started collecting art in the mid-'90s and began attending the Venice Biennale, which showed me yet another completely different aspect of Italy. In this amazing city, probably the most concentrated collection of the greatest art and architecture of the most consistent quality in the world, the art-appreciating world comes together to immerse themselves in Venice's legendary beauty and to pay attention to contemporary art. It is a fabulous sensation—and often a revelation—to be a part of the dialogue between this ancient house of treasures and the totally unexpected new forms of artistic expression that make their appearance at the Biennale.

Slowly but surely, Italy has taken over much of my life and much of my heart. Throughout these years, I have been exceptionally blessed to have had remarkable Italian friends who have generously unlocked for me some of the innumerable secrets this country holds. To those I have mentioned above I must add Victoria Fernández, Riccardo Lanza, Emanuele Mascioni, and Antonio Monfreda, who have guided me to the right place or person at the right time and unlocked the mysteries, unexpected treasures, and unforgettable experiences that have lined the winding road of my Italian odyssey.

Ciao, Italia!

ITALY
ALAIN ELKANN

Through his images, Mario Testino has expressed "his" Italy across the years. Italy and its people, Italy and fashion, cinema, monuments and sea. It is fascinating just how many artists, writers, and filmmakers have been determined to travel through Italy. Some have expressed "their" Italy by writing memorable pages, such as Goethe, President De Brosses, Stendhal, Paul Morand, Henry James, John Ruskin, and Marcel Proust. Others—including Turner, Claude Lorrain, Nicolas Poussin, De Chirico and Mantegna—have felt the need to paint it. There is an Italy narrated by the neorealist cinema of De Sica and Rossellini, and another Italy in the films of Fellini and Antonioni…

If I had to talk about Italy, my Italy, I wouldn't know where to start…or where to finish. If for example I was in Bologna, after visiting the Archiginnasio, the Morandi Museum and the Basilica of Santo Stefano, I could travel to Ferrara to see the Palazzo dei Diamanti, then go up from Rovigo to Padua, visit the Scrovegni Chapel and continue on to Venice and Trieste. I could stop in Vicenza to admire Palladio's masterpieces or in Verona to visit the Basilica of San Zeno, I could go to see Palazzo Te in Mantua or the Palatine Library in Parma, perhaps stopping at the Colorno Palace. If instead, again starting from Bologna, I decided to drive south along the Adriatic coast, I could stop in Ravenna to ponder its mosaics or the tomb of Dante and then in Cesena to visit the Malatesta Library. I could go to Rimini to admire the Malatesta Temple, Alberti's masterpiece, and then continue to Urbino, then Puglia, to Andria to see Castel del Monte…and continue like this, more or less to infinity, or at least to Gallipoli or Otranto. But, if I'd done that, I'd have missed Umbria, Tuscany, Rome, Naples, Amalfi, the Amalfi Coast. I'd have missed the

OPPOSITE *Hierogamia* (detail)
PAGES 12–13 *Piritoo* (detail) – Courtesy of the Ministero per i Beni e le Attività Culturali – Museo Archeologico Nazionale di Napoli, 2018

islands, Sicily, Sardinia, the Aeolian Islands and Ponza. And how could I see the South without its volcanoes? Vesuvius, Stromboli, Etna? Or the ruins of Paestum, Herculaneum, Pompeii, and in Sicily the ruins of Piazza Armerina, Syracuse, Agrigento, and Selinunte? And Rome? The Etruscan, Roman, Gothic, Renaissance, Baroque, Neoclassical, Umbertine, and Fascist city. And Milan, with Leonardo, *The Last Supper*, the Pinacoteca Ambrosiana, Brera, Michelangelo's Rondanini Pietà, Fontana, Manzoni ... And Turin, with its Shroud and the Savoy royal palaces. And then the sea, Liguria, the Gulf of Tigullio, Genoa—which the French historian Braudel called the most beautiful city in the Mediterranean with its historic buildings in Via Garibaldi—and again the Cinque Terre with the Gulf of Poets, where Shelley died and so many poets were inspired. Then again we have La

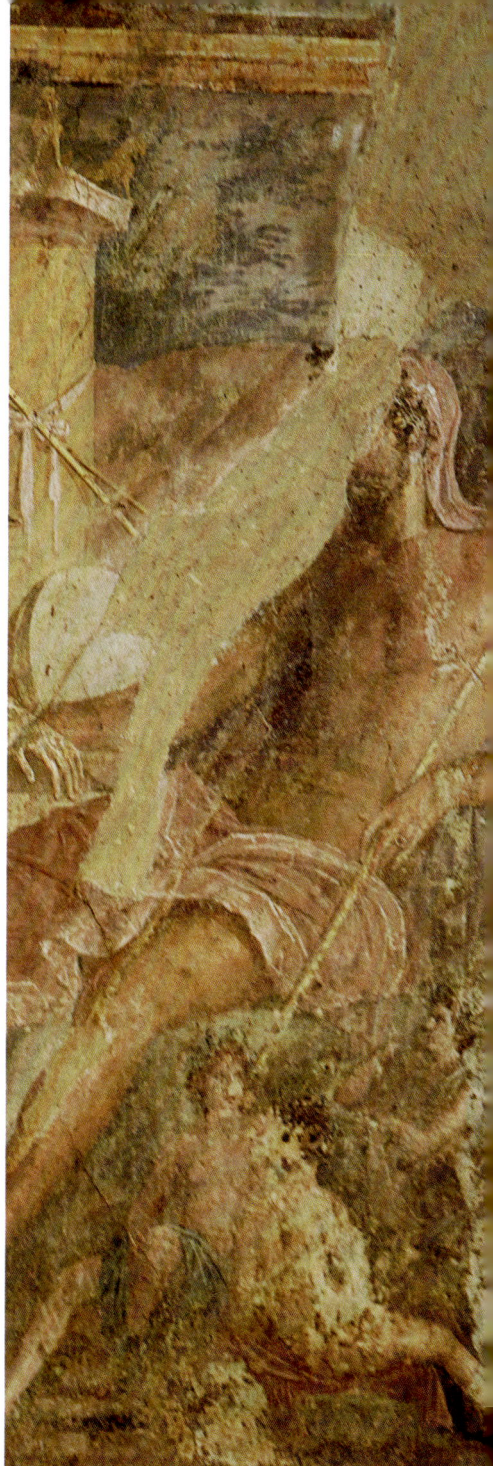

Versilia, Pisa—the Lungarno and the Tower—southwards to the Argentario promontory and on to Naples. Greek Naples, Baroque Naples, Archaeological Naples with its Gulf and islands: Capri, Ischia, Procida. Every city has its own musical dialect, its own language. Each main city is a capital, complete with royal palace, cathedral, and opera house. As I said before, the journey to every Italy is endless ... and can be done by train, car, boat, bicycle, or plane.

And what about the Italians? So alike and so different. From north to south, from east to west, how many types of different pasta, different sauces, different wines, from Friuli to Etna, from Tuscany to Piedmont! Who are the Italians? It's not easy to say, or to know. Superficial and profound, ancient and young. They're quarrelsome and polemical. The majority are Roman Catholics, politically they've been monarchists, fascists, socialists, Christian Democrats, communists, Five Star Movement followers or supporters of the League. They speak one language in many accents, as well as many different dialects. The cliché says they're good at improvising and bad at teamwork. What unites them and also sets them against each other? Soccer teams, of course. Italians have been arguing with each other since long before Dante was born, but usually their quarrels end in nothing. There are many issues with delinquency, the mafia, the camorra, and the 'ndrangheta. And it's true: some

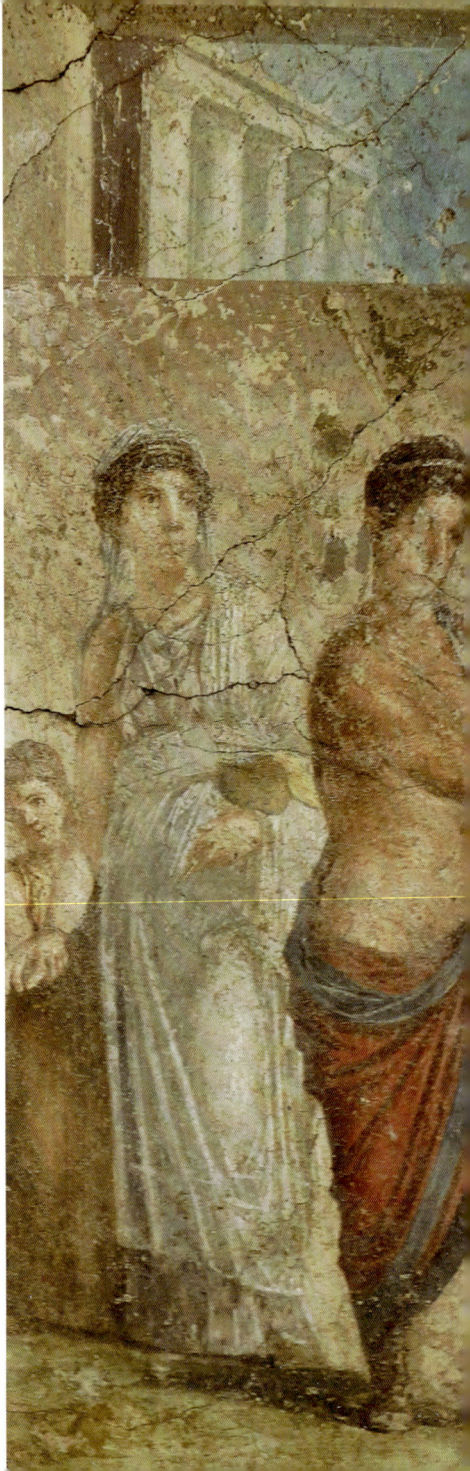

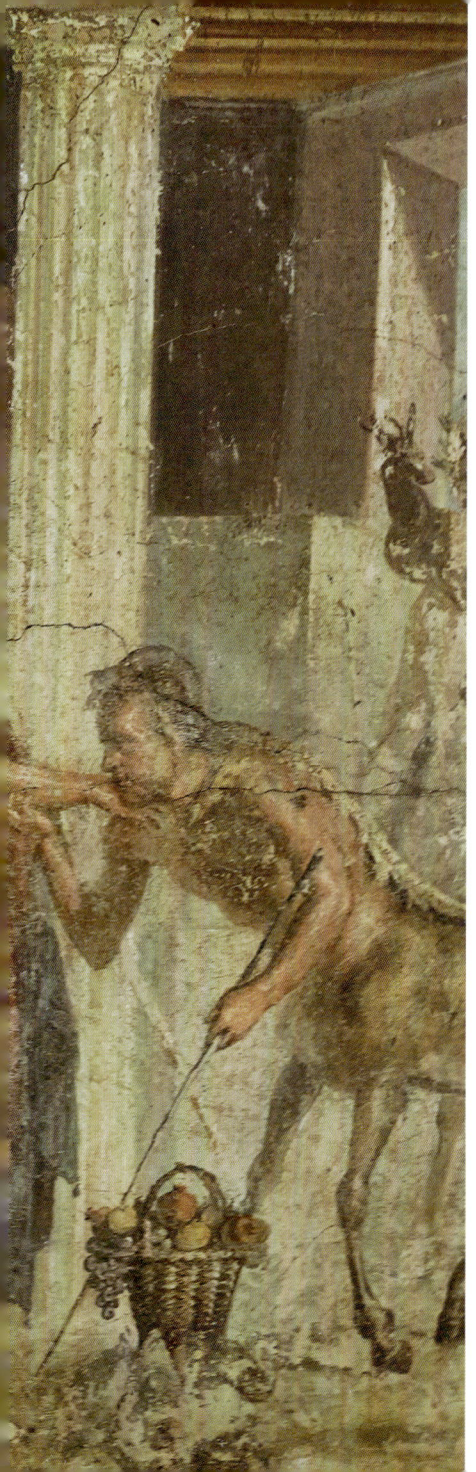

regions of the south – and not only the south – are under blackmail by the underworld, despite law enforcement bodies and the judiciary doing their best to fight against this.

So what is Italy? A fascinating country with a thousand contradictions. A country loved the world over and looked on as the land of beauty. Despite which Italians love to complain: they're convinced that everything is better abroad, but in the end they feel good only in Italy. Yes indeed, because in the midst of so many dramas and so many unresolved problems, Italy also maintains a special lightness, a generosity, a simplicity in facing life, which is a rare and precious gift in today's world.

And then there is the family, always a central nucleus of the community. Families come first and help to cushion the discomforts of life. Families mean solidarity, love, little things, and a degree of humility. They mean common sense, deep roots, and solidity.

OUT
AND
ABOUT

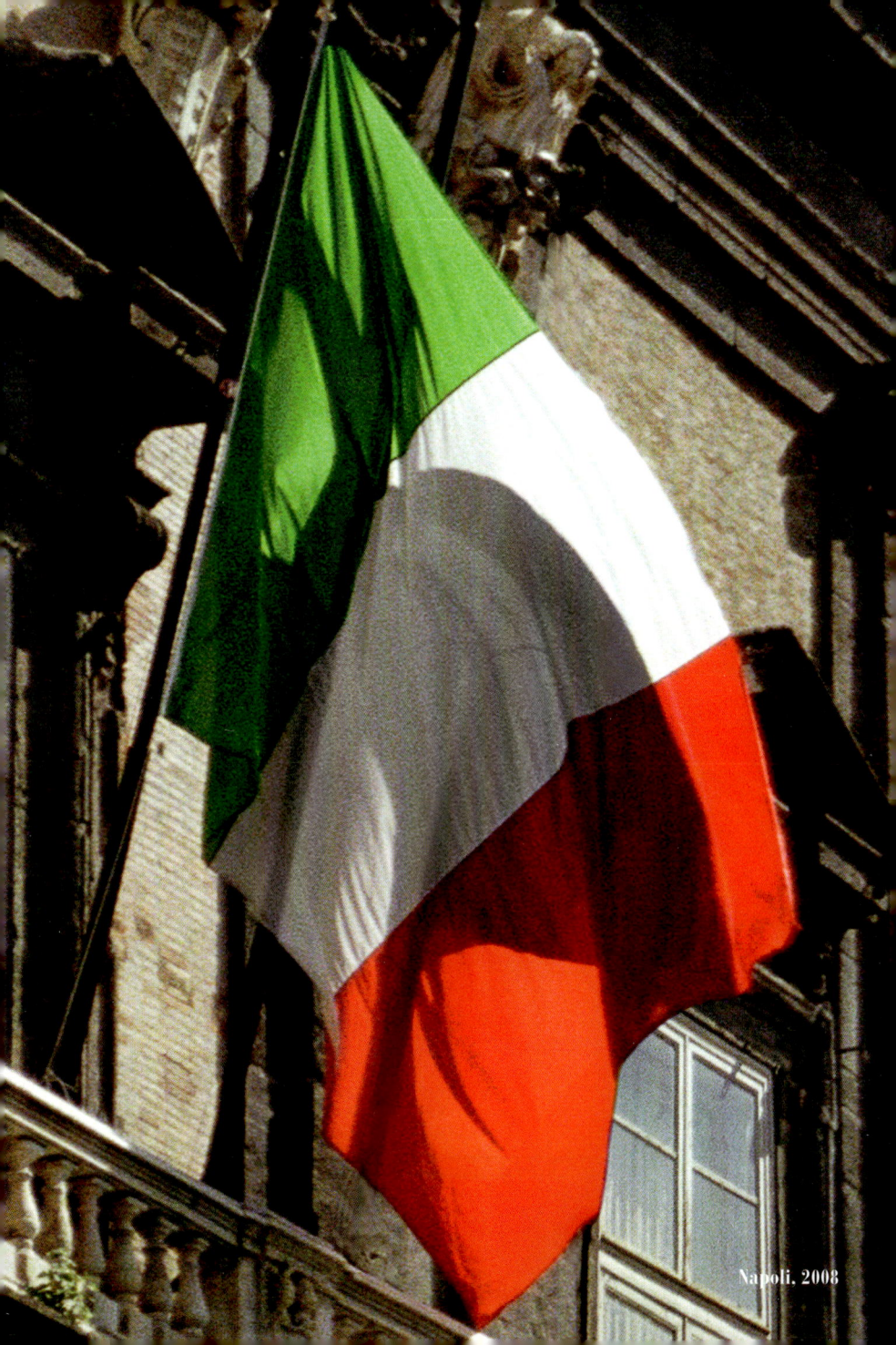

Napoli. 2008

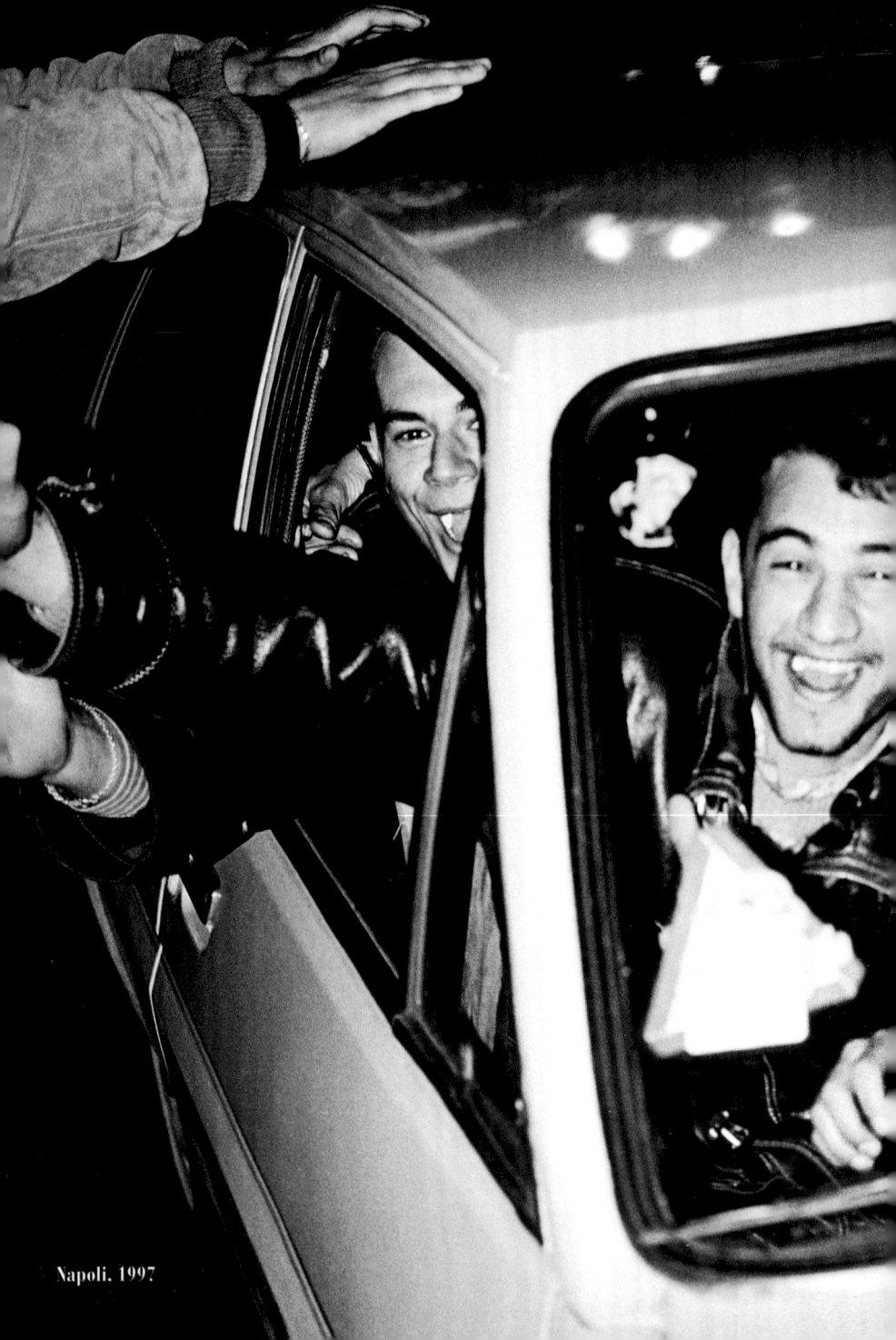

Napoli, 1997

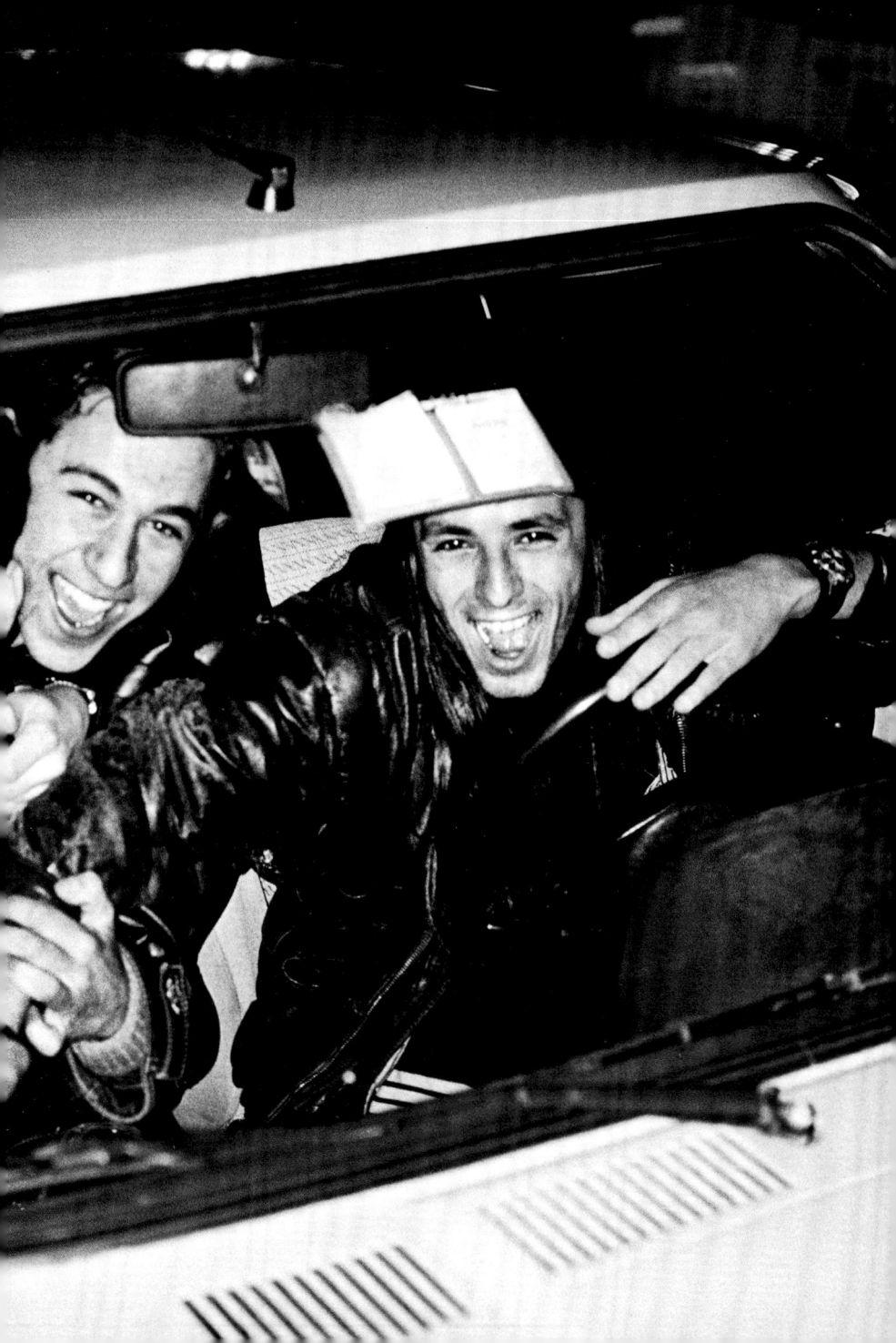

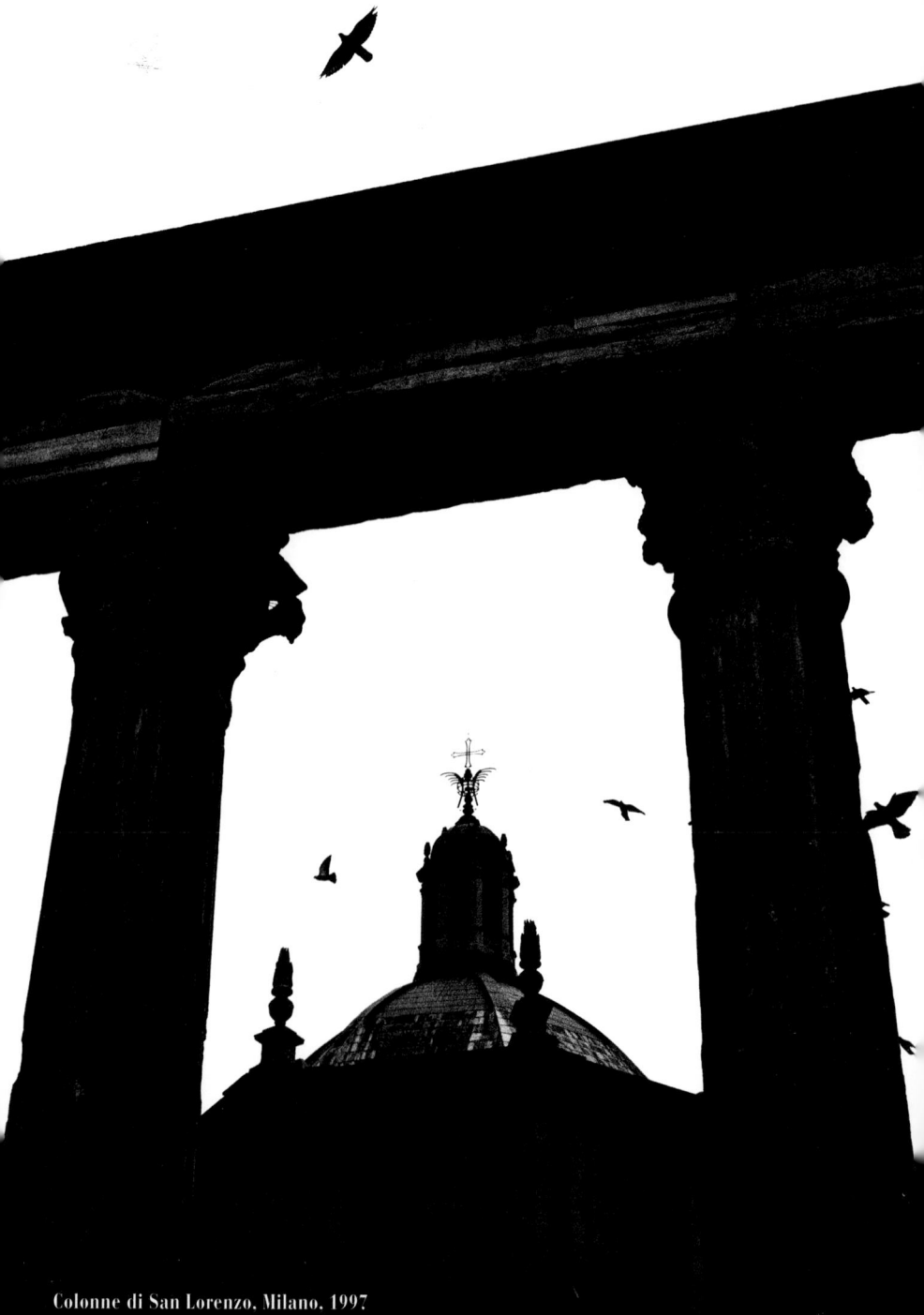

Colonne di San Lorenzo, Milano, 1997

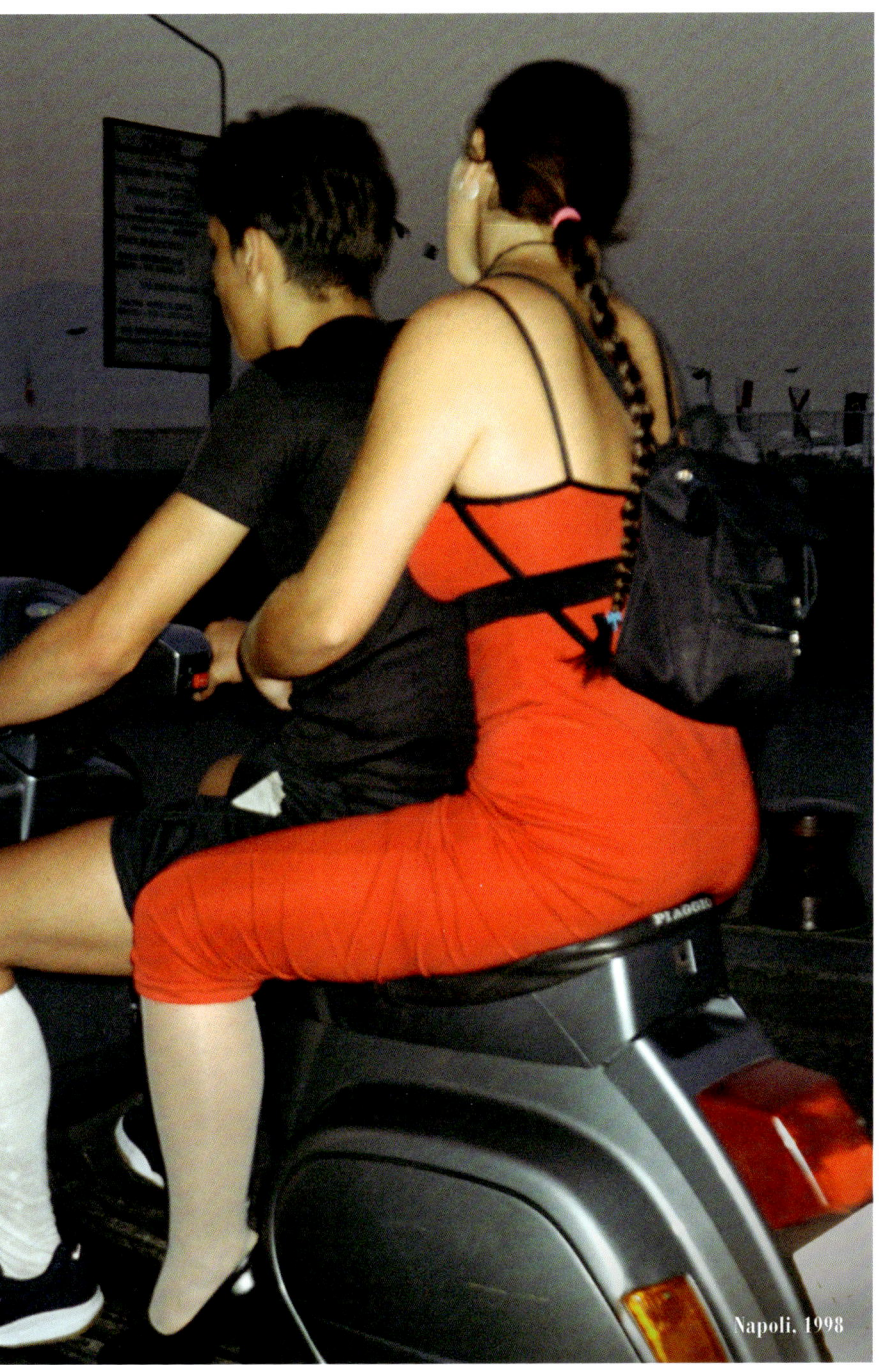

Napoli, 1998

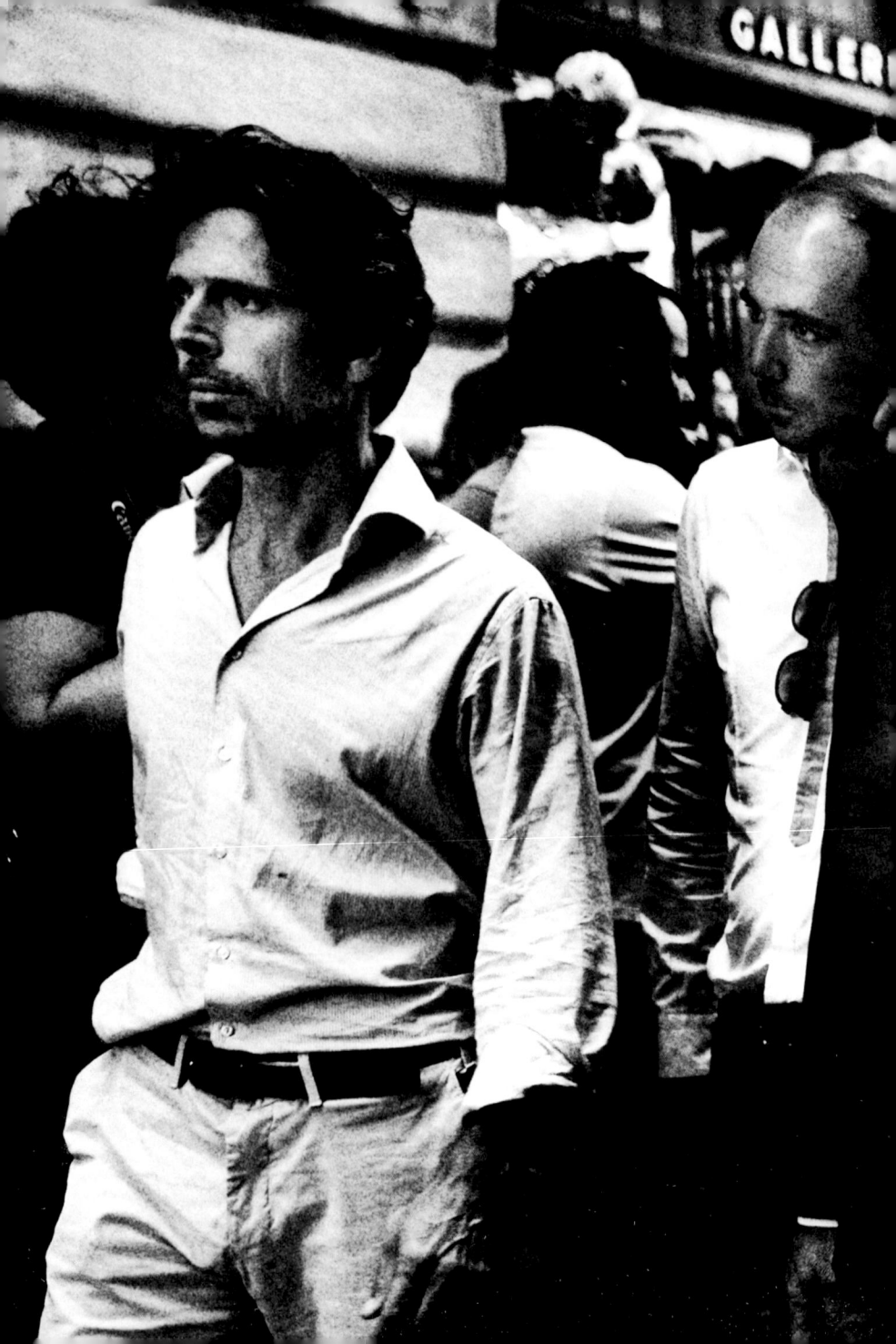

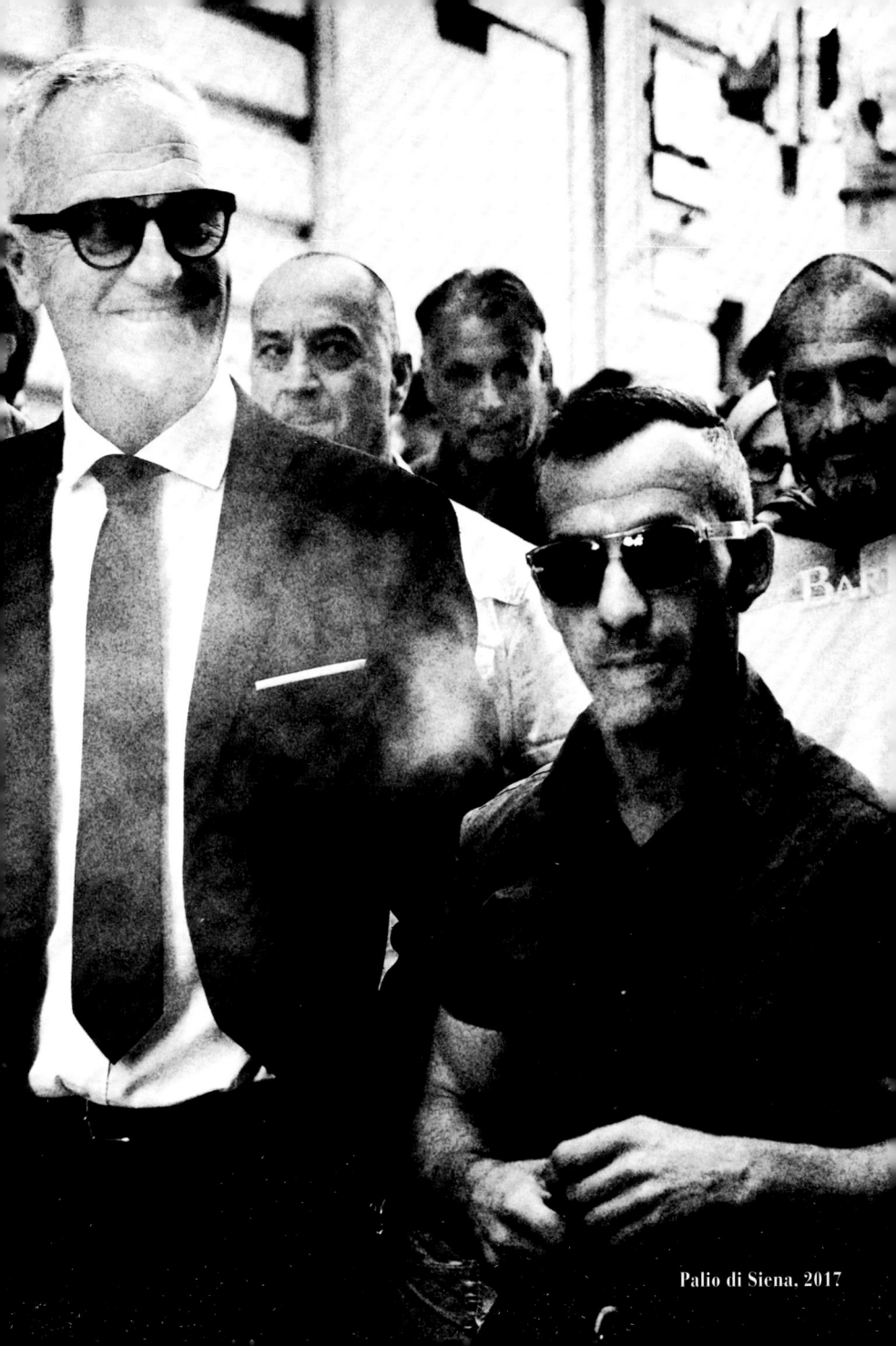

Palio di Siena, 2017

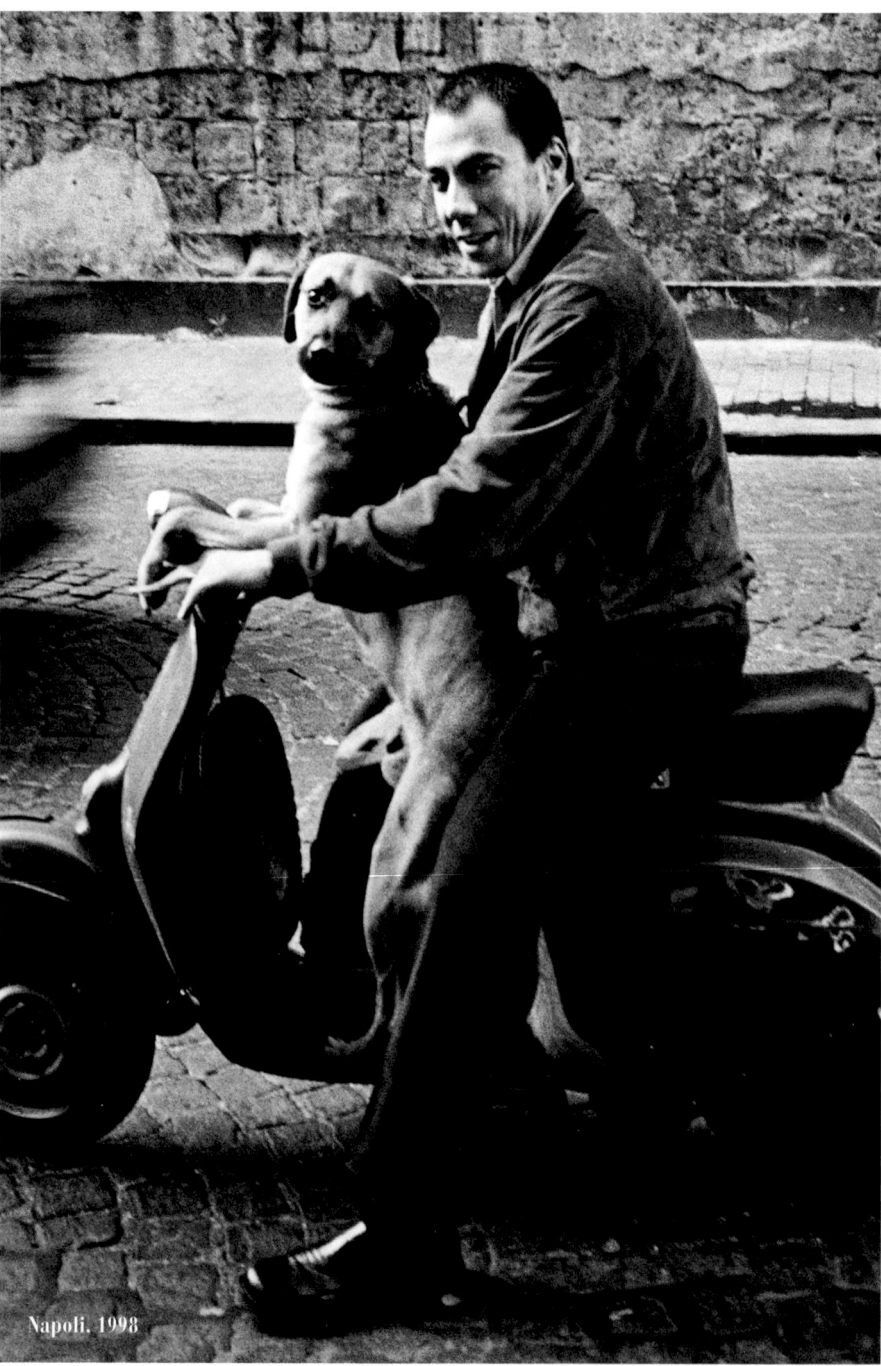

Napoli, 1998

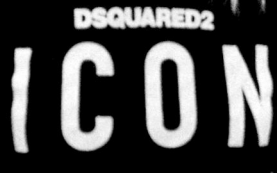

Via del Babuino, Roma, 2018

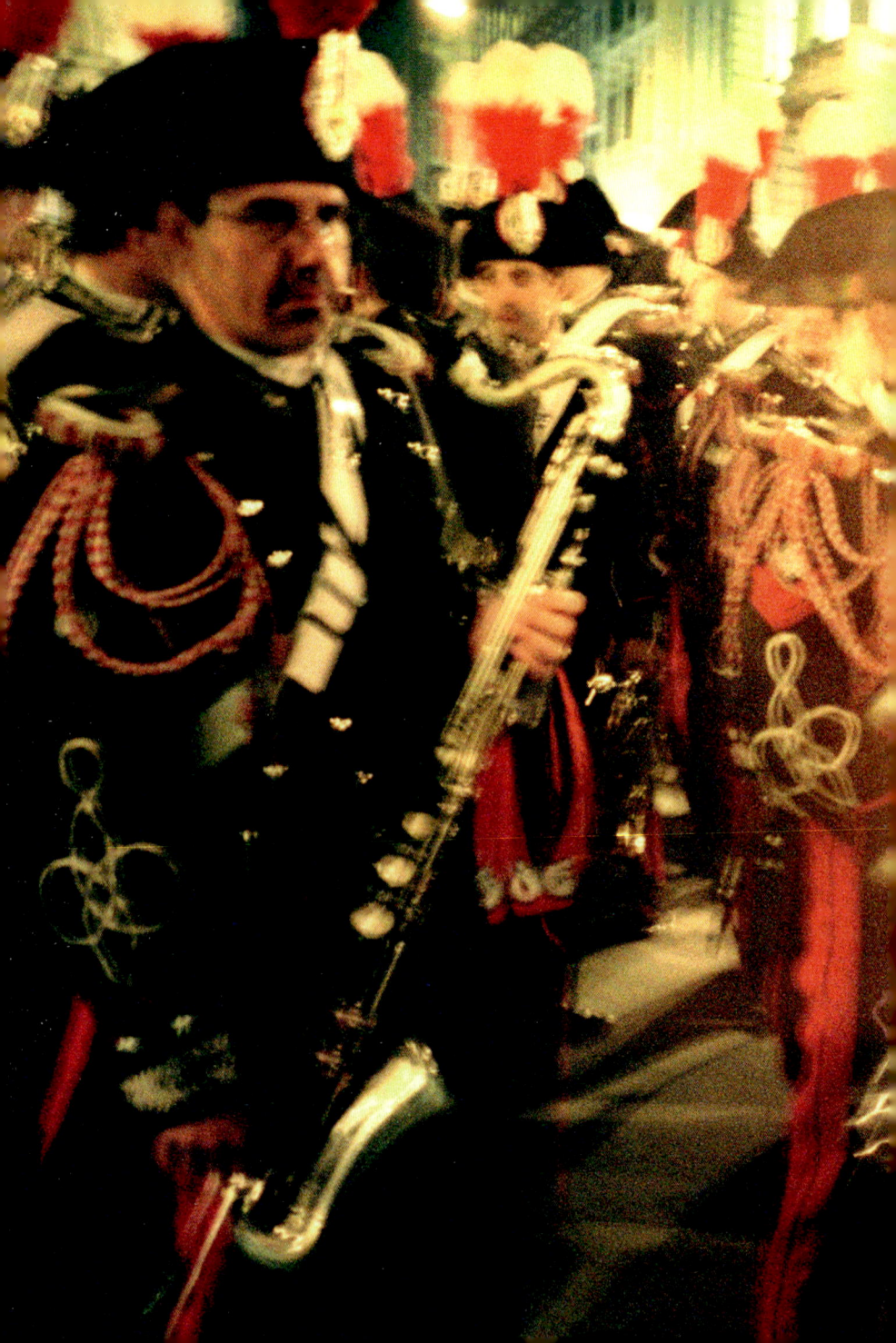

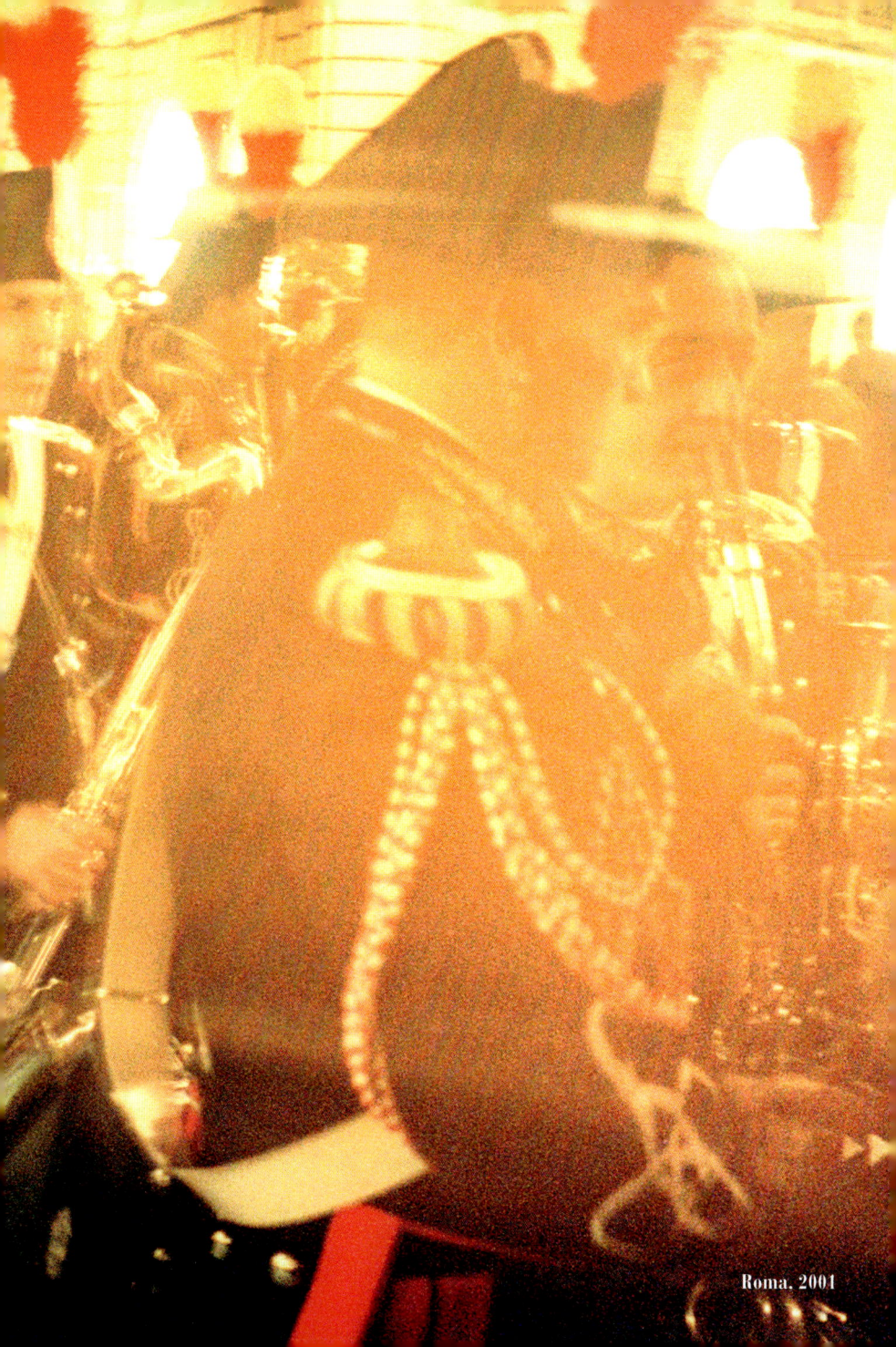

Roma, 2001

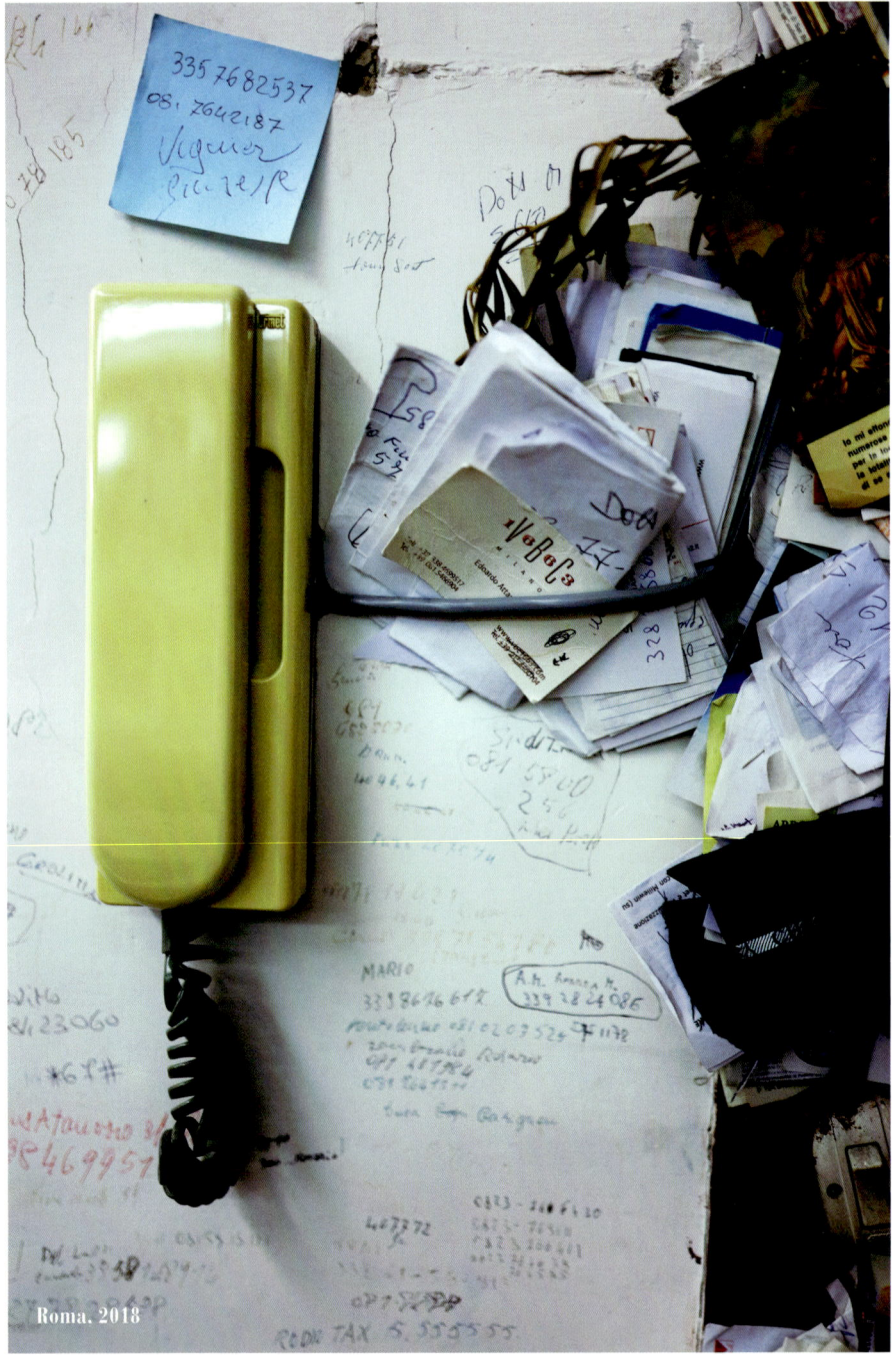

Roma, 2018

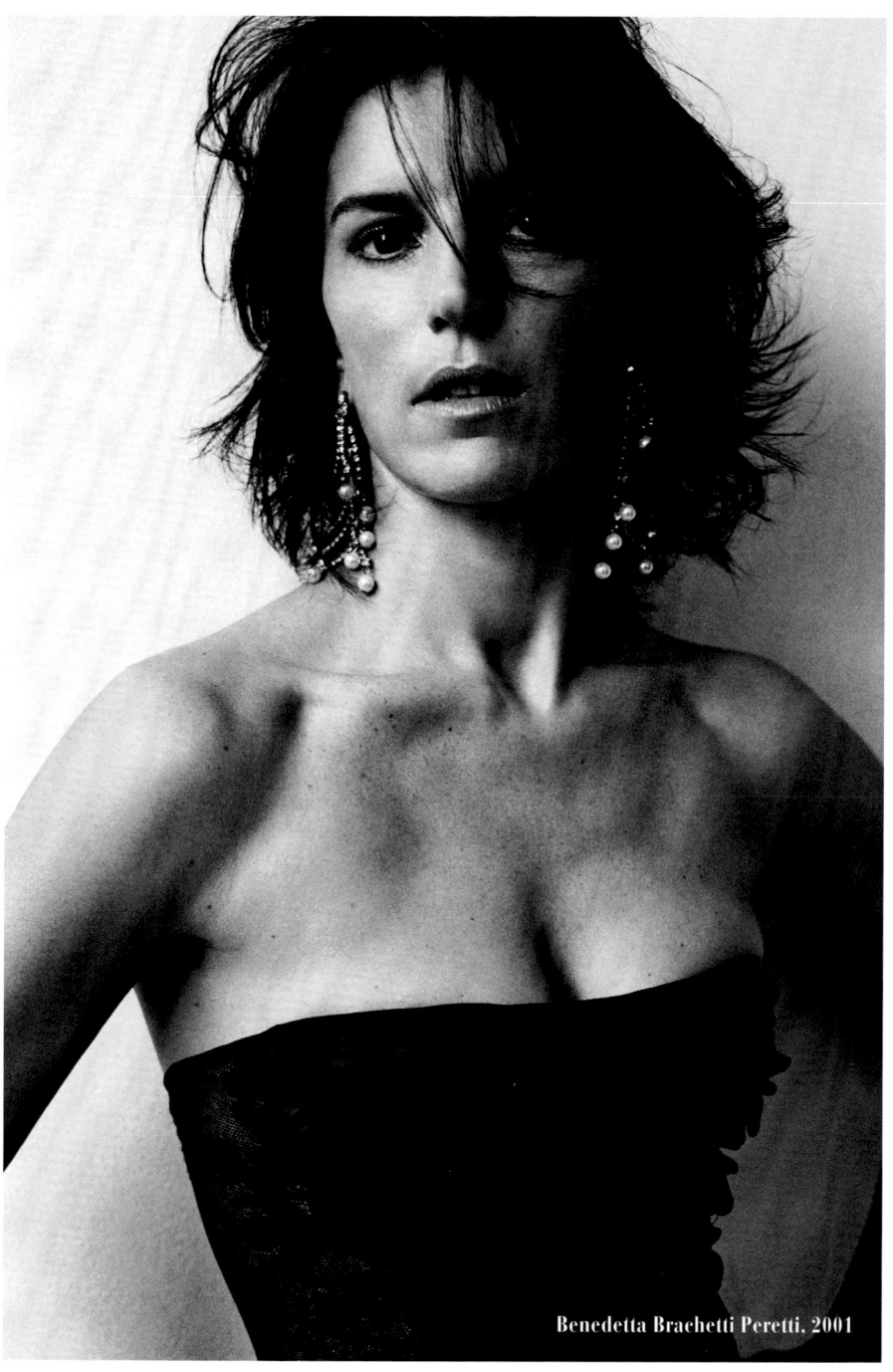

Benedetta Brachetti Peretti, 2001

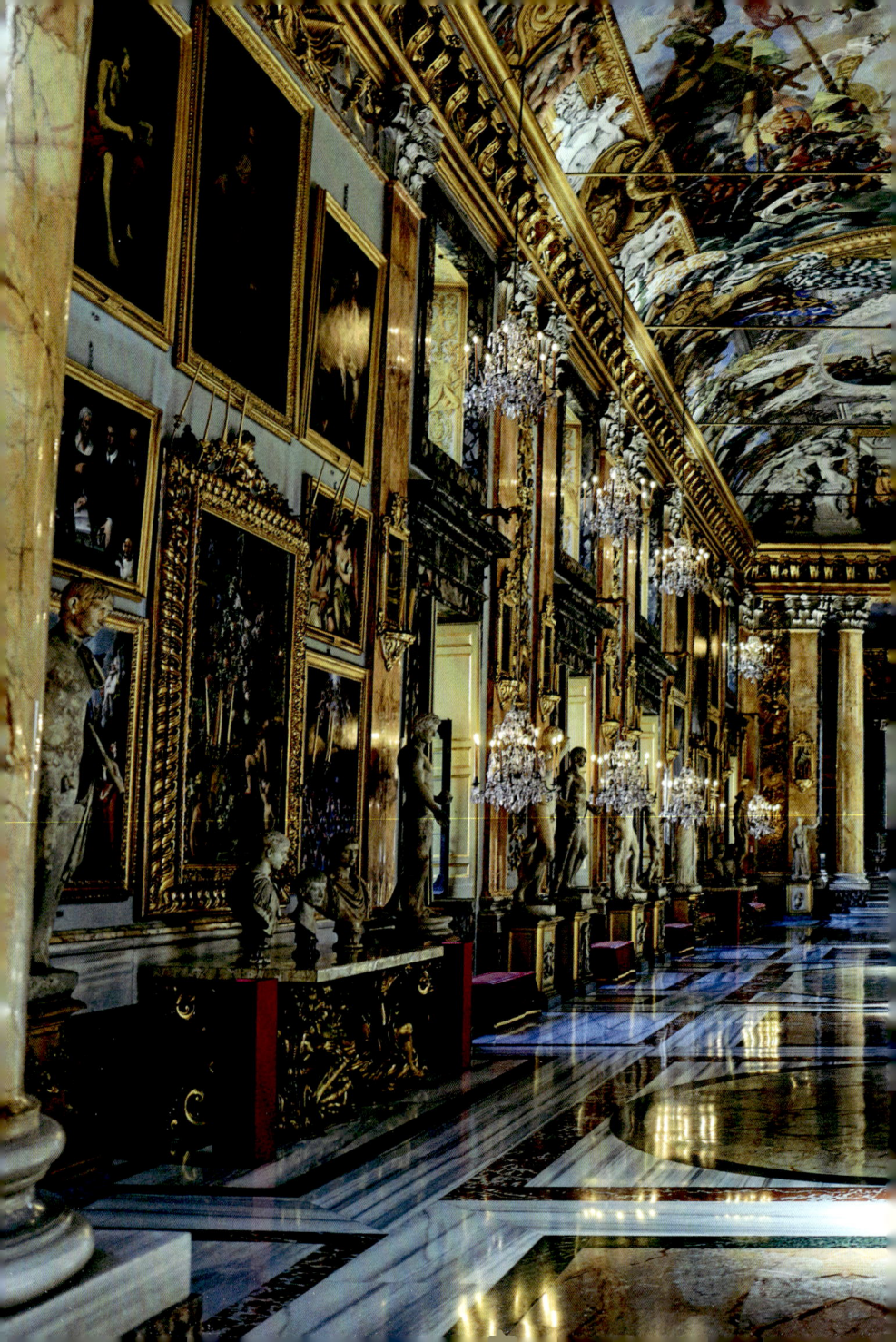

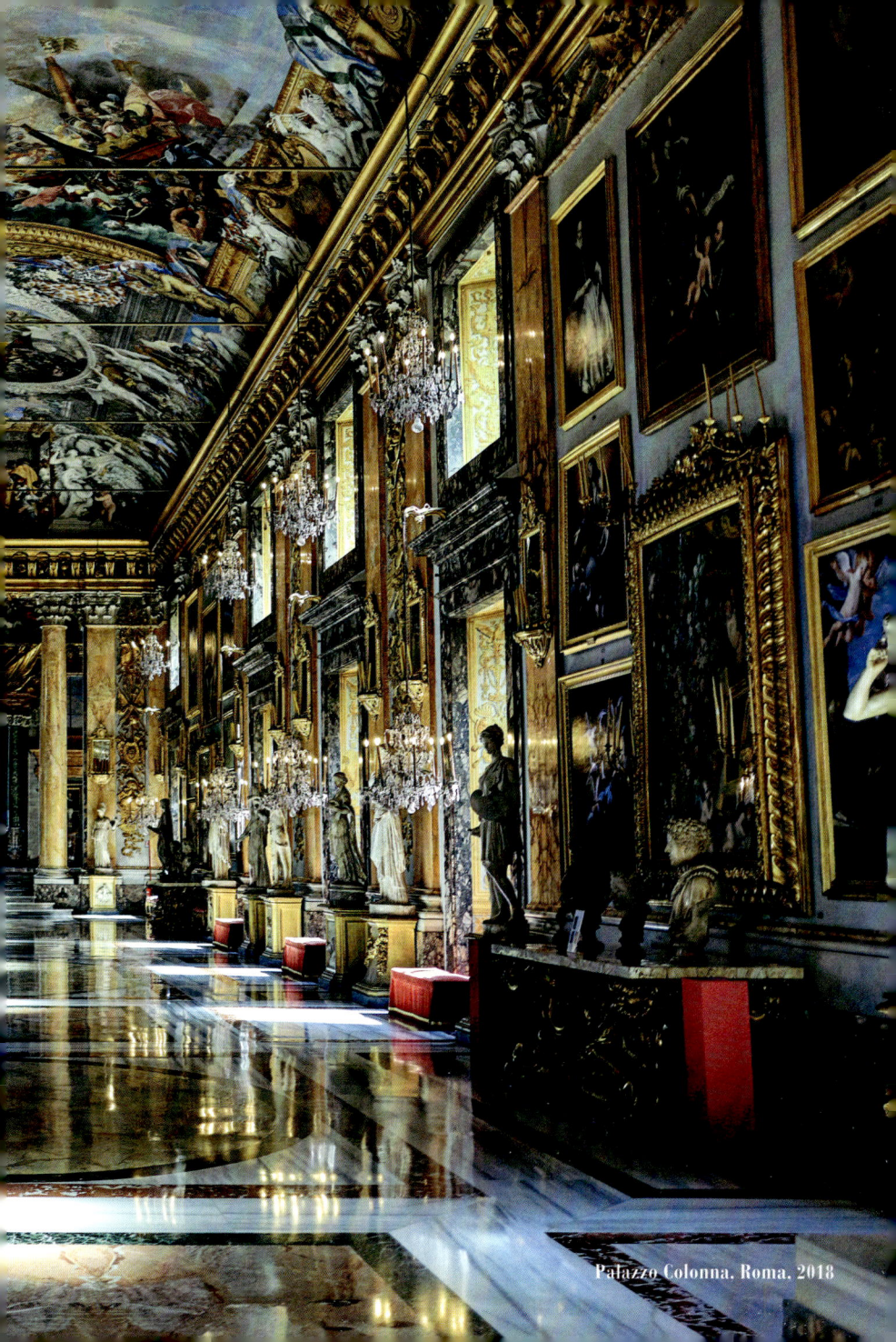

Palazzo Colonna, Roma, 2018

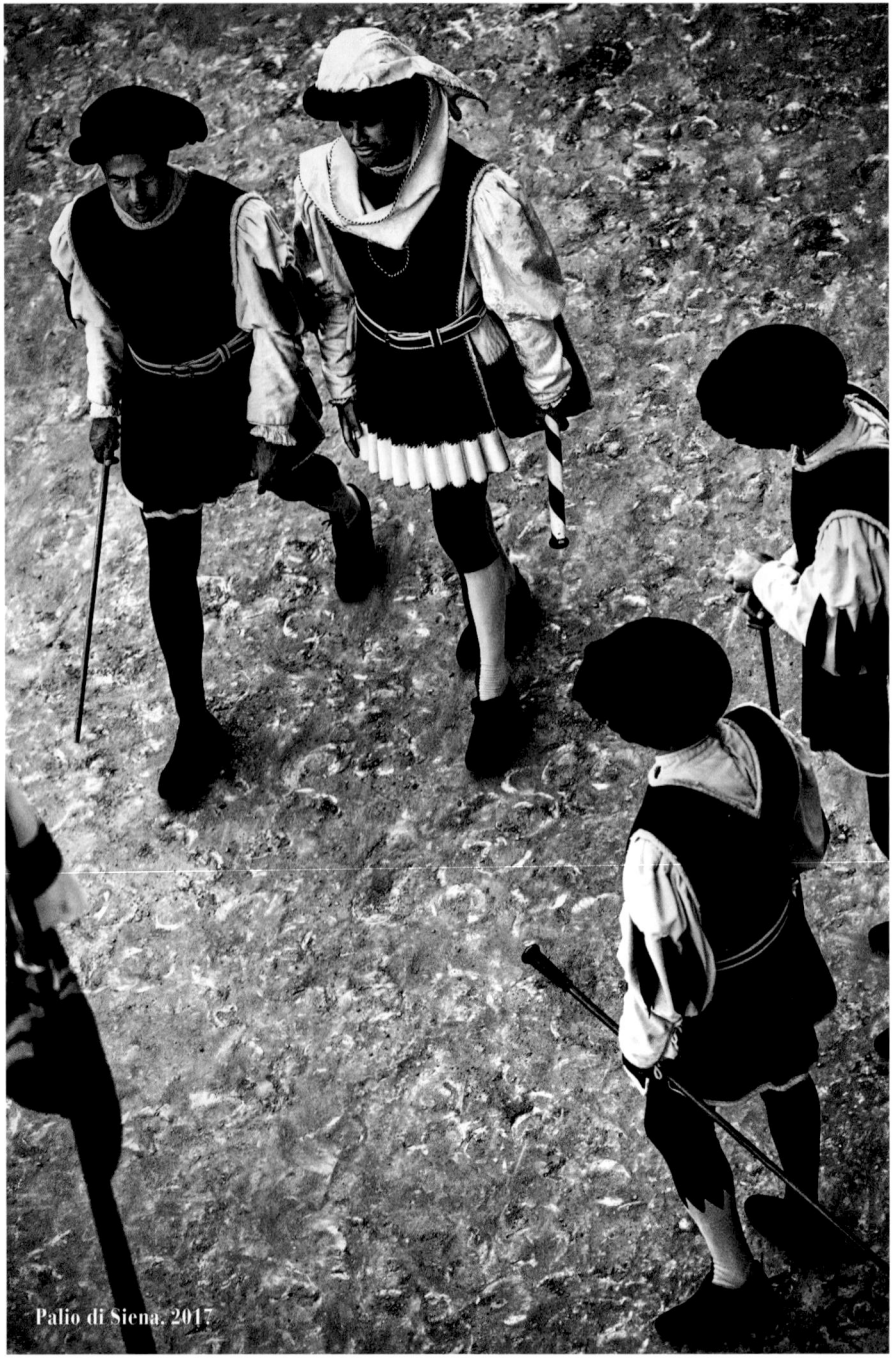

Palio di Siena, 2017

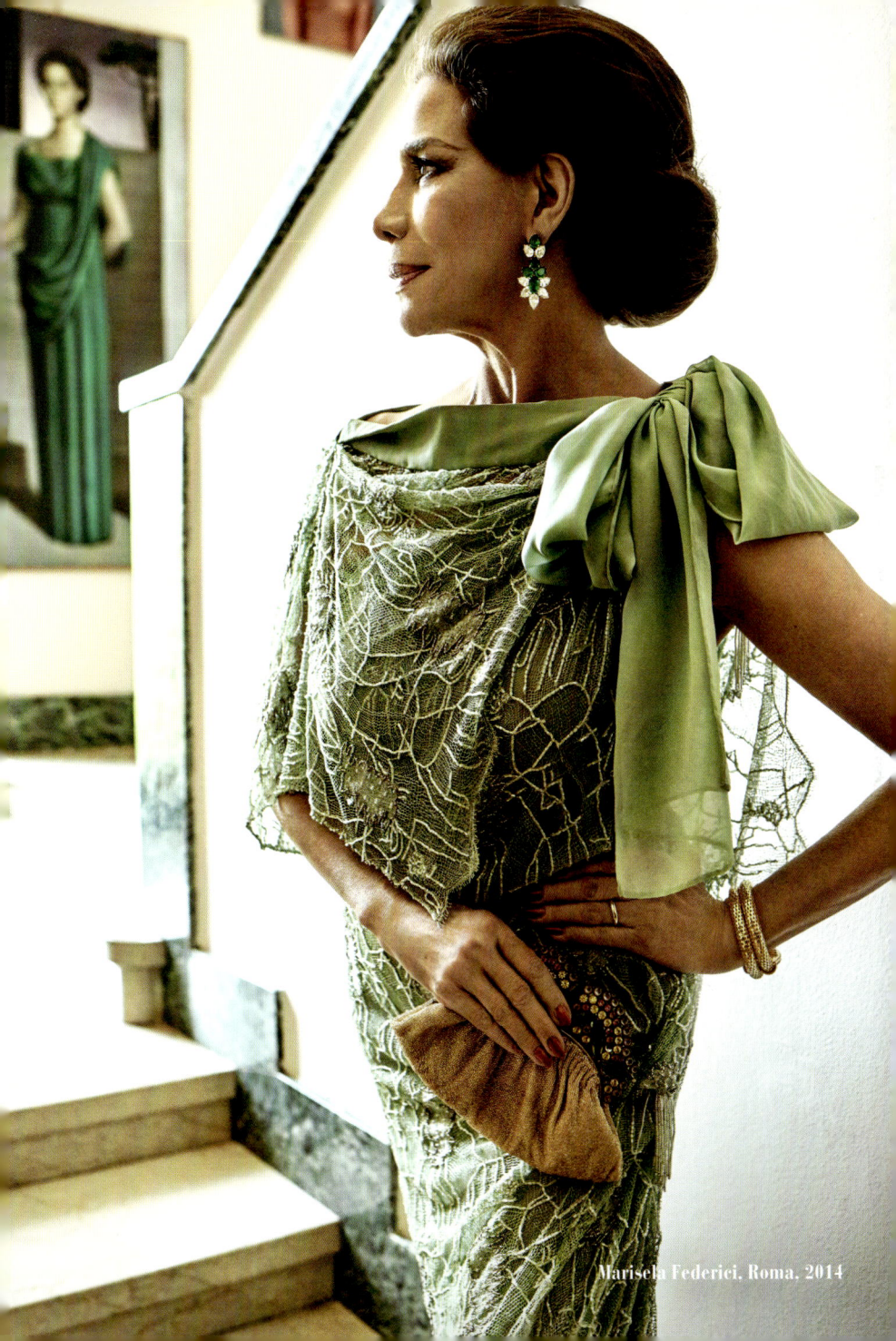

Marisela Federici, Roma, 2014

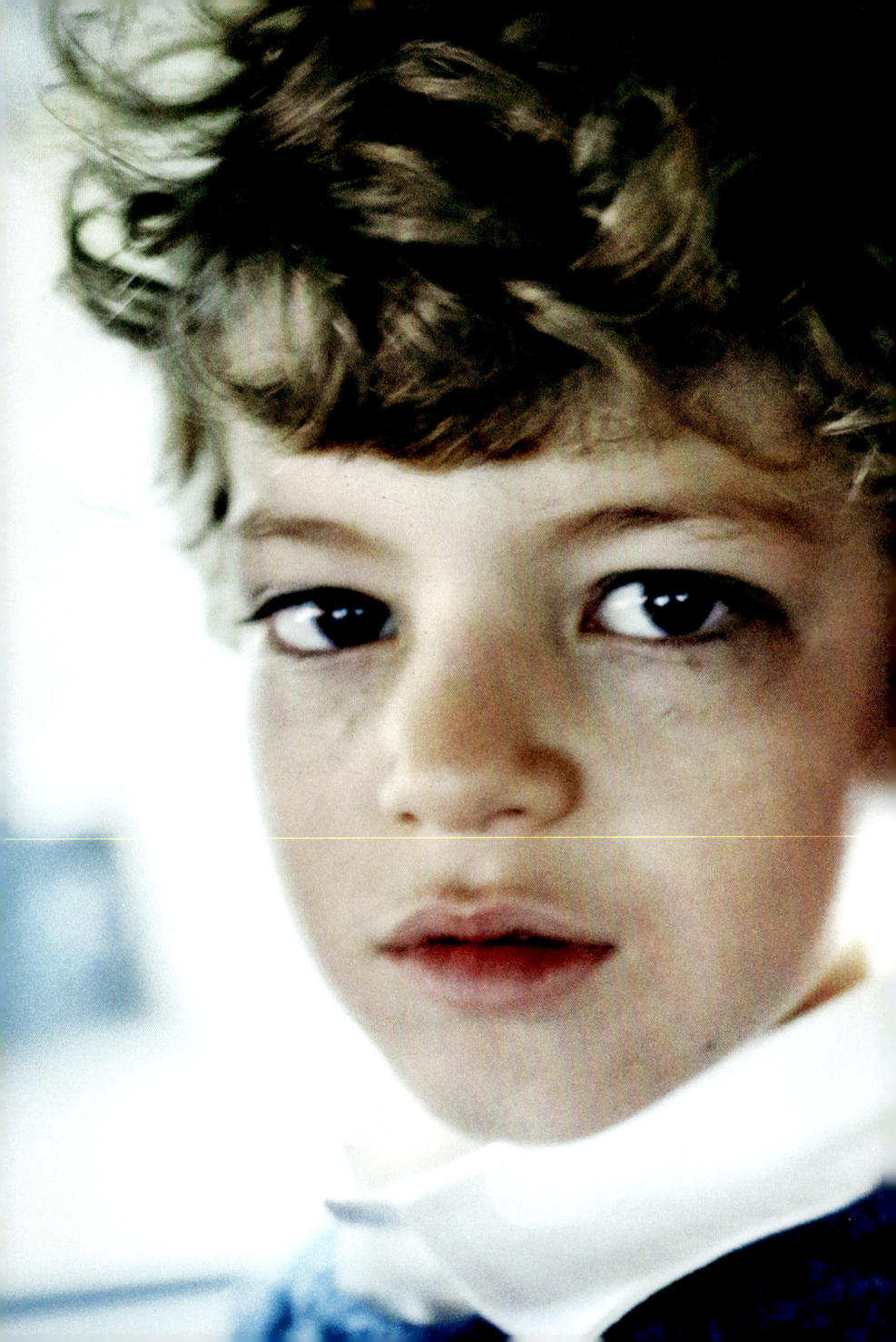

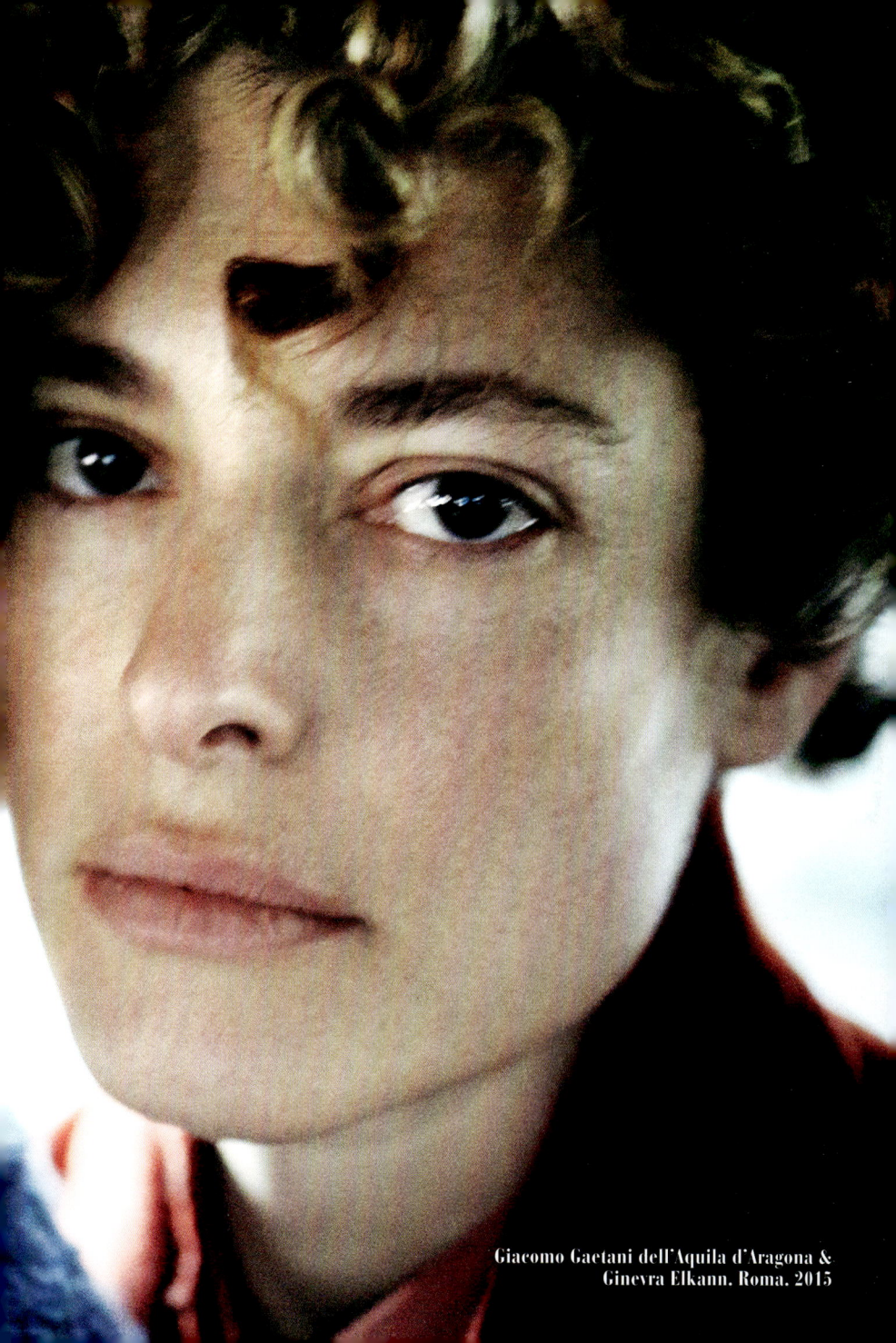

Giacomo Gaetani dell'Aquila d'Aragona &
Ginevra Elkann. Roma. 2015

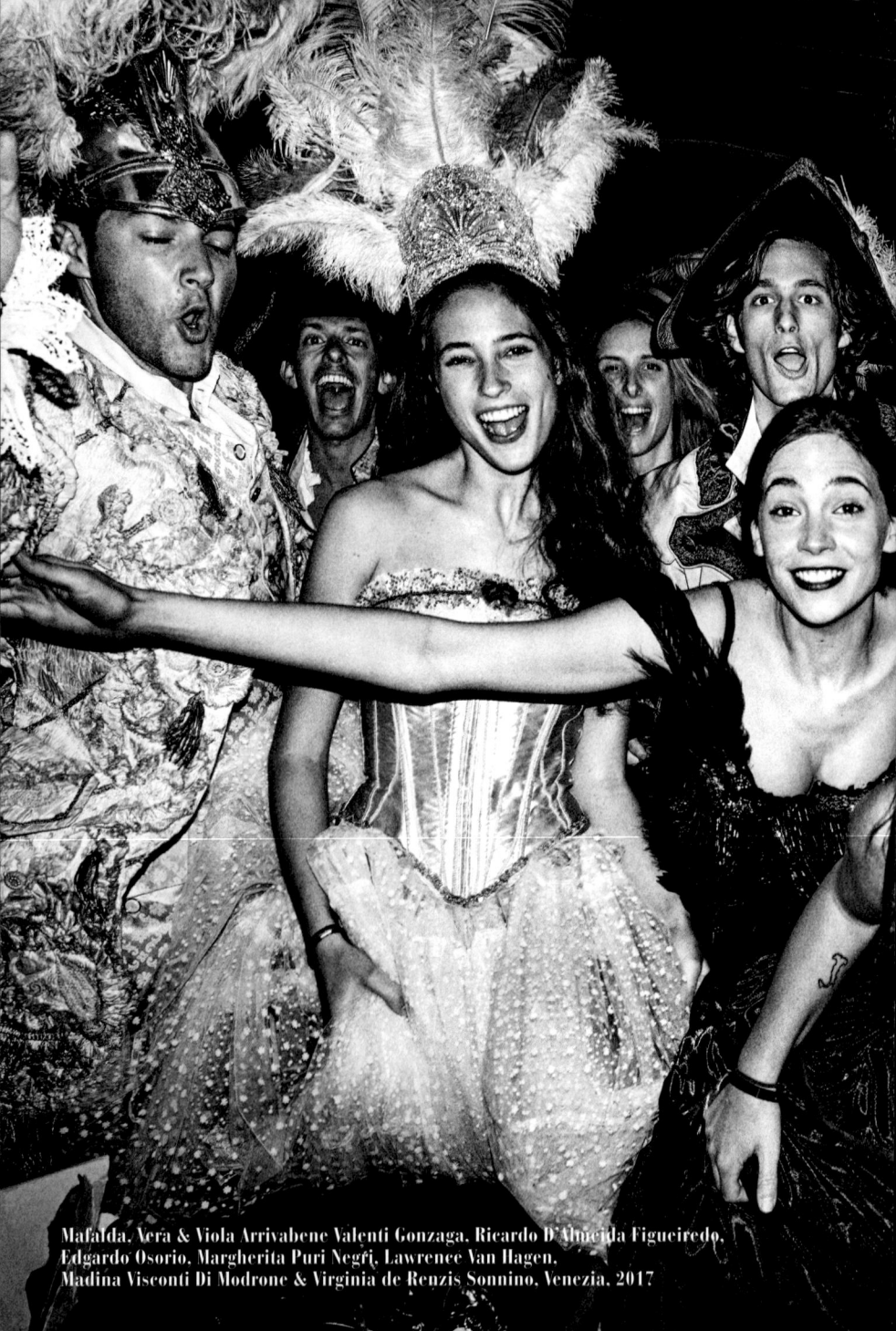

Mafalda, Vera & Viola Arrivabene Valenti Gonzaga, Ricardo D'Almeida Figueiredo, Edgardo Osorio, Margherita Puri Negri, Lawrence Van Hagen, Madina Visconti Di Modrone & Virginia de Renzis Sonnino, Venezia, 2017

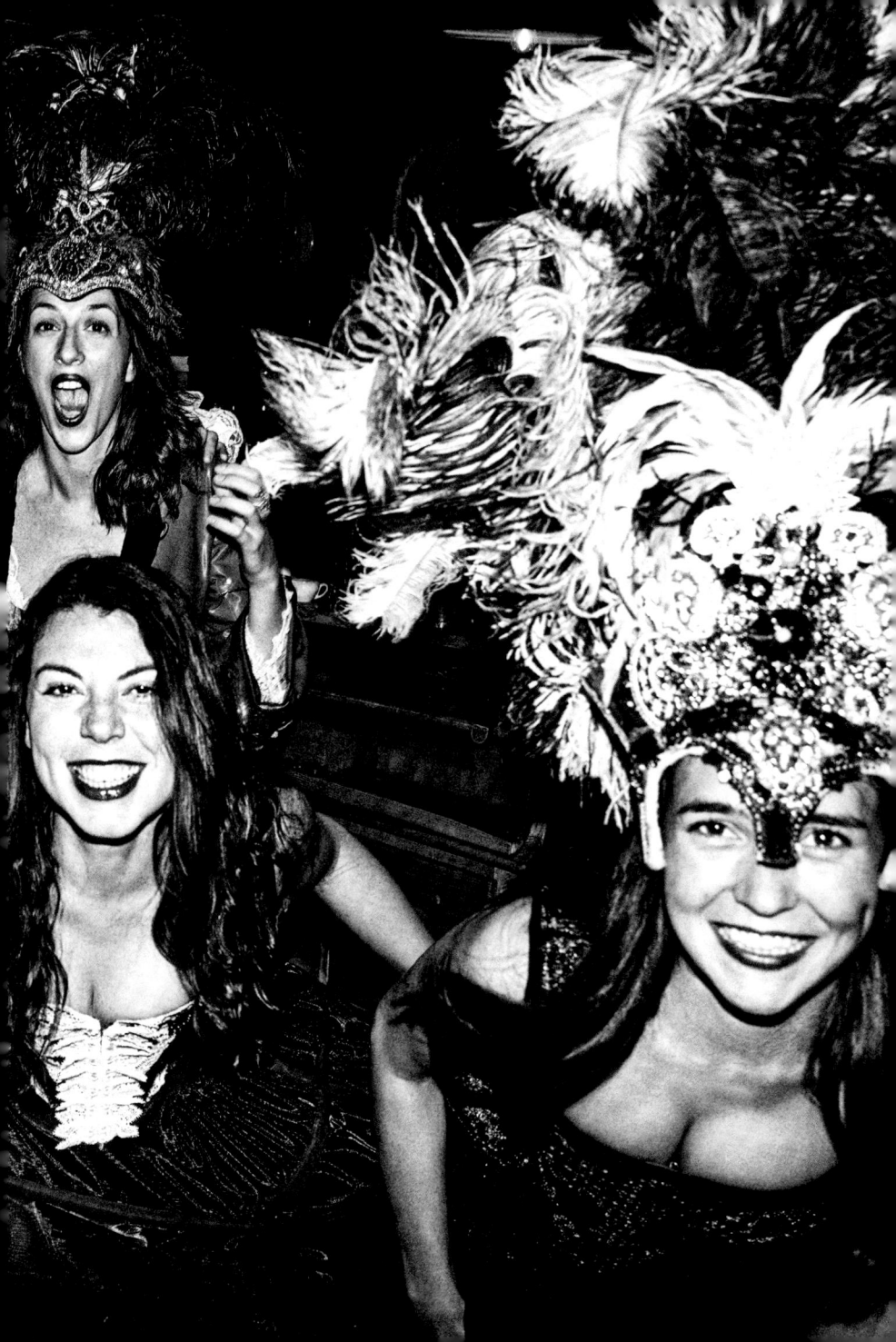

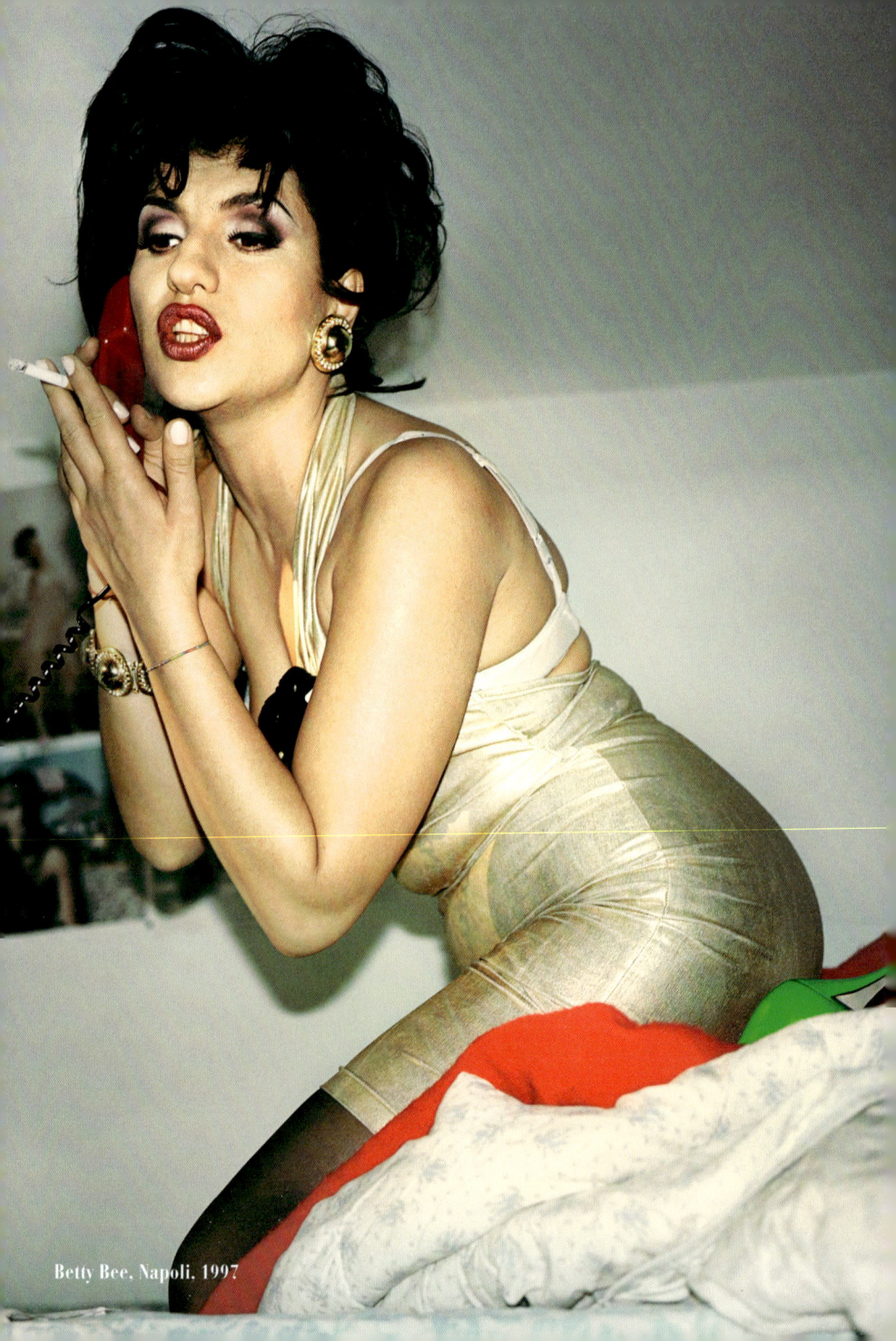

Betty Bee, Napoli, 1997

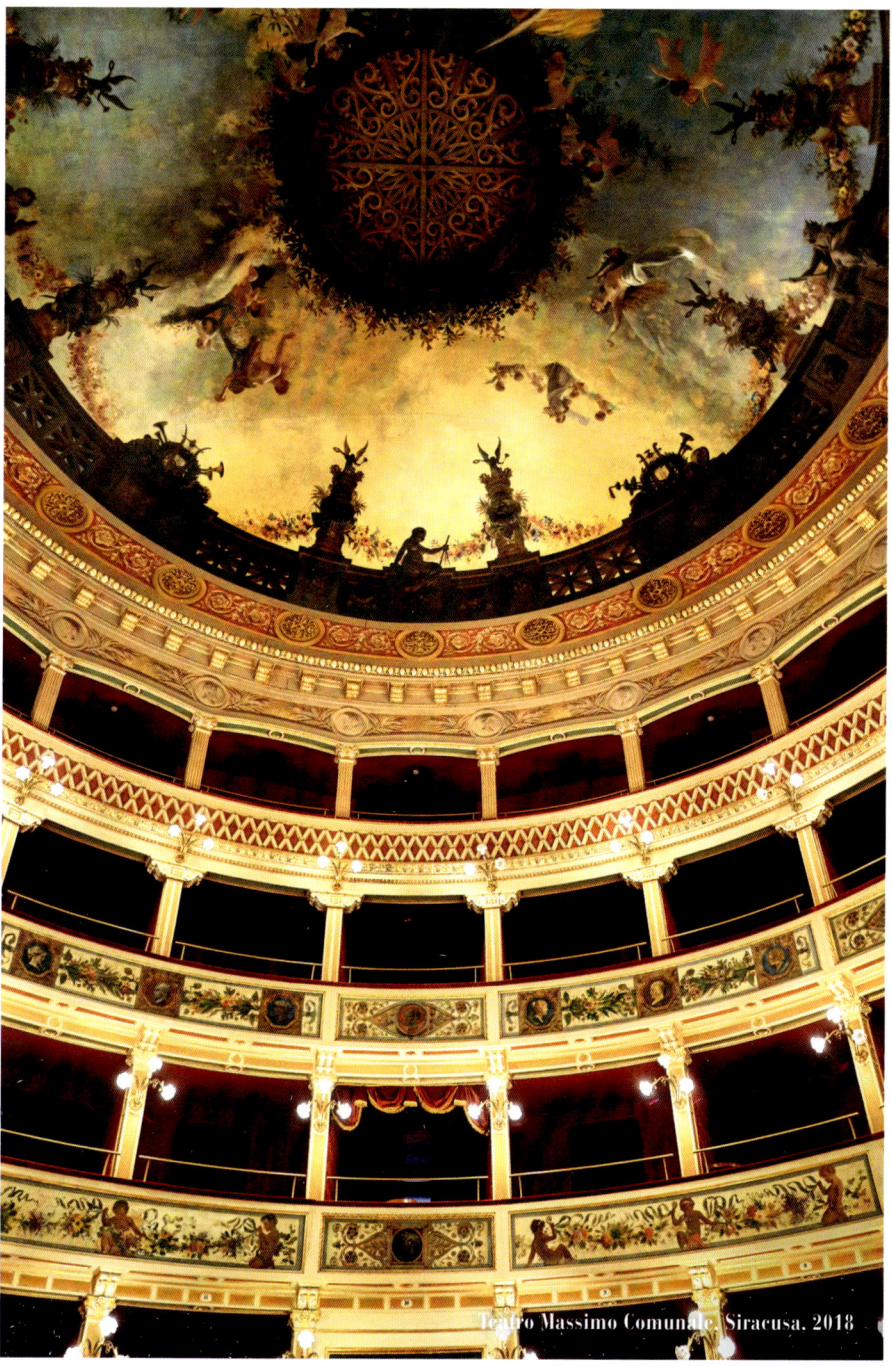

Teatro Massimo Comunale, Siracusa, 2018

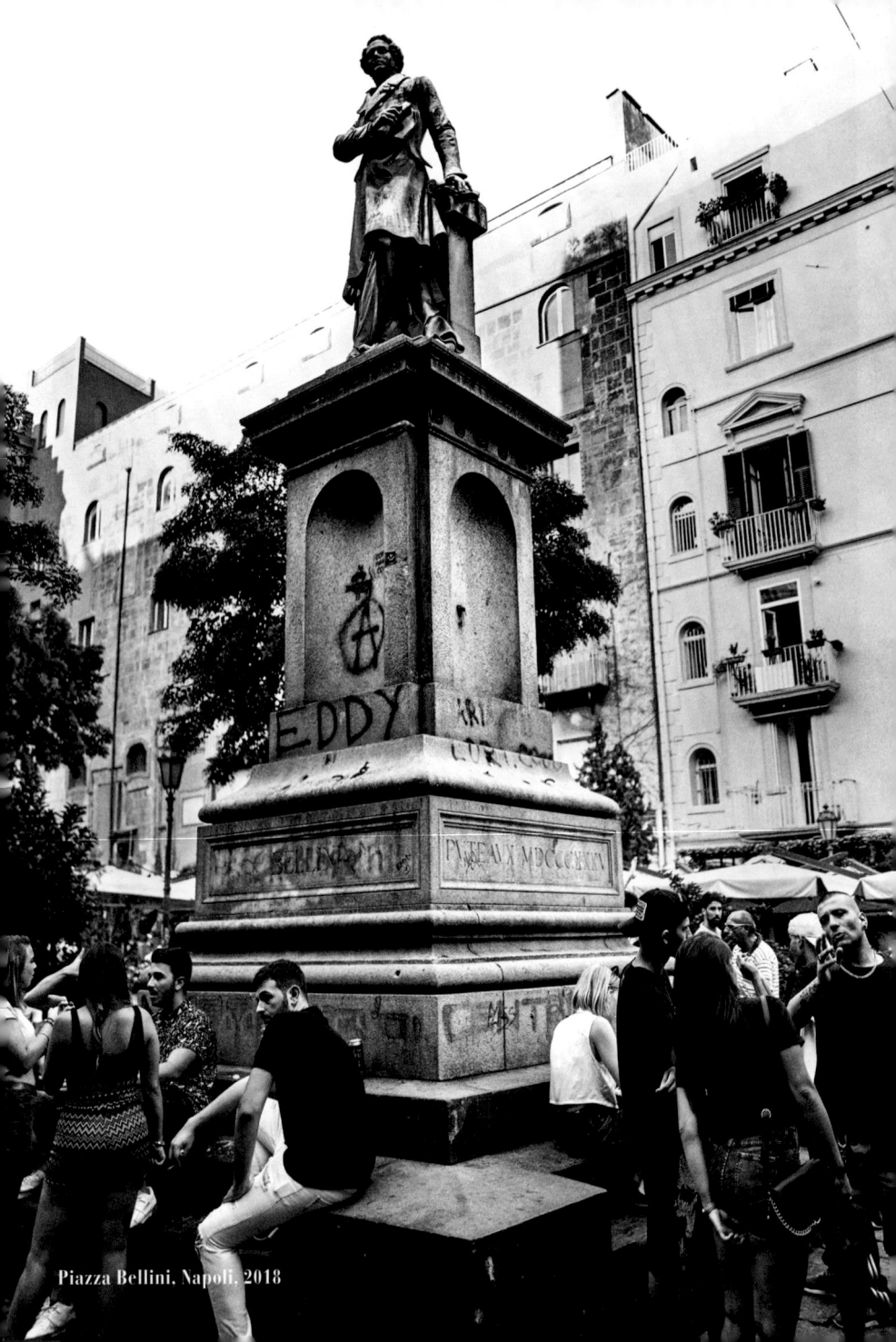

Piazza Bellini, Napoli, 2018

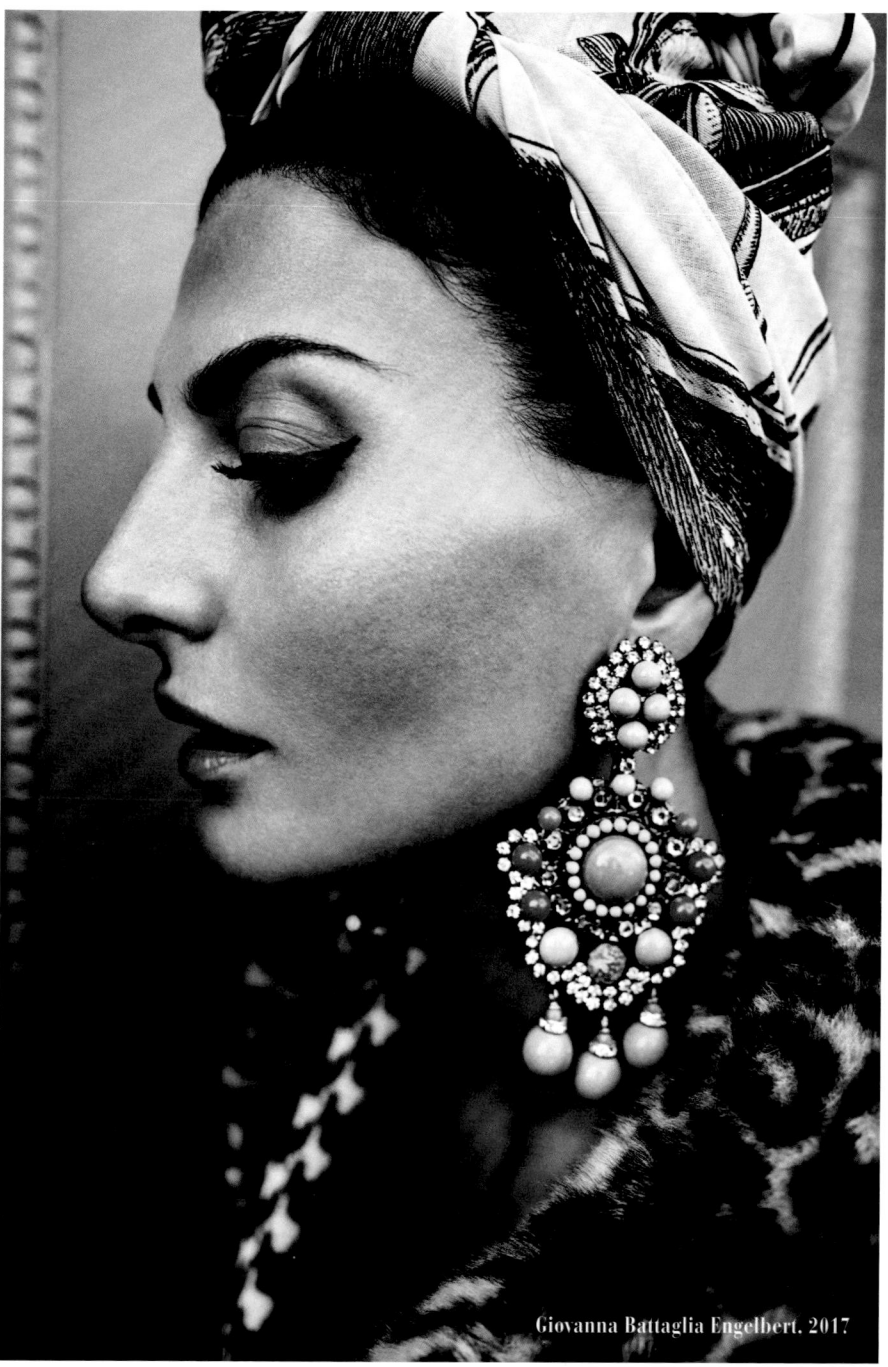

Giovanna Battaglia Engelbert. 2017

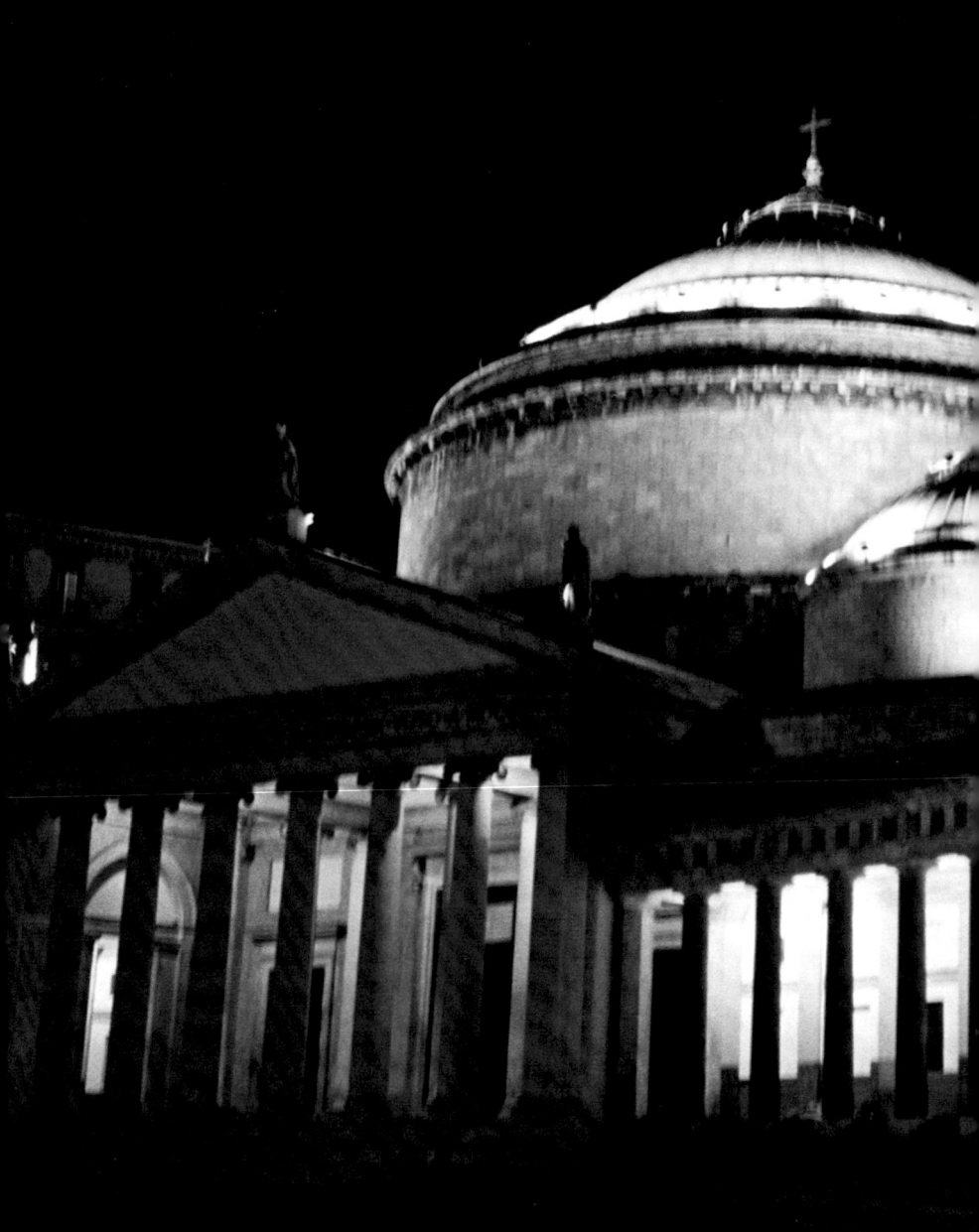

Piazza del Plebiscito, Napoli, 1998

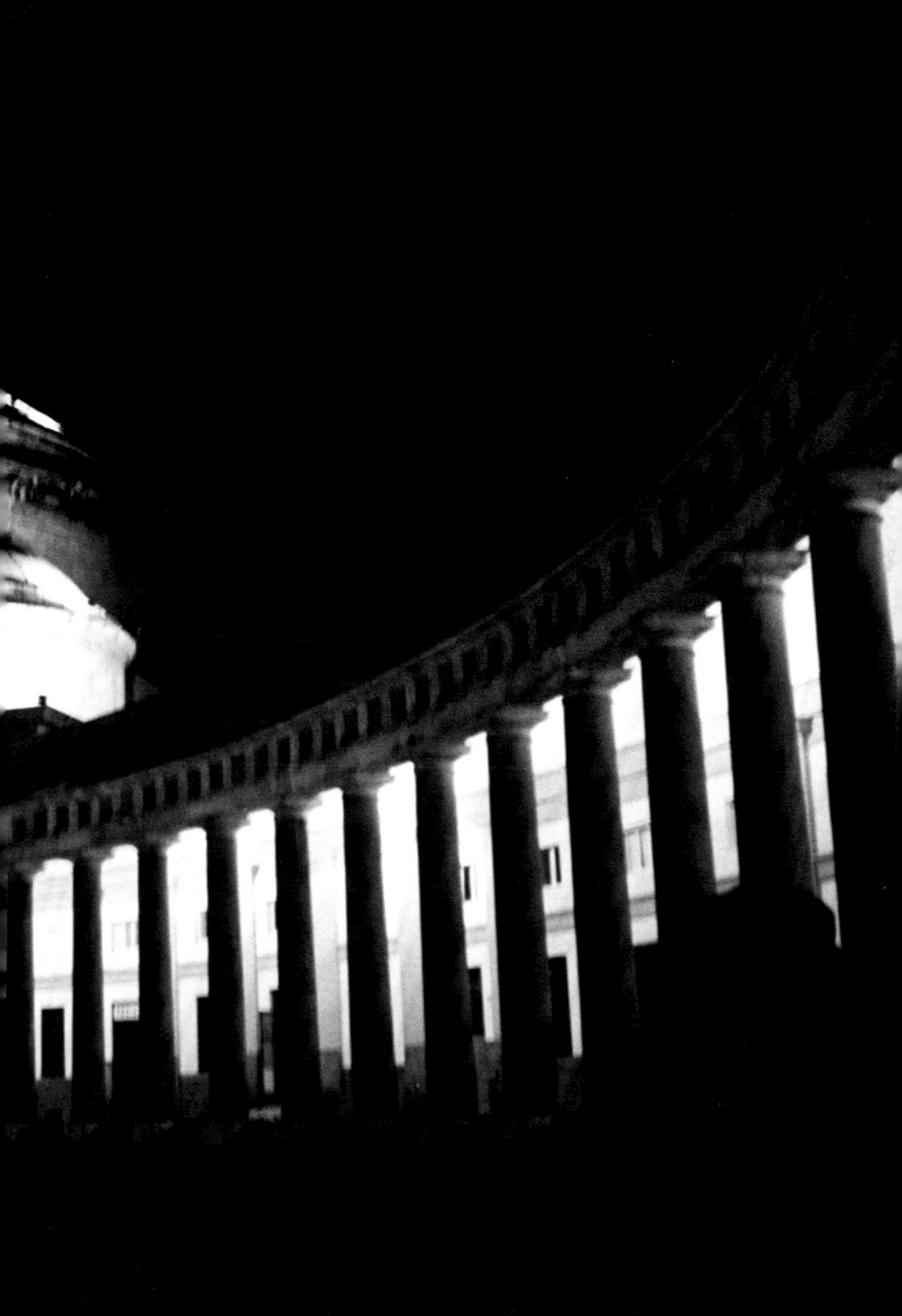

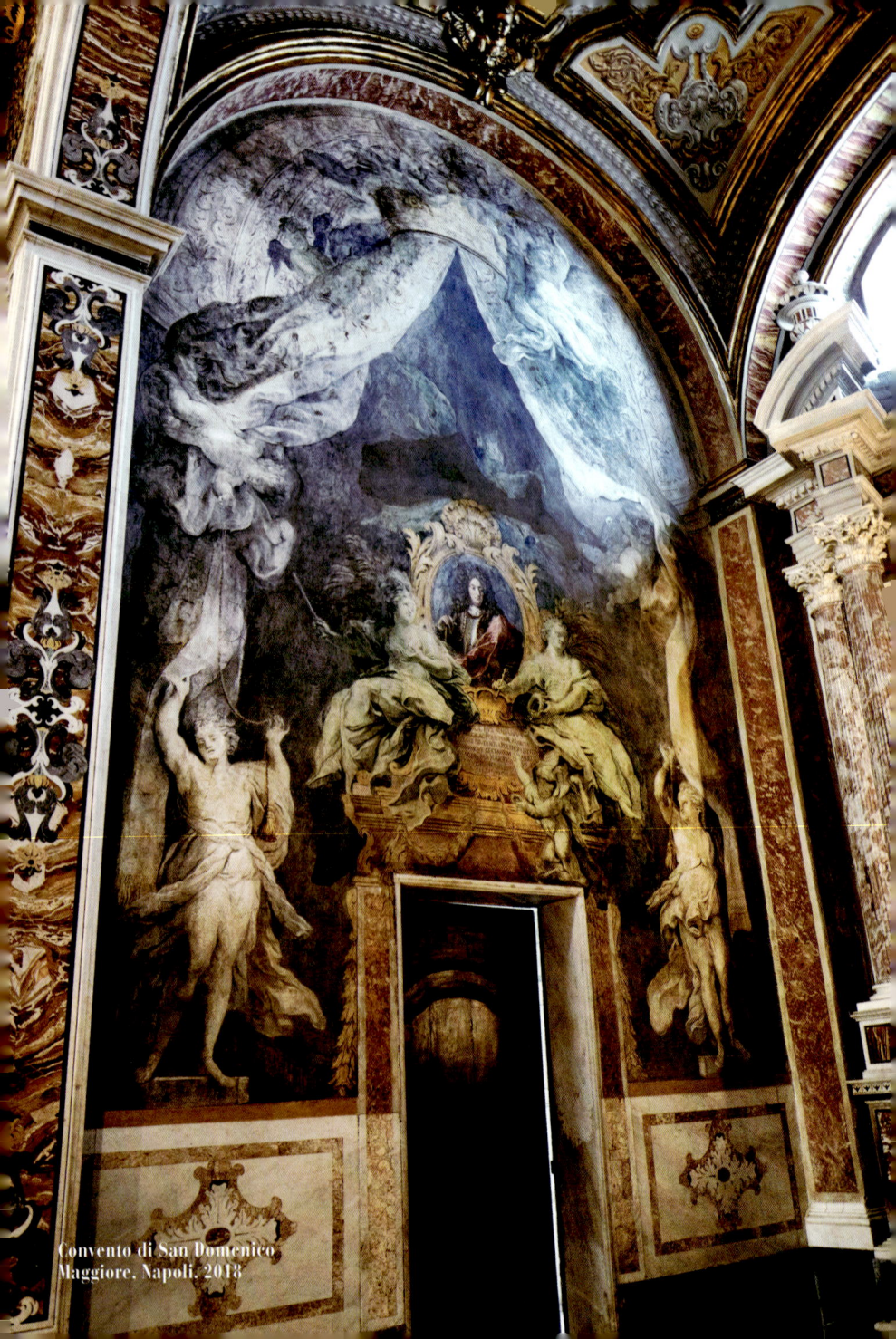

Convento di San Domenico
Maggiore, Napoli, 2018

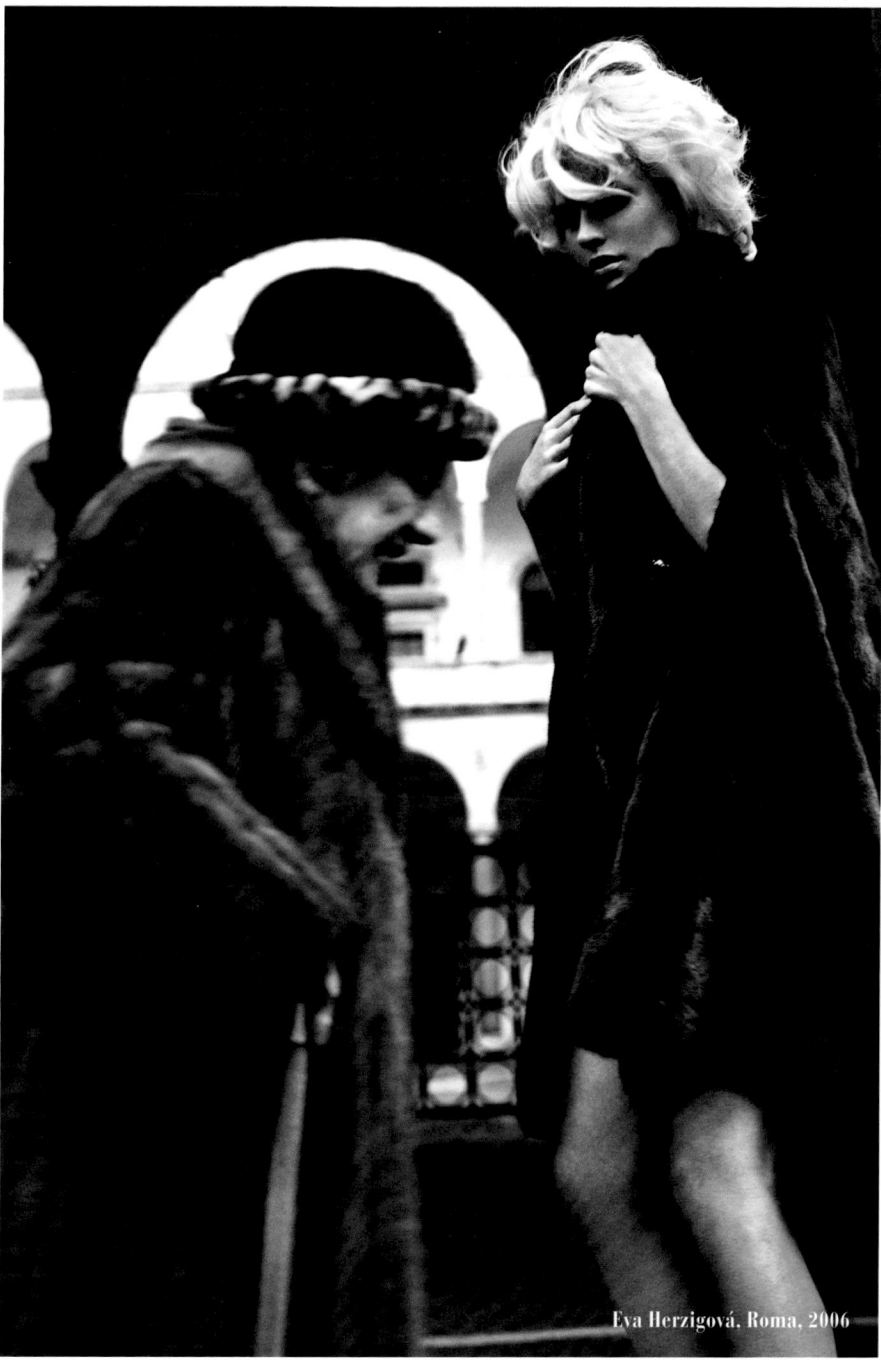

Eva Herzigová, Roma, 2006

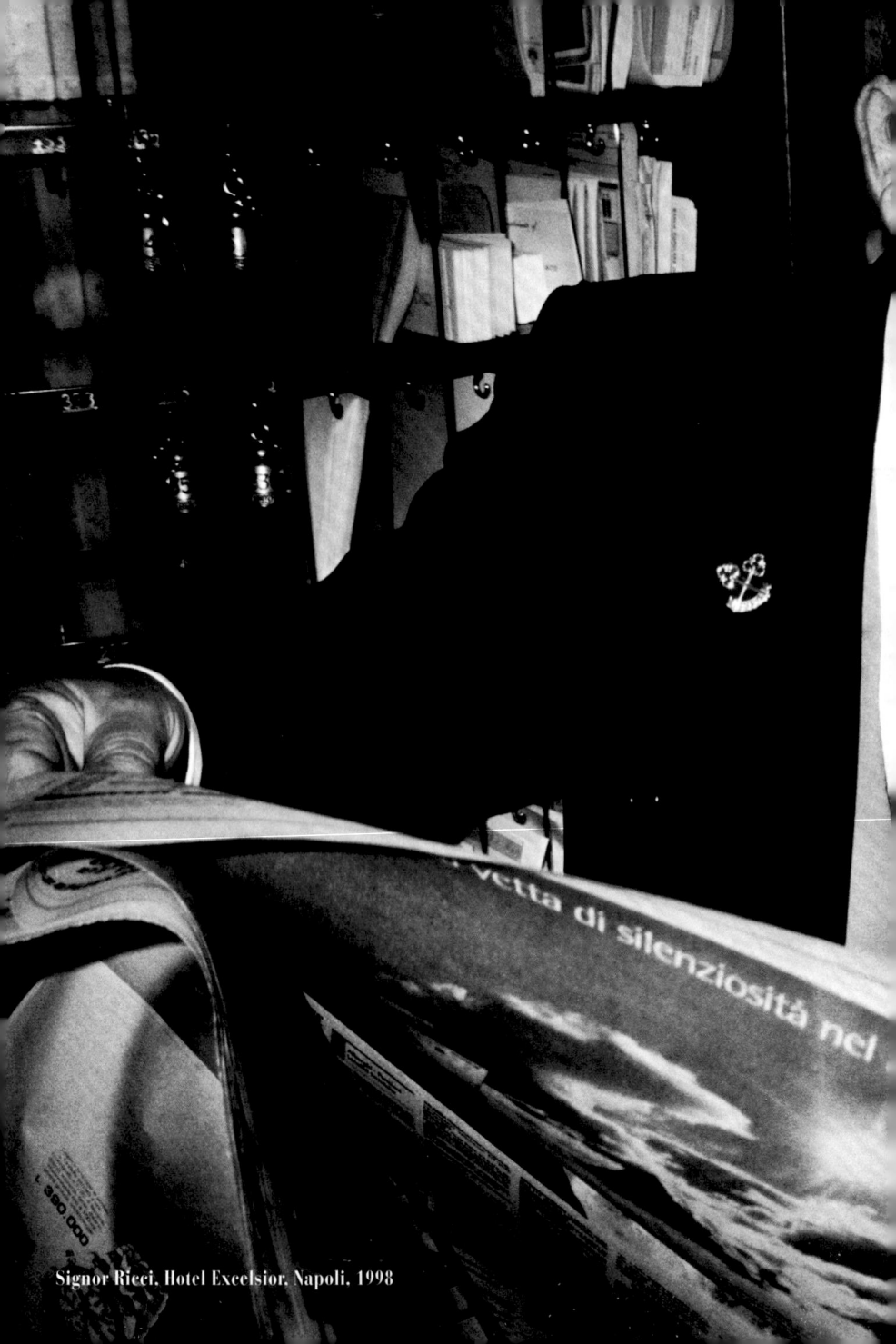

Signor Ricci, Hotel Excelsior, Napoli, 1998

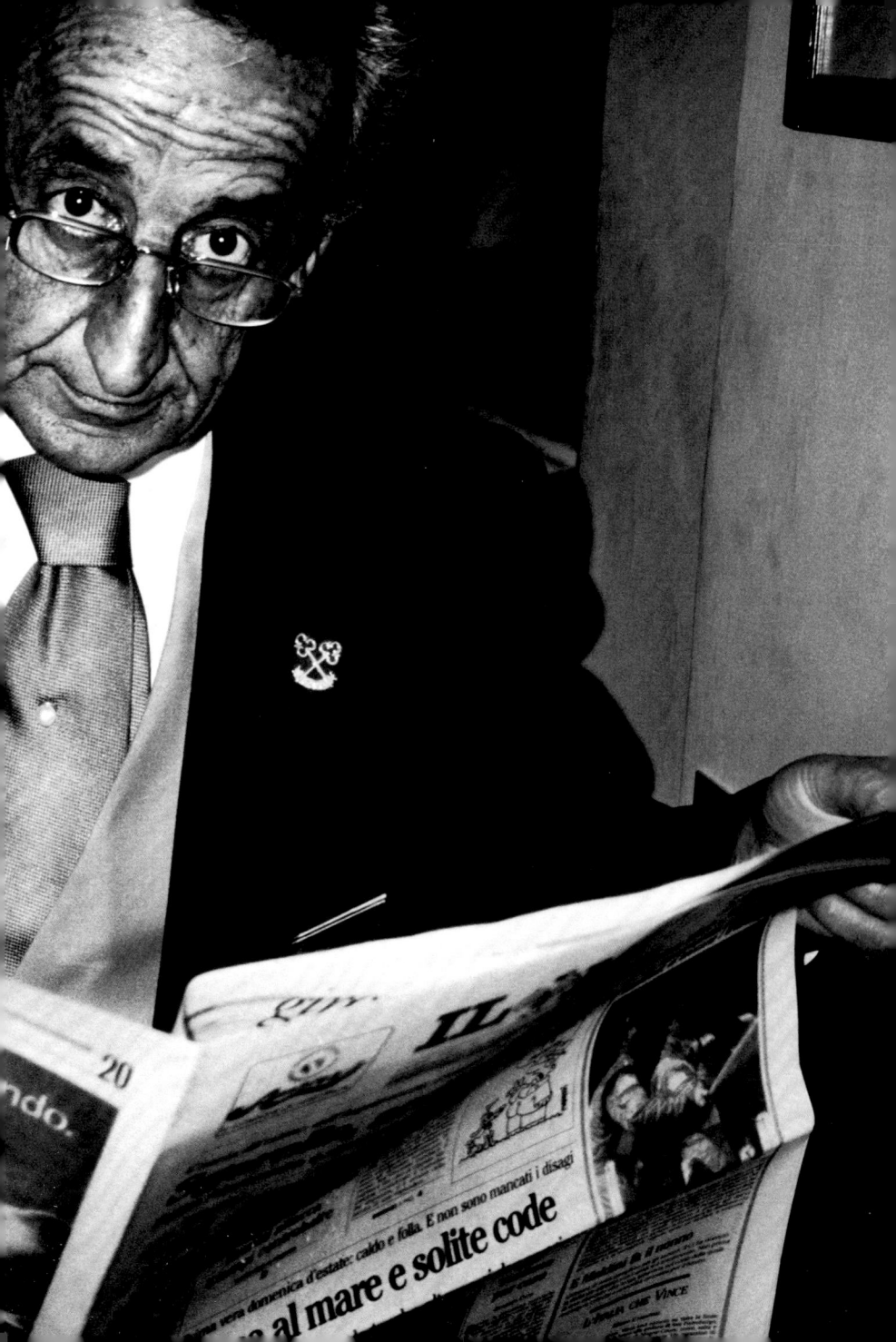

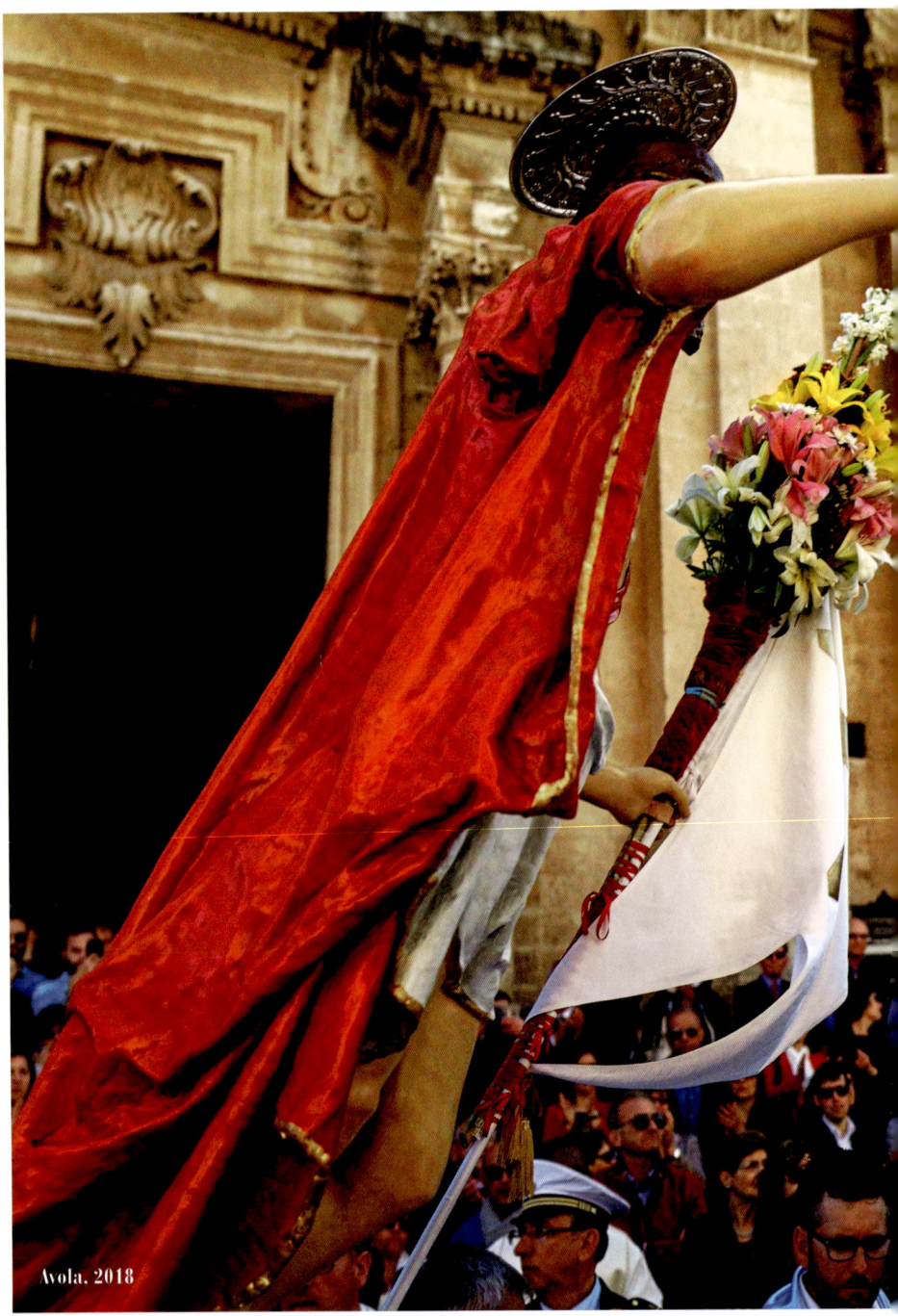

Avola. 2018

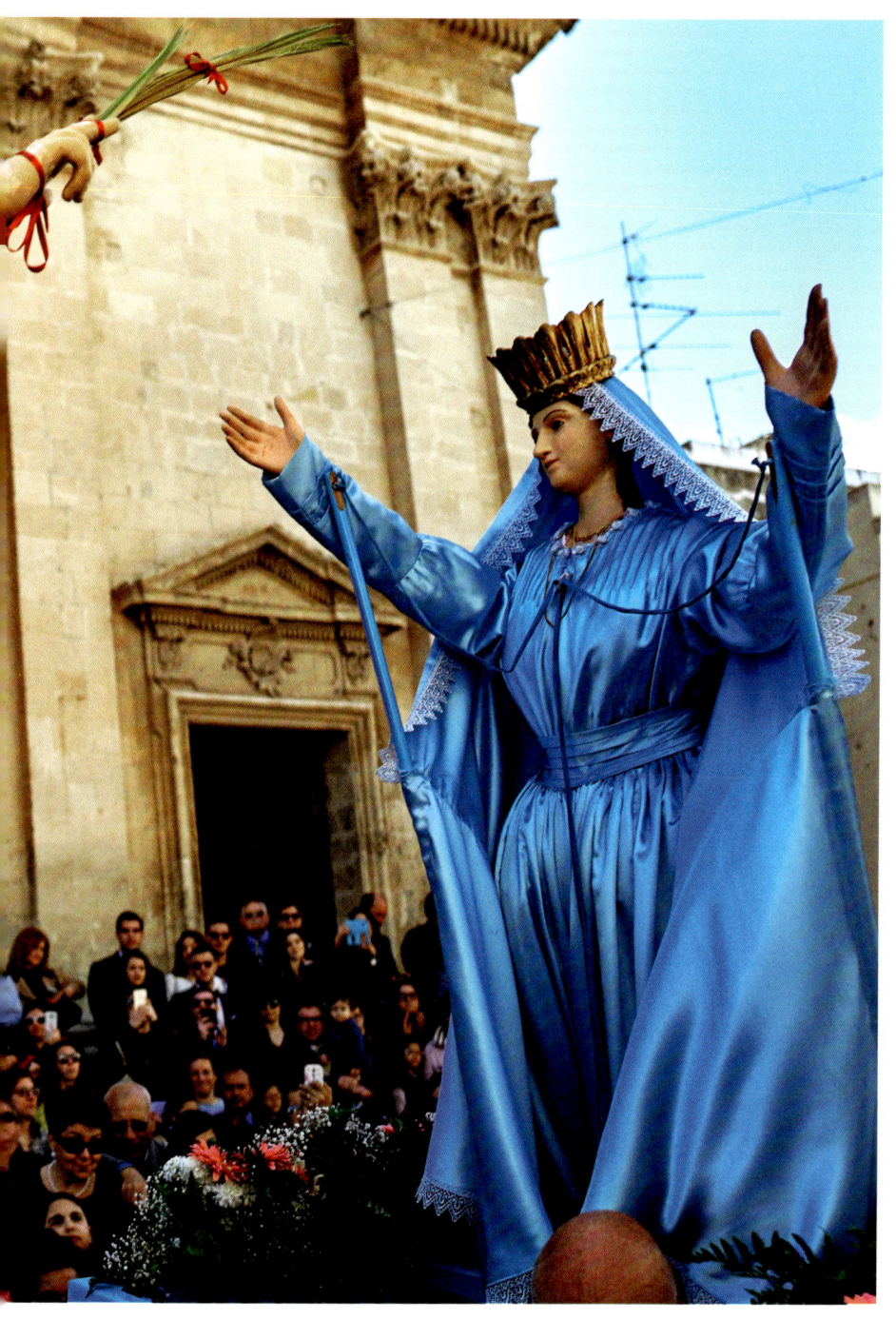

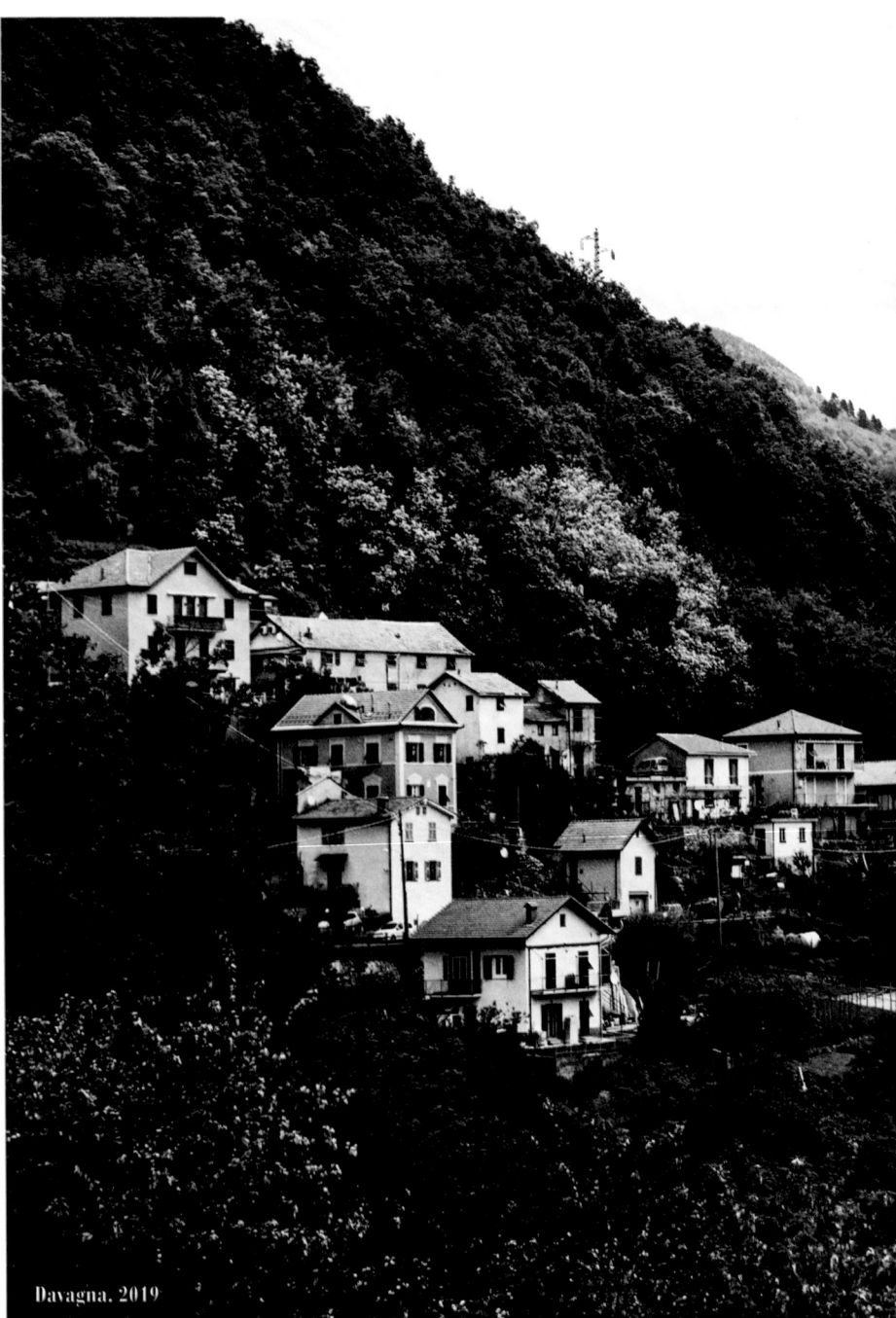

Davagna. 2019

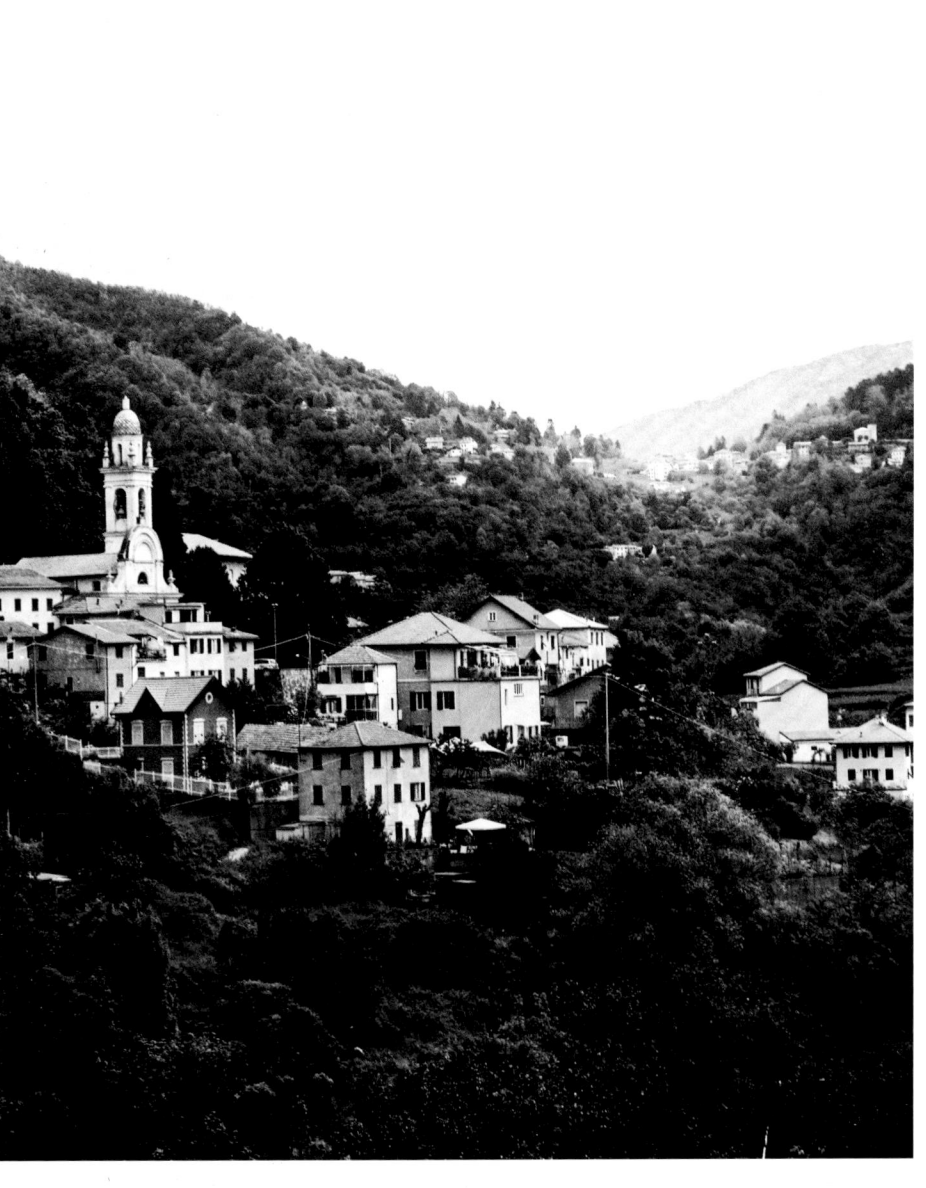

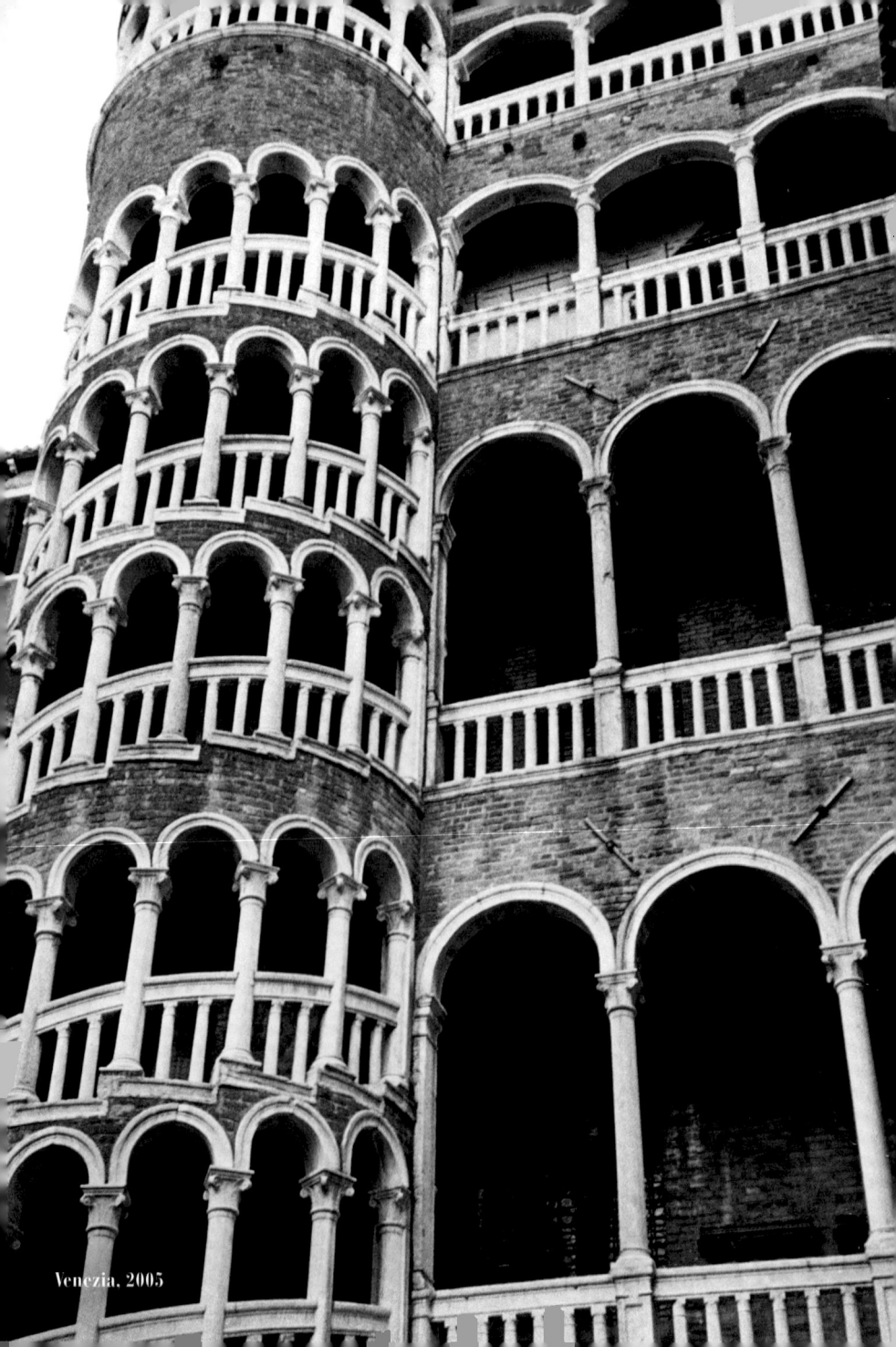

Venezia, 2005

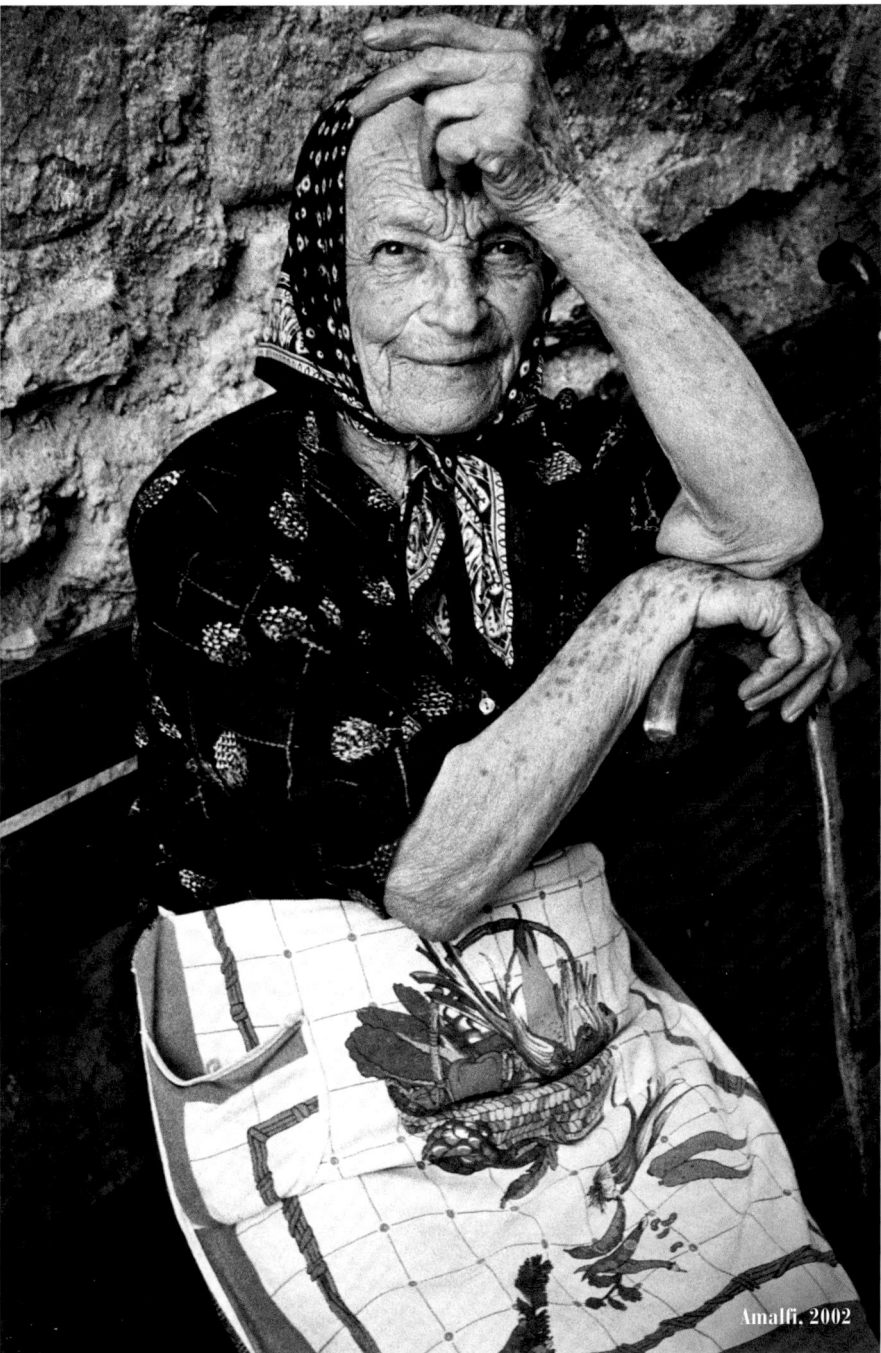

Amalfi, 2002

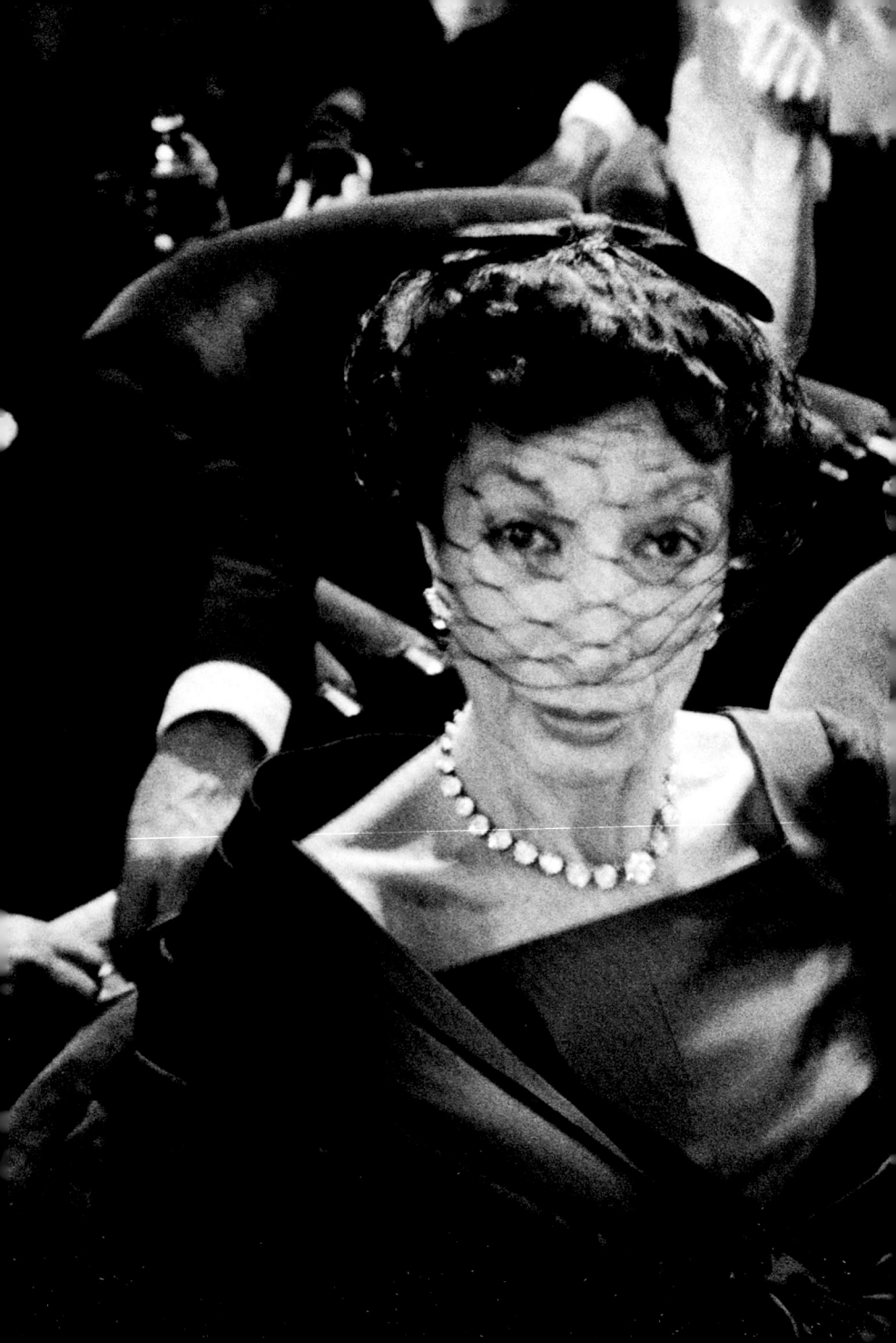

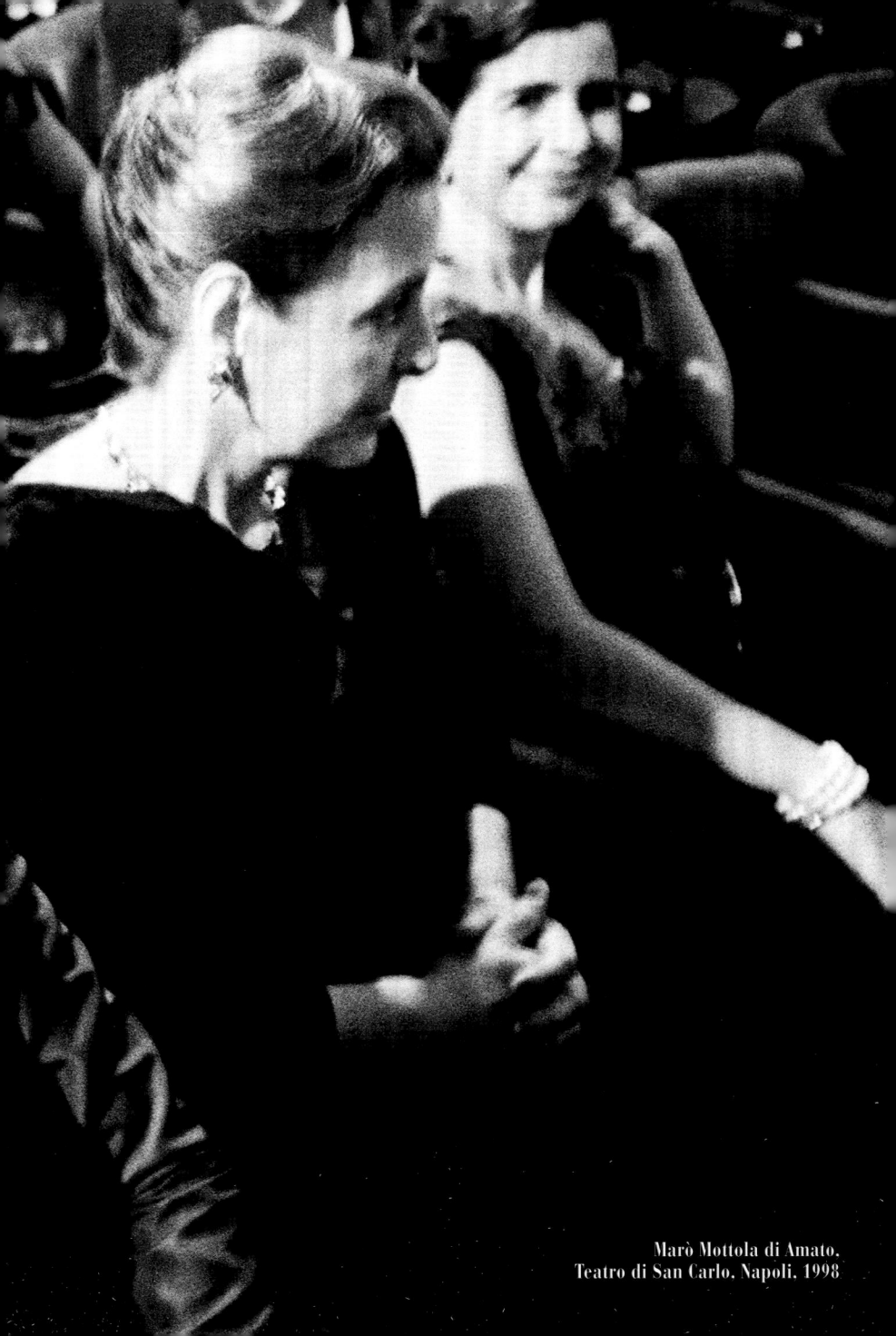

Marò Mottola di Amato.
Teatro di San Carlo, Napoli, 1998

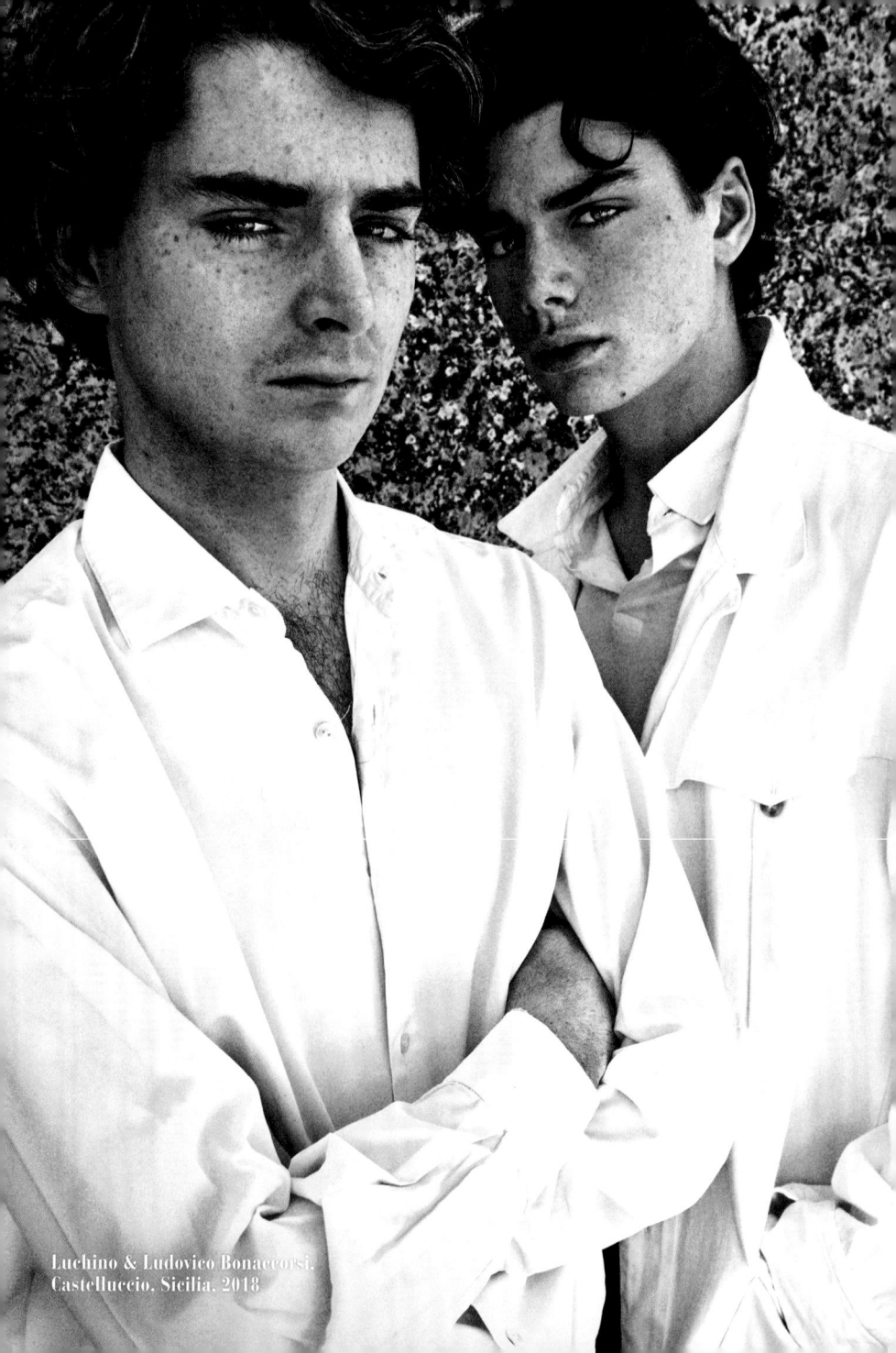

Luchino & Ludovico Bonaccorsi,
Castelluccio, Sicilia, 2013

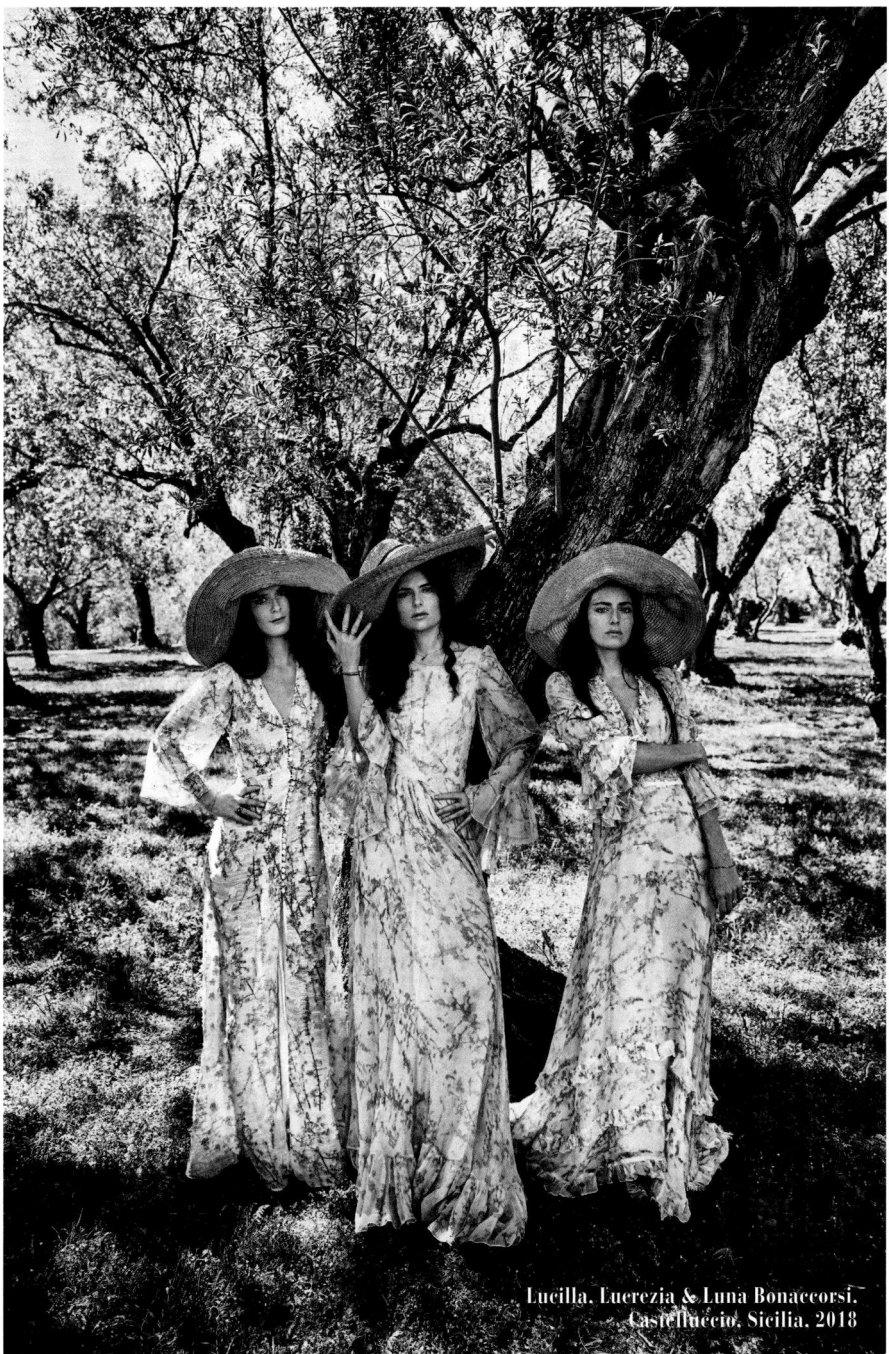

Lucilla, Lucrezia & Luna Bonaccorsi.
Castelluccio, Sicilia, 2018

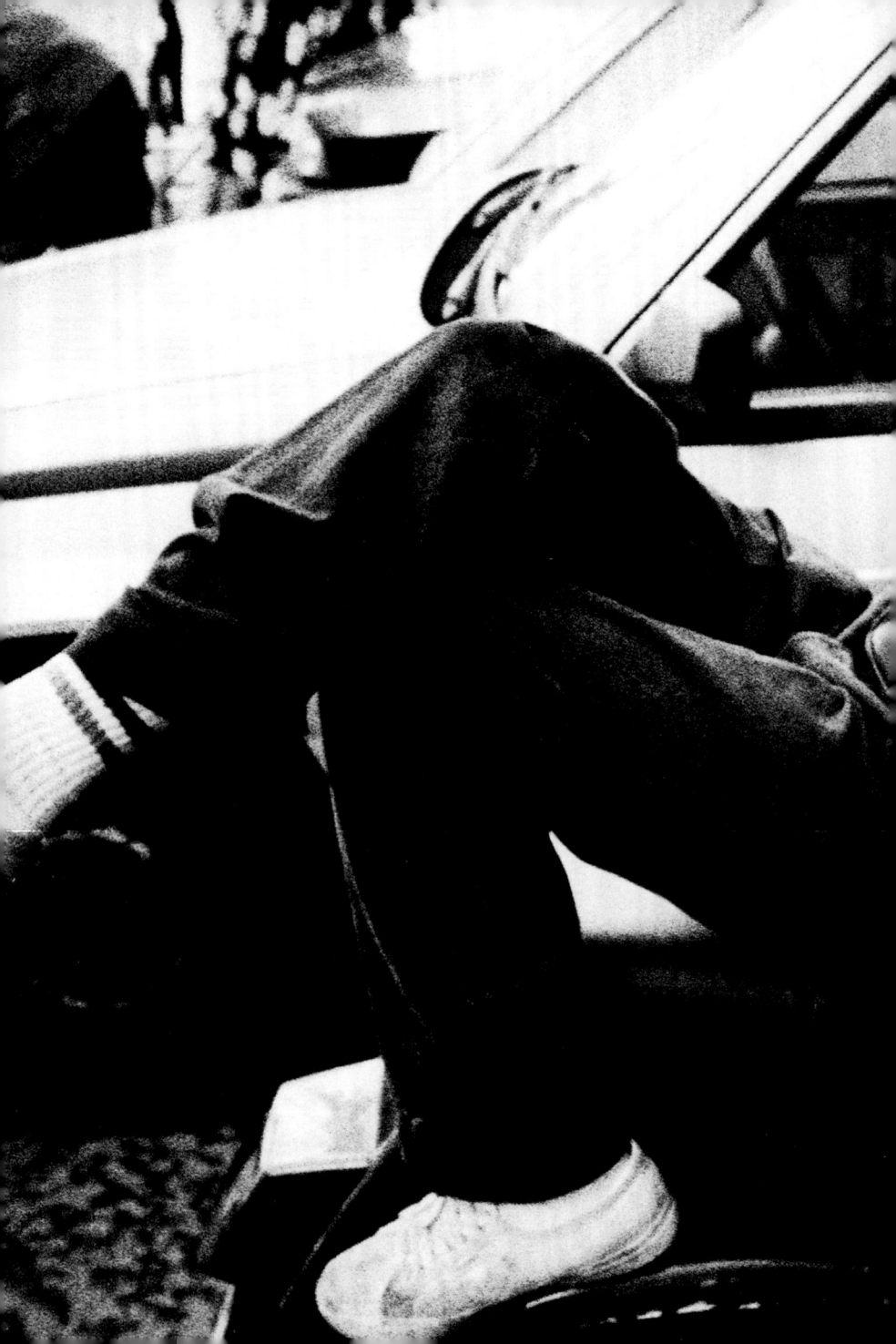

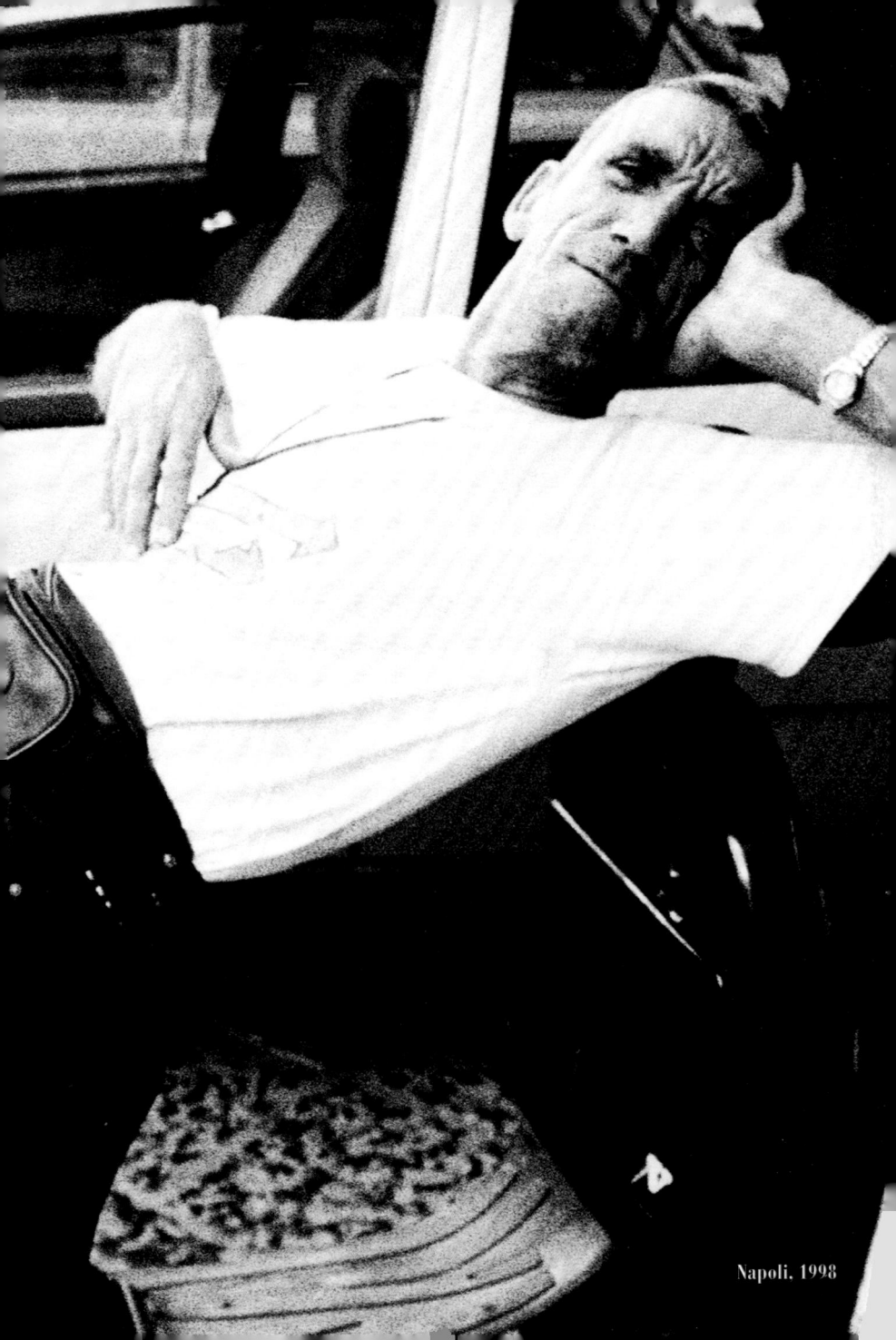

Napoli, 1998

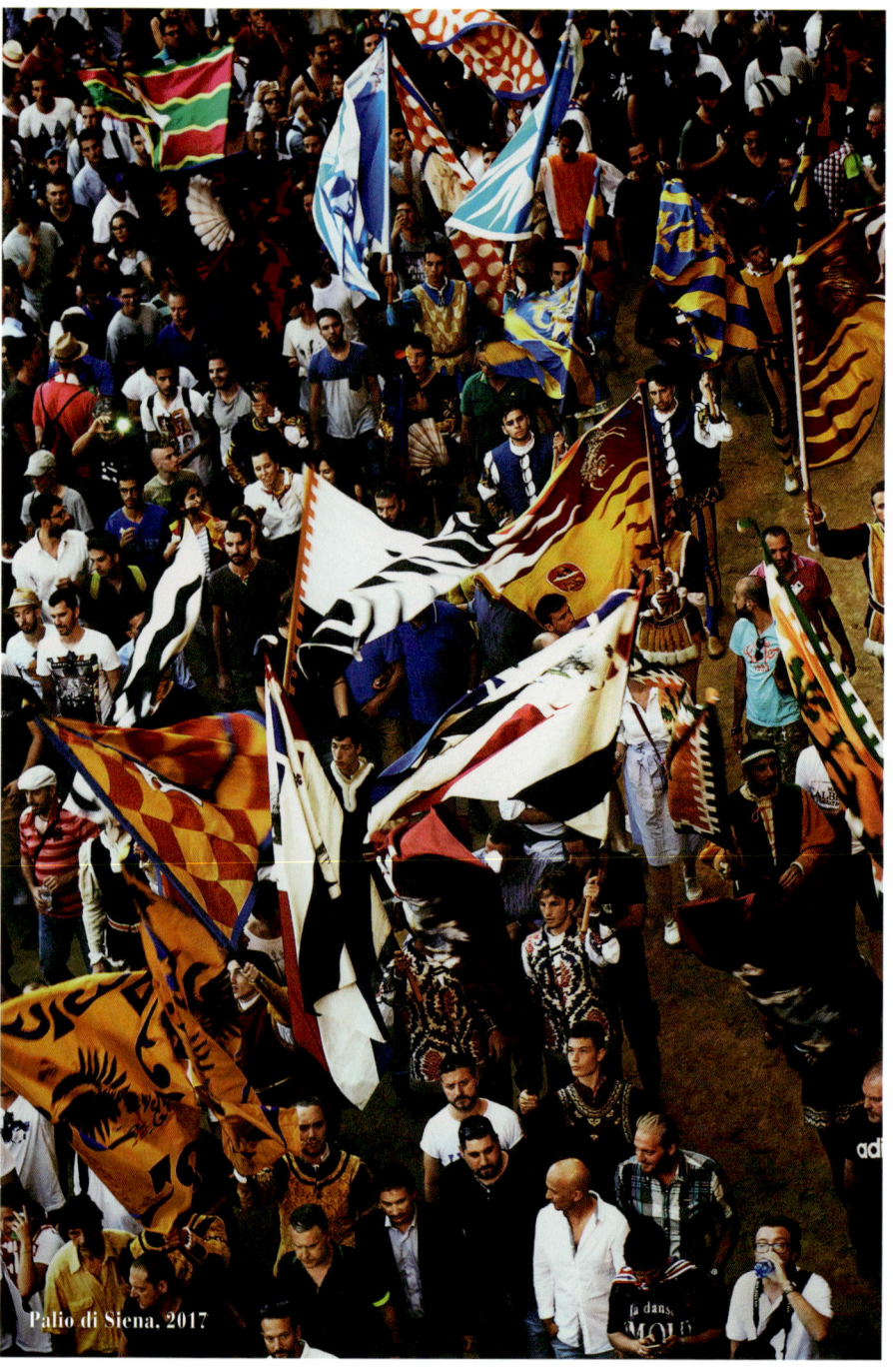

Palio di Siena, 2017

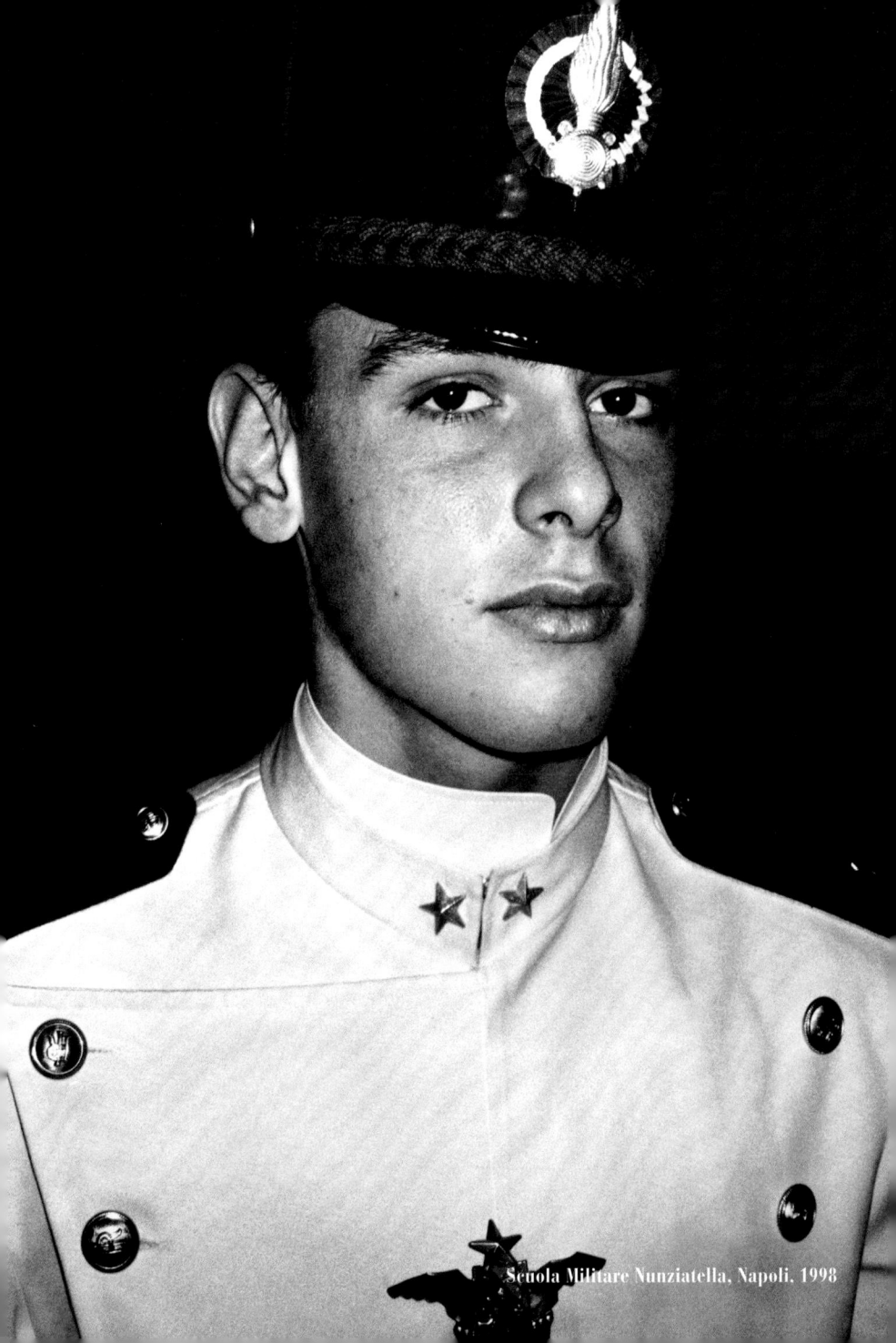

Scuola Militare Nunziatella, Napoli, 1998

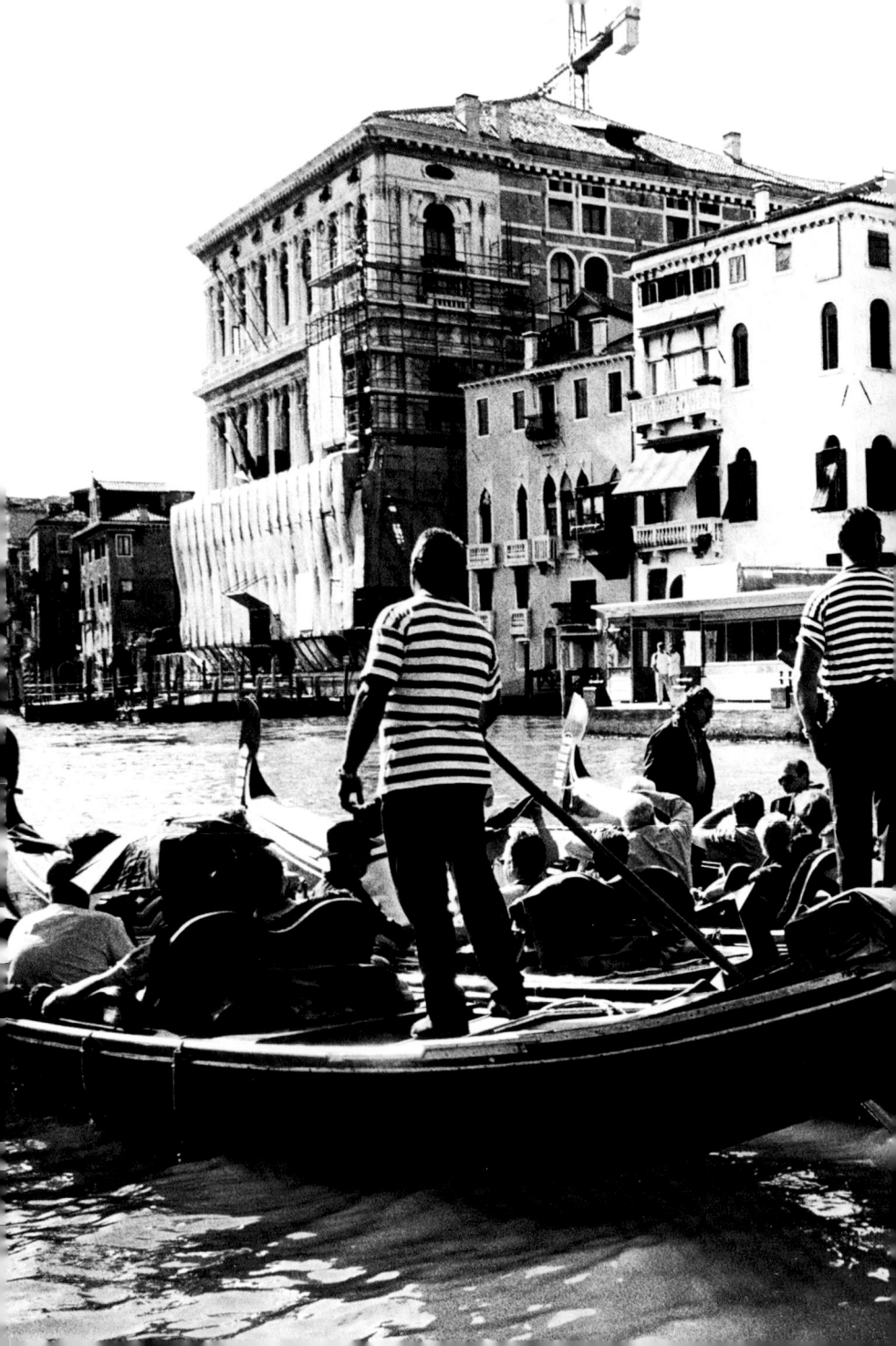

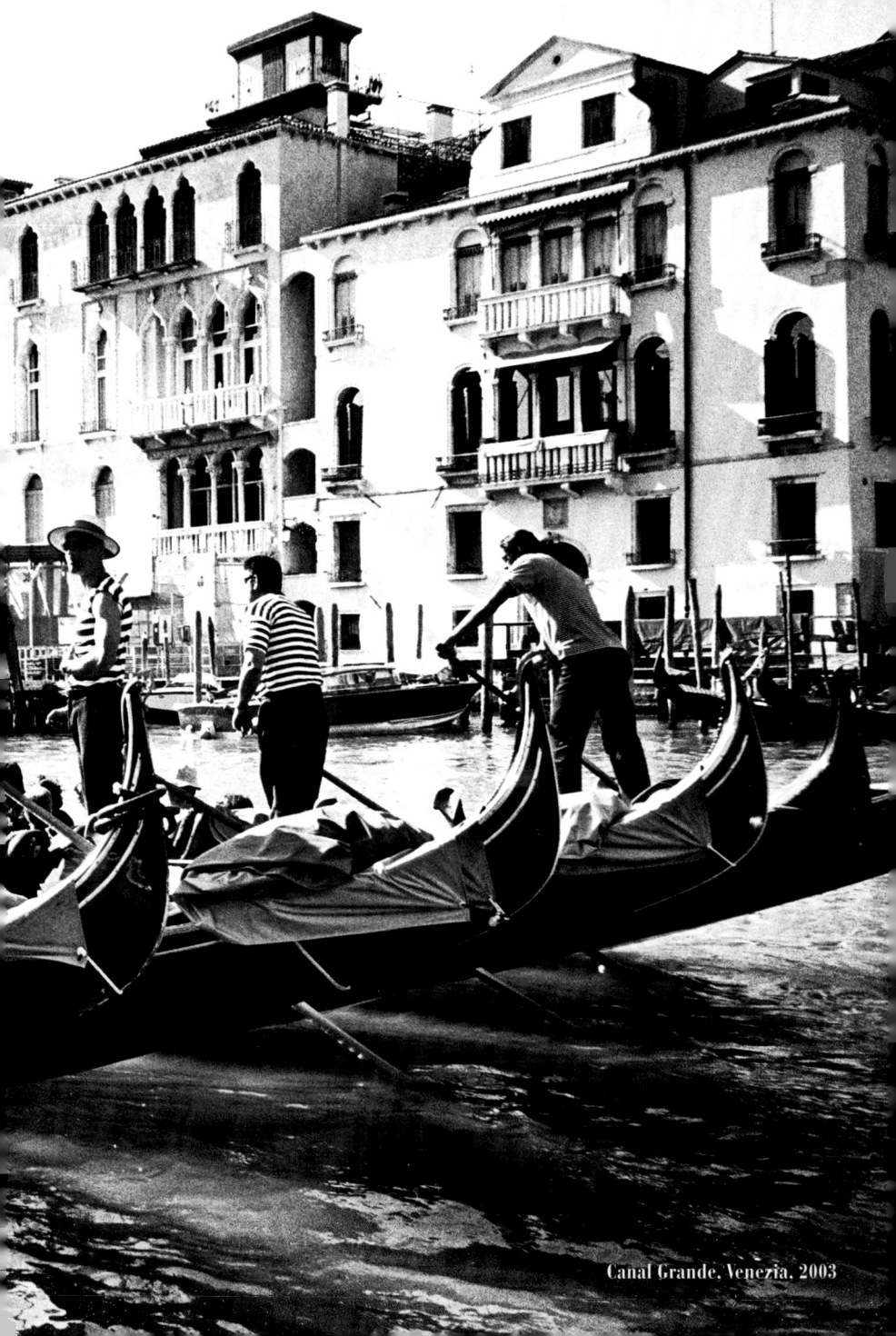

Canal Grande, Venezia, 2003

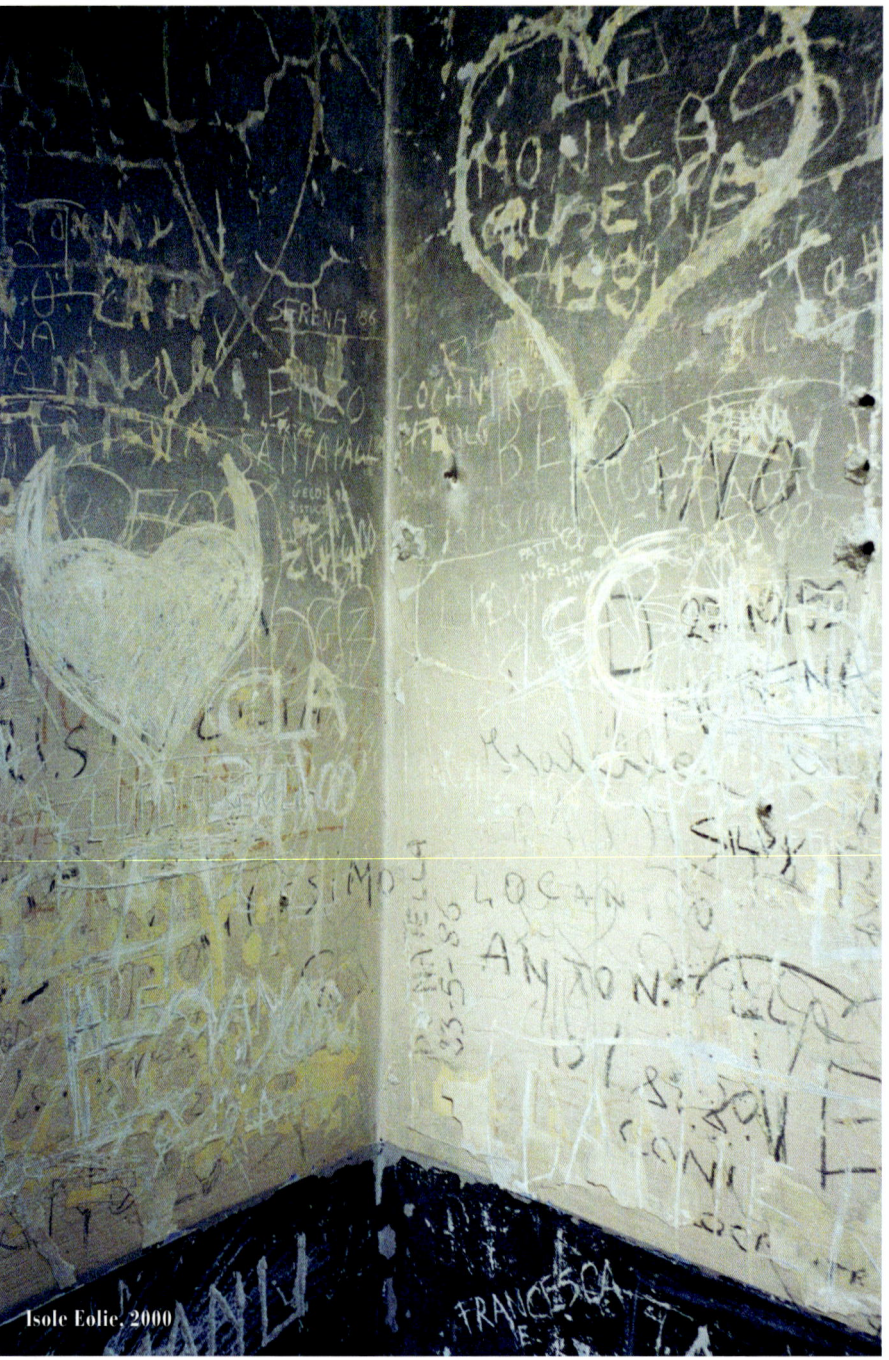

Isole Eolie, 2000

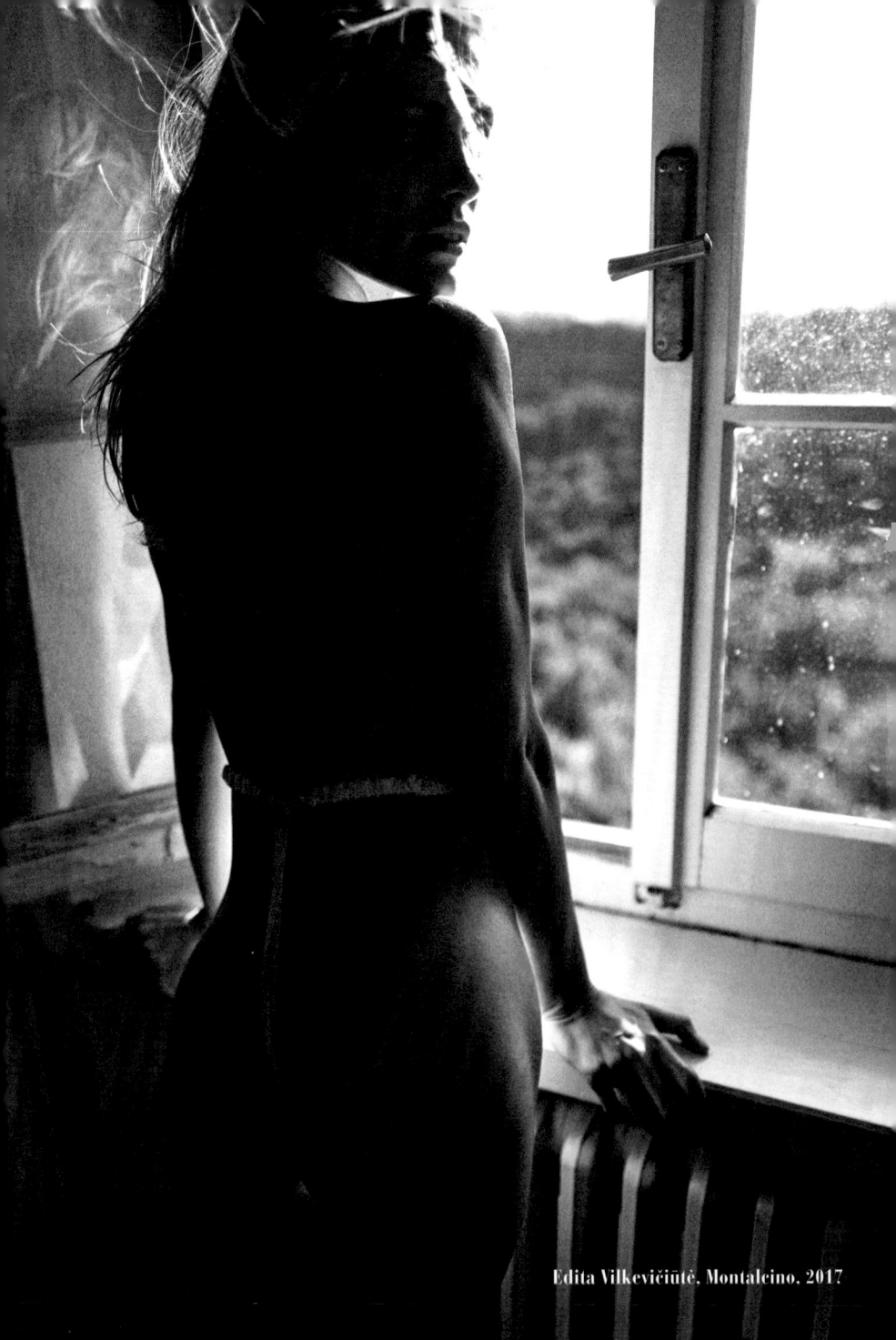

Edita Vilkevičiūtė, Montalcino, 2017

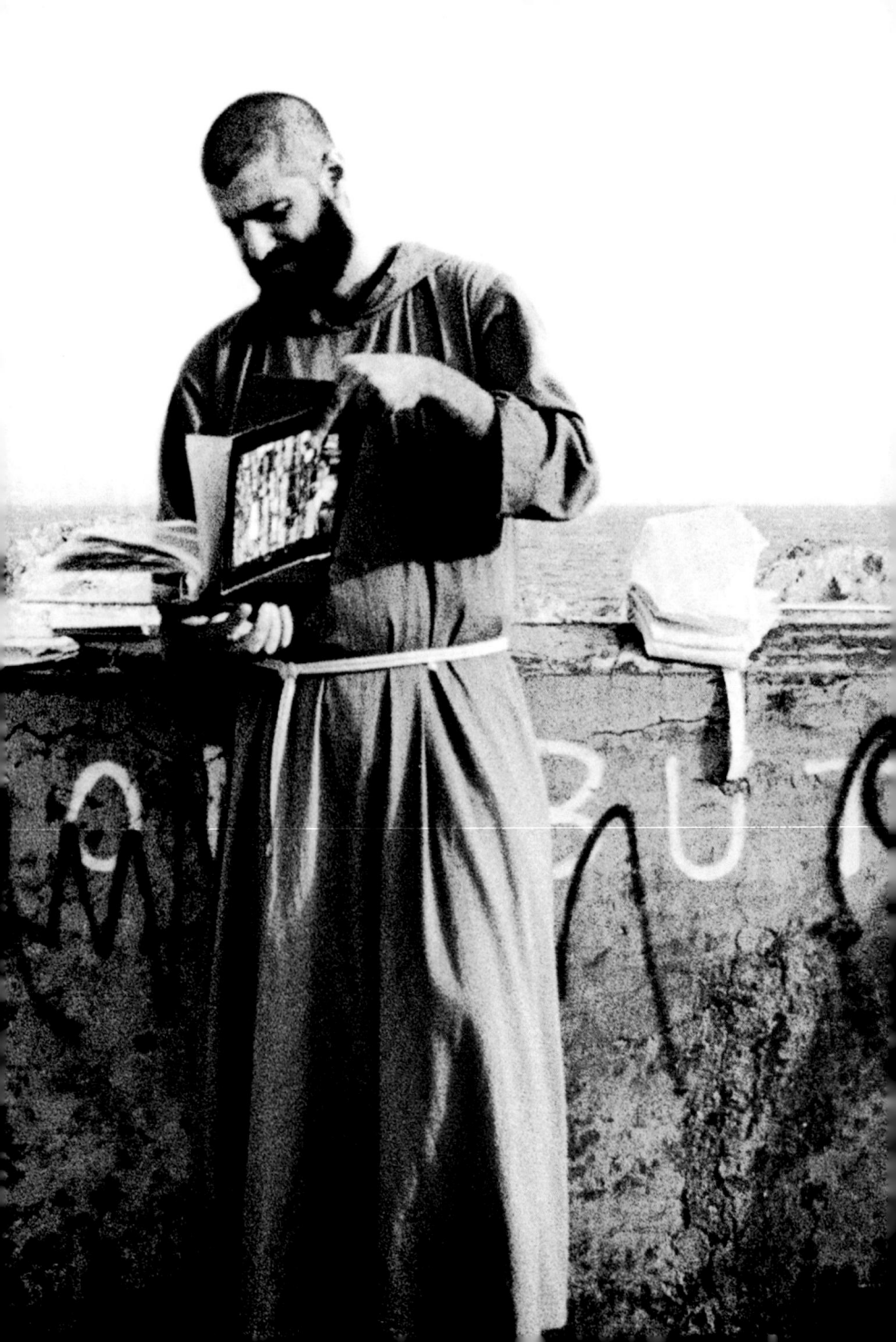

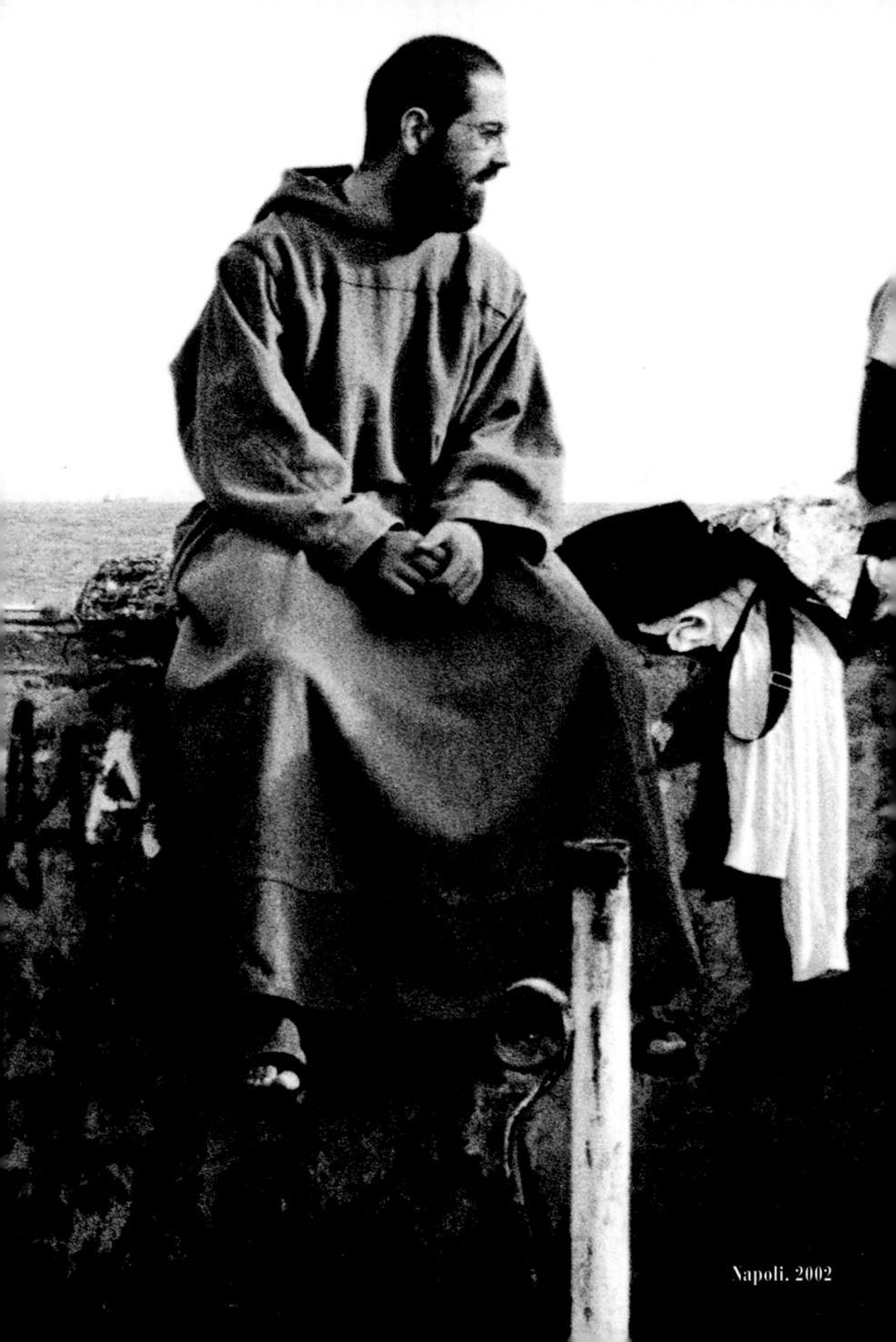

Napoli. 2002

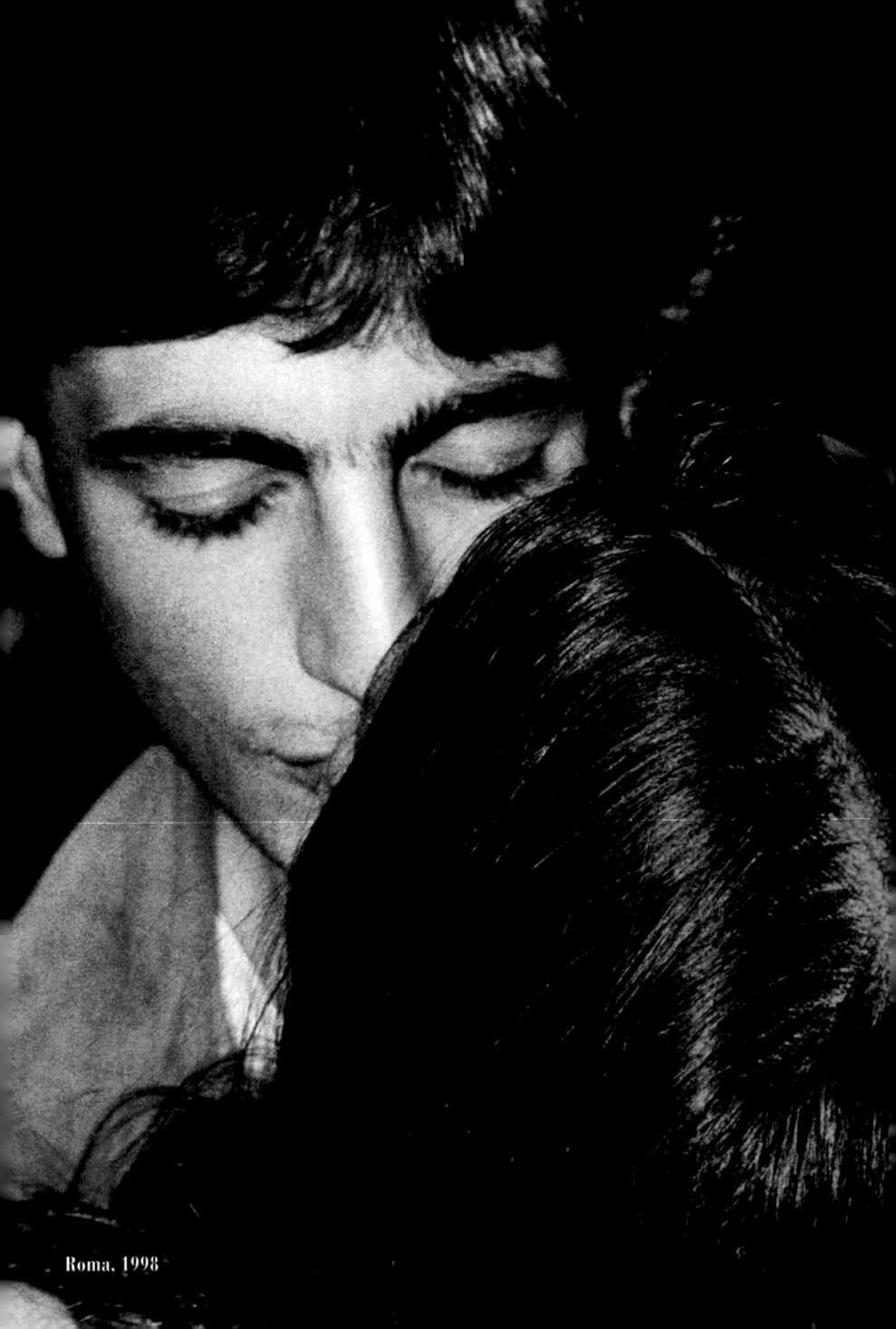

Roma, 1998

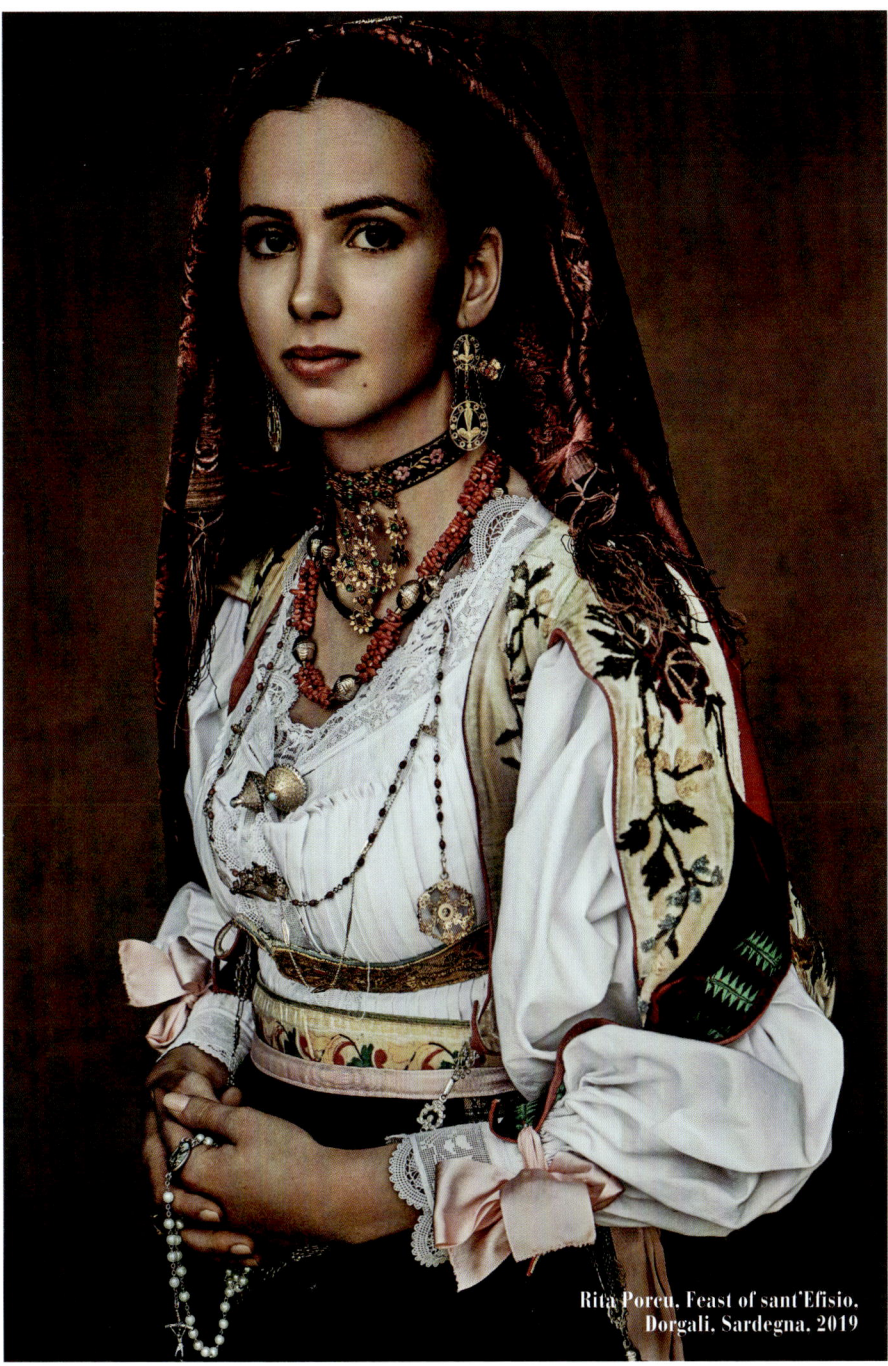

Rita Porcu. Feast of sant'Efisio.
Dorgali. Sardegna. 2019

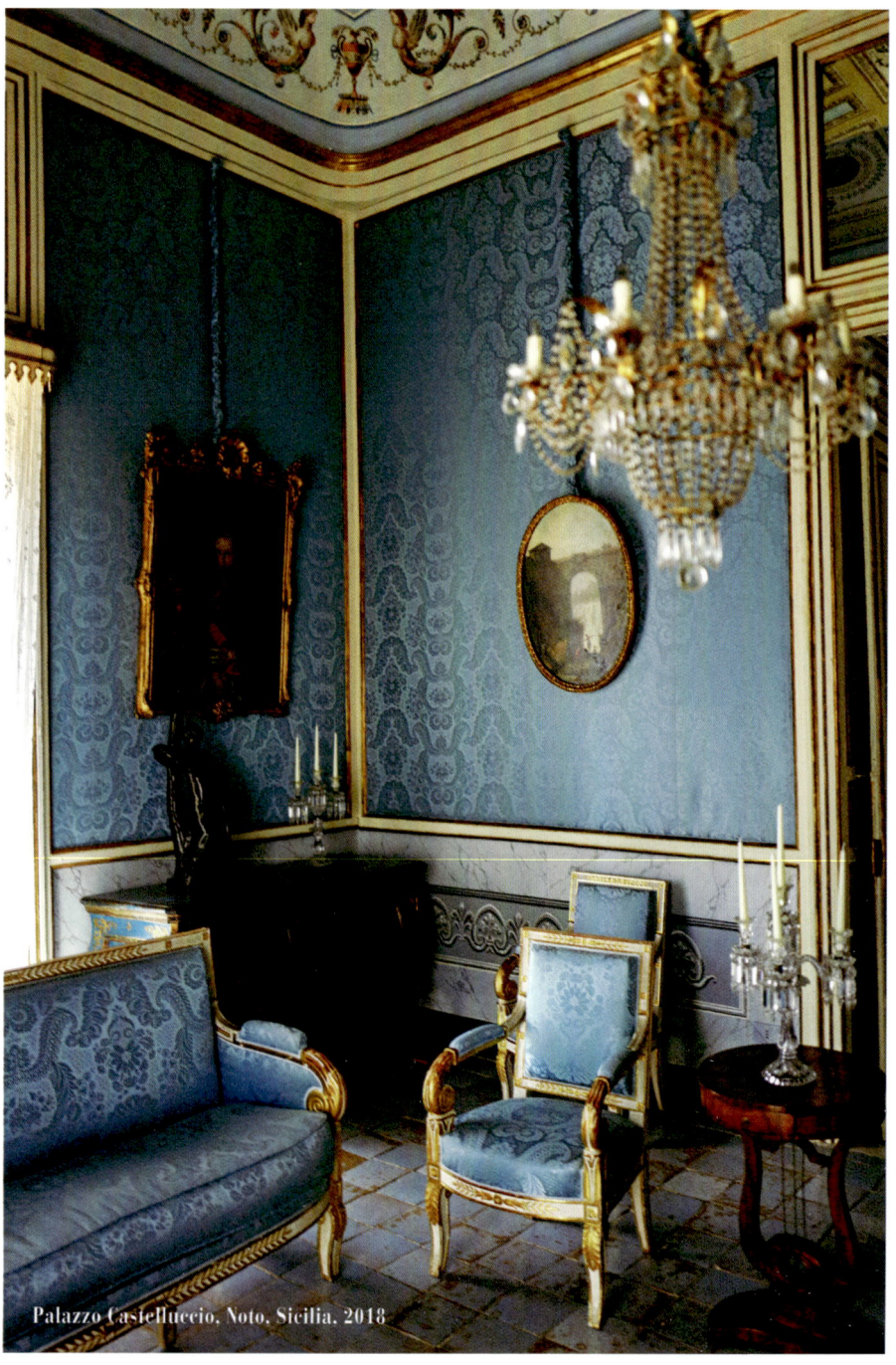

Palazzo Castelluccio, Noto, Sicilia, 2018

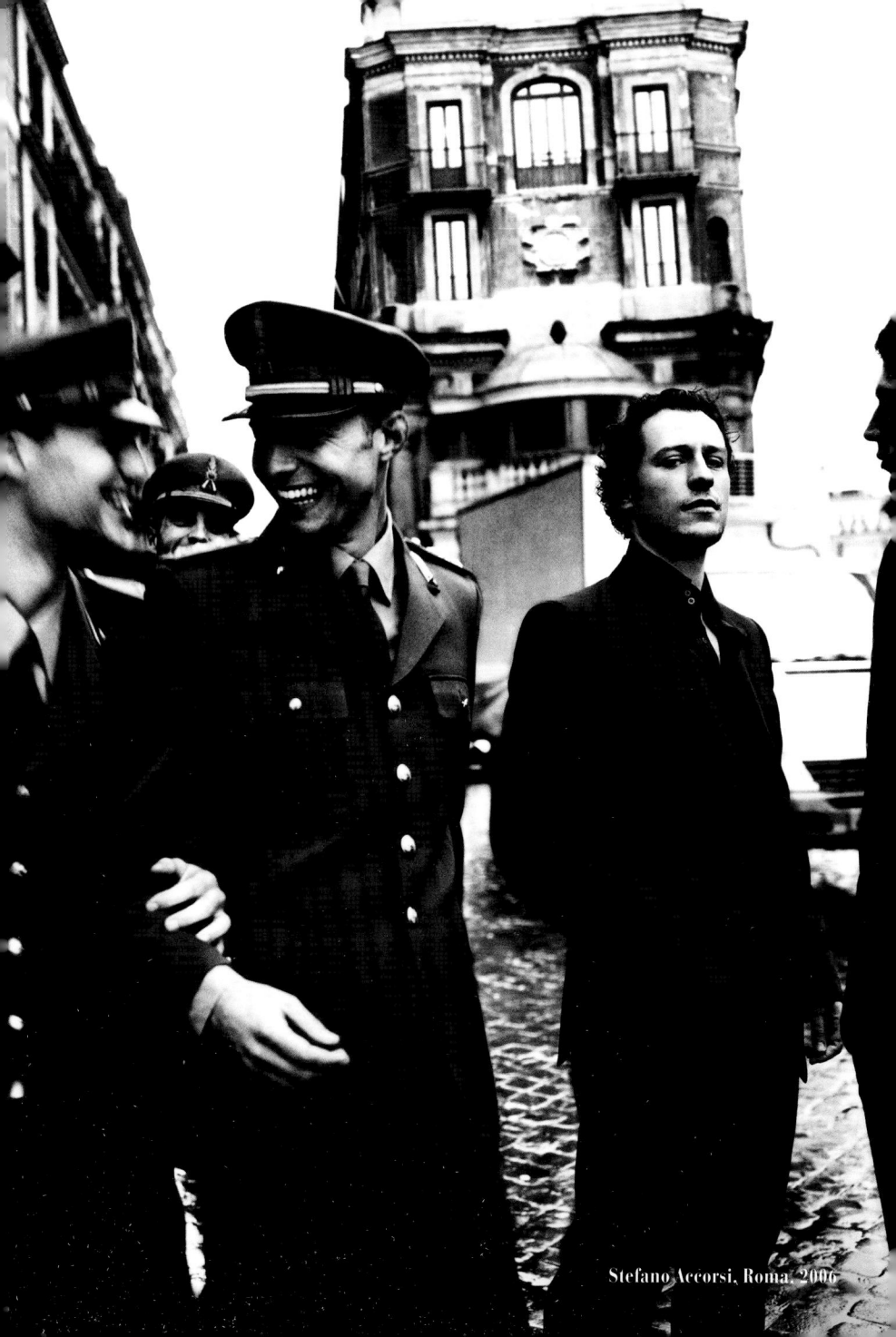

Stefano Accorsi, Roma, 2006

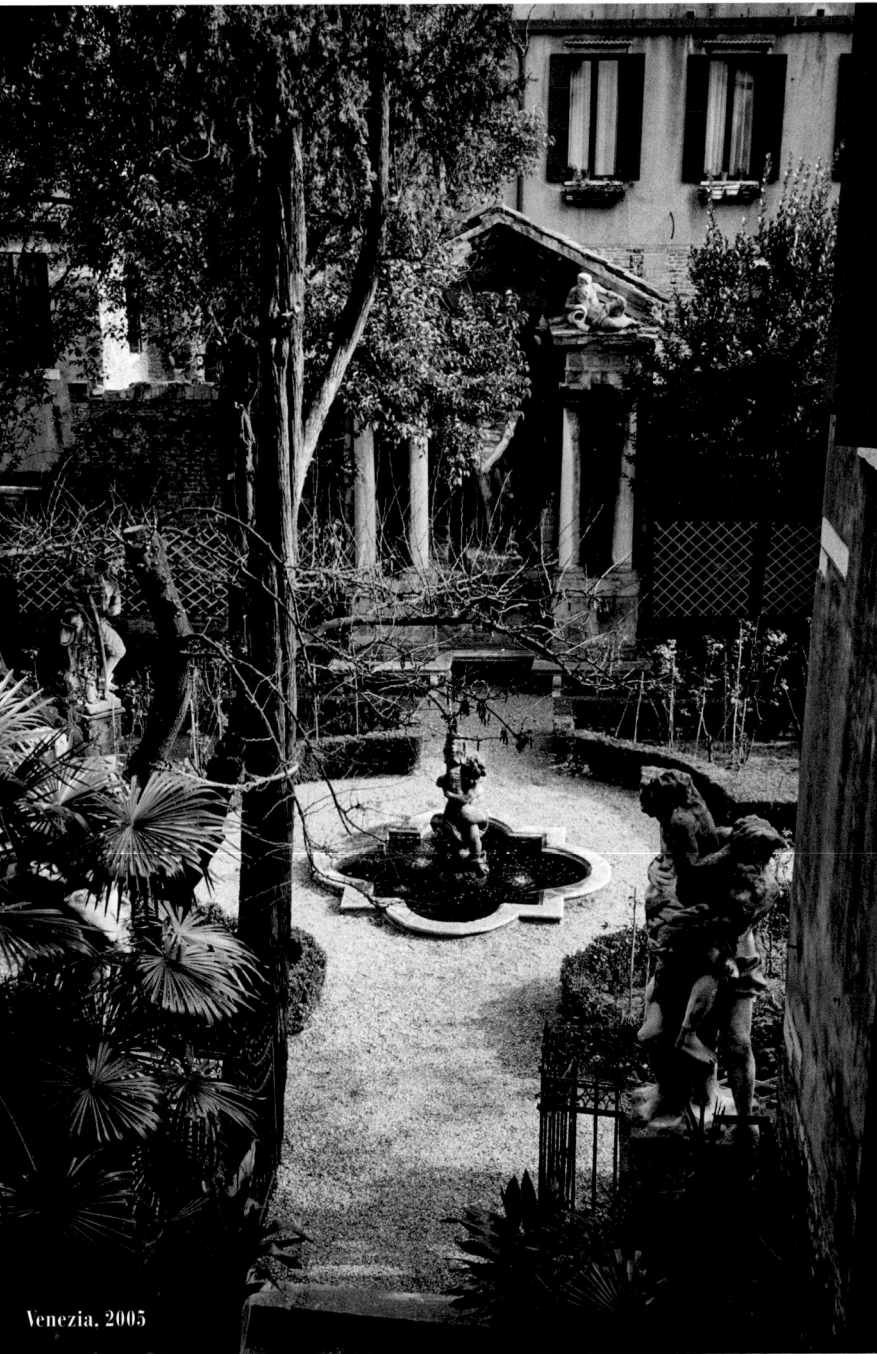

Venezia. 2005

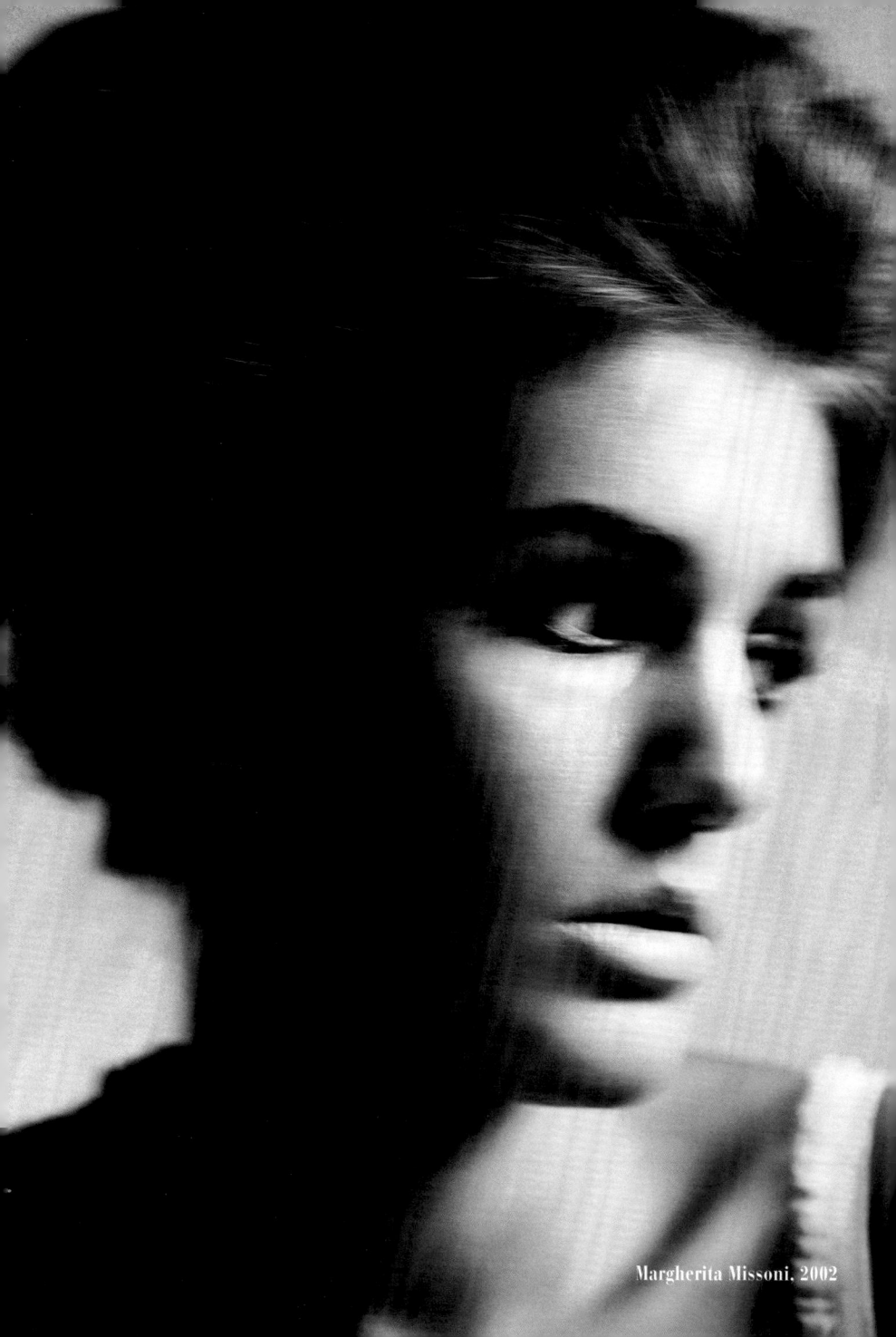

Margherita Missoni, 2002

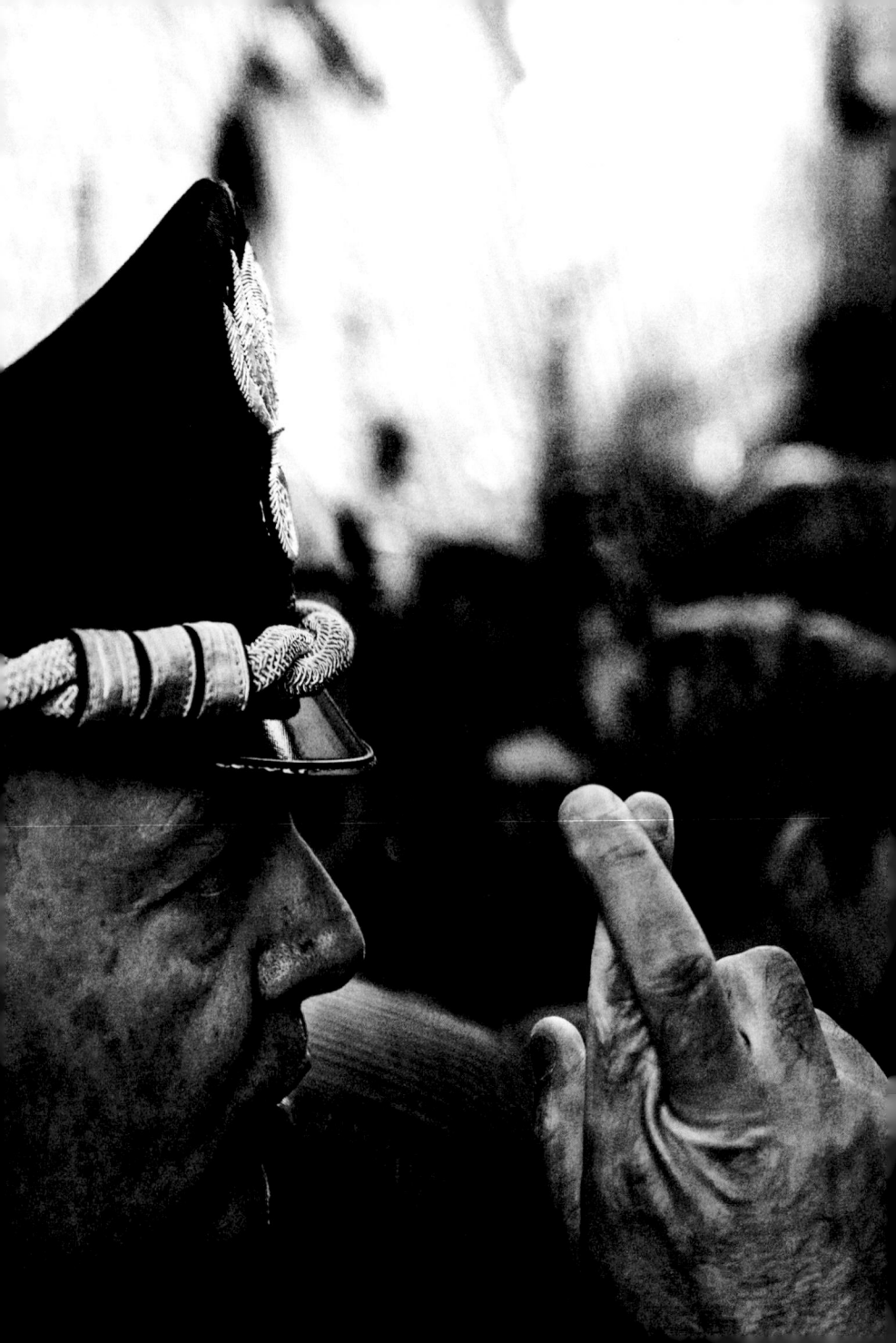

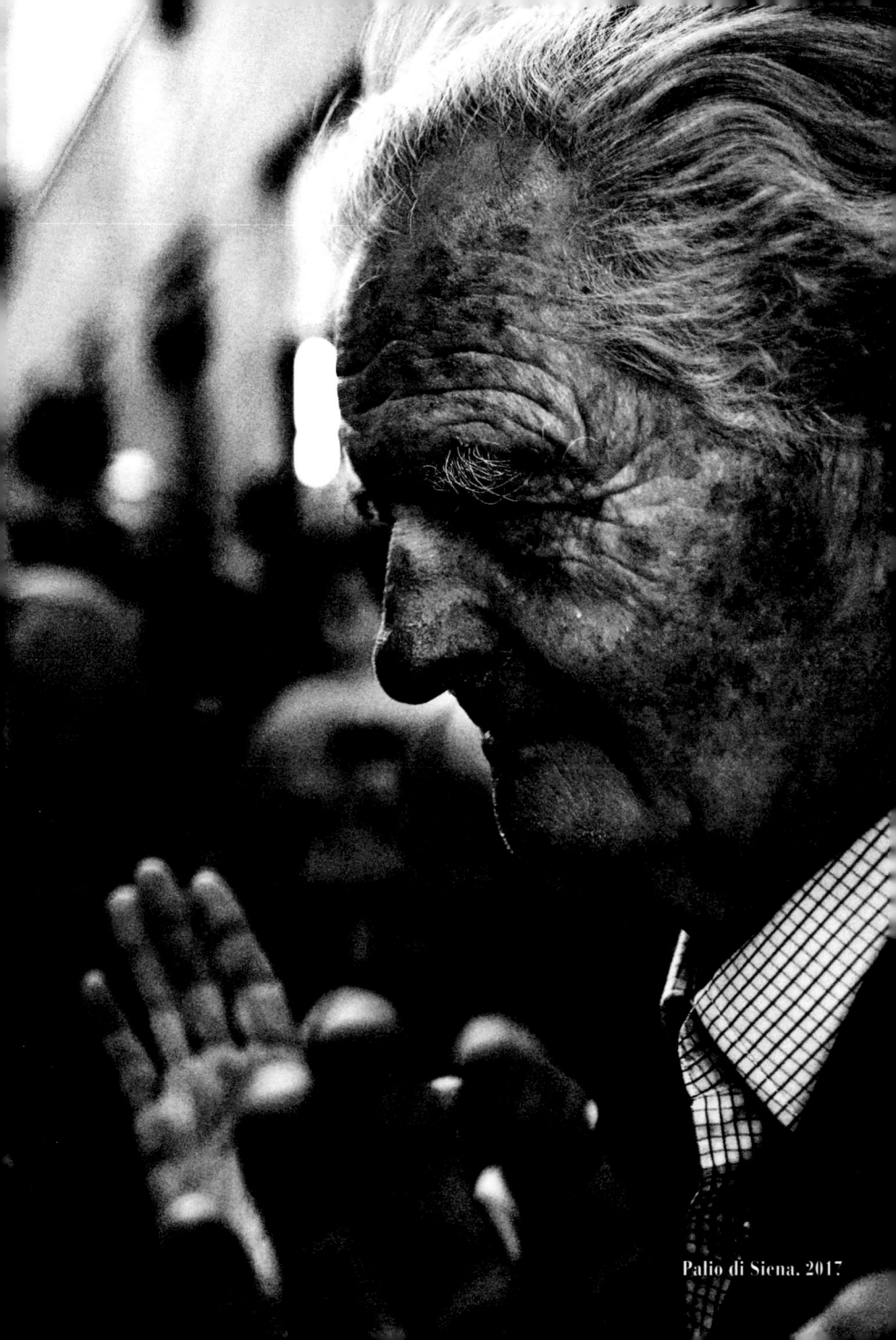

Palio di Siena, 2017

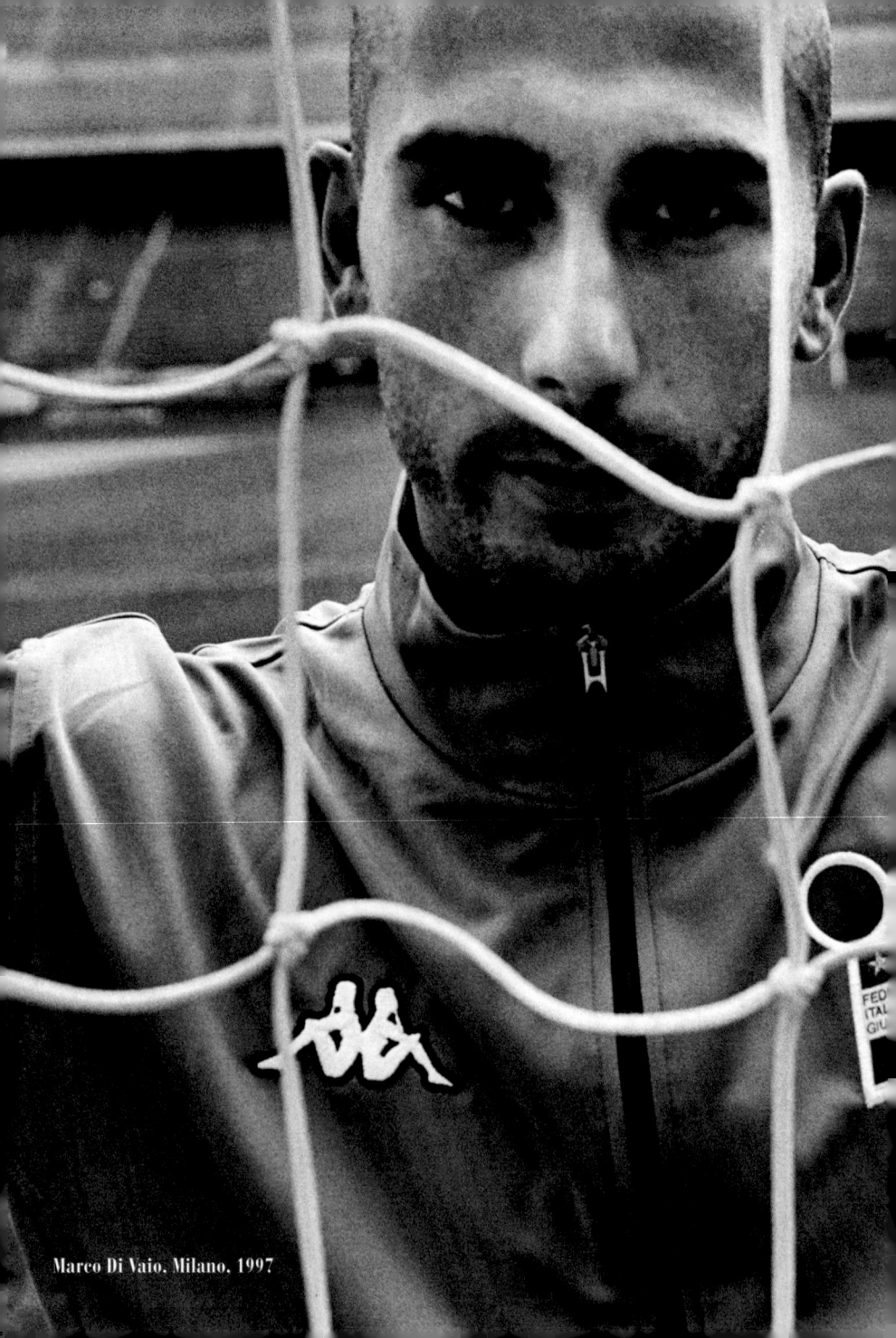
Marco Di Vaio, Milano, 1997

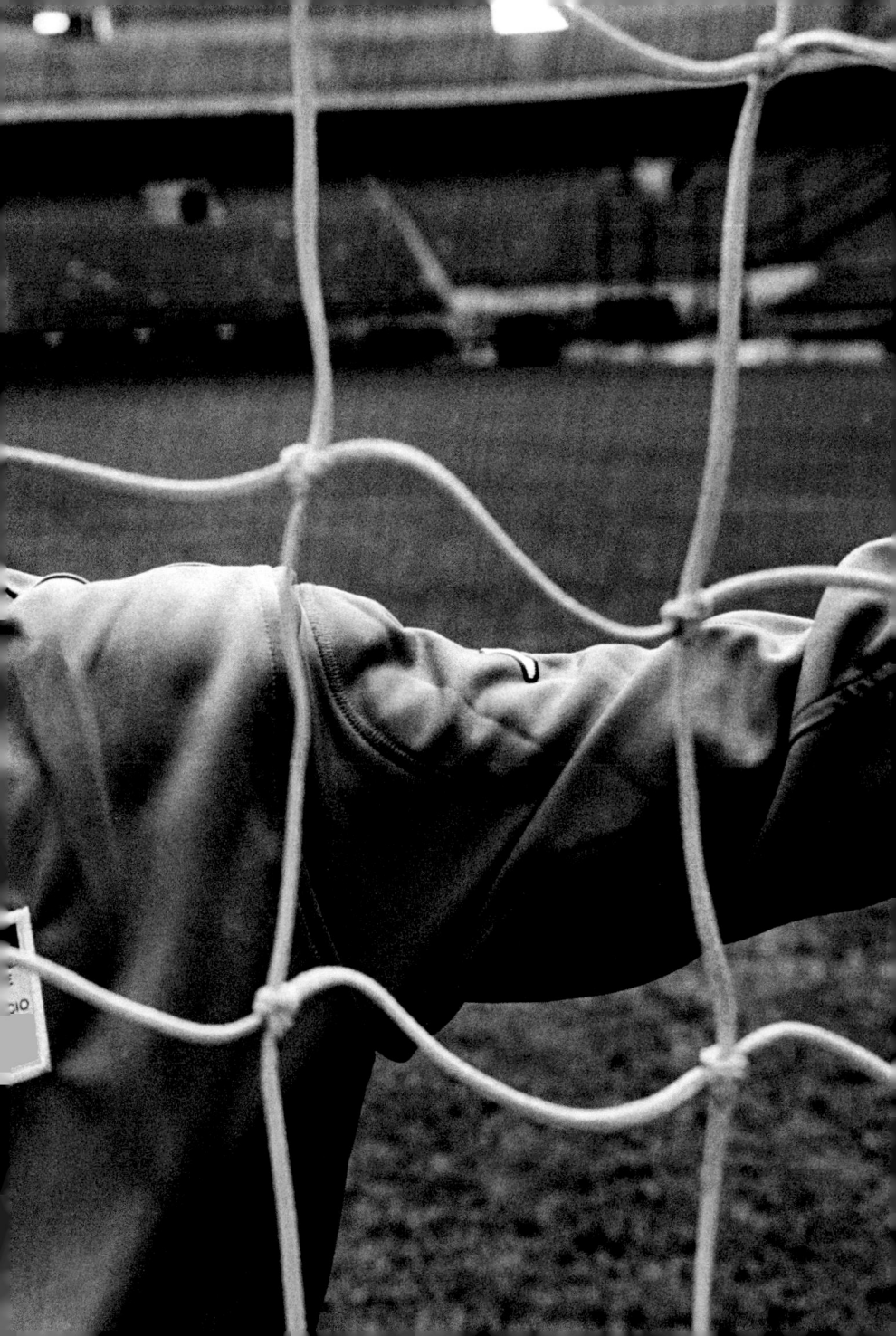

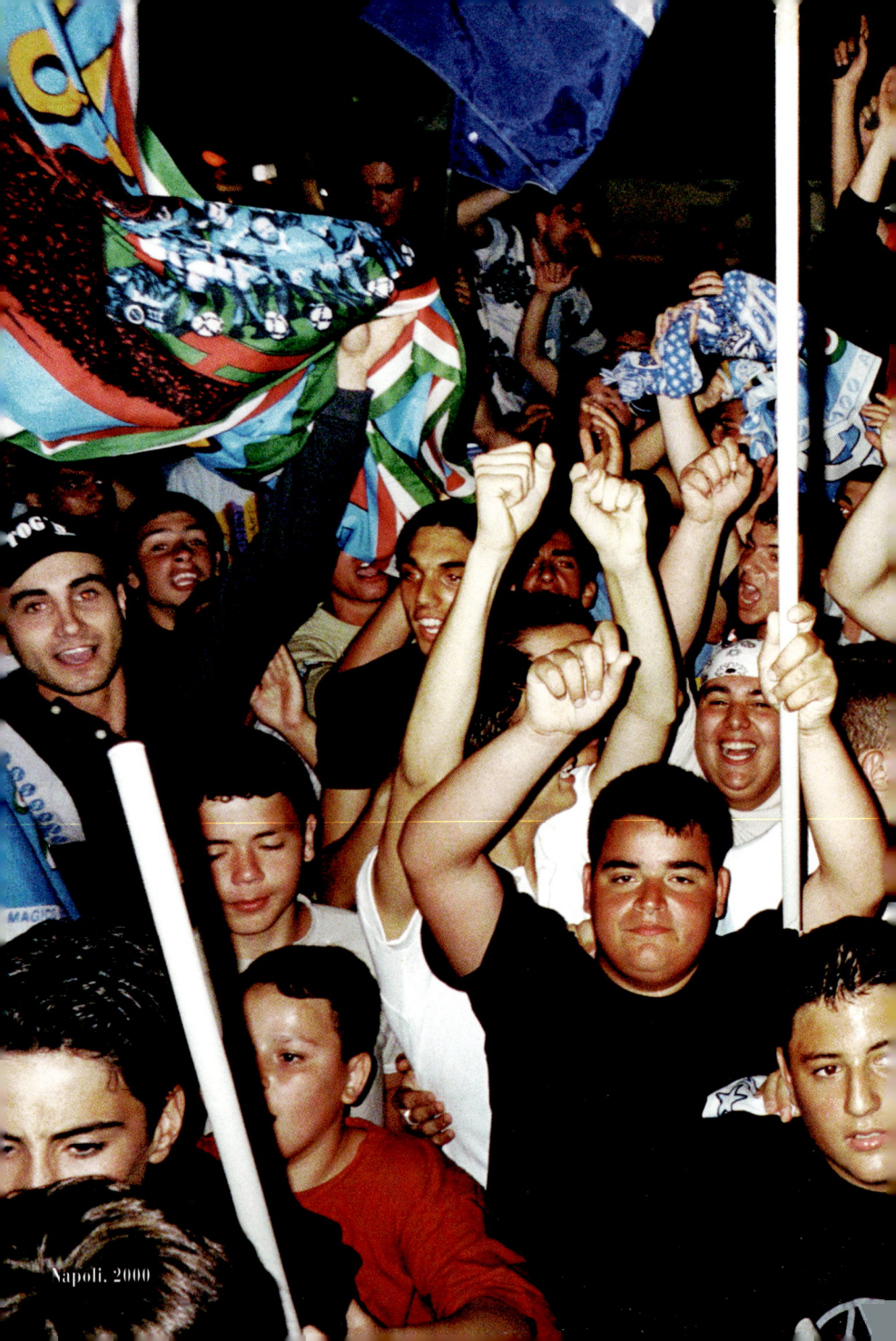

Napoli, 2000

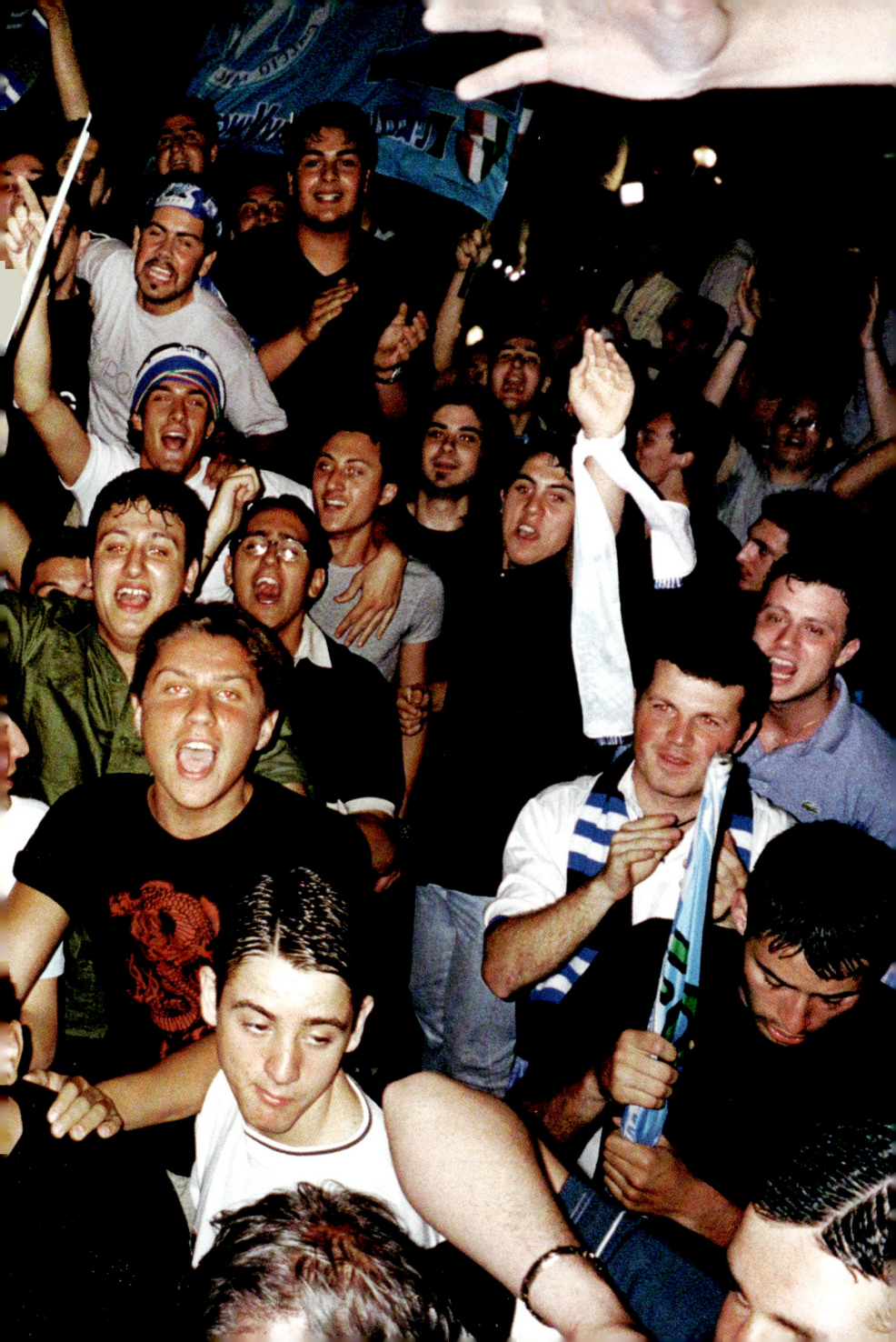

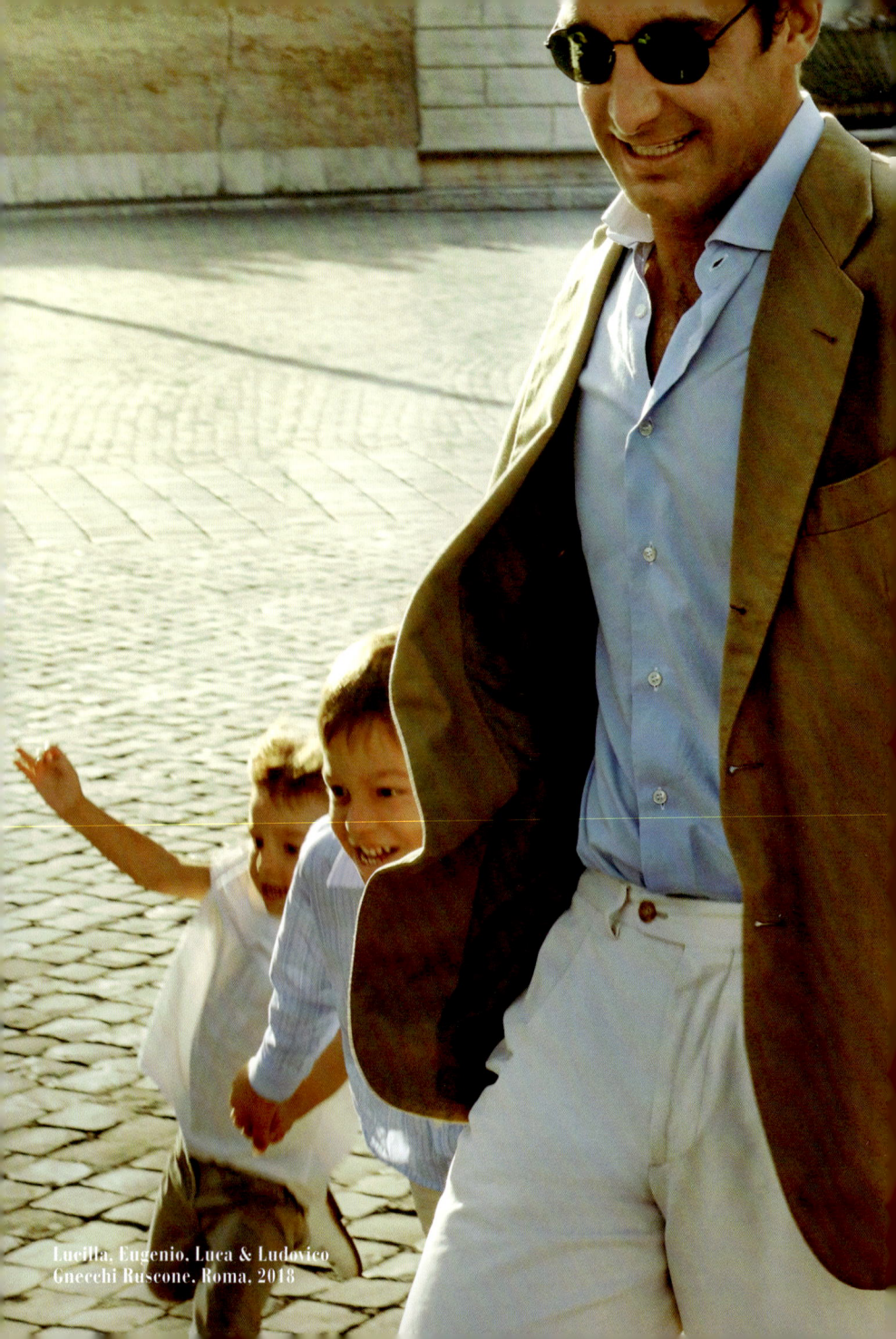

Lucilla, Eugenio, Luca & Ludovico
Gnecchi Ruscone, Roma, 2018

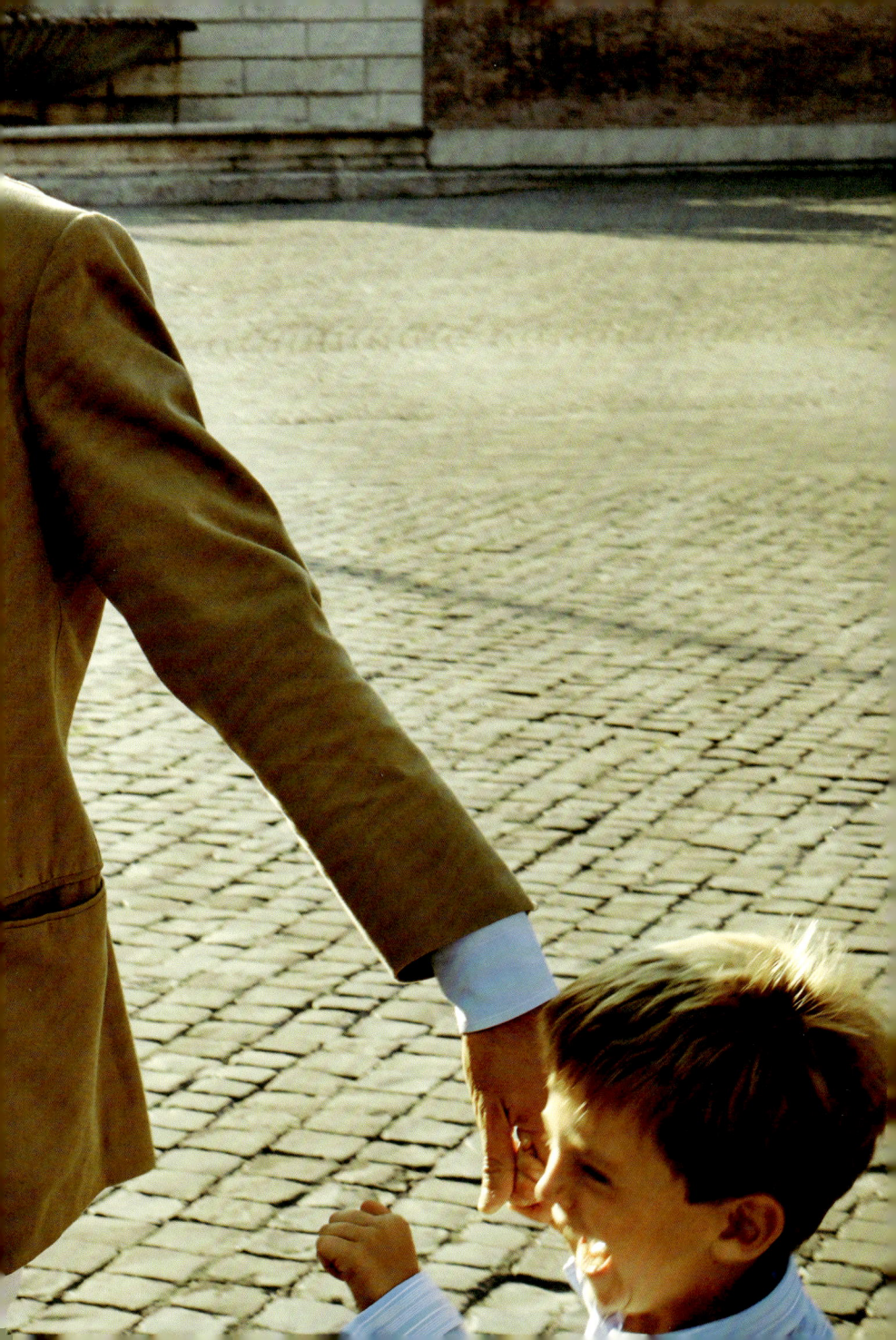

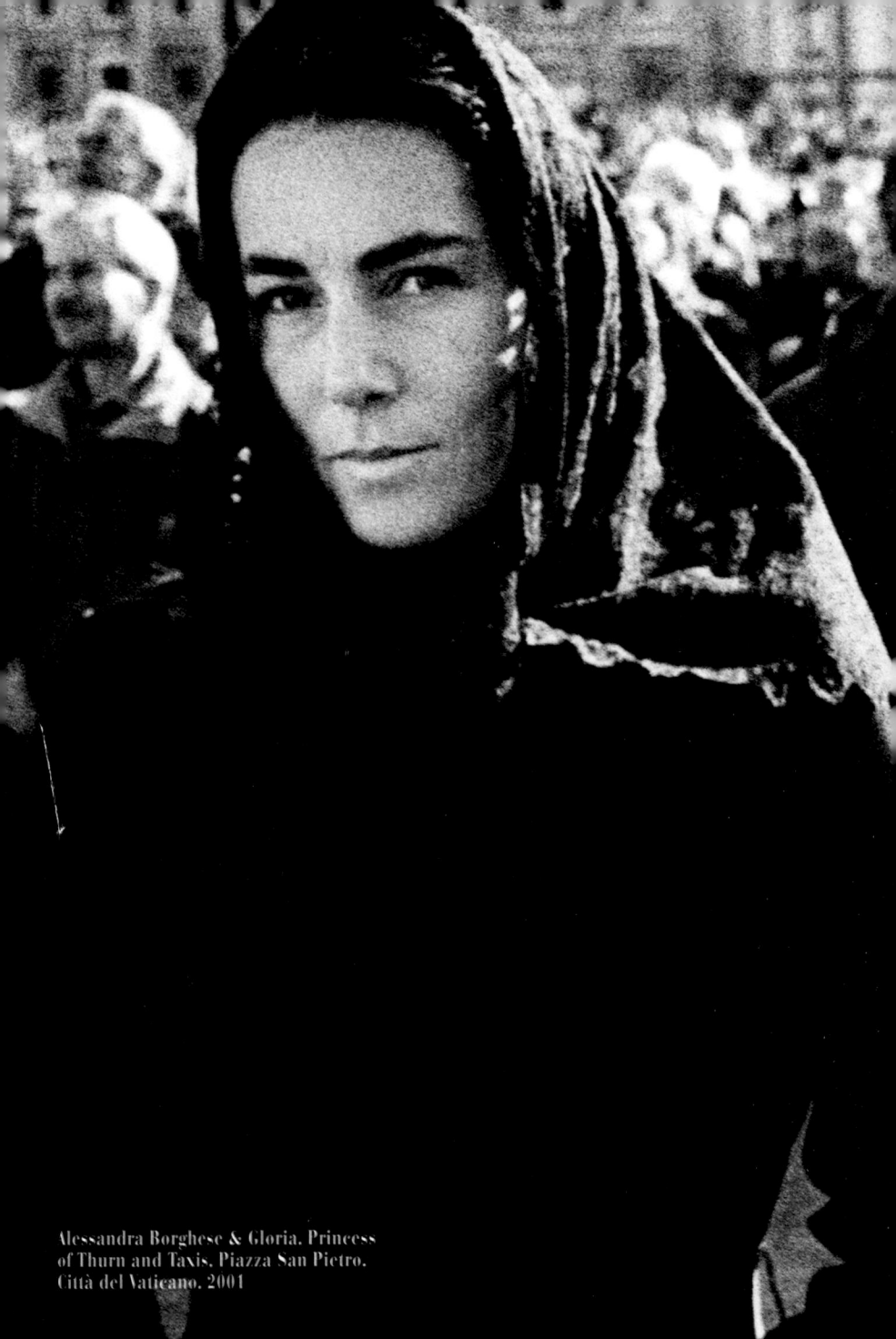

Alessandra Borghese & Gloria, Princess
of Thurn and Taxis, Piazza San Pietro,
Città del Vaticano, 2001

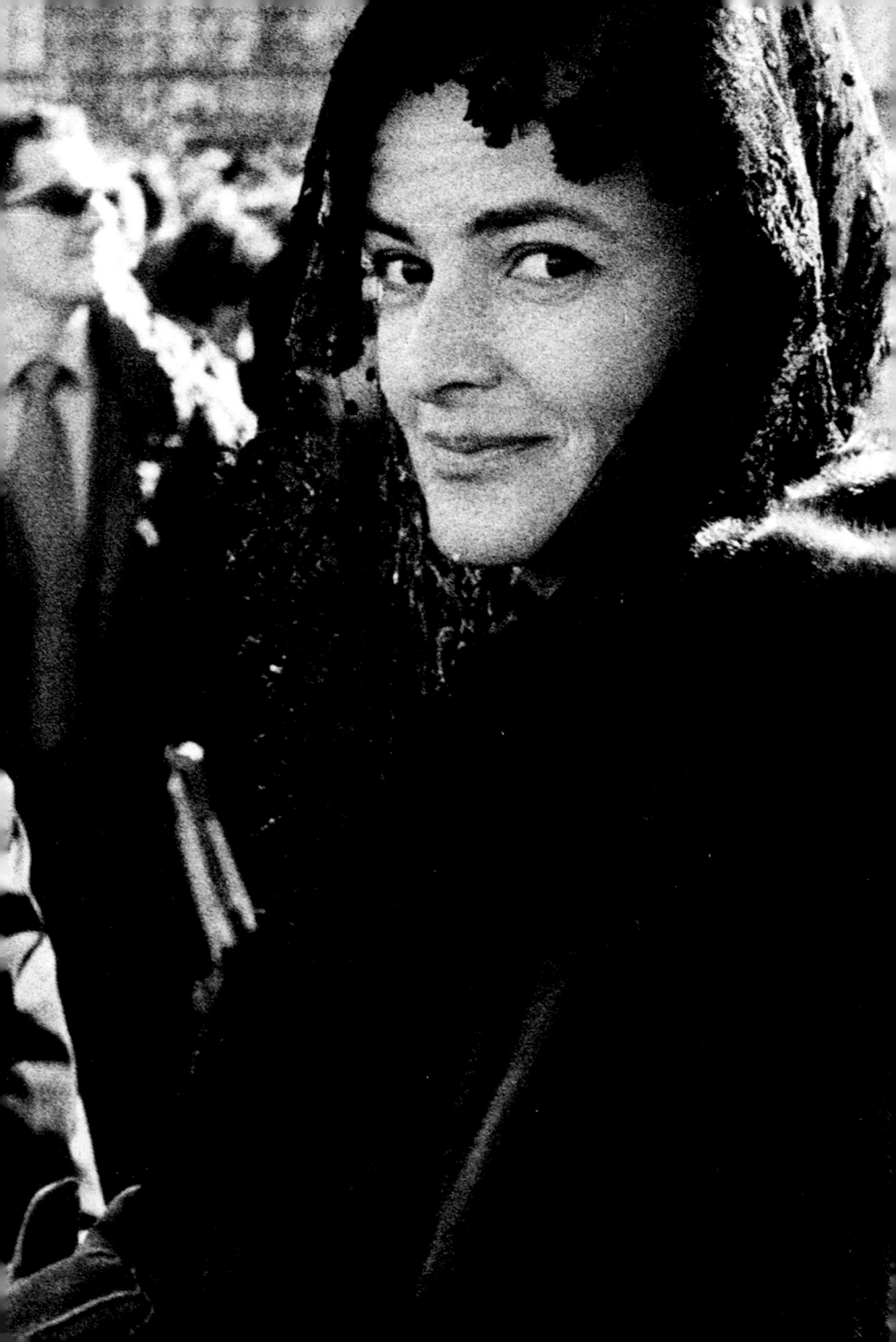

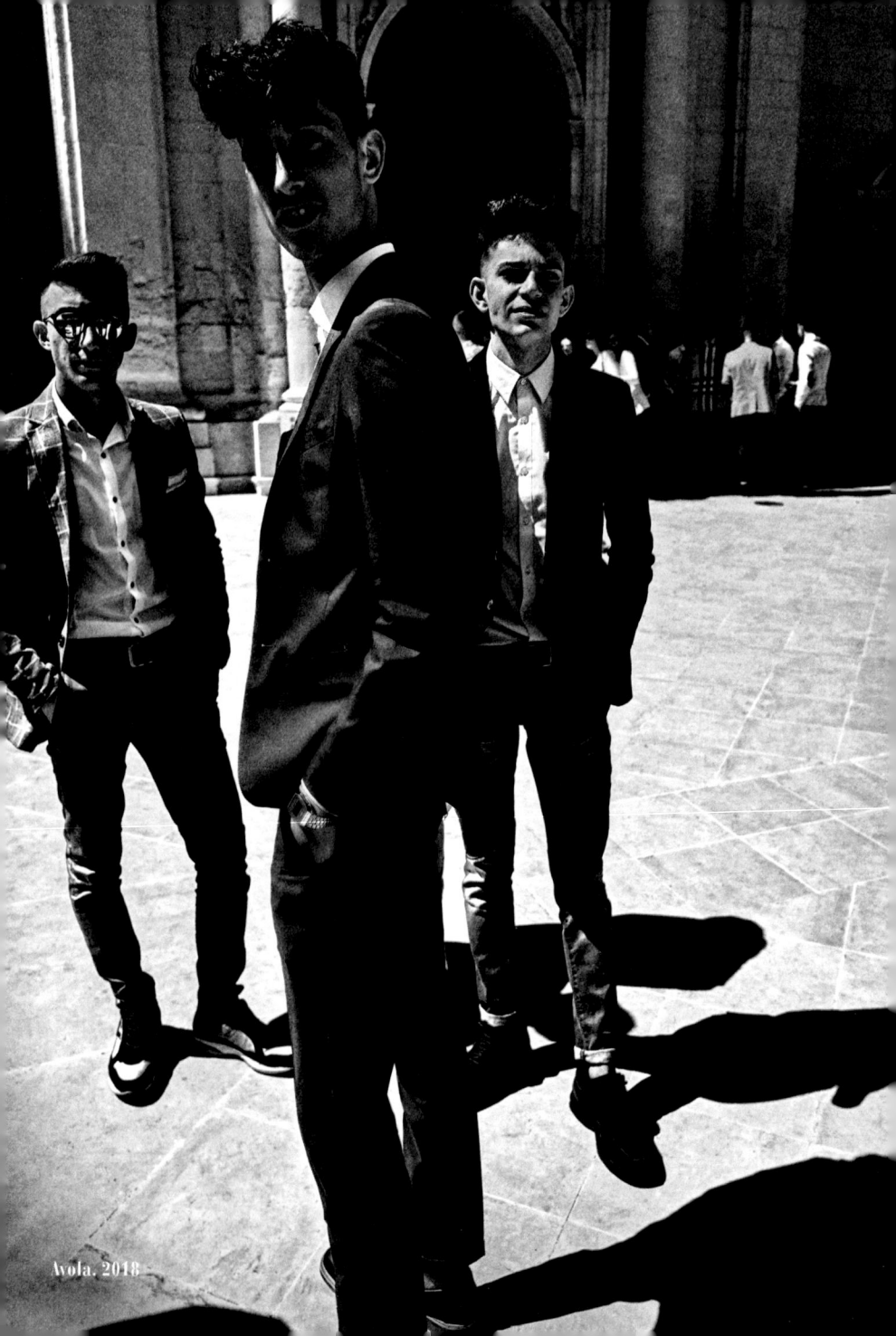

Avola, 2018

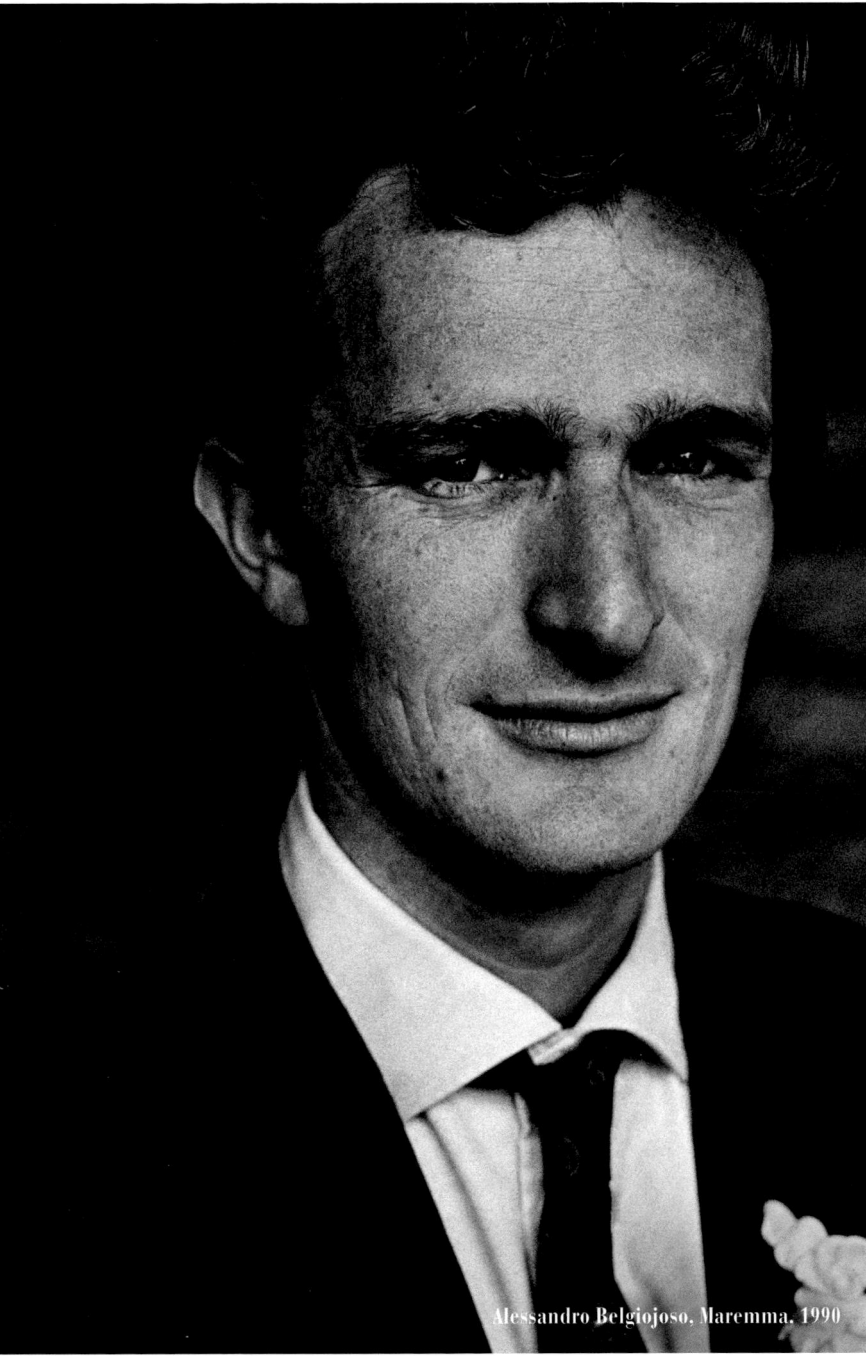

Alessandro Belgiojoso, Maremma, 1990

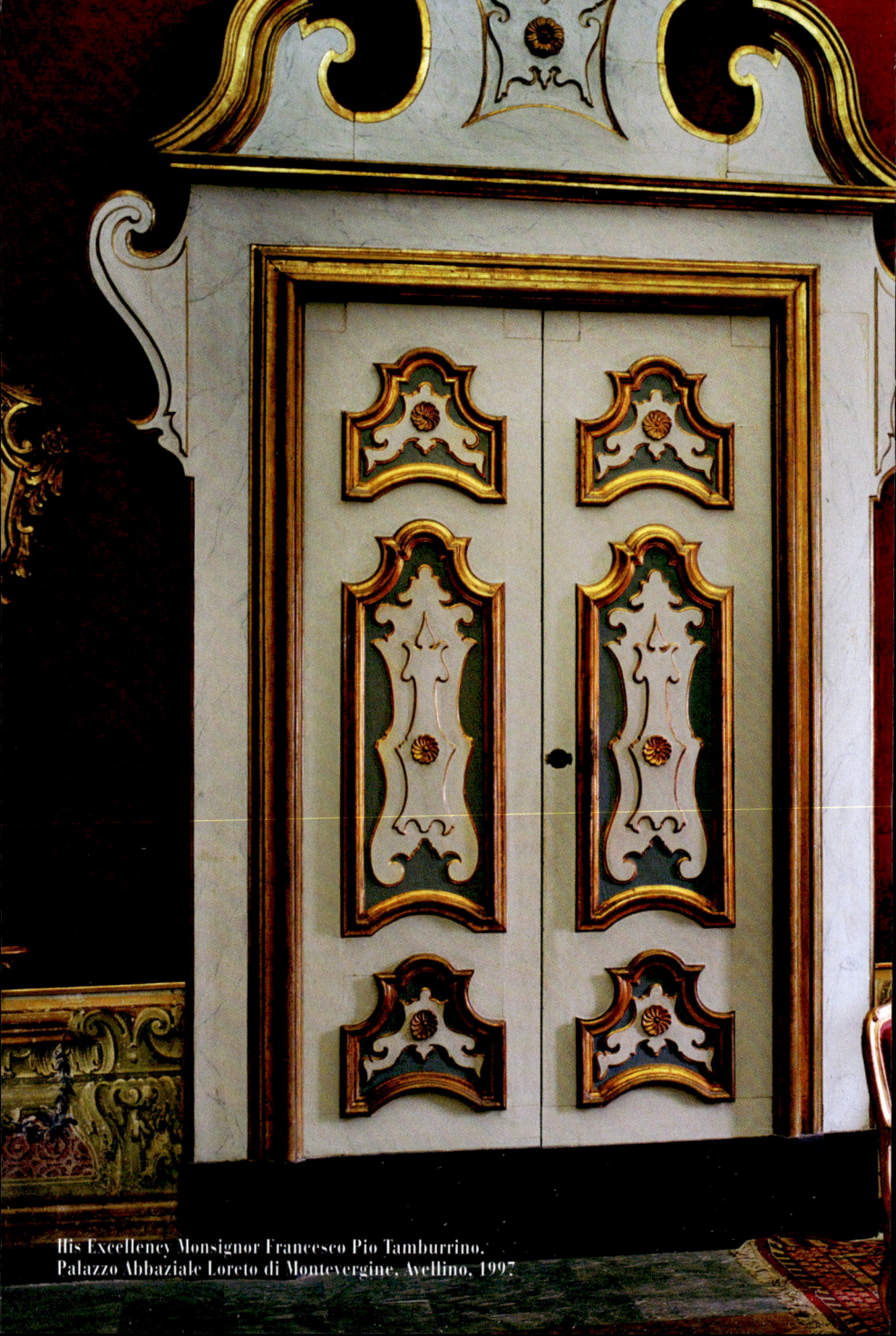

His Excellency Monsignor Francesco Pio Tamburrino,
Palazzo Abbaziale Loreto di Montevergine, Avellino, 1997

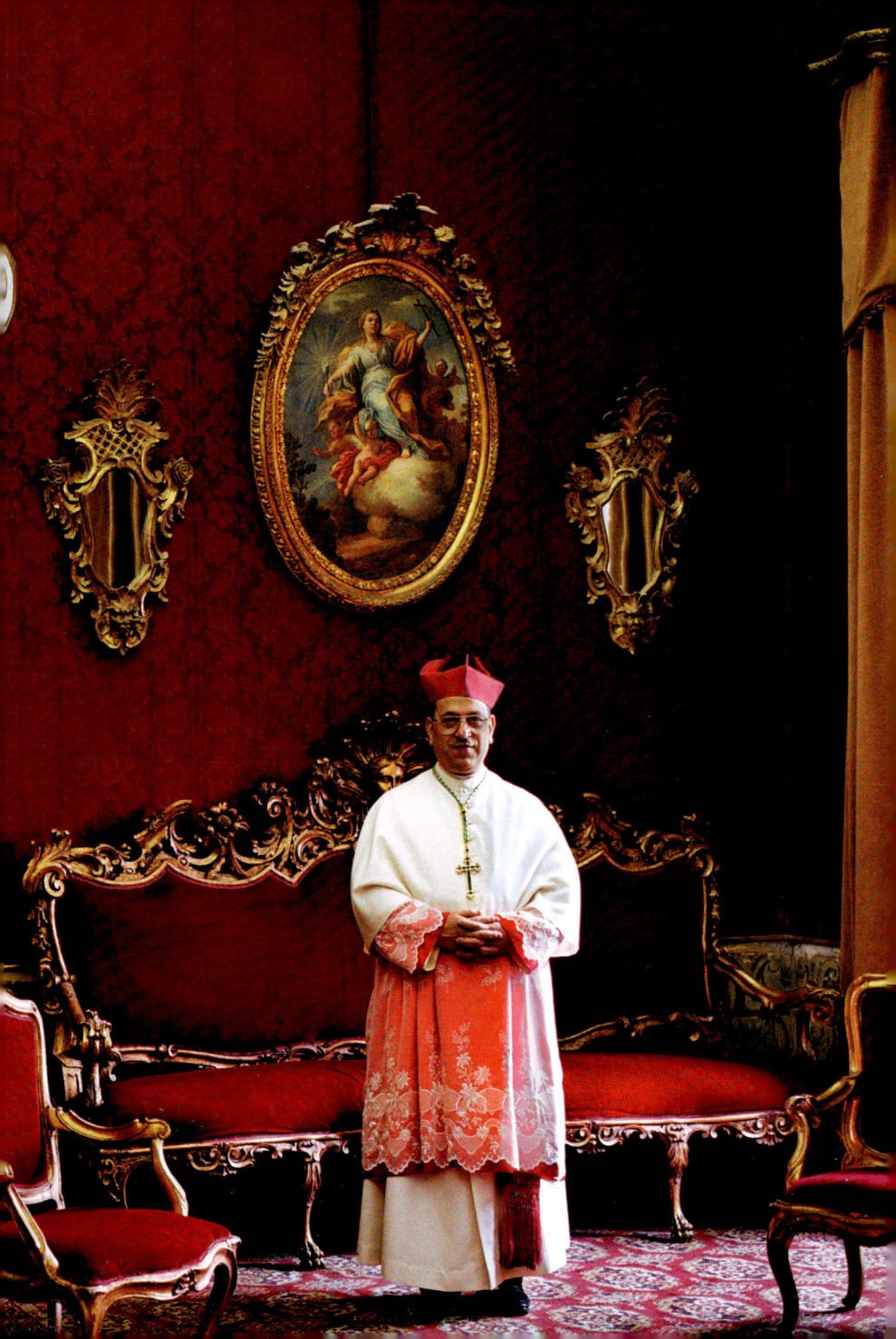

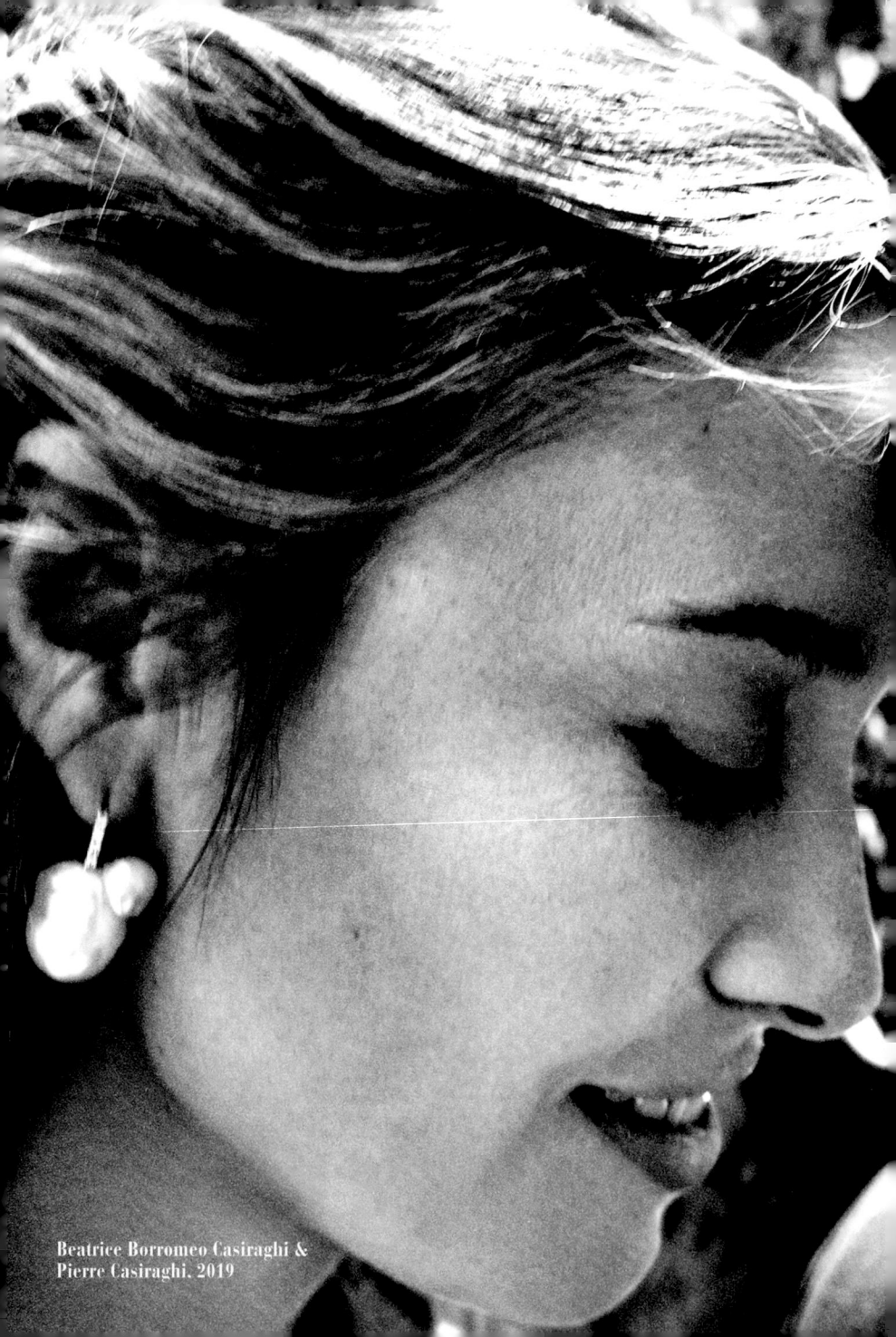

Beatrice Borromeo Casiraghi &
Pierre Casiraghi, 2019

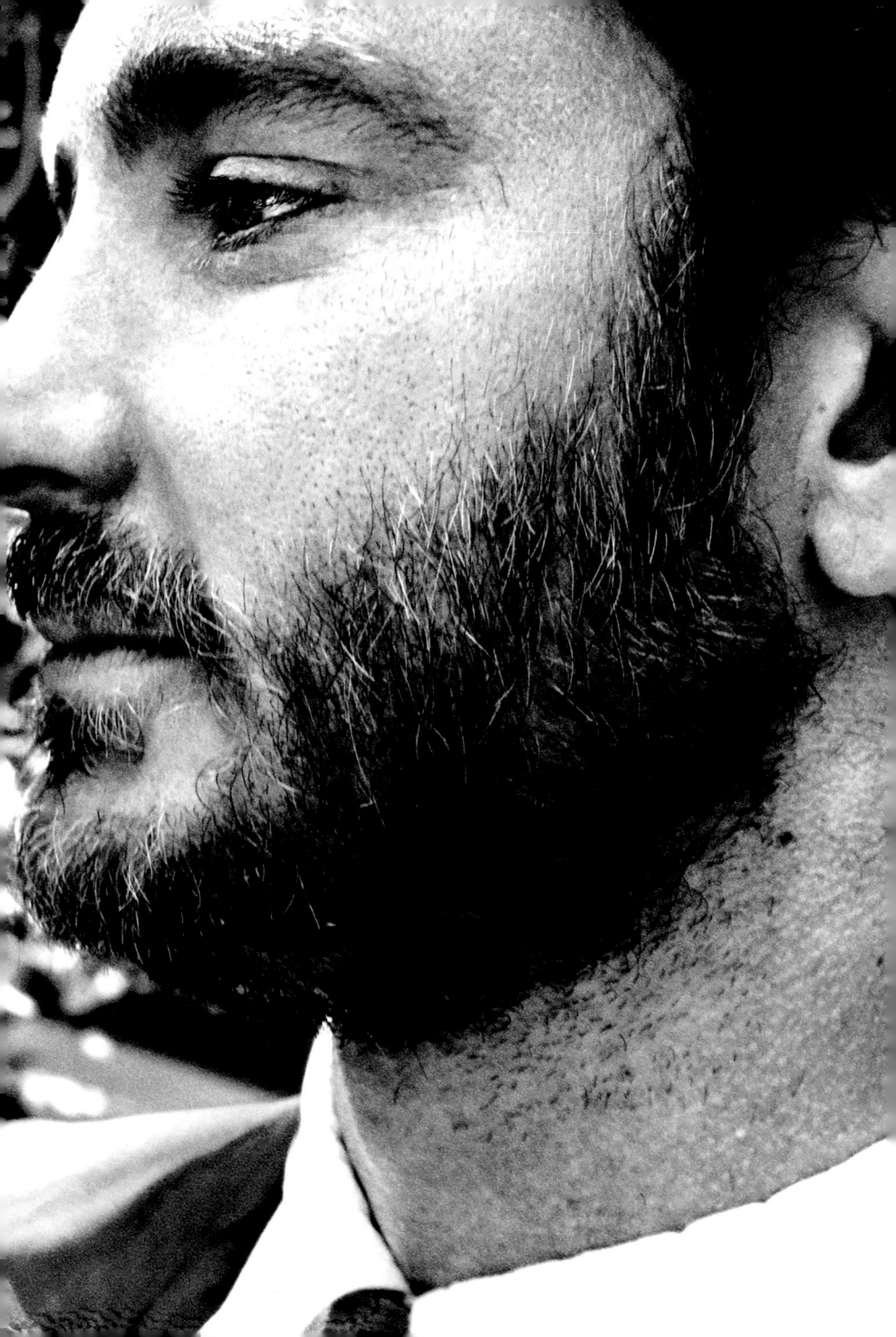

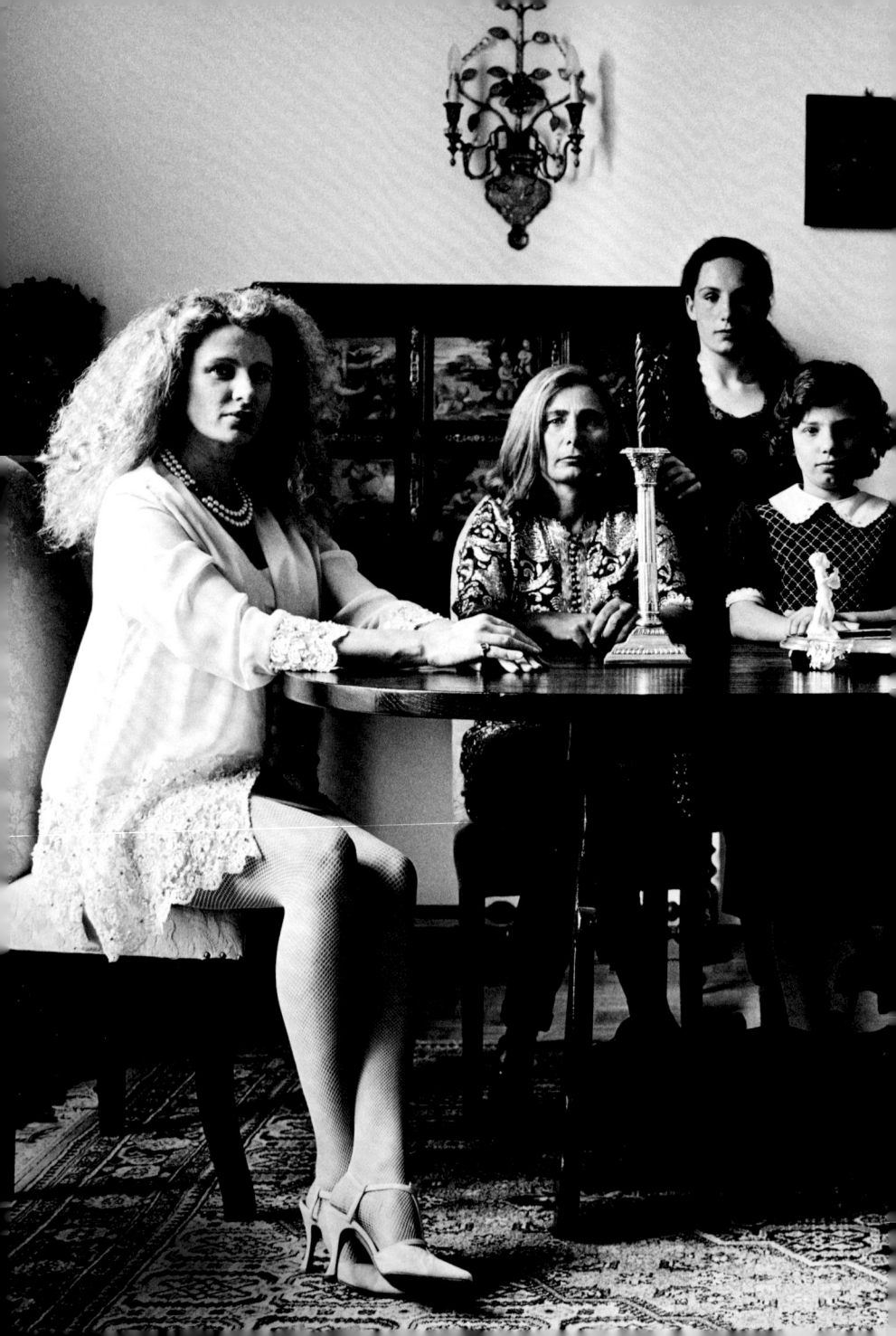

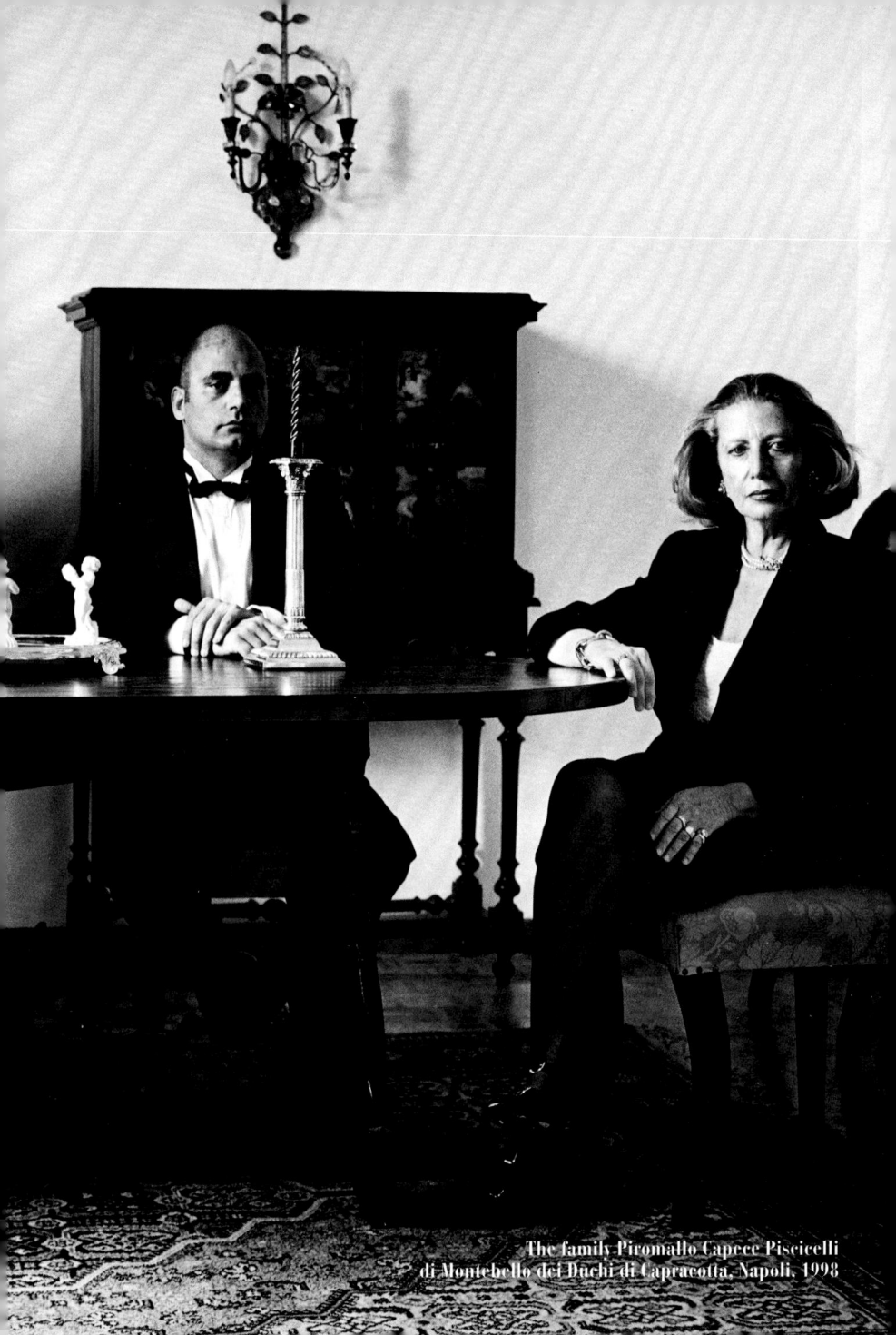

The family Piromallo Capece Piscicelli
di Montebello dei Duchi di Capracotta, Napoli, 1998

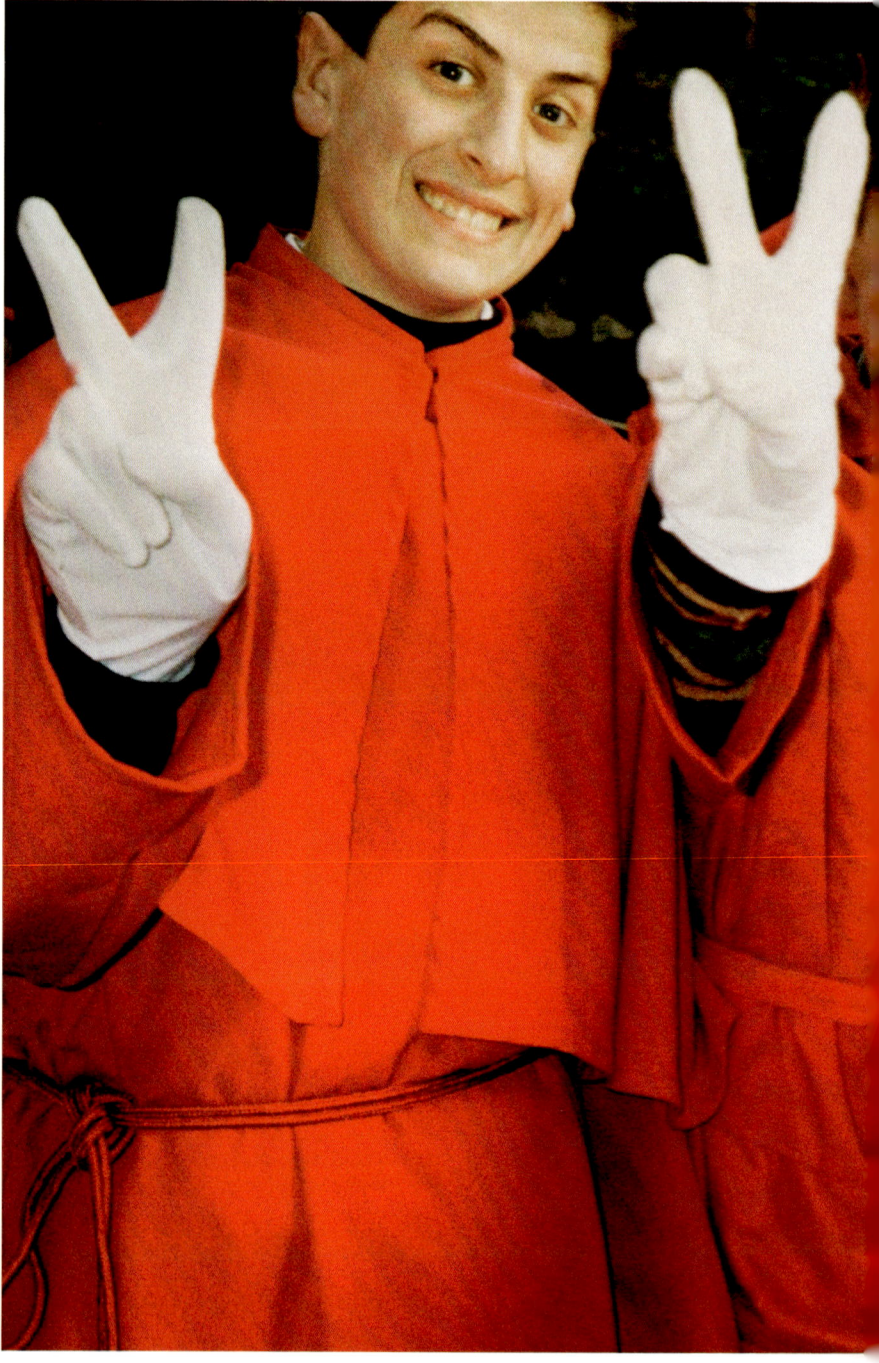

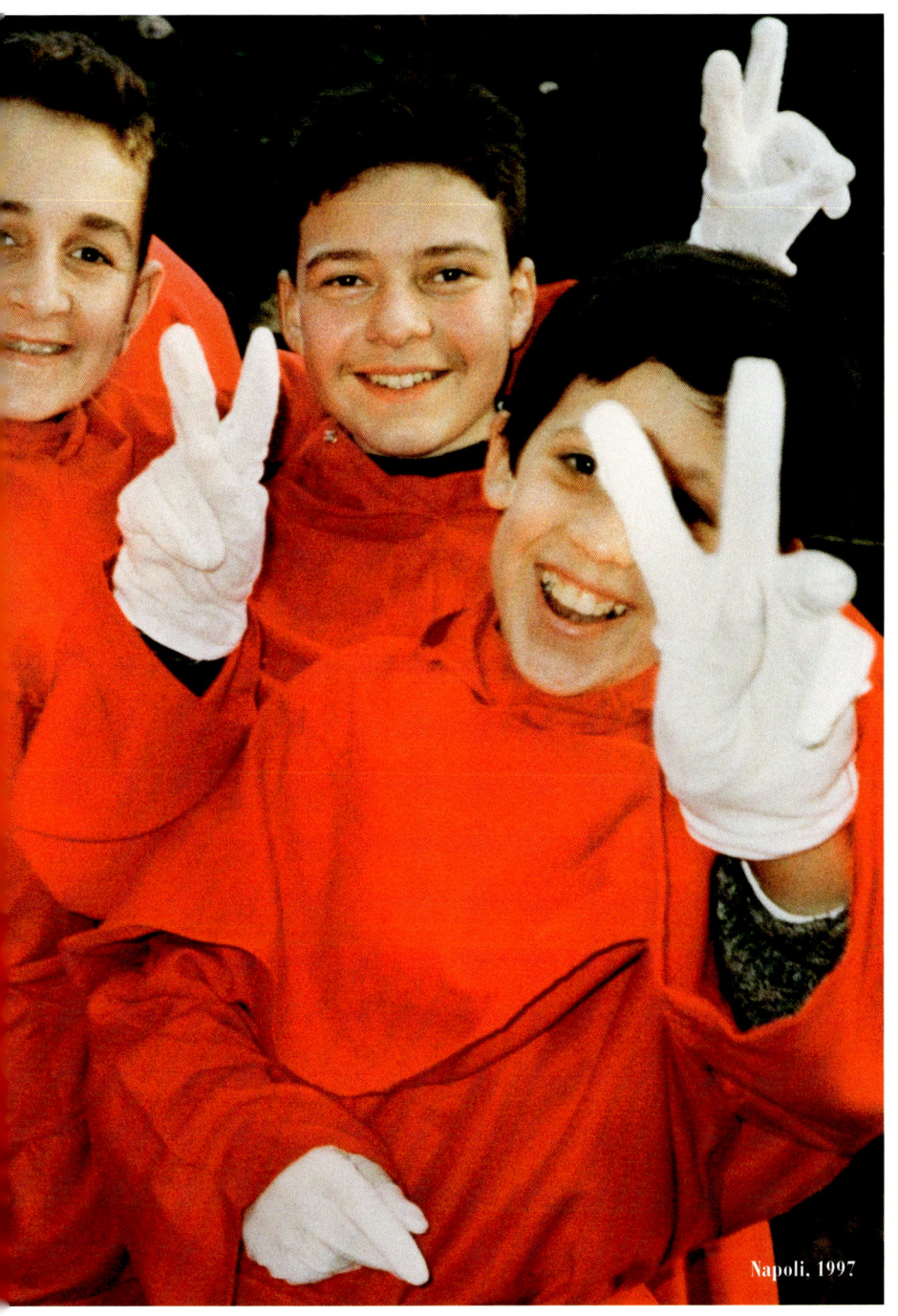

Napoli, 1997

IN
FASHION

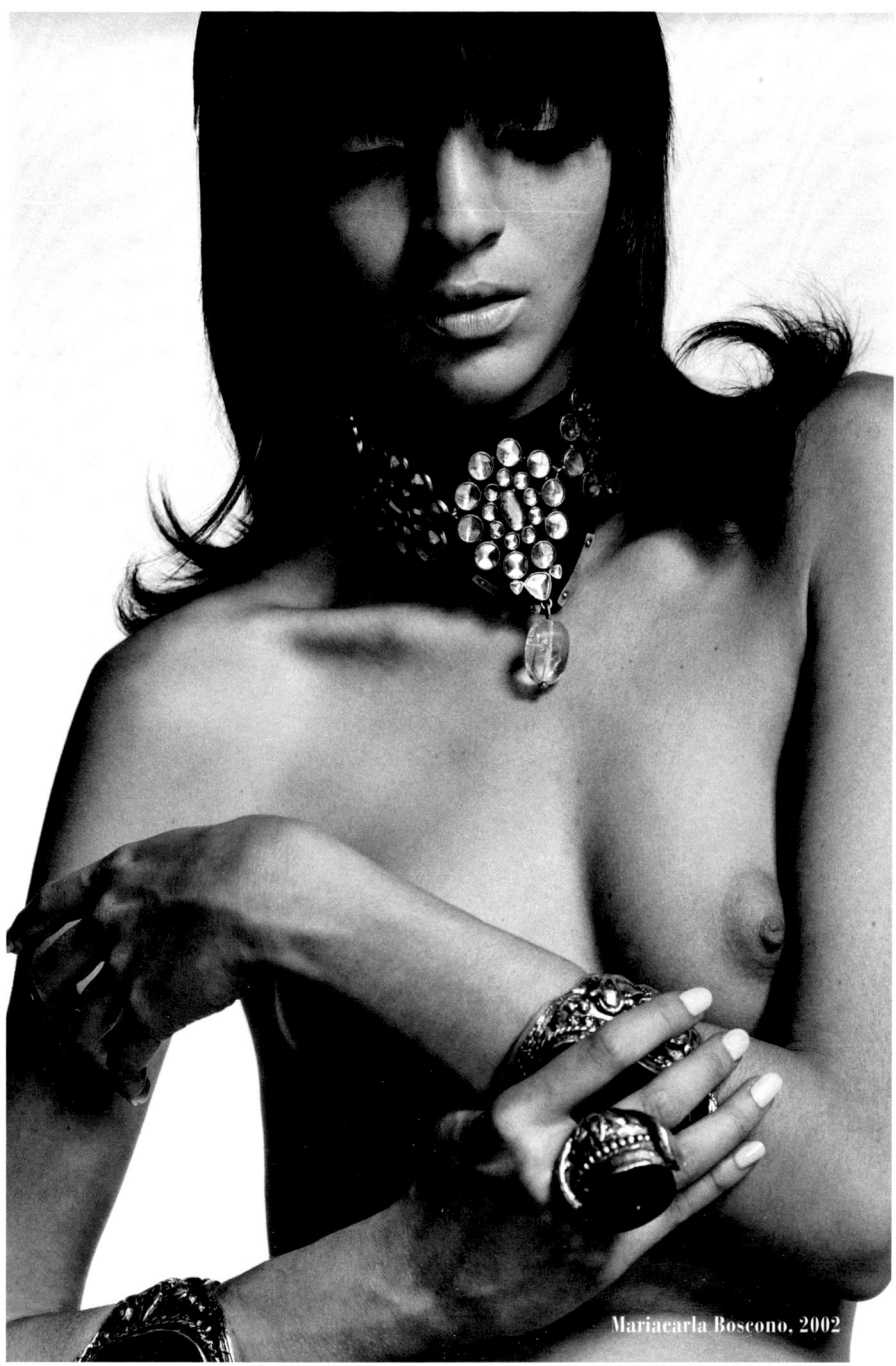

Mariacarla Boscono, 2002

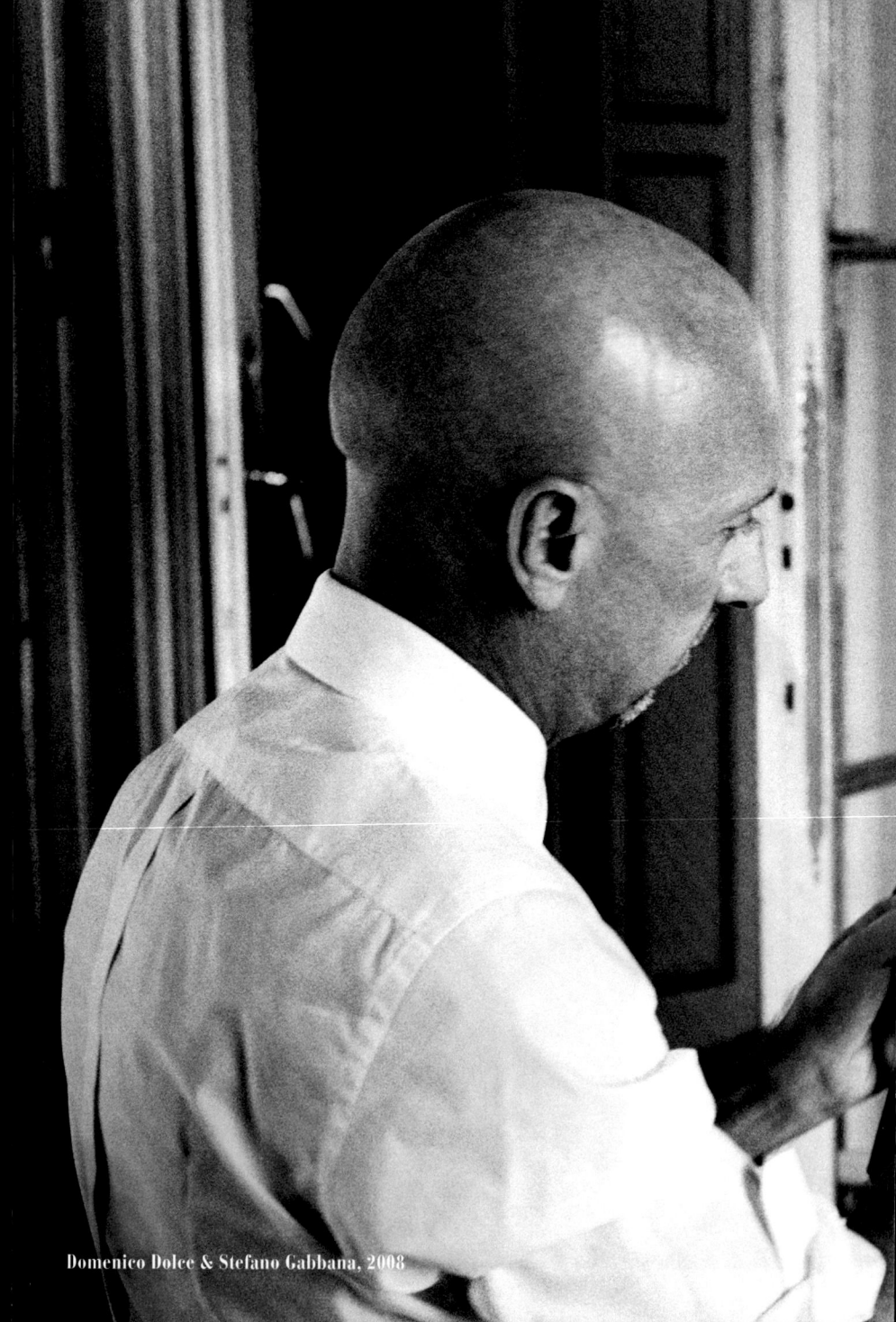

Domenico Dolce & Stefano Gabbana, 2008

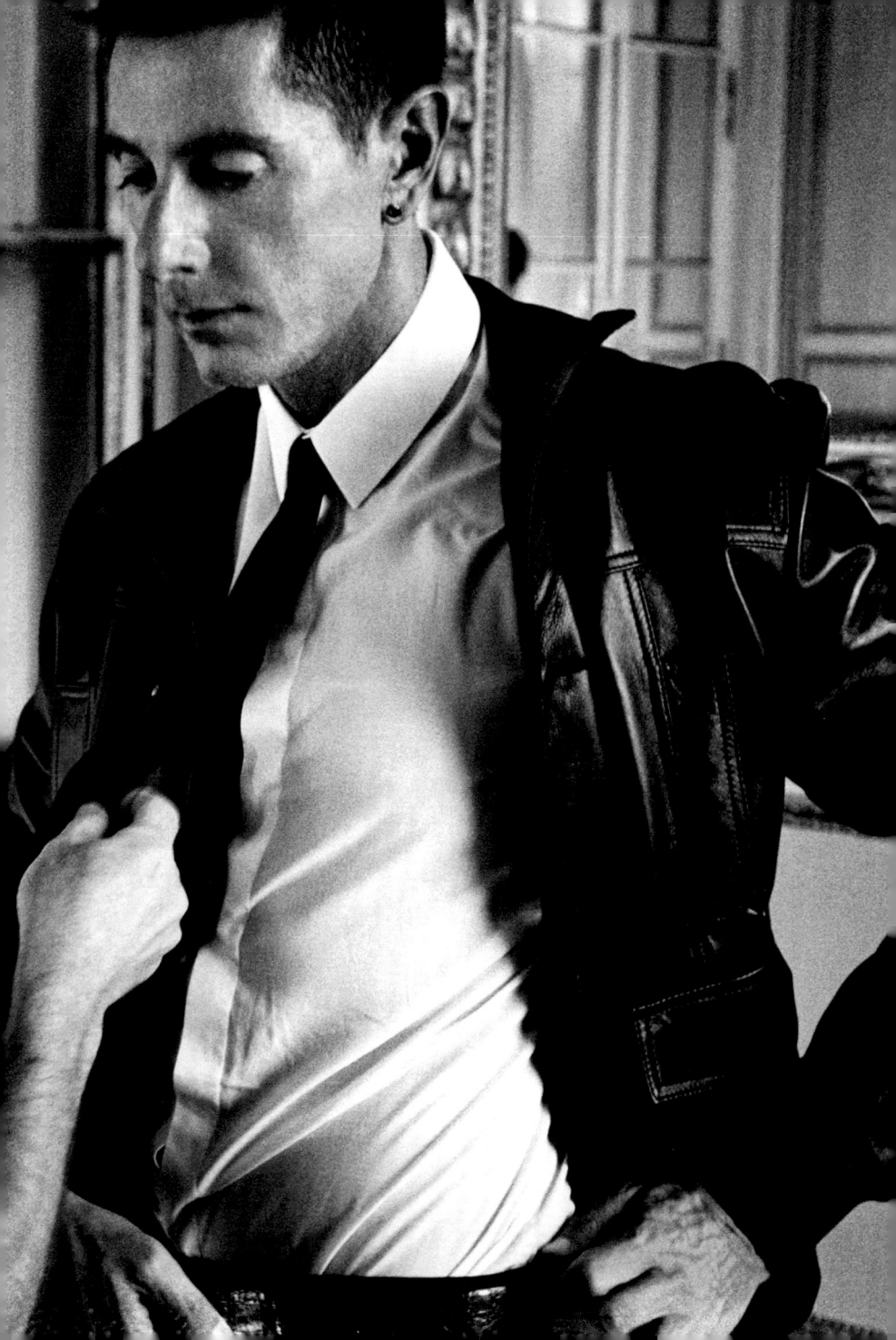

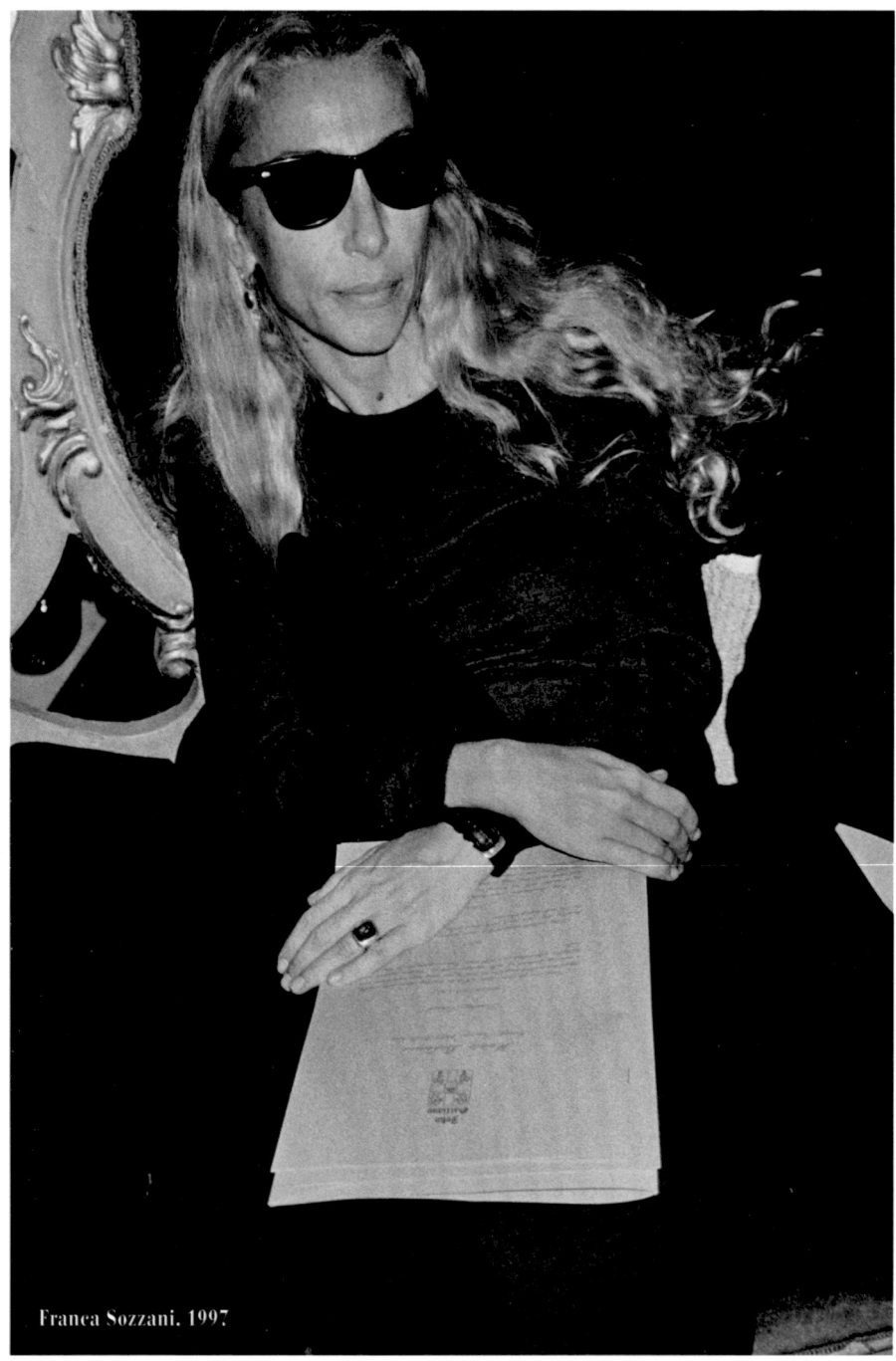

Franca Sozzani. 1997

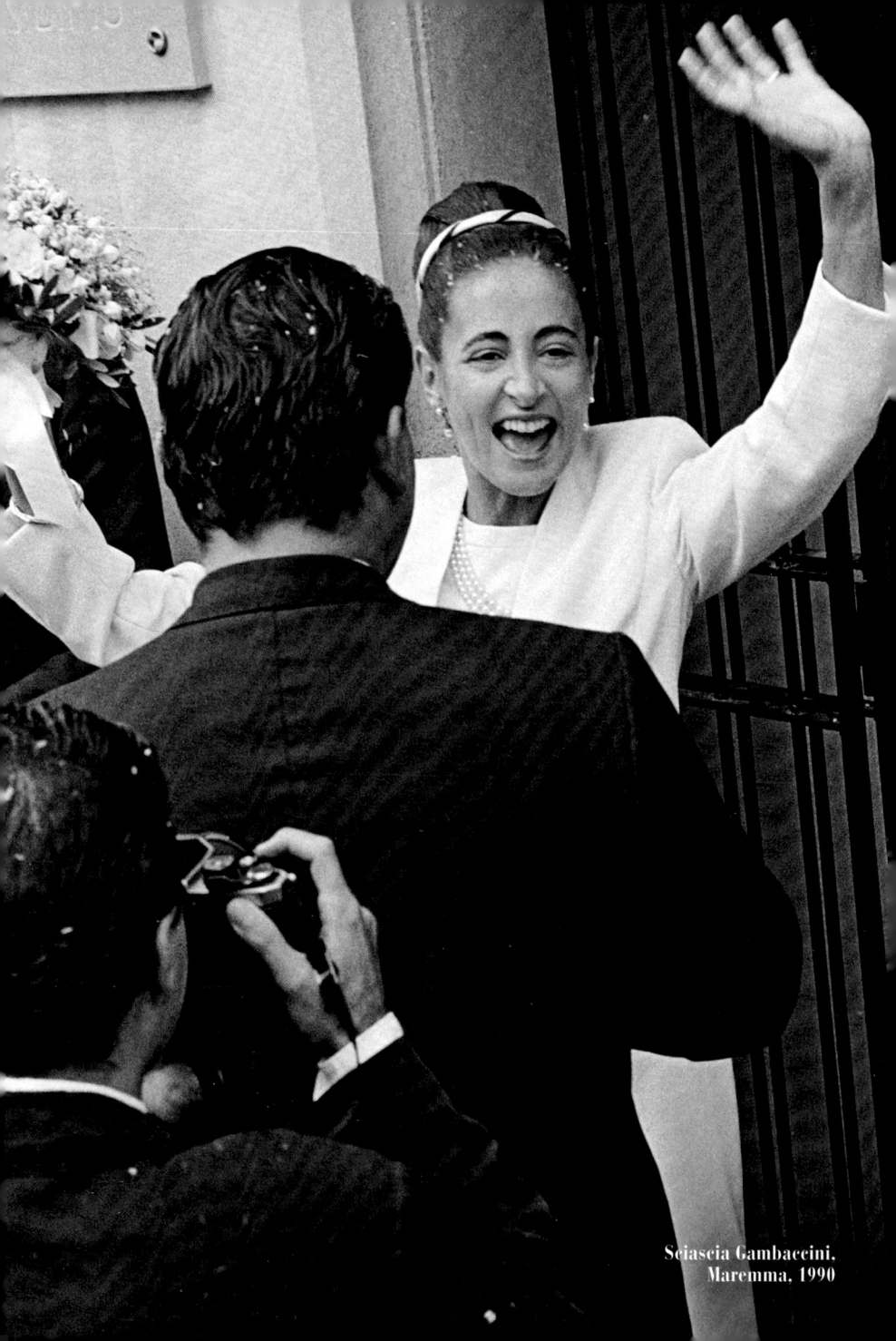

Sciascia Gambaccini,
Maremma, 1990

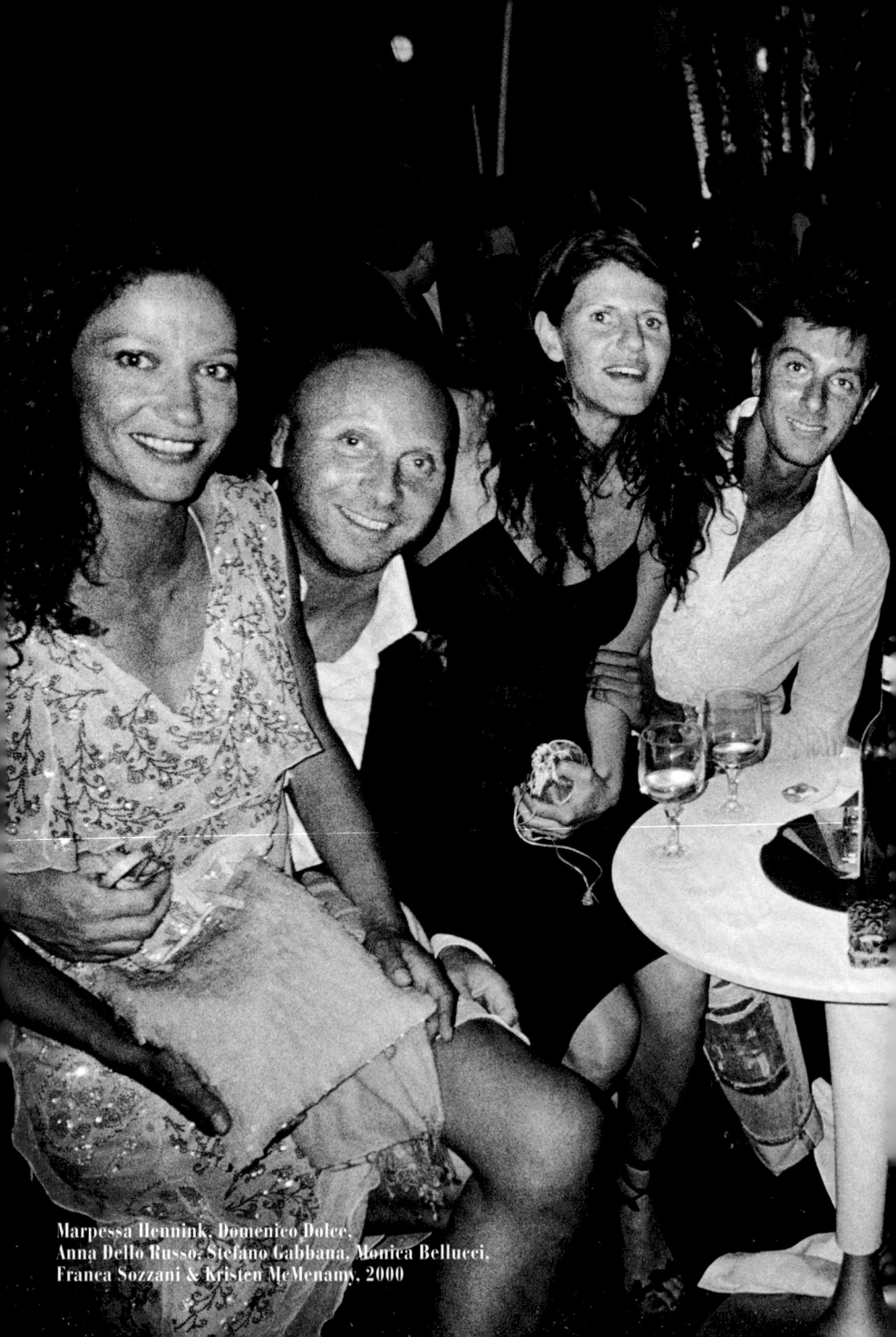

Marpessa Hennink, Domenico Dolce,
Anna Dello Russo, Stefano Gabbana, Monica Bellucci,
Franca Sozzani & Kristen McMenamy, 2000

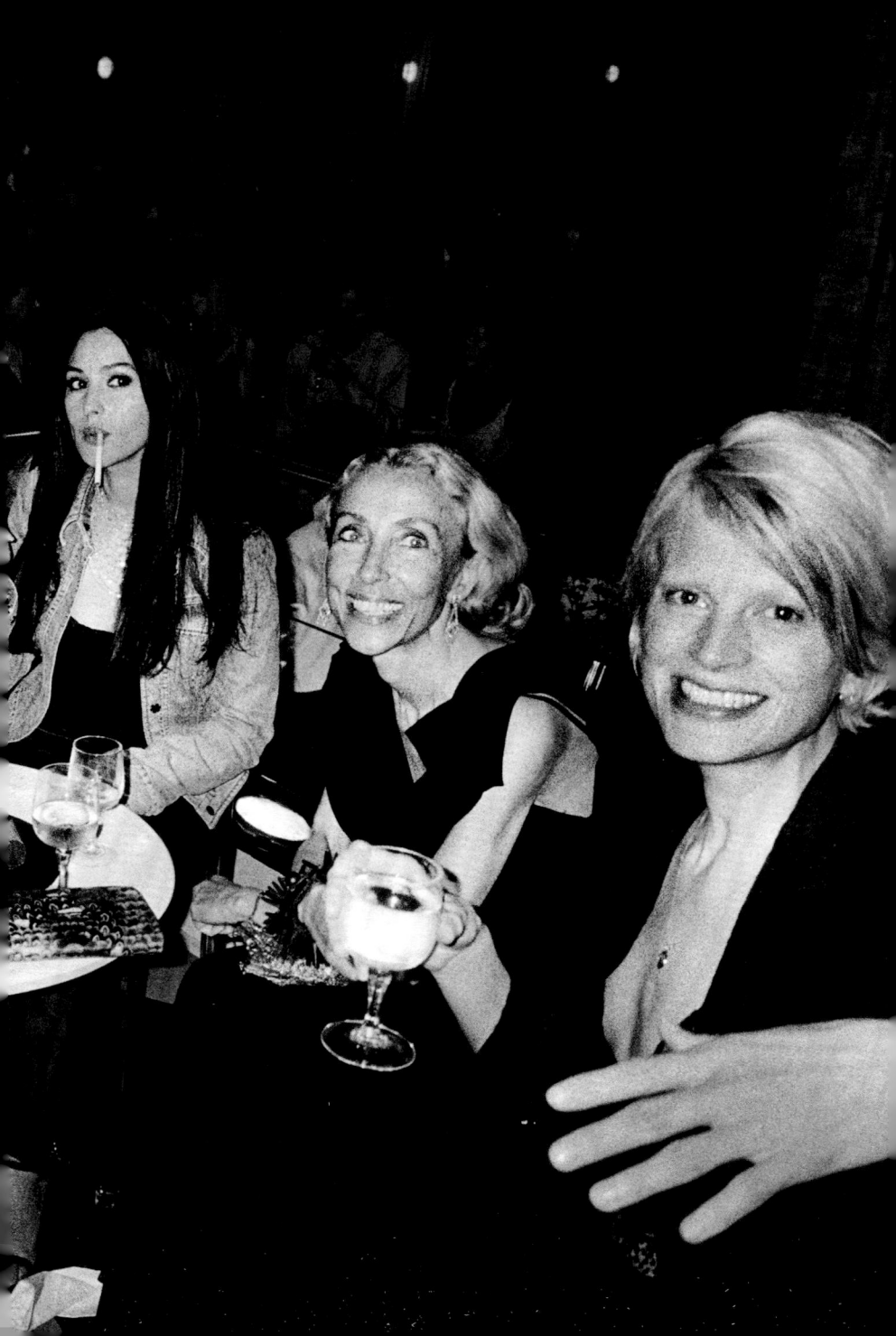

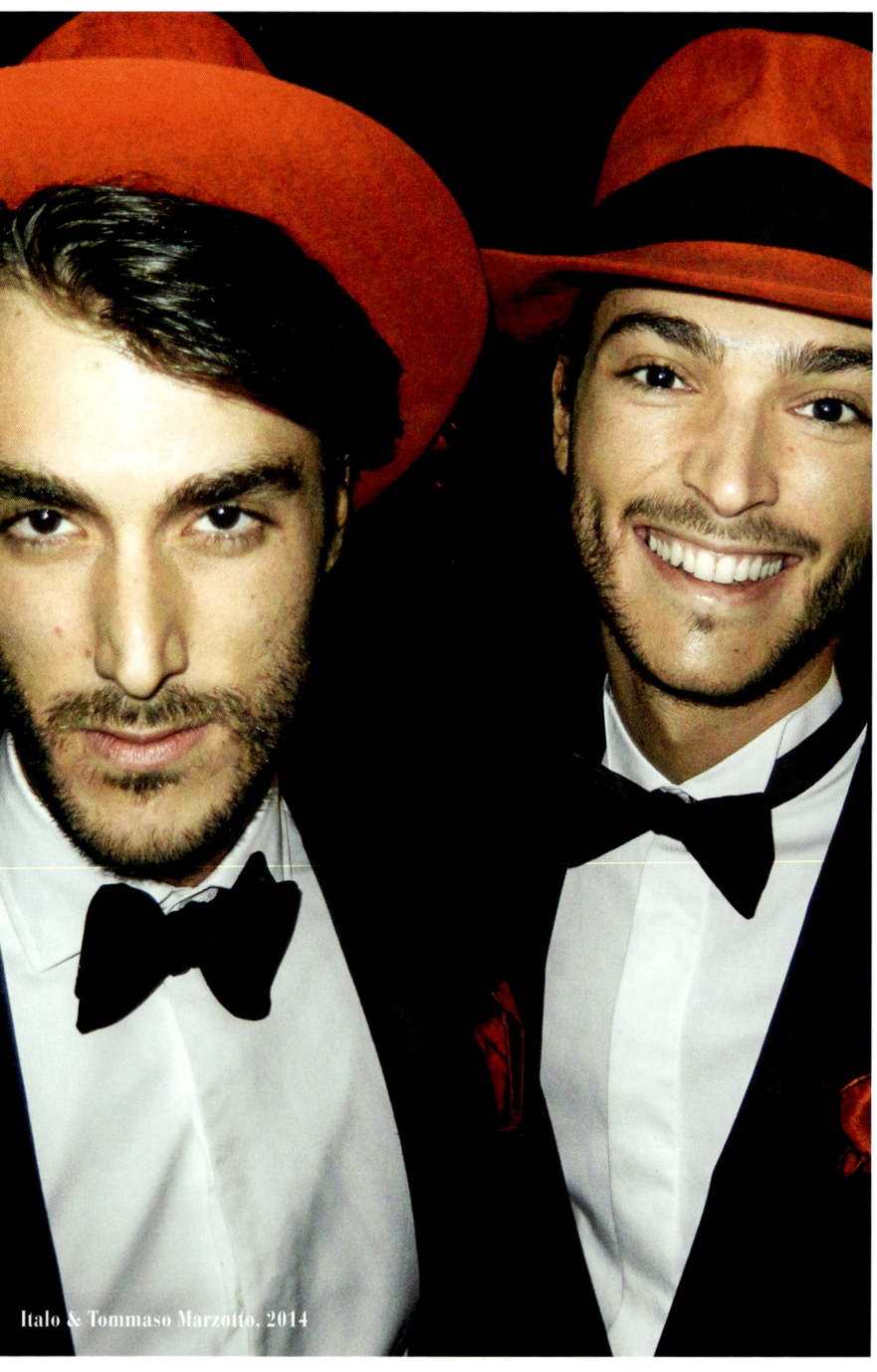

Italo & Tommaso Marzotto, 2014

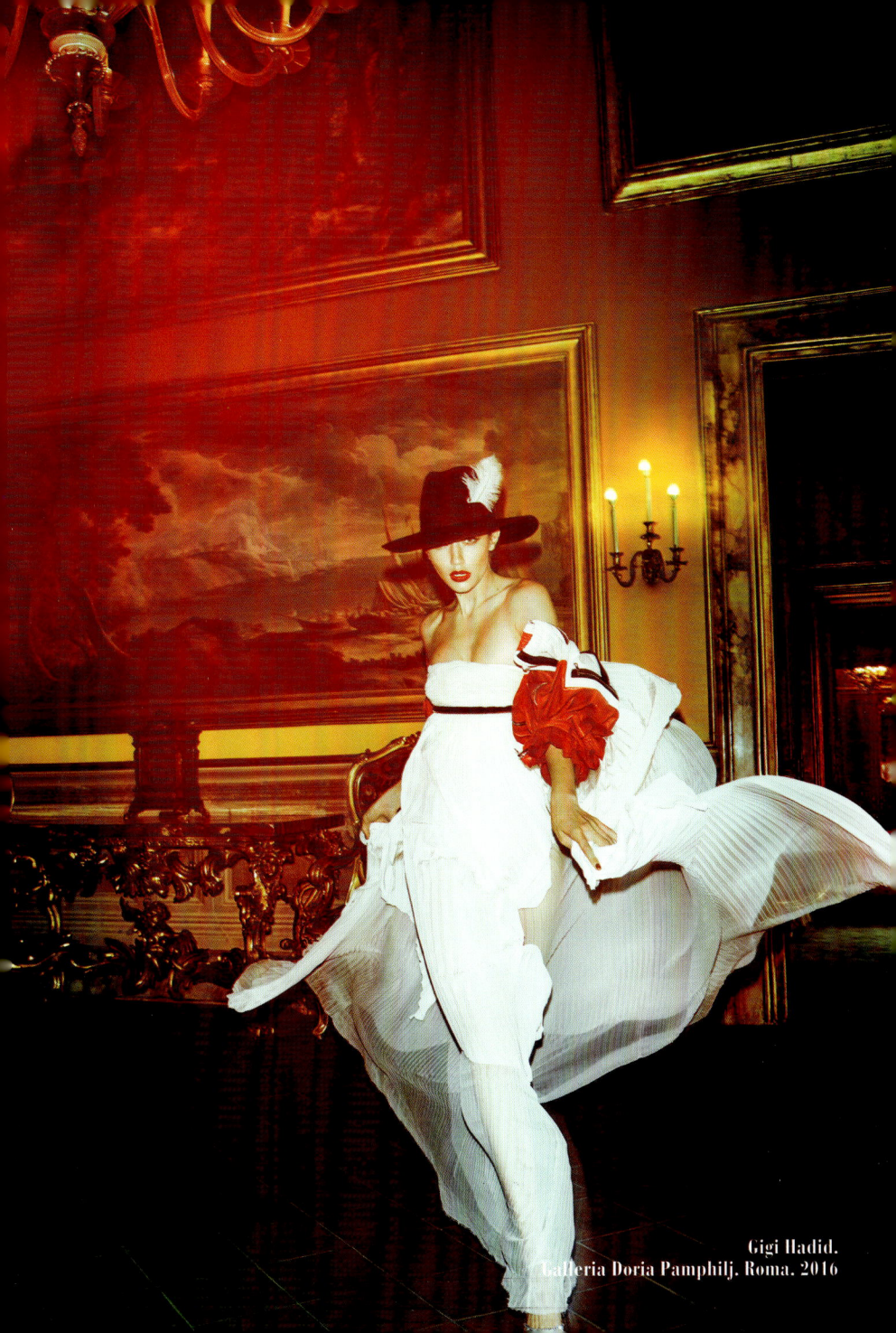

Gigi Hadid.
Galleria Doria Pamphilj. Roma. 2016

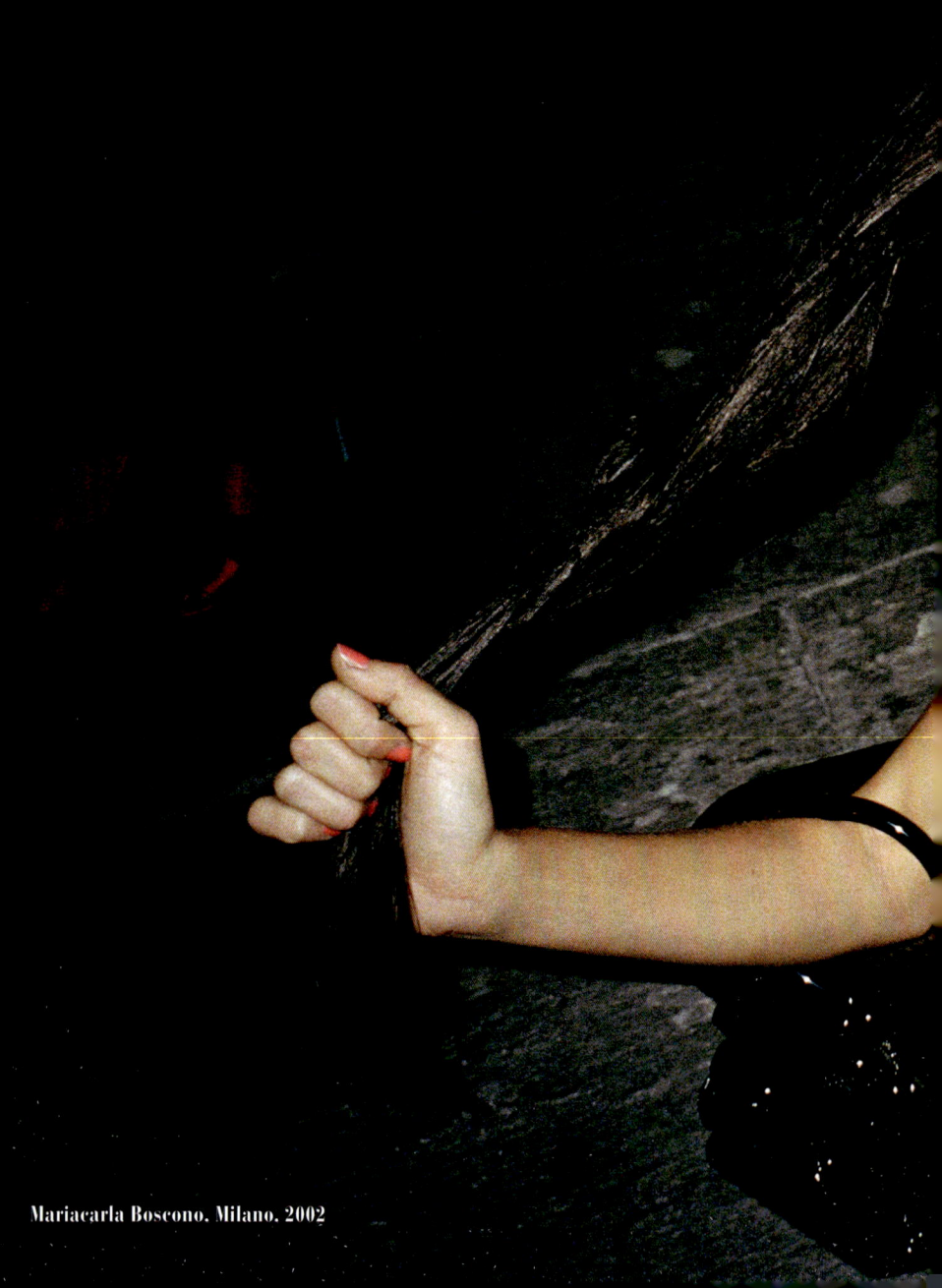

Mariacarla Boscono. Milano. 2002

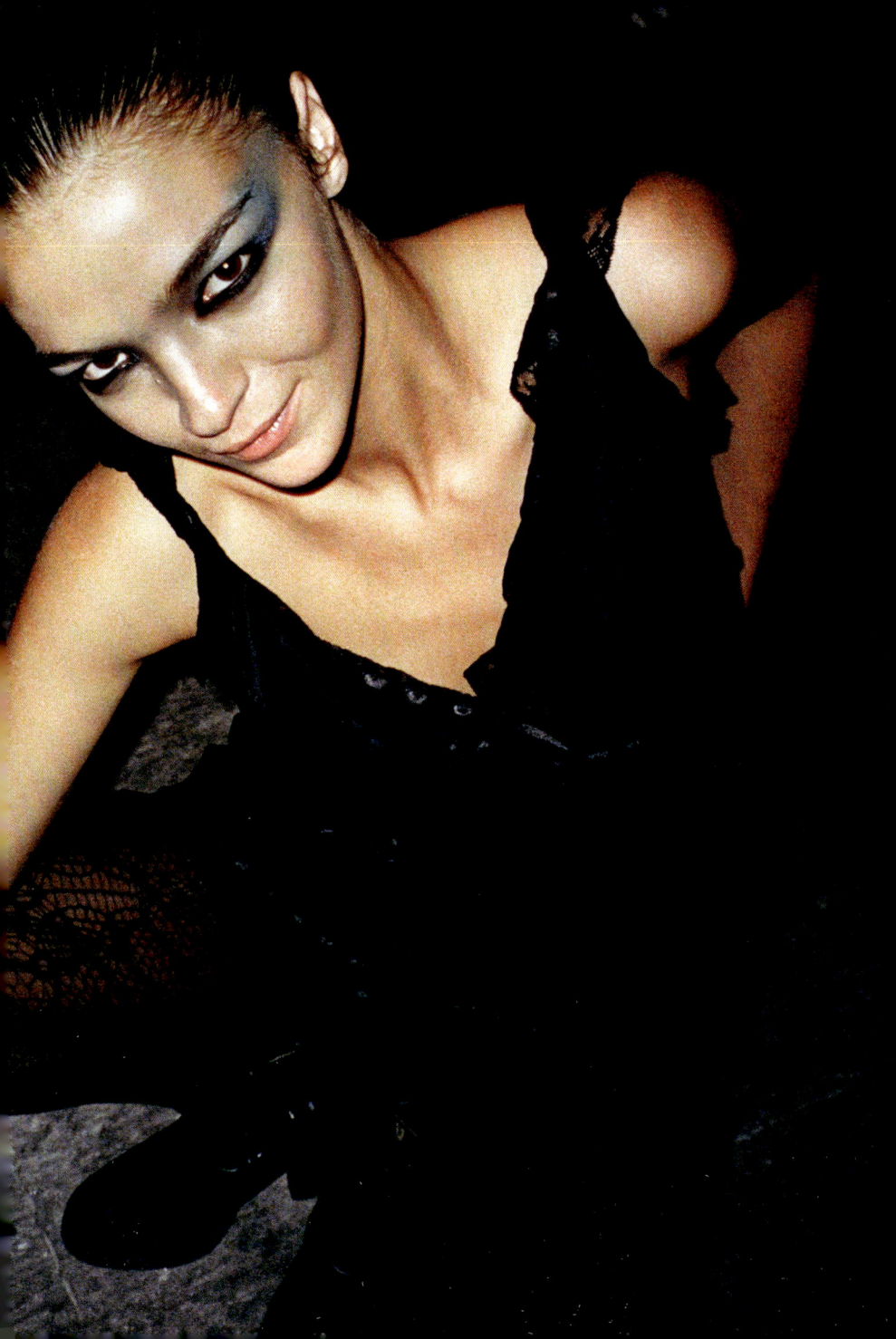

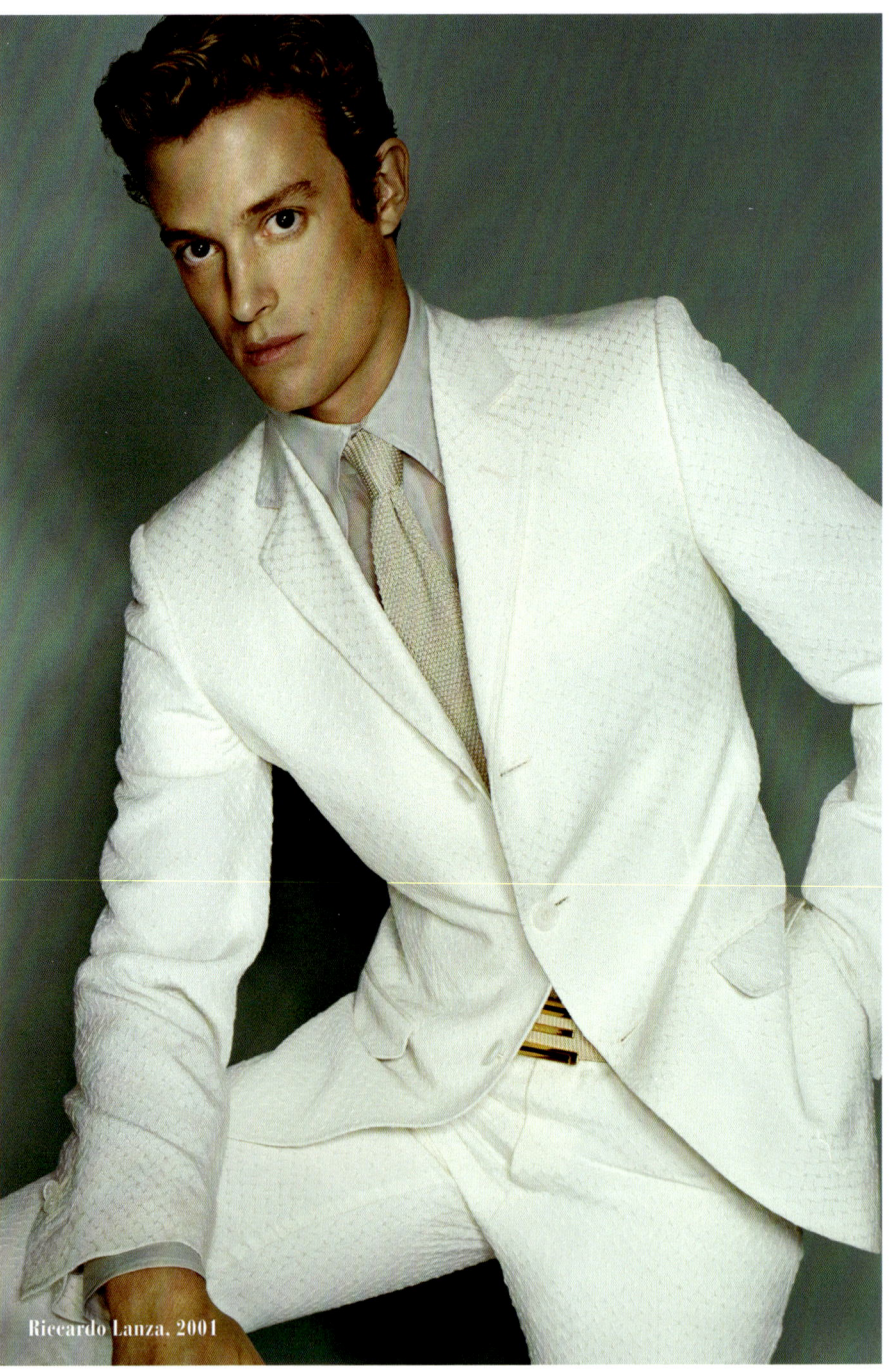

Riccardo Lanza, 2001

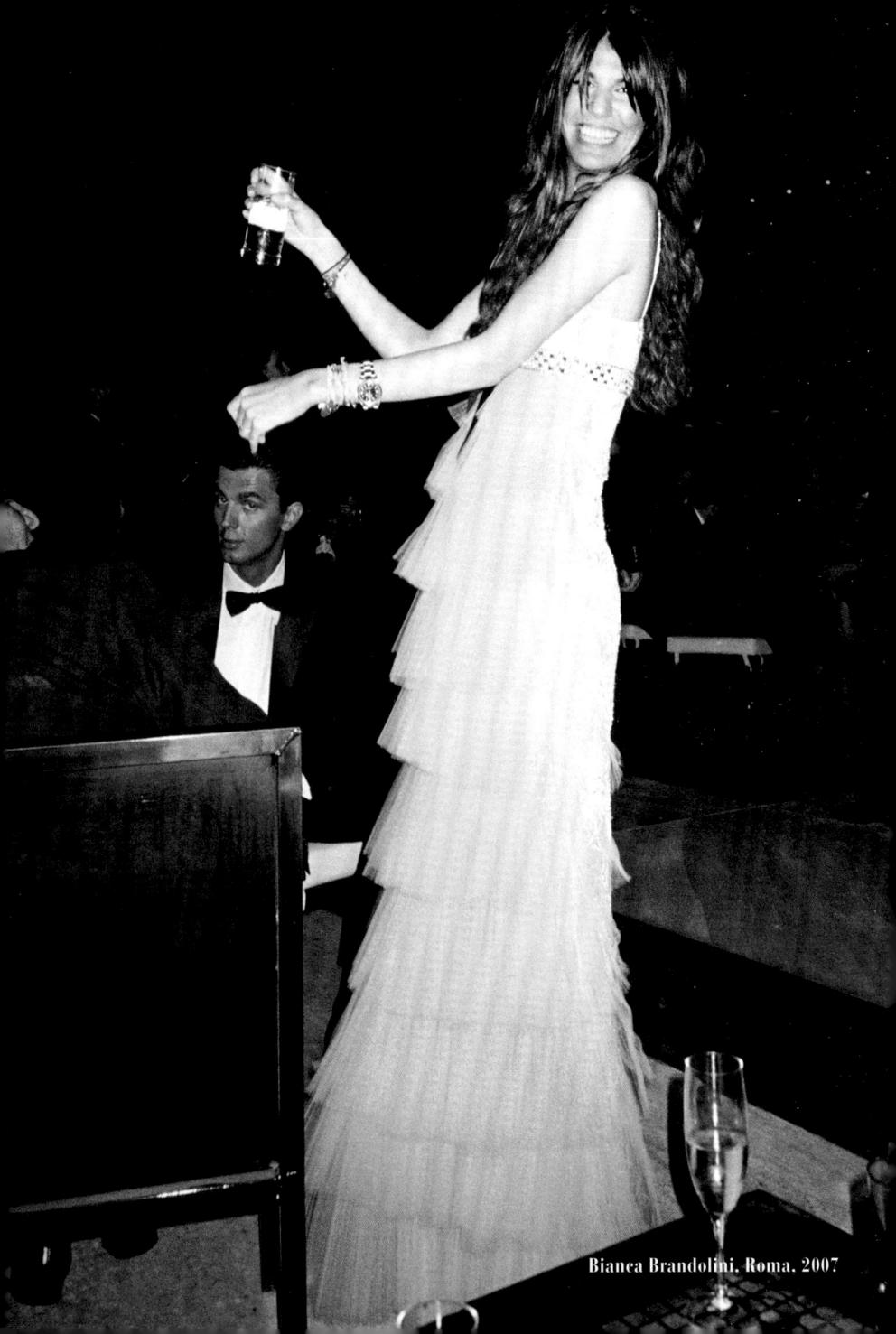

Bianca Brandolini, Roma, 2007

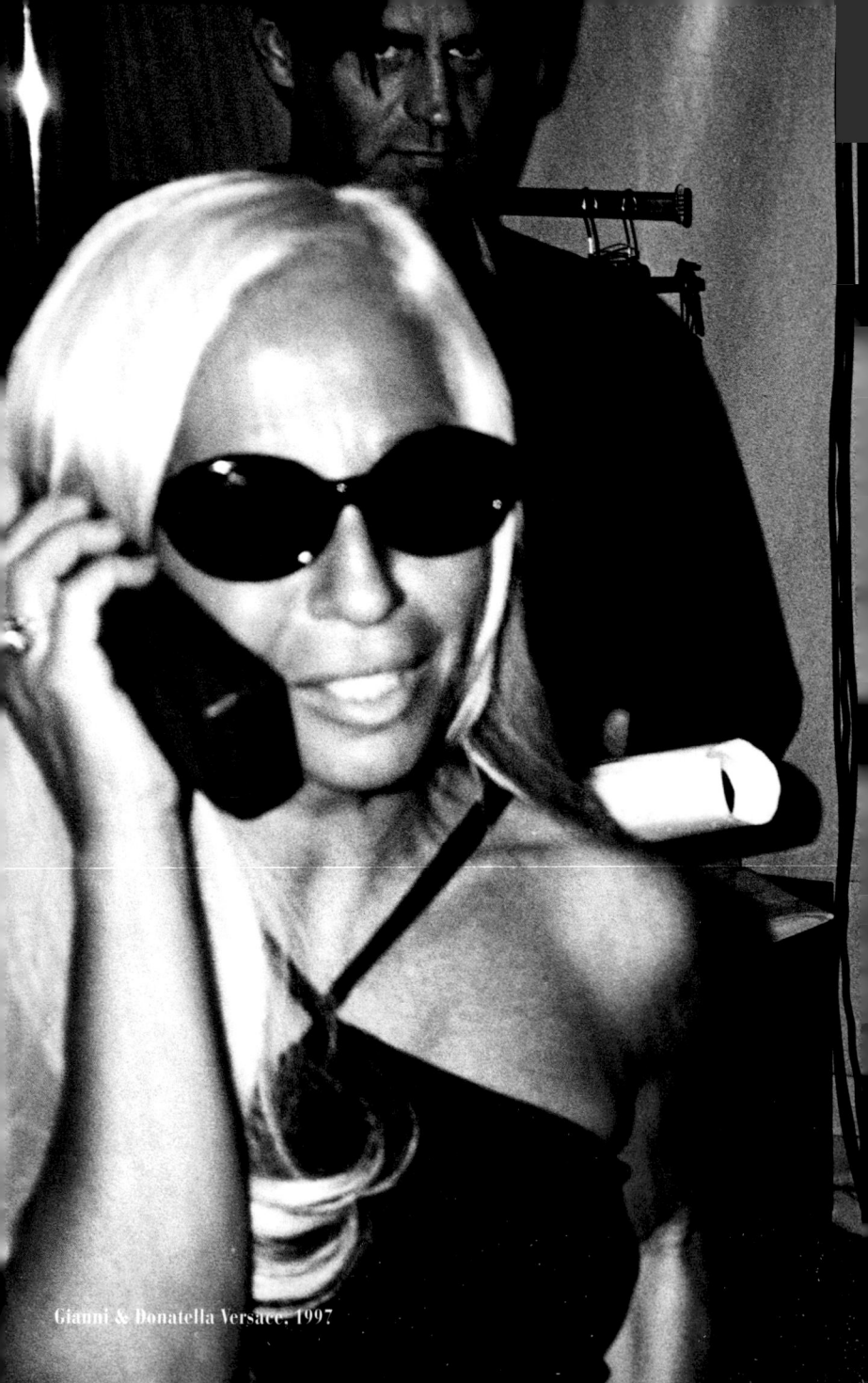

Gianni & Donatella Versace, 1997

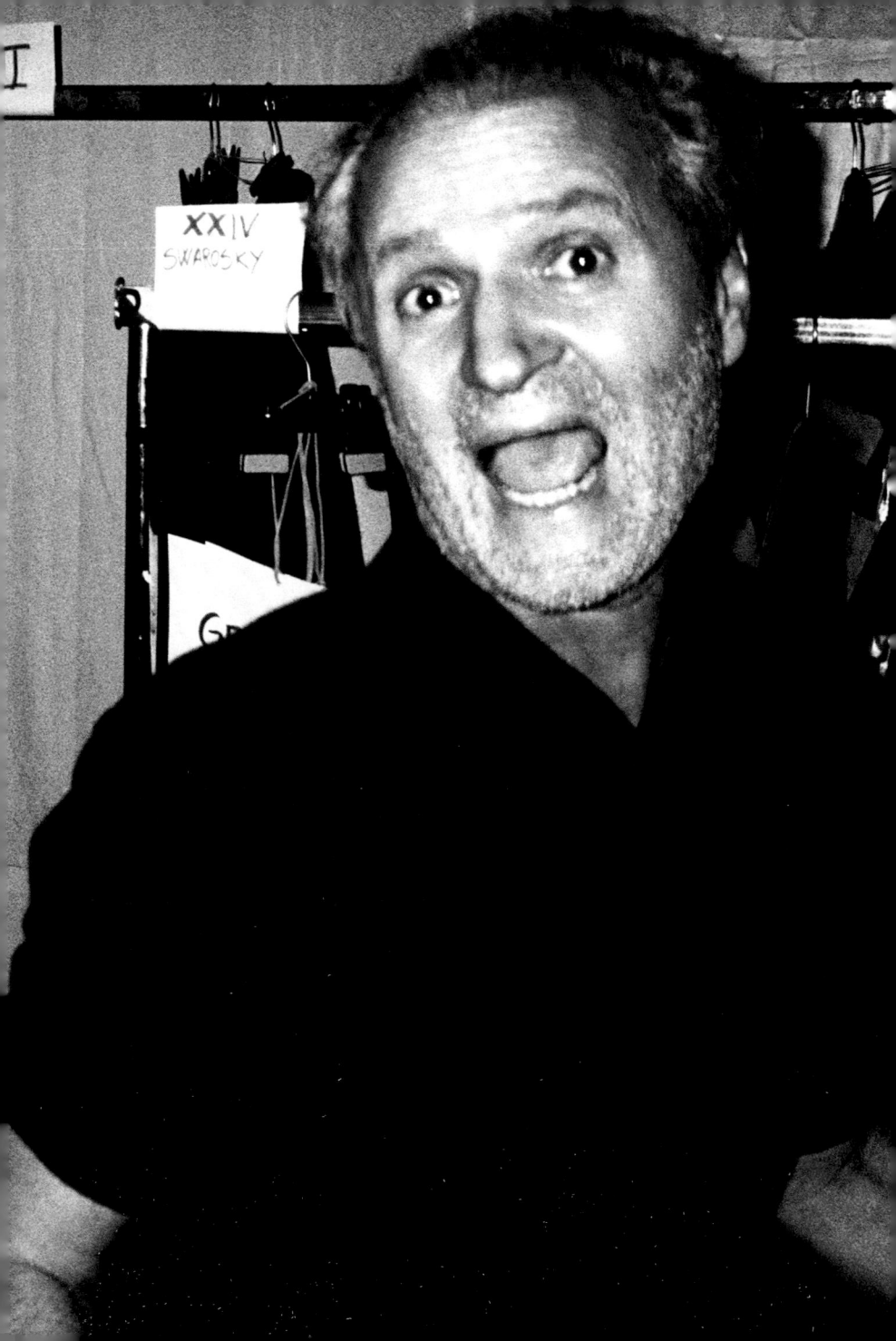

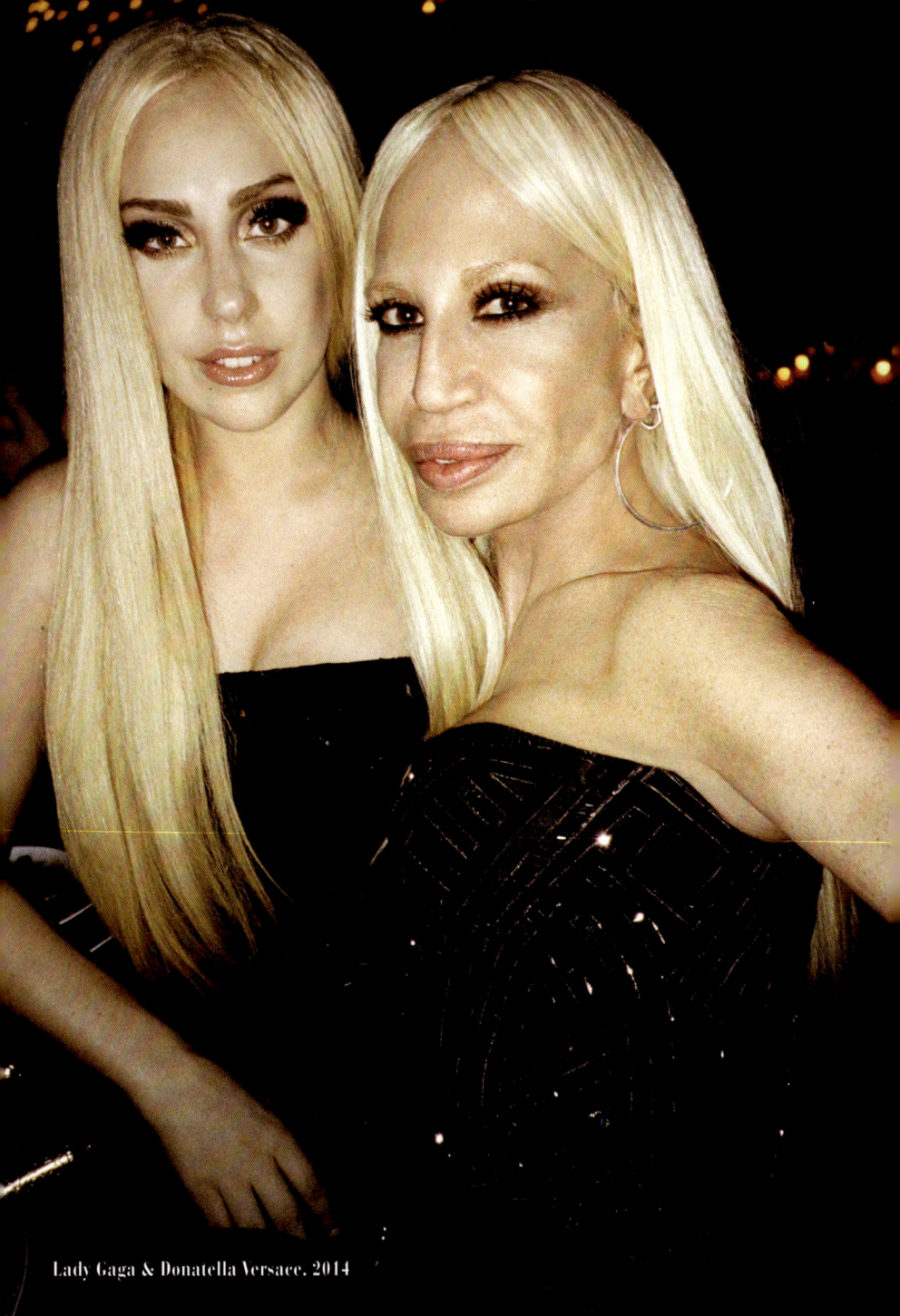

Lady Gaga & Donatella Versace. 2014

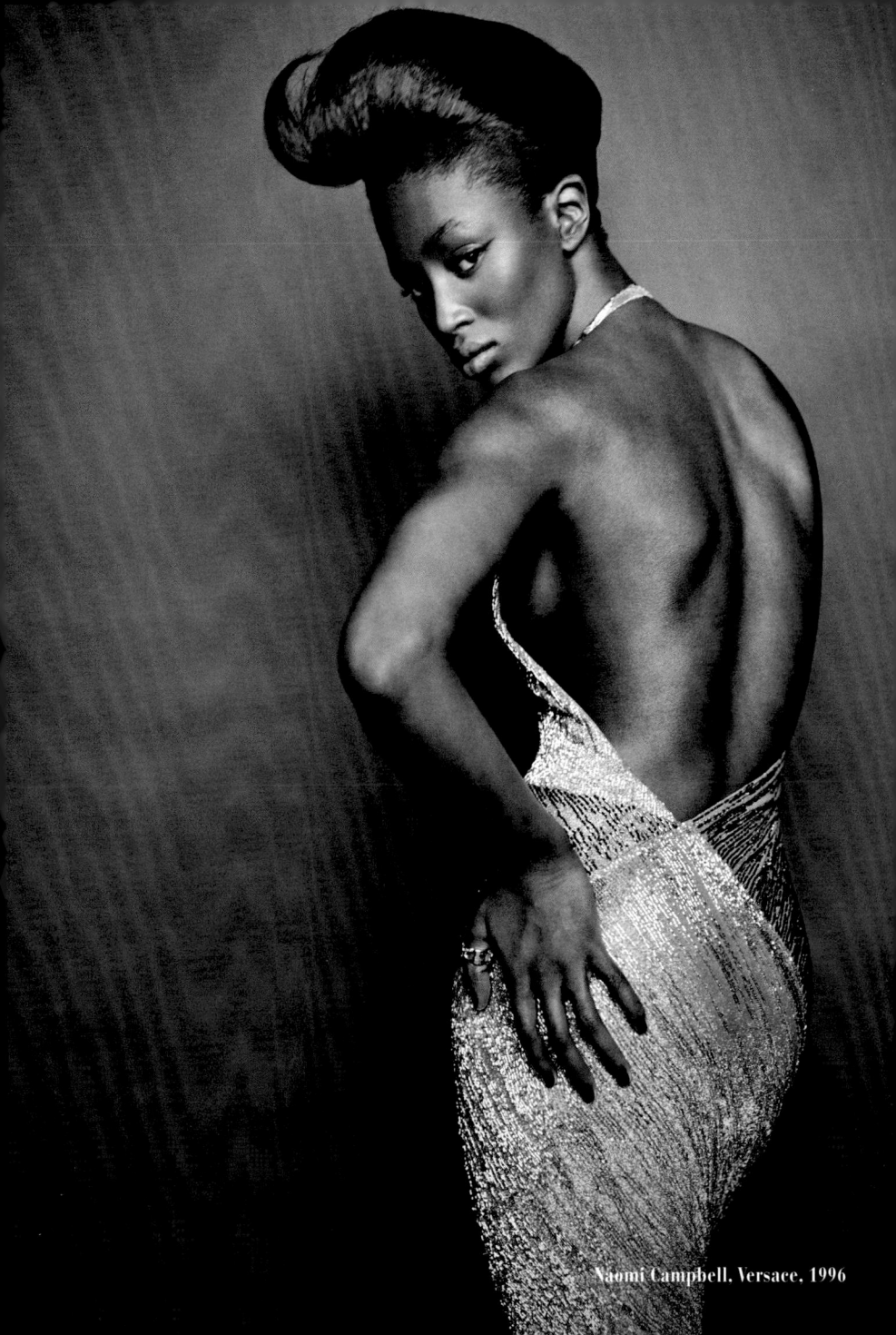

Naomi Campbell, Versace, 1996

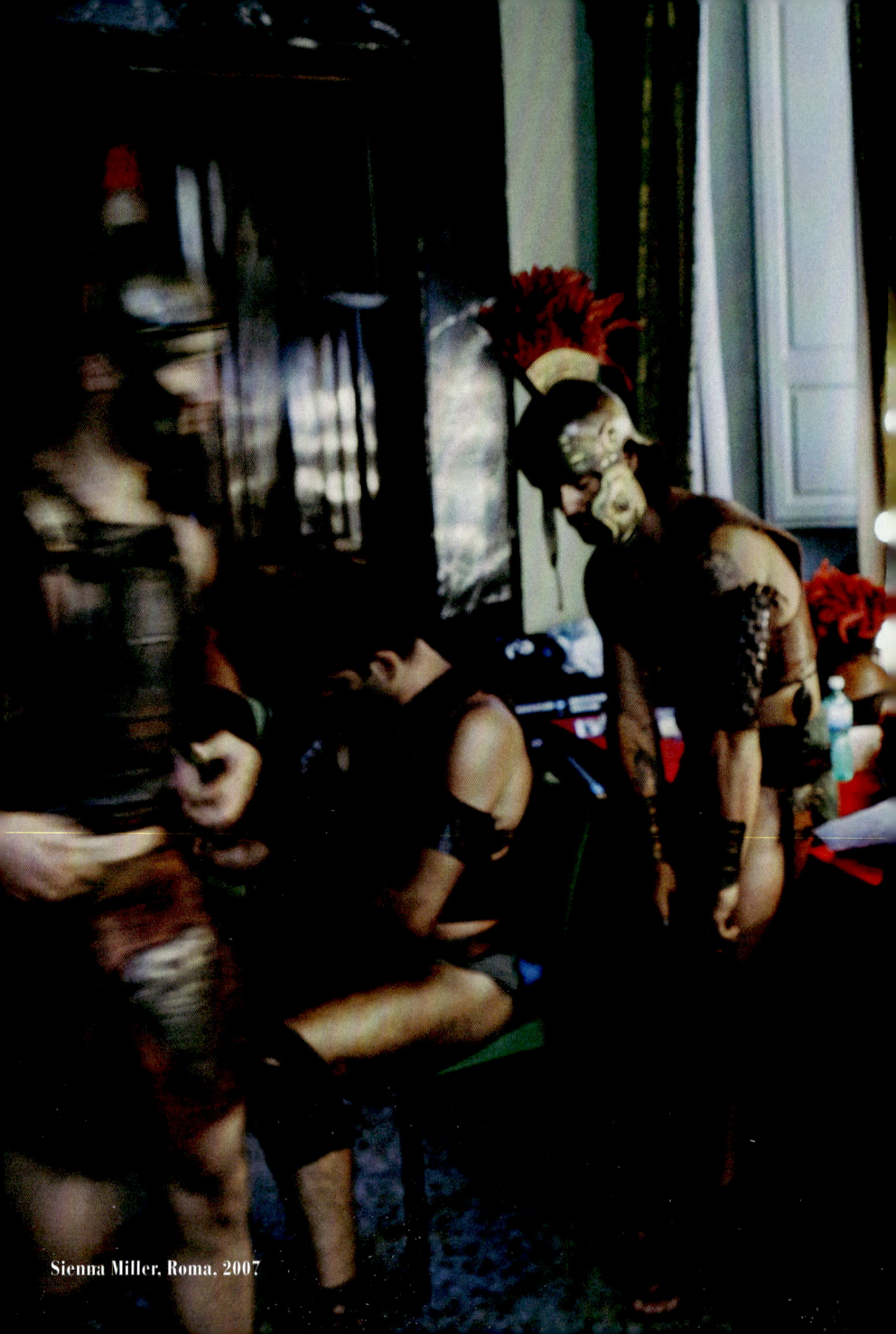

Sienna Miller, Roma, 2007

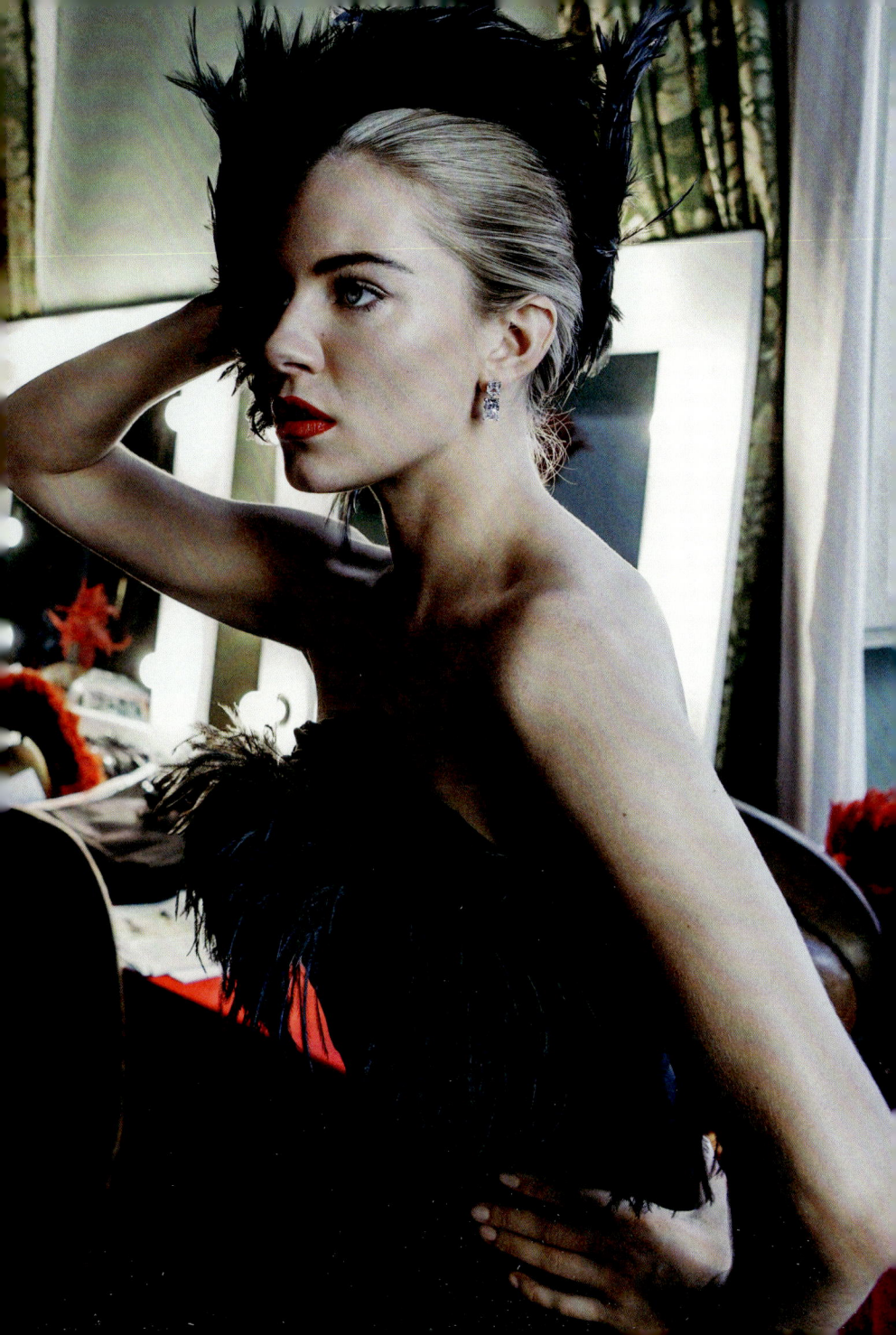

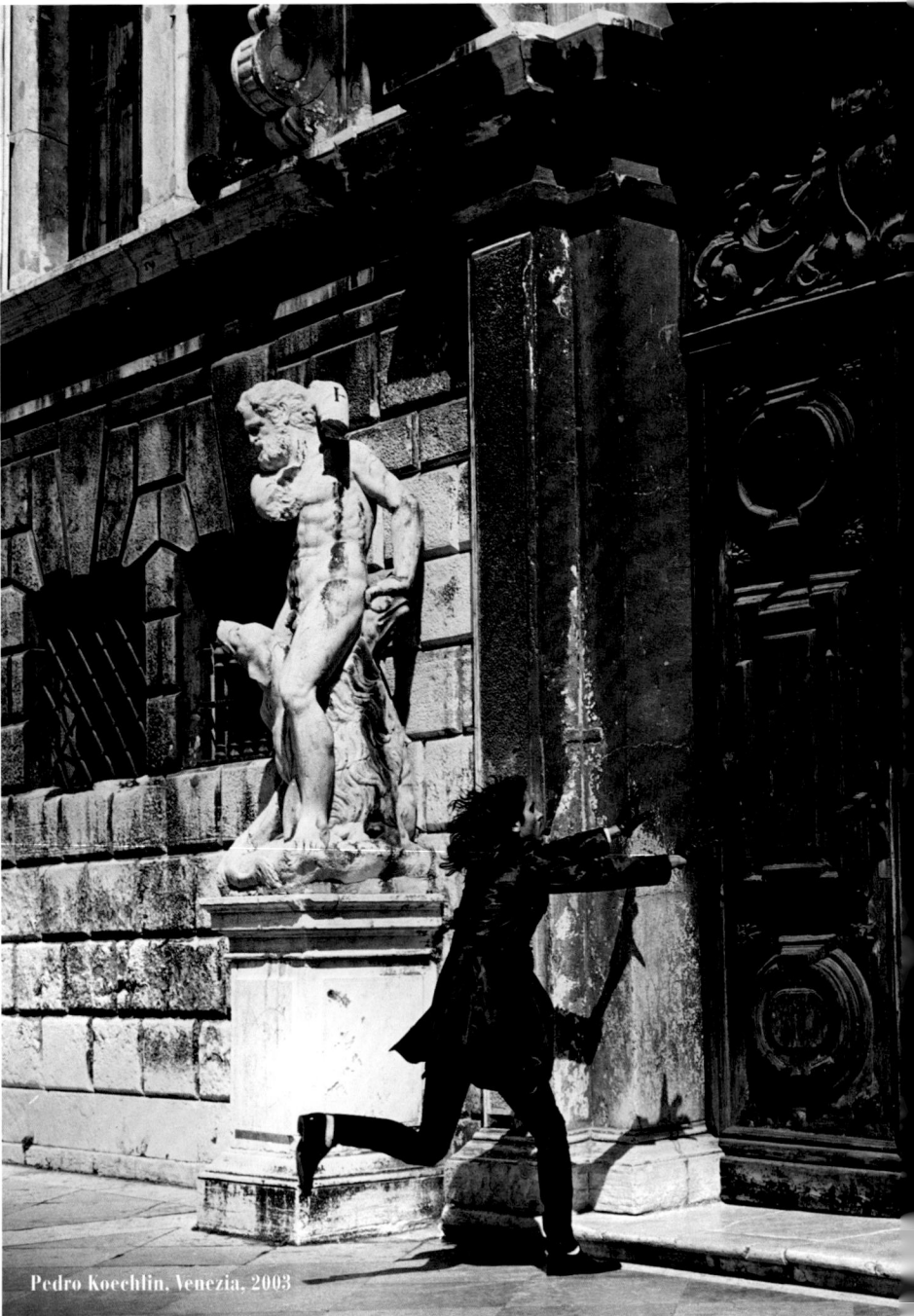
Pedro koechlin, Venezia, 2003

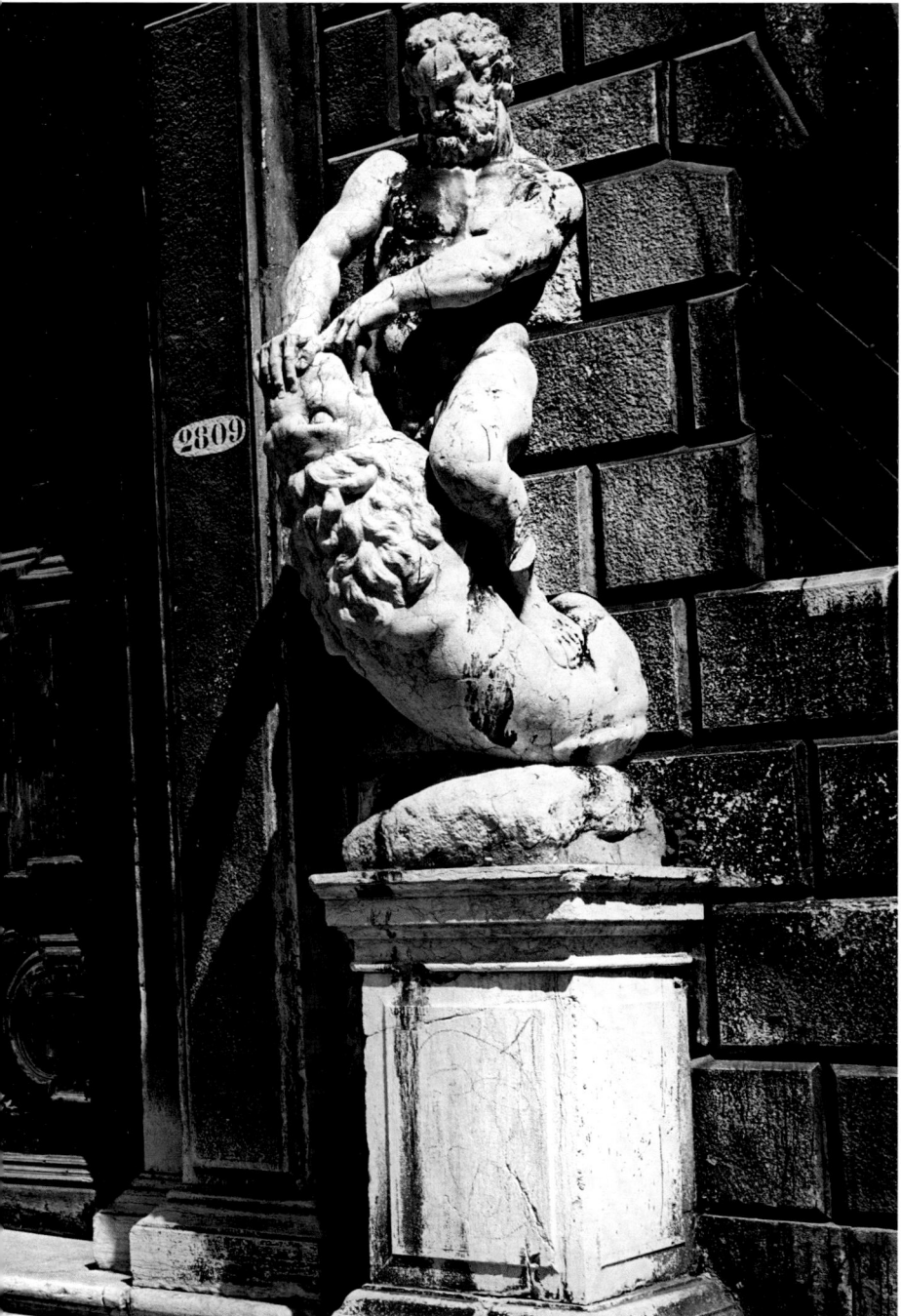

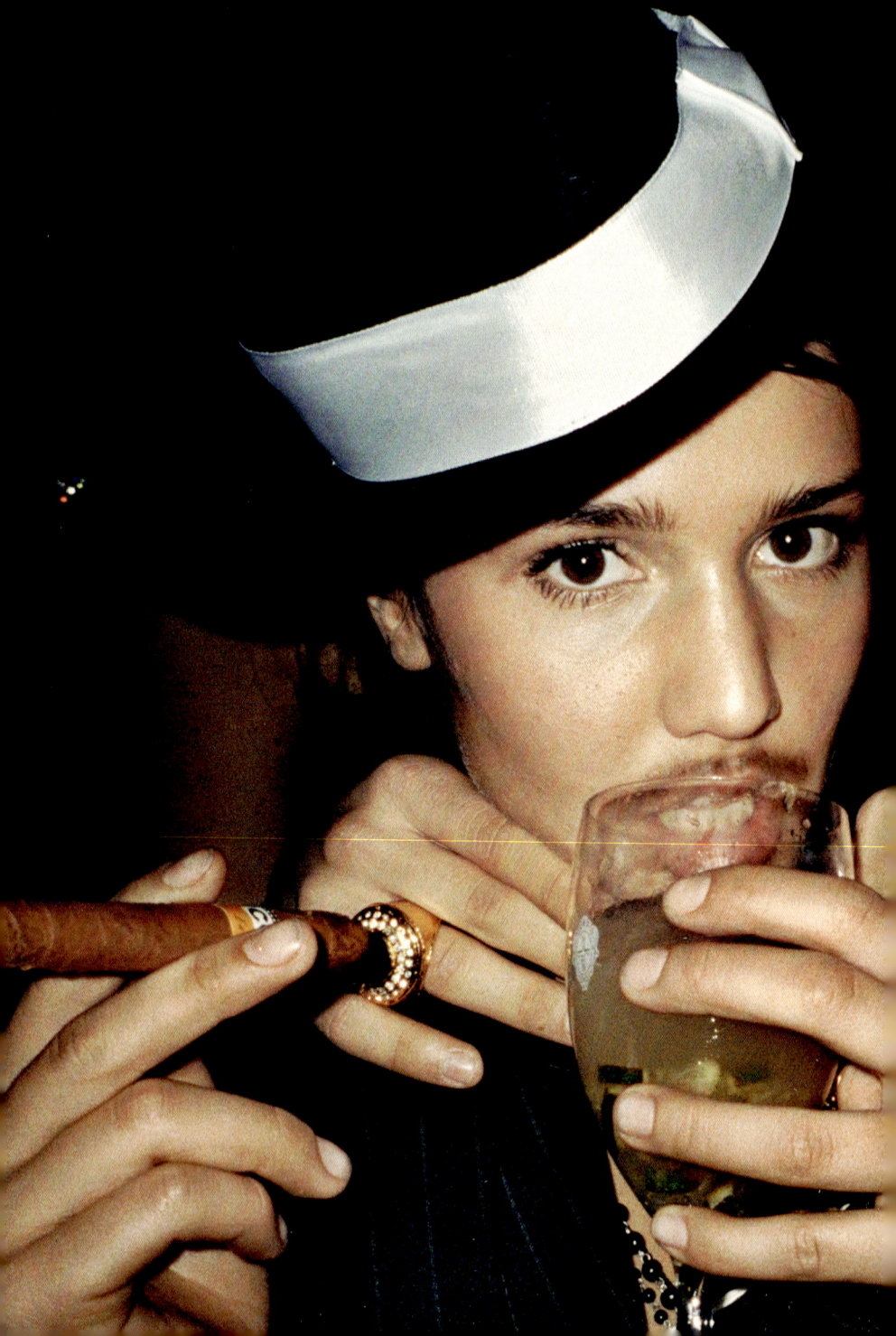

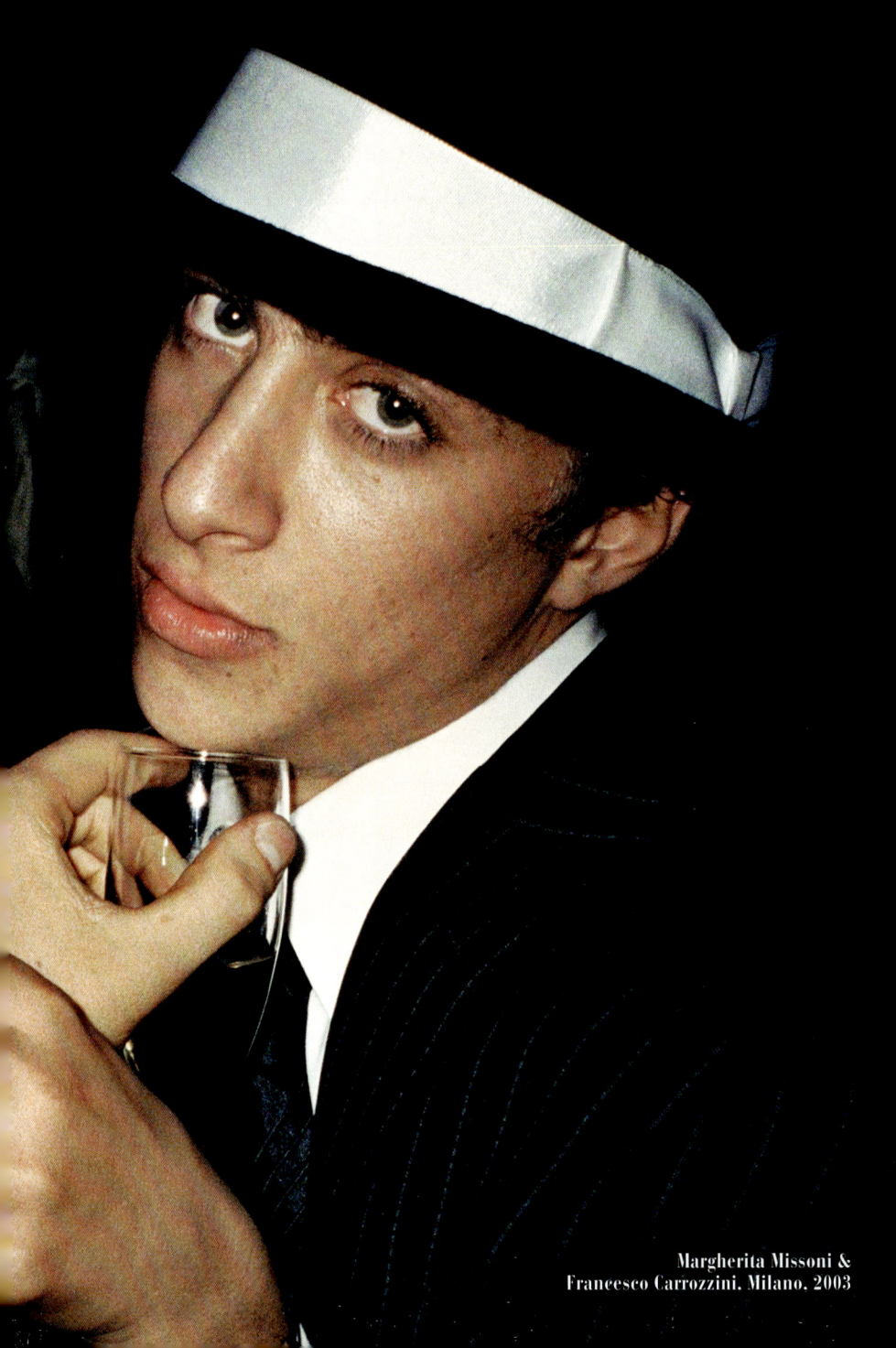

Margherita Missoni &
Francesco Carrozzini, Milano, 2003

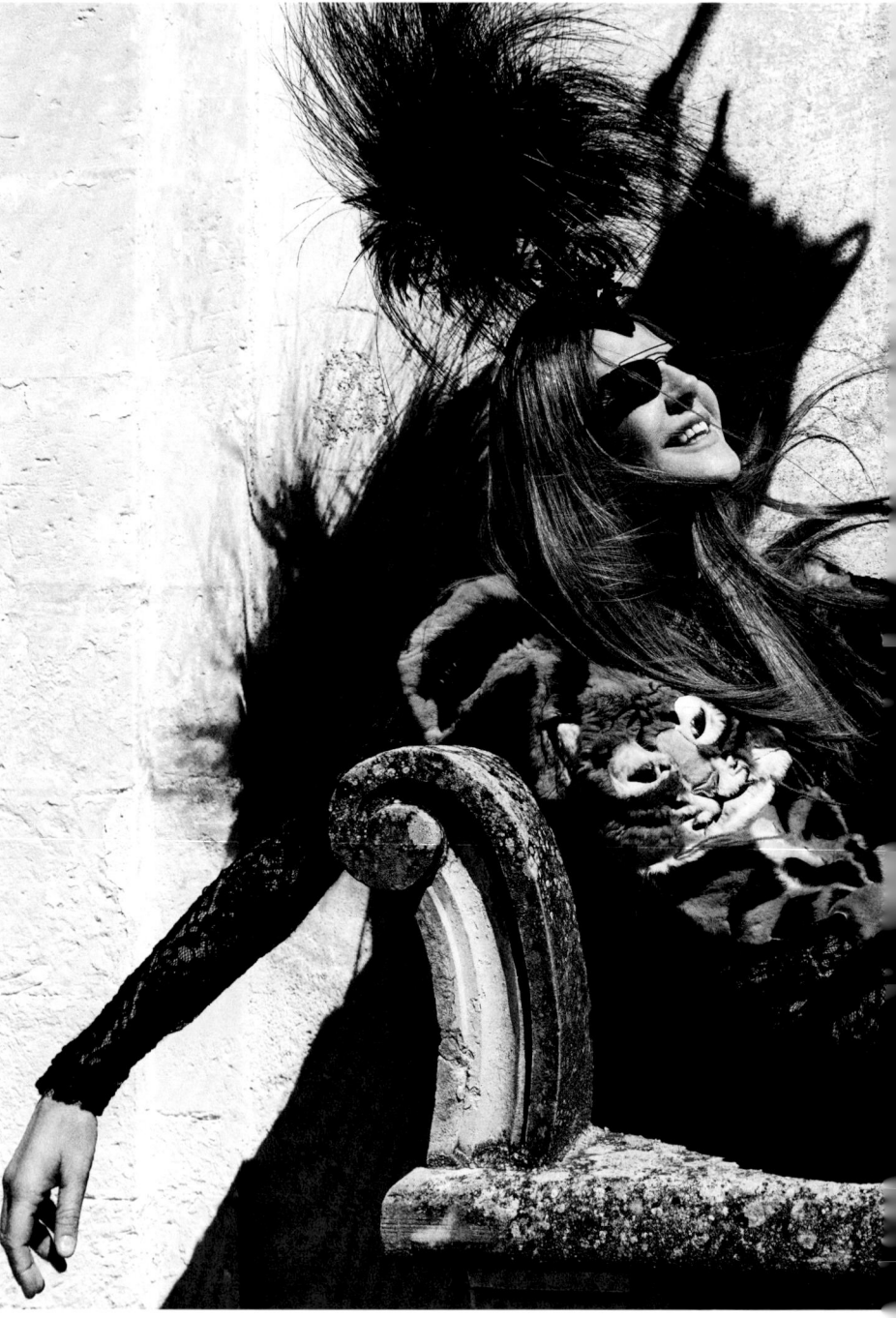

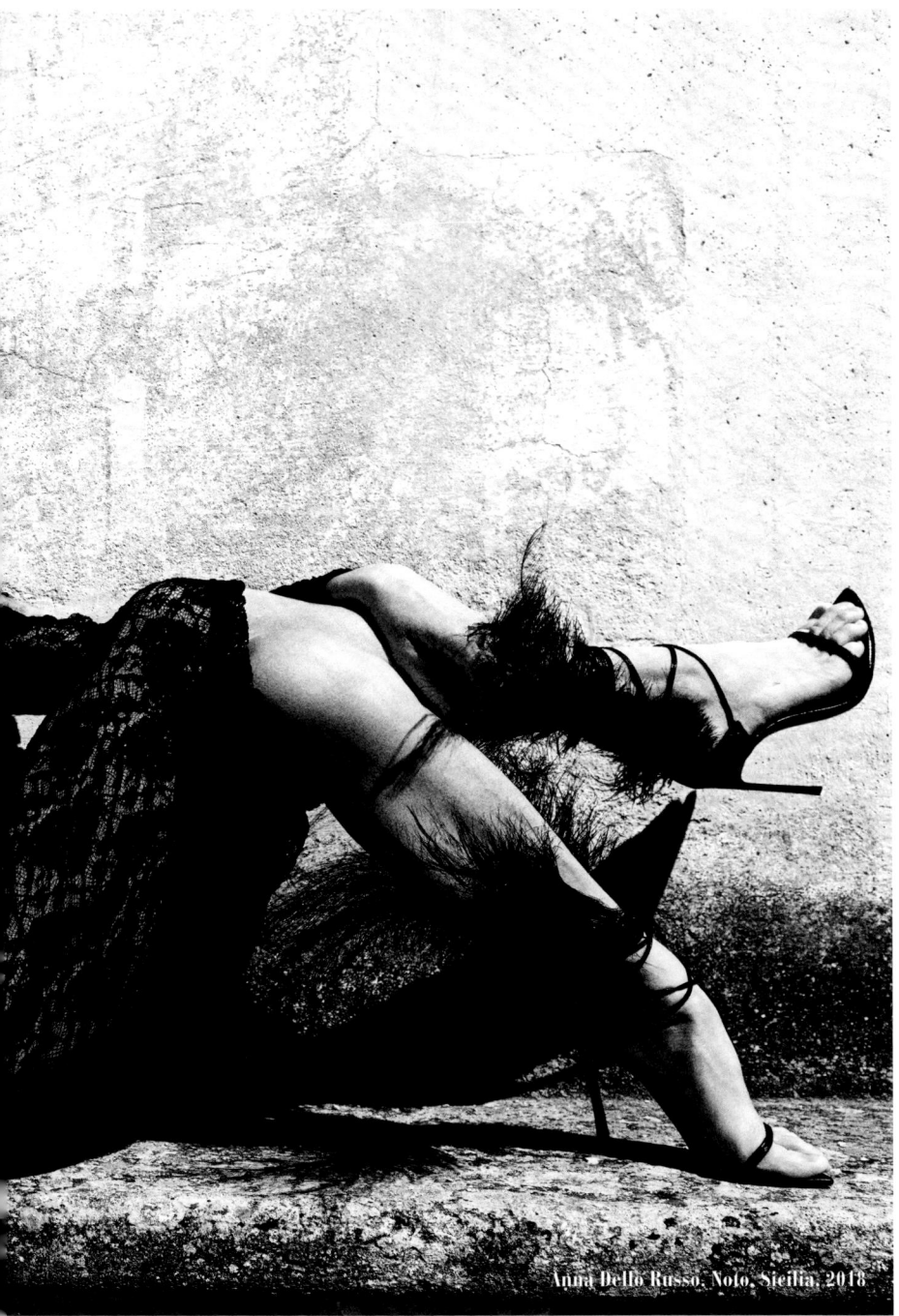

Anna Dello Russo, Noto, Sicilia, 2018

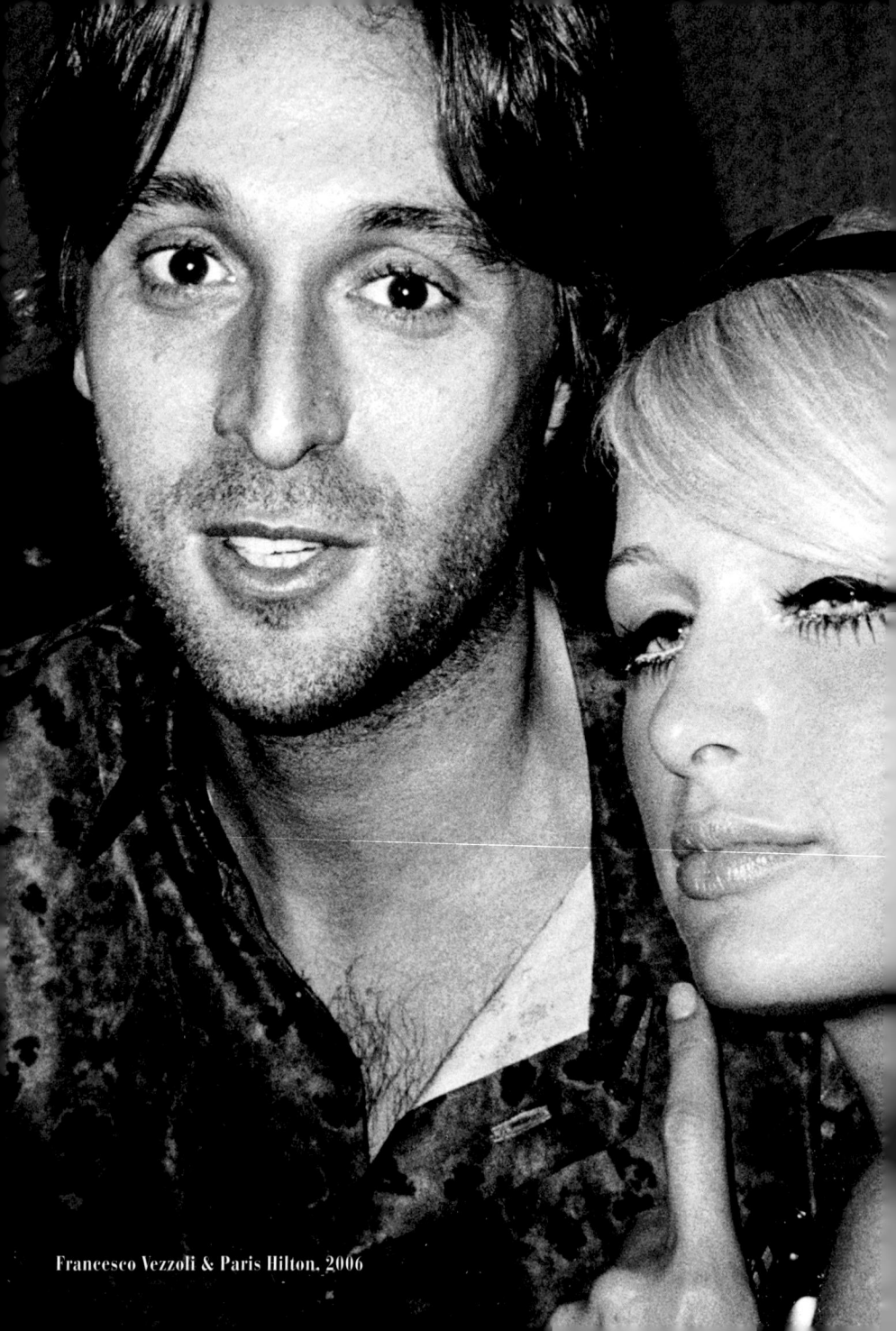

Francesco Vezzoli & Paris Hilton, 2006

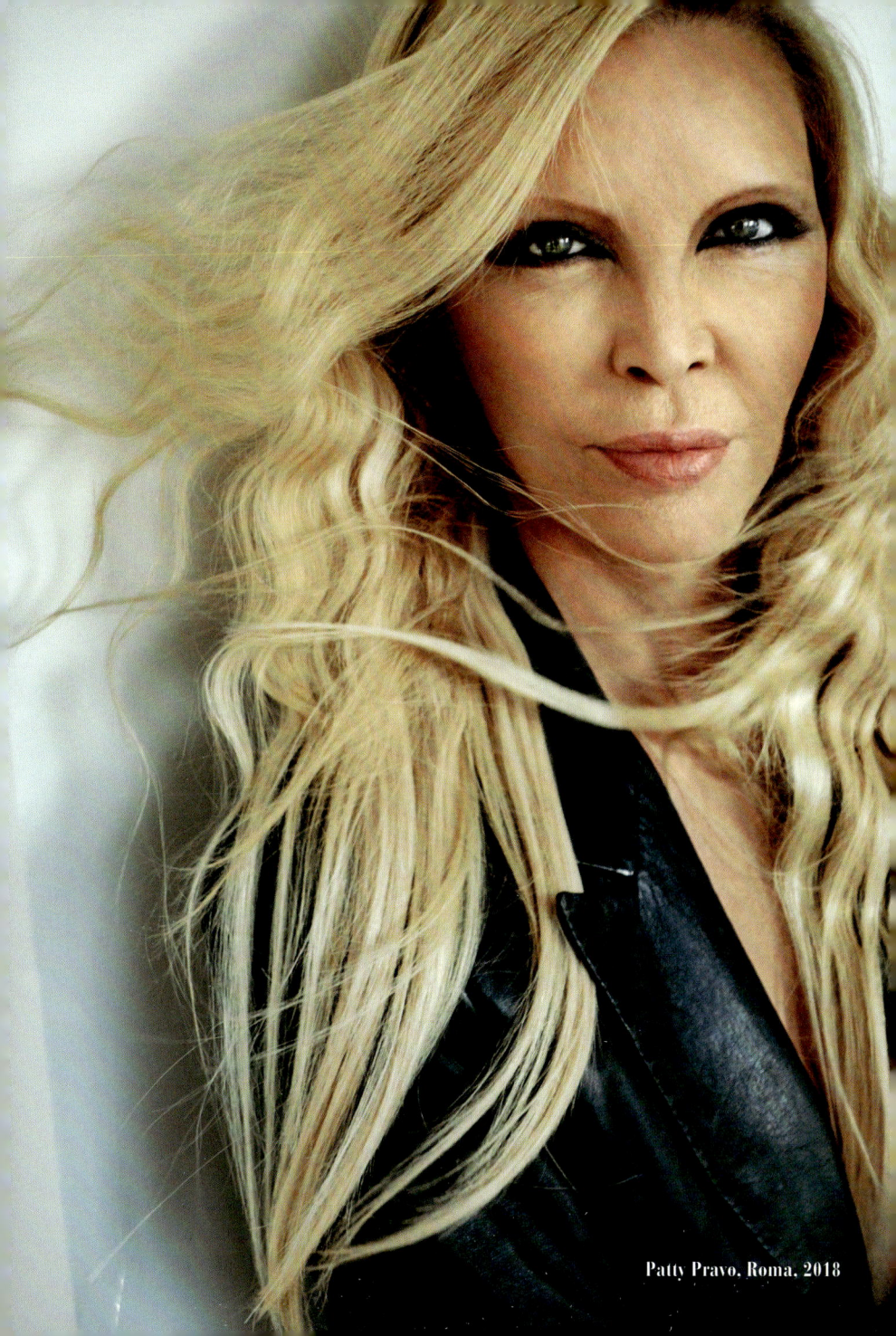

Patty Pravo, Roma, 2018

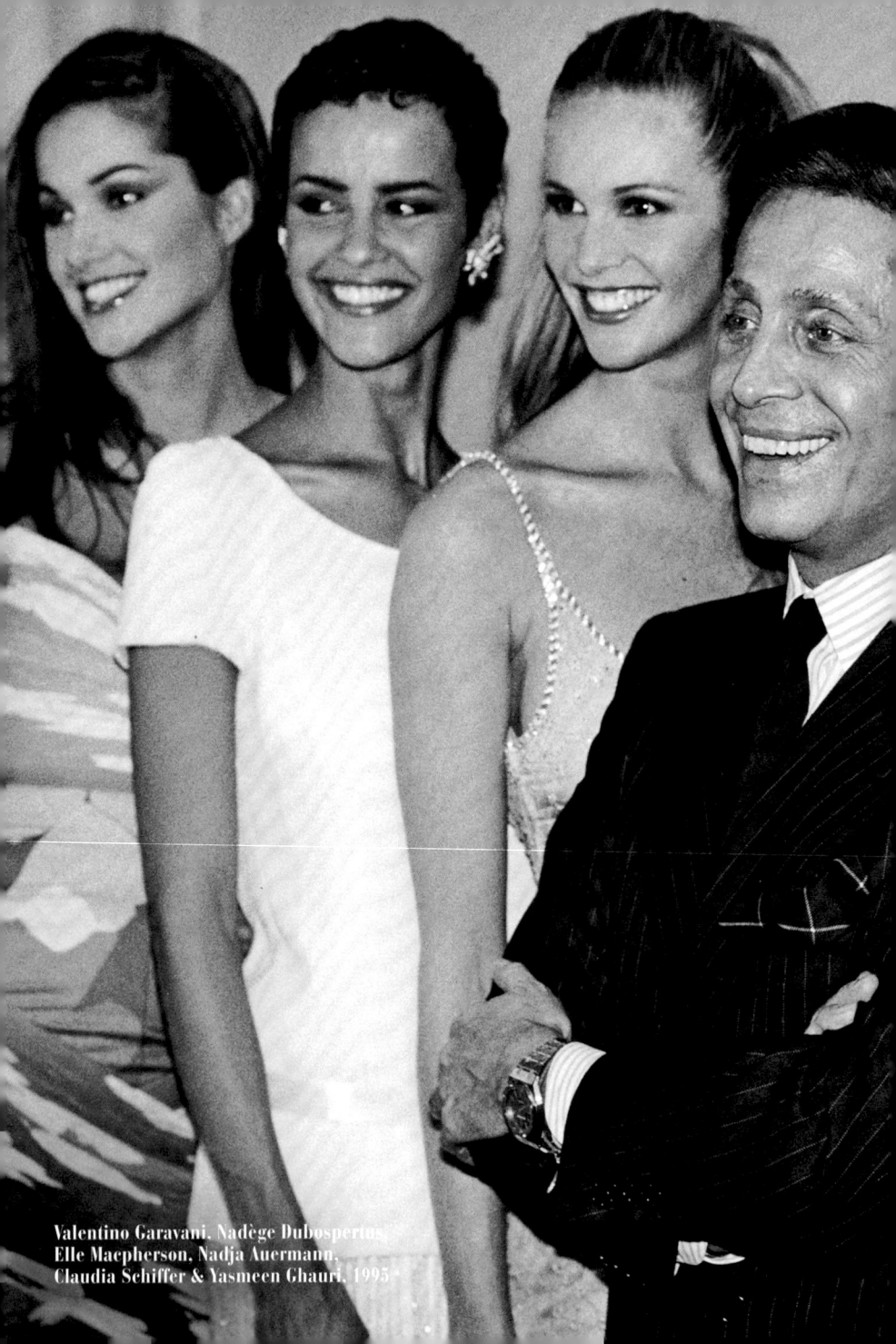

Valentino Garavani. Nadège Dubospertus.
Elle Macpherson, Nadja Auermann.
Claudia Schiffer & Yasmeen Ghauri, 1995.

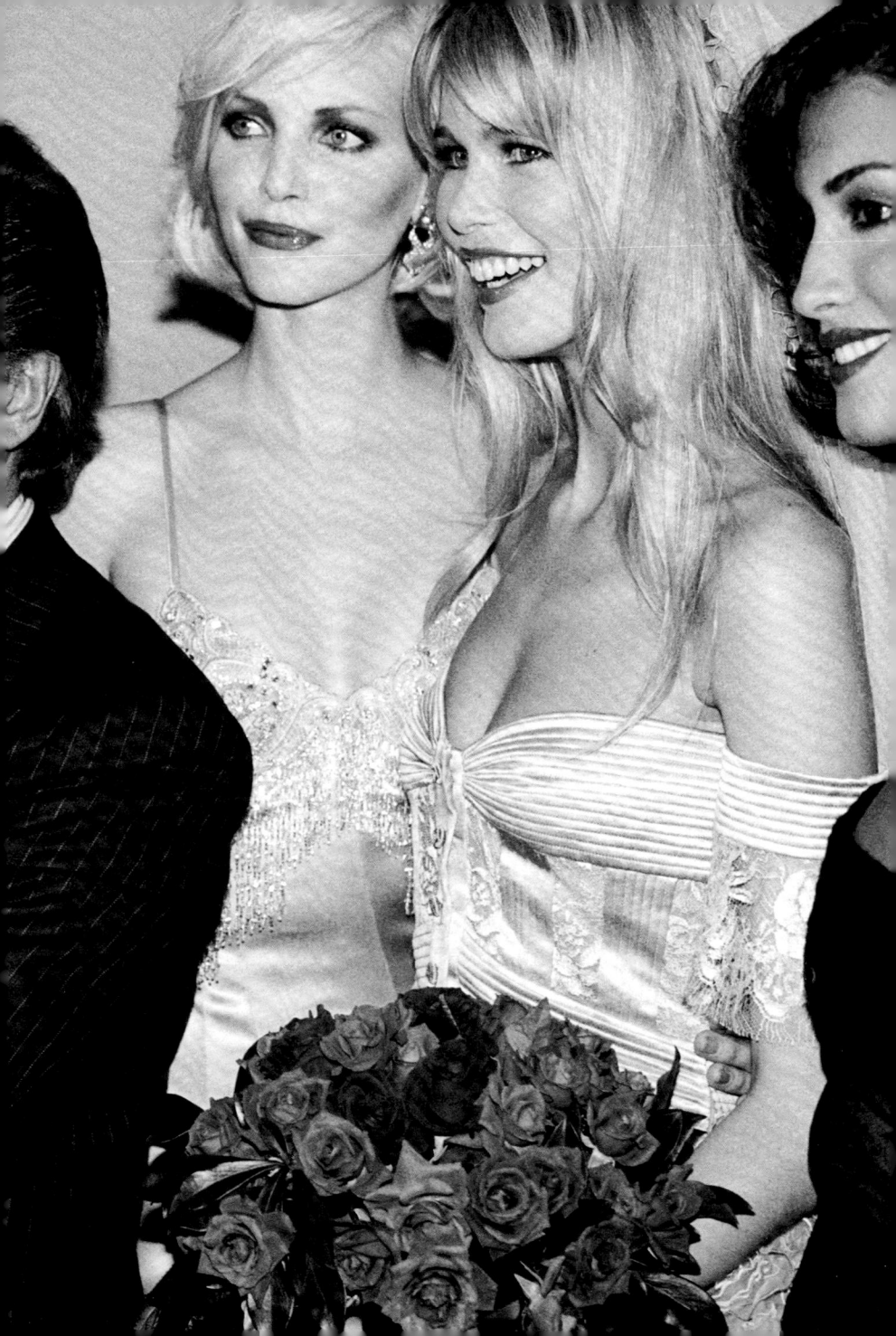

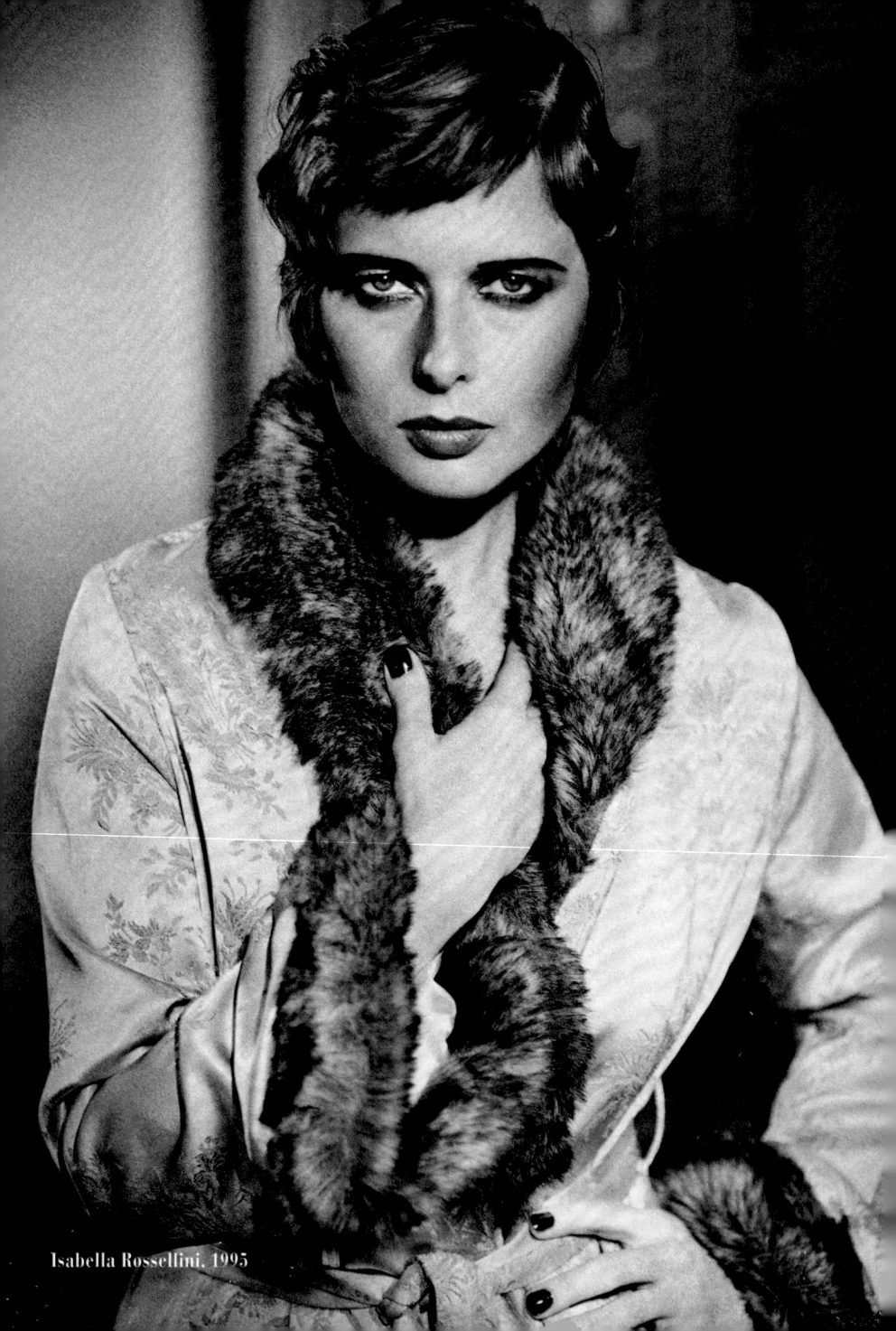

Isabella Rossellini, 1995

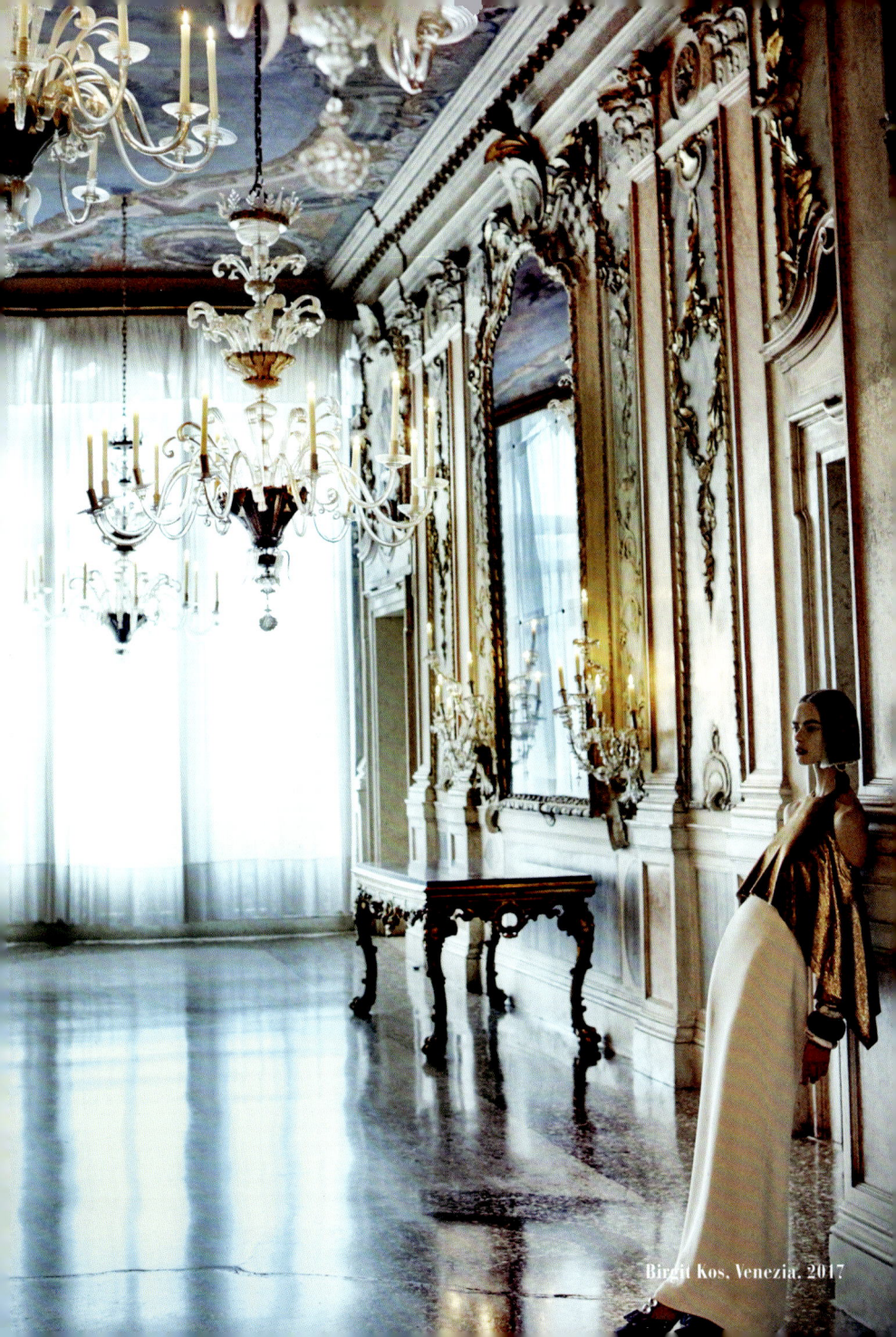

Birgit Kos, Venezia, 2017

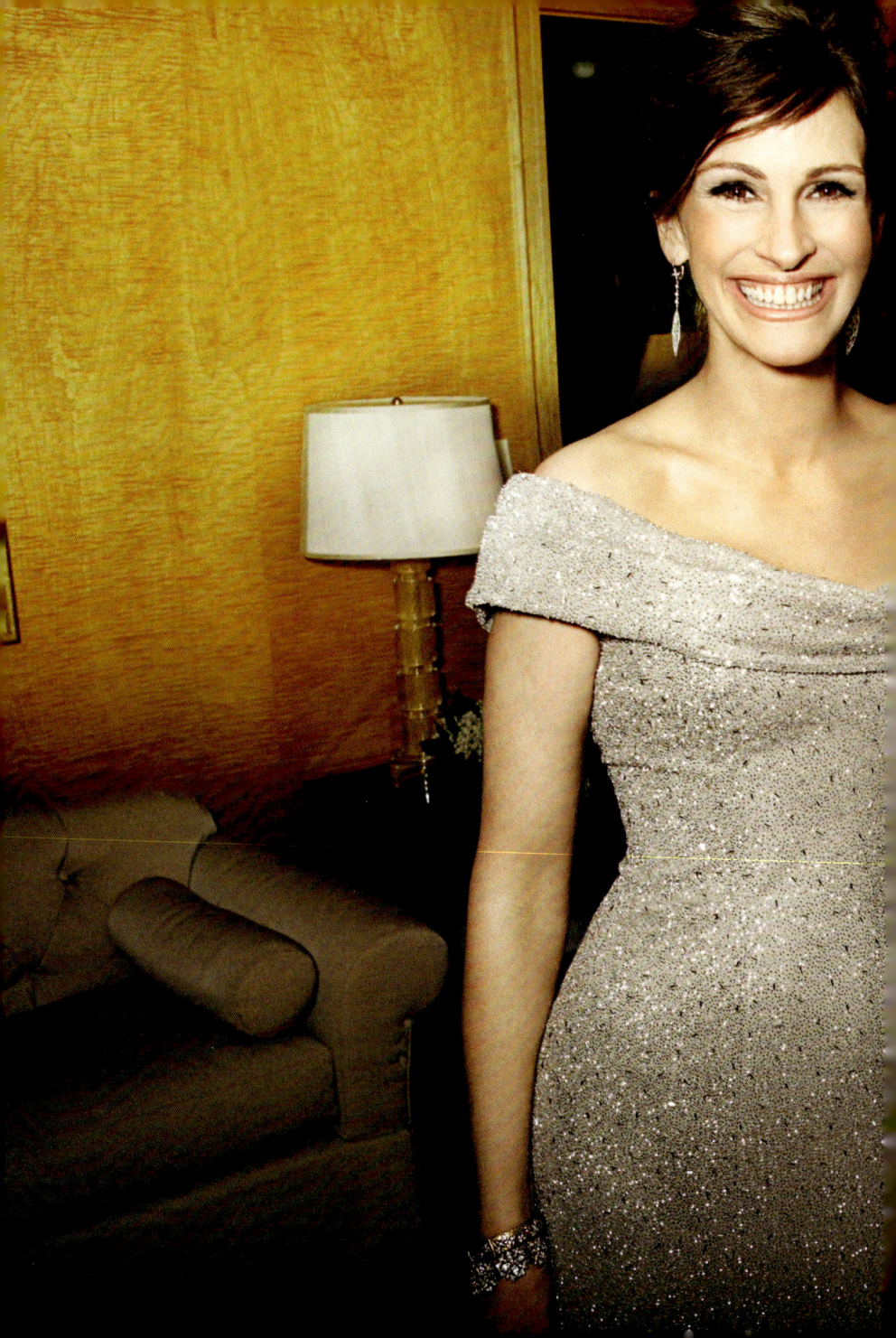

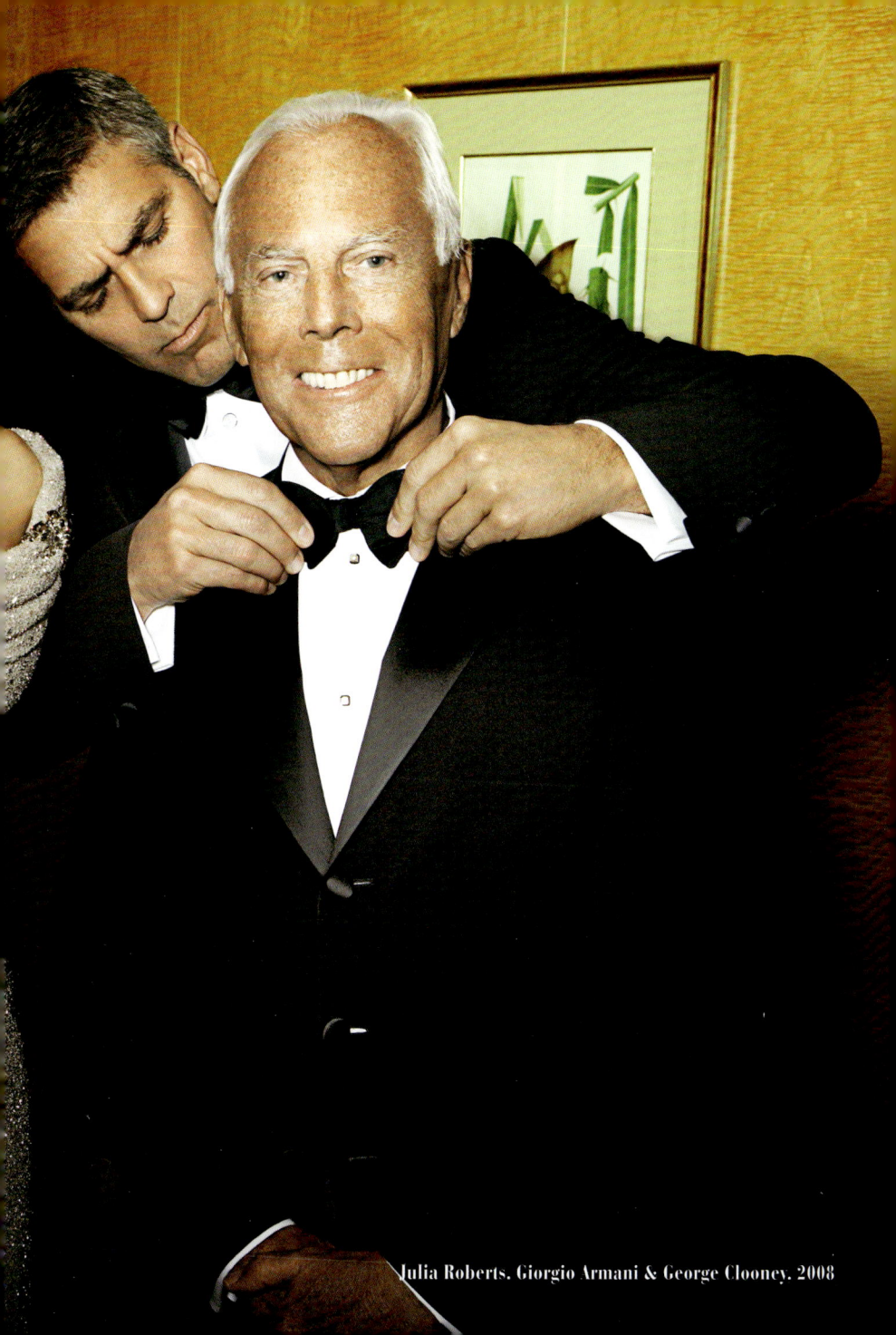

Julia Roberts. Giorgio Armani & George Clooney. 2008

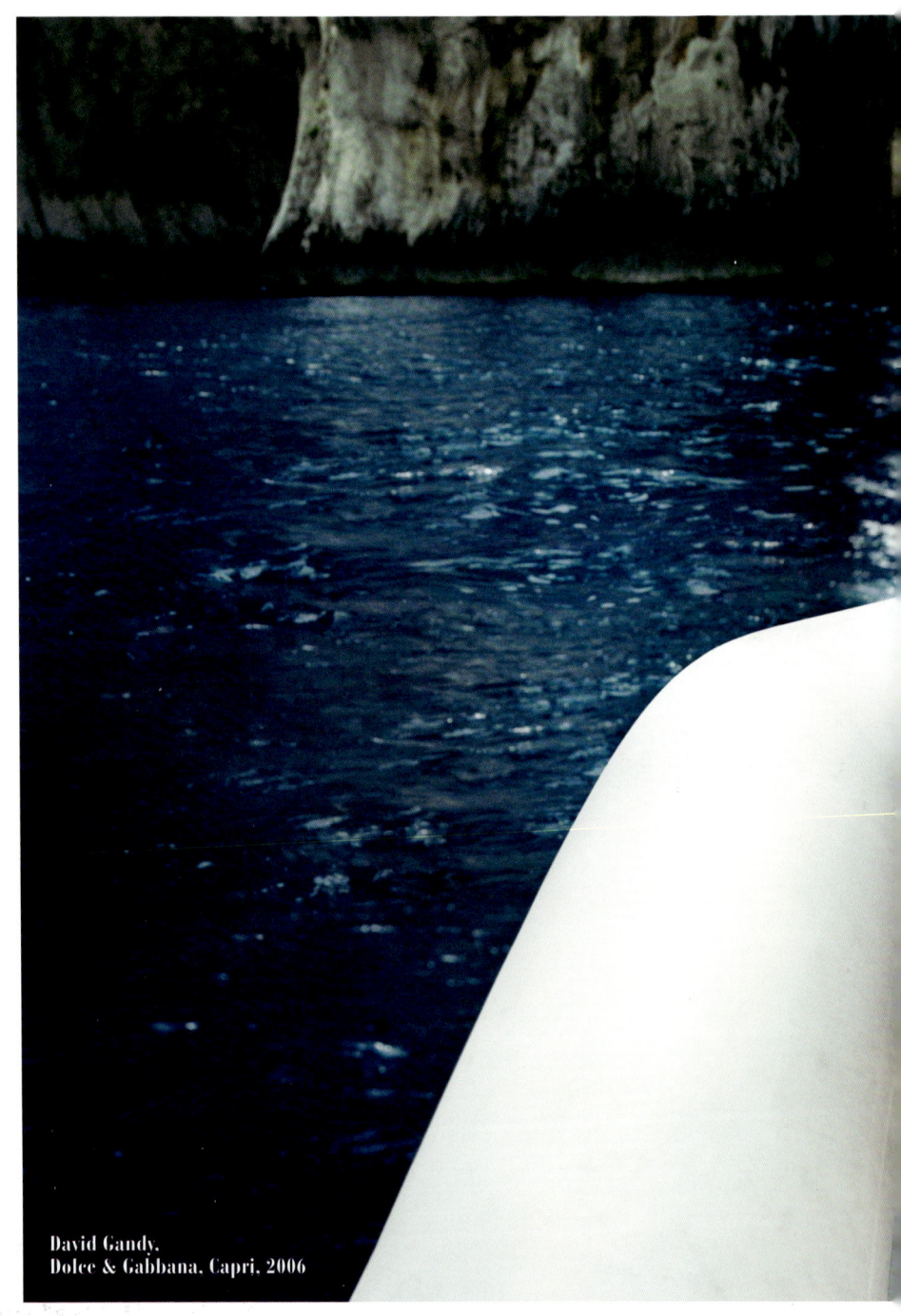

David Gandy.
Dolce & Gabbana, Capri, 2006

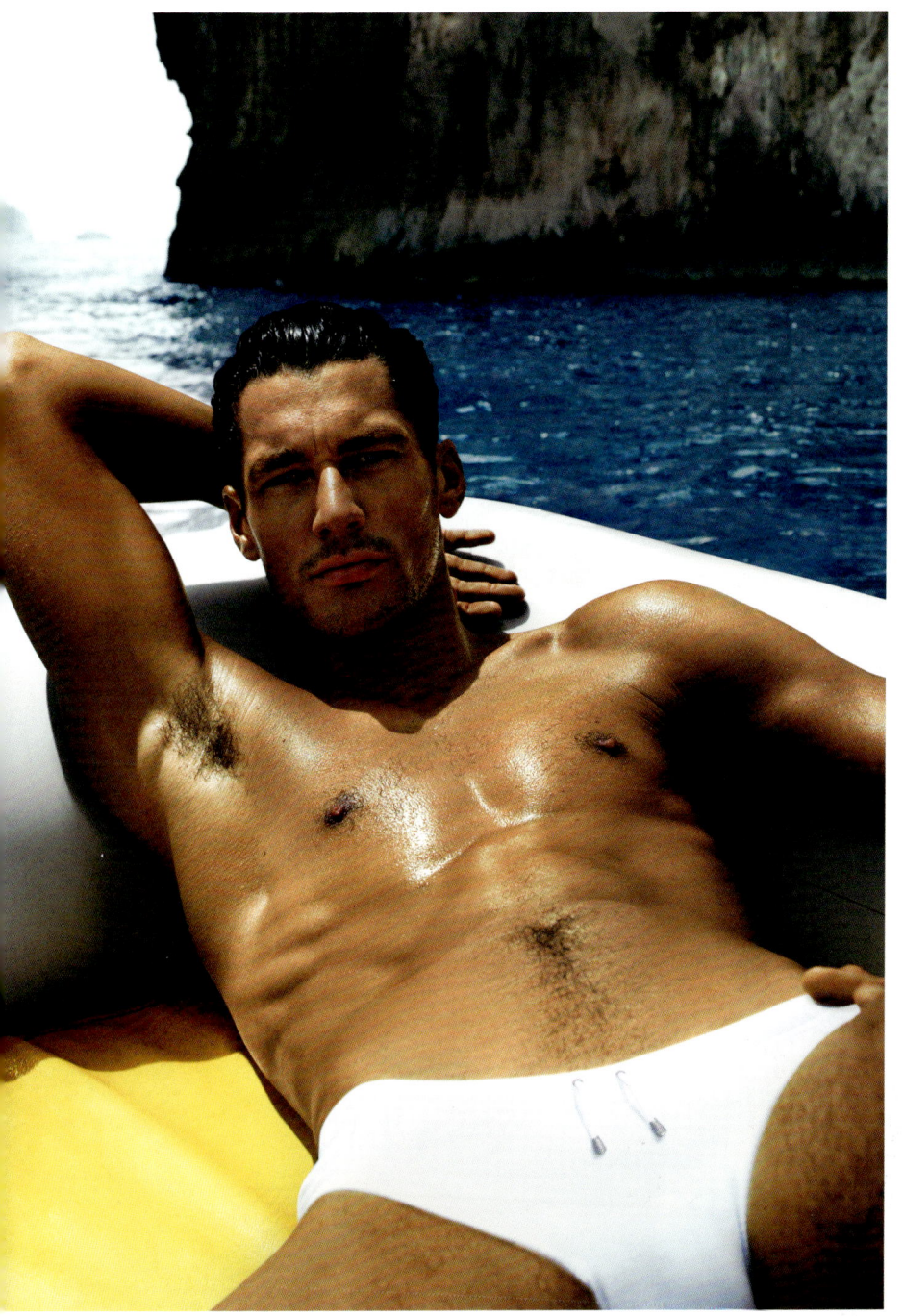

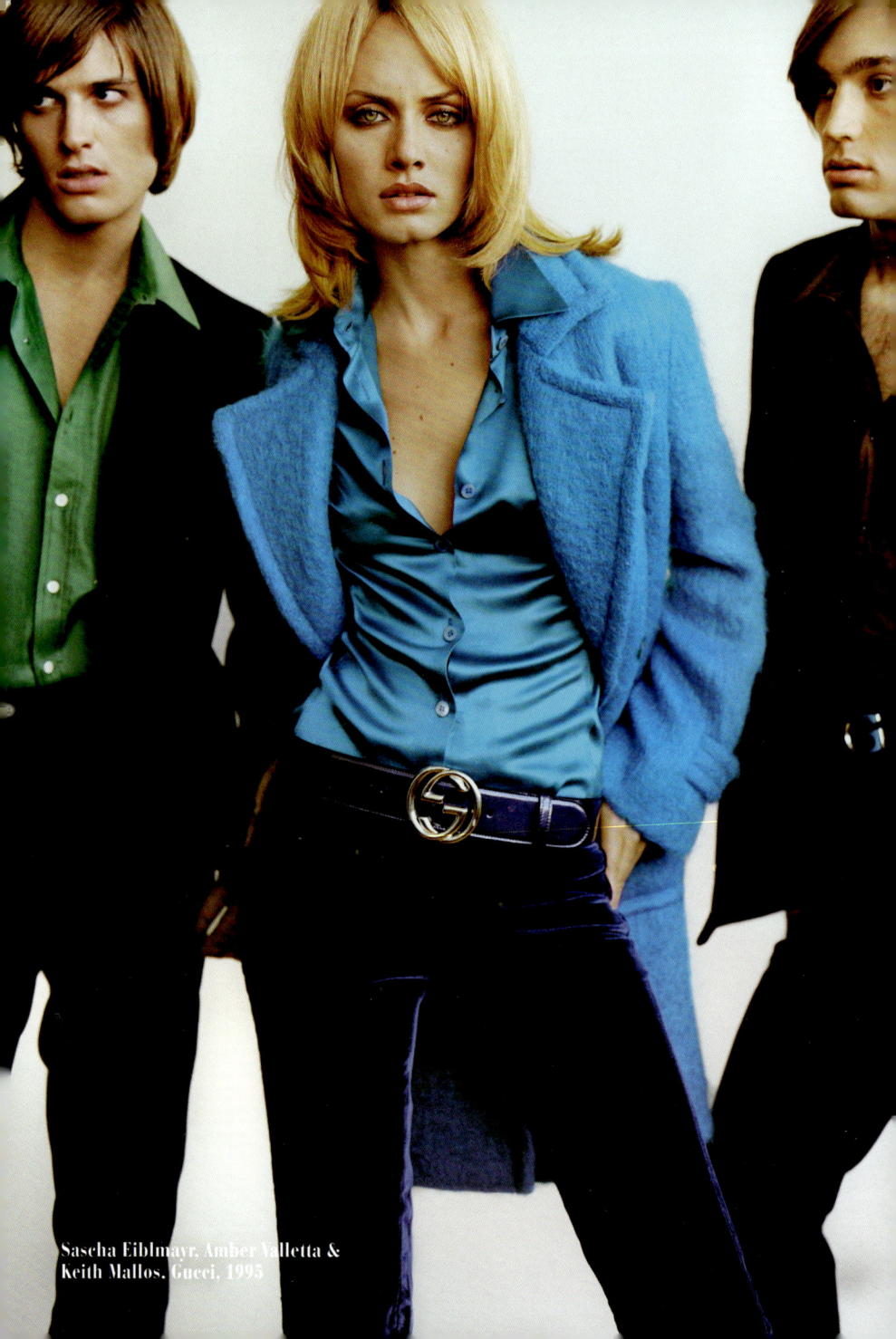

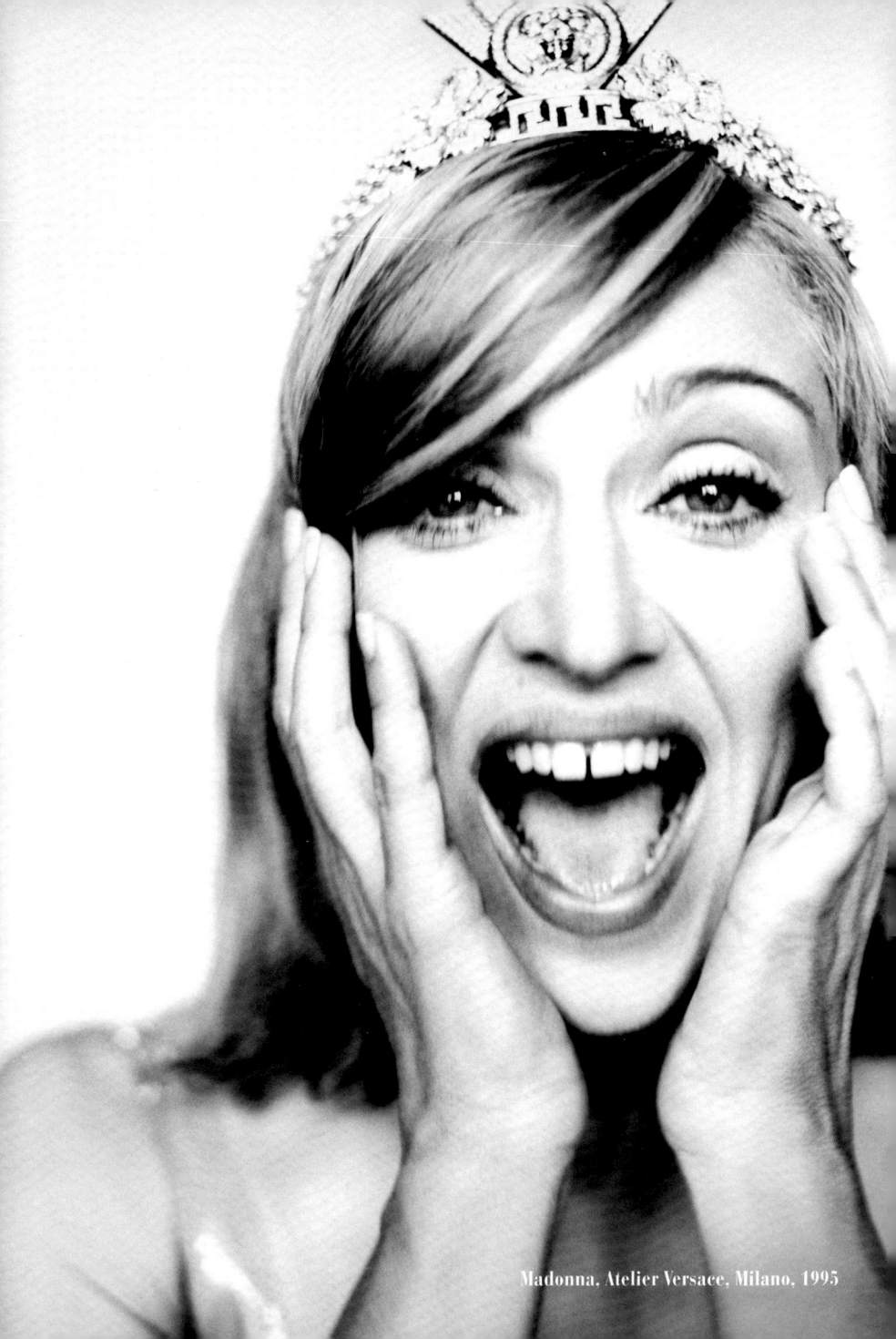

Madonna, Atelier Versace, Milano, 1995

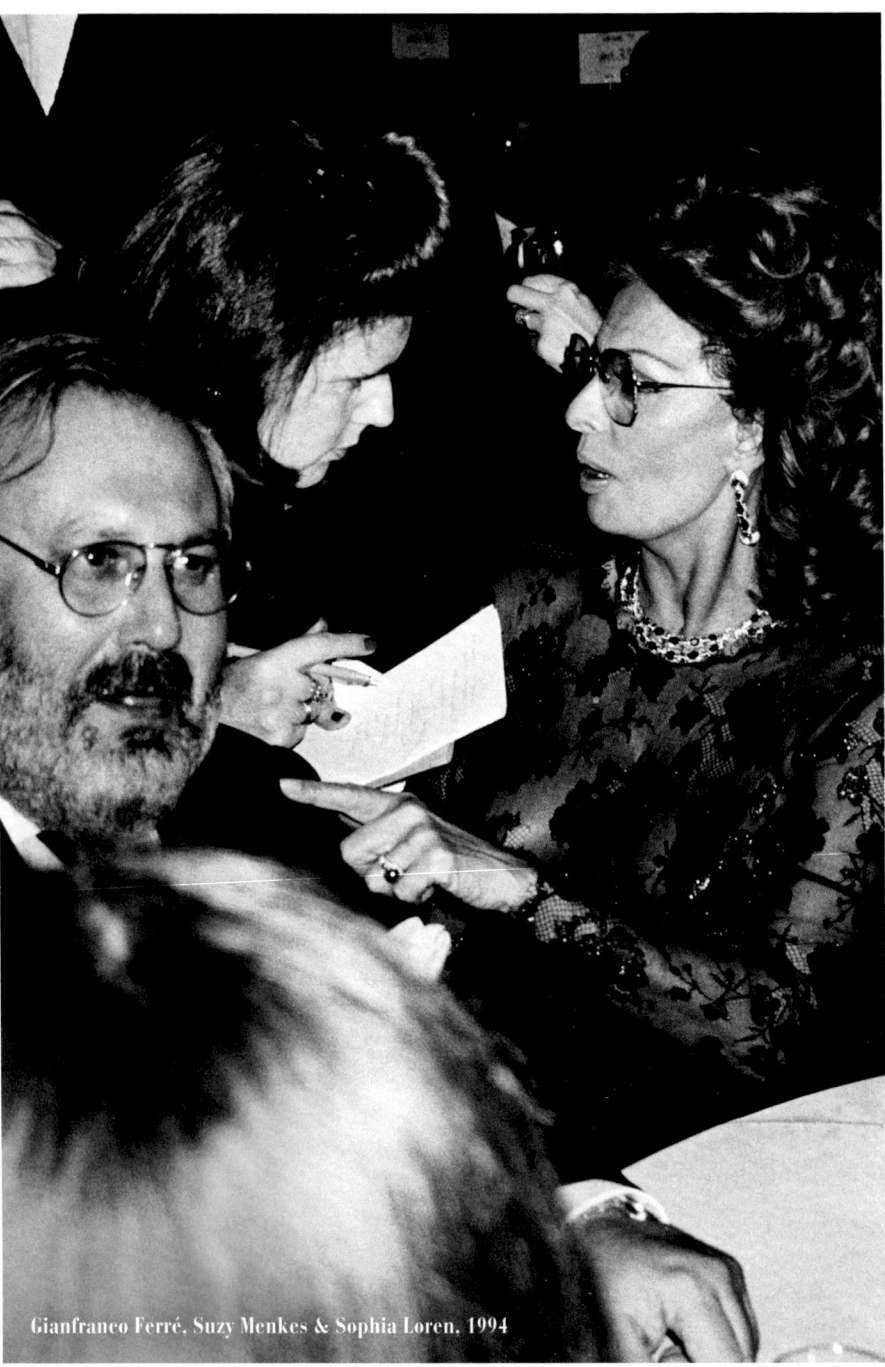

Gianfranco Ferré, Suzy Menkes & Sophia Loren, 1994

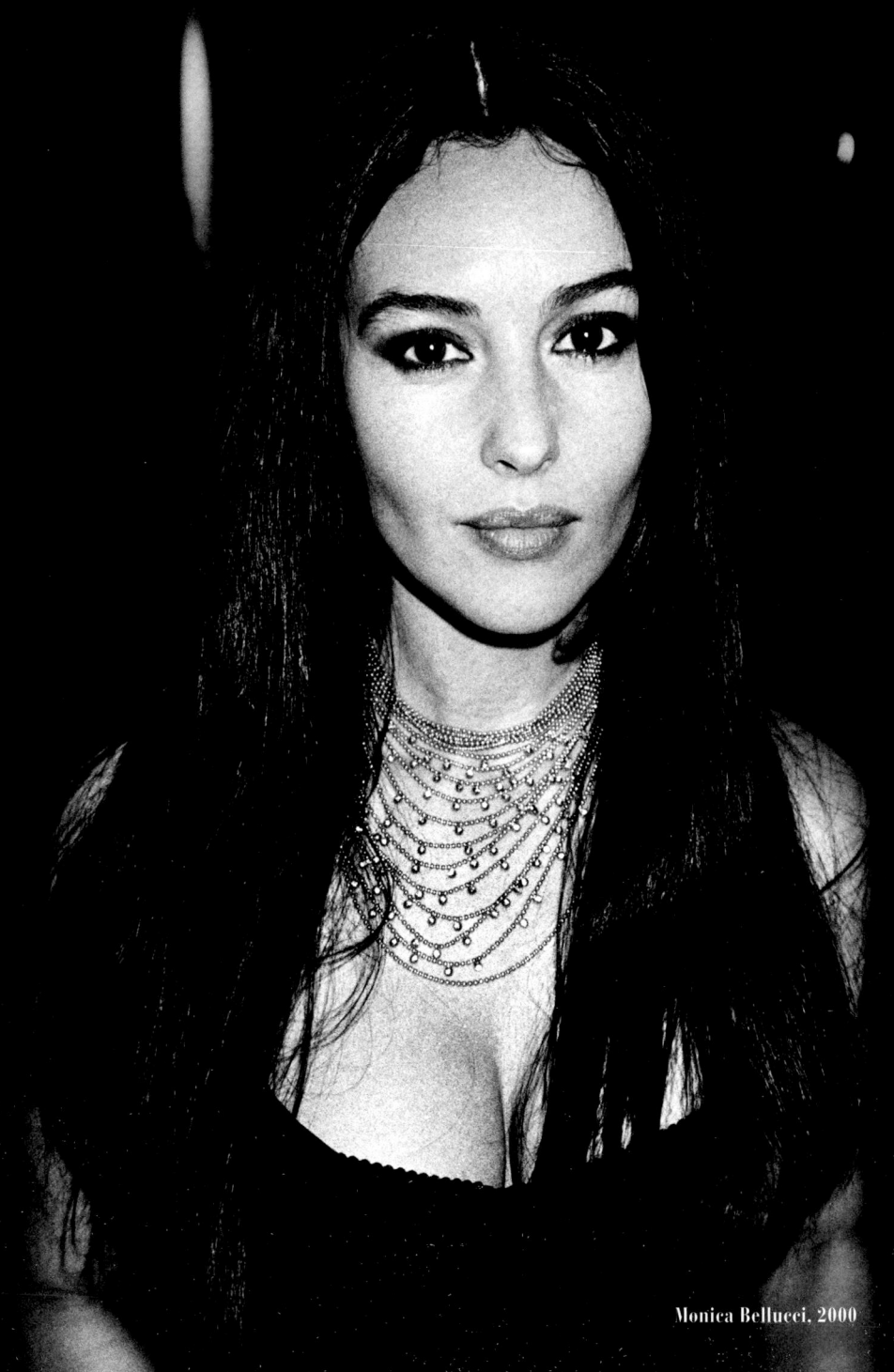

Monica Bellucci, 2000

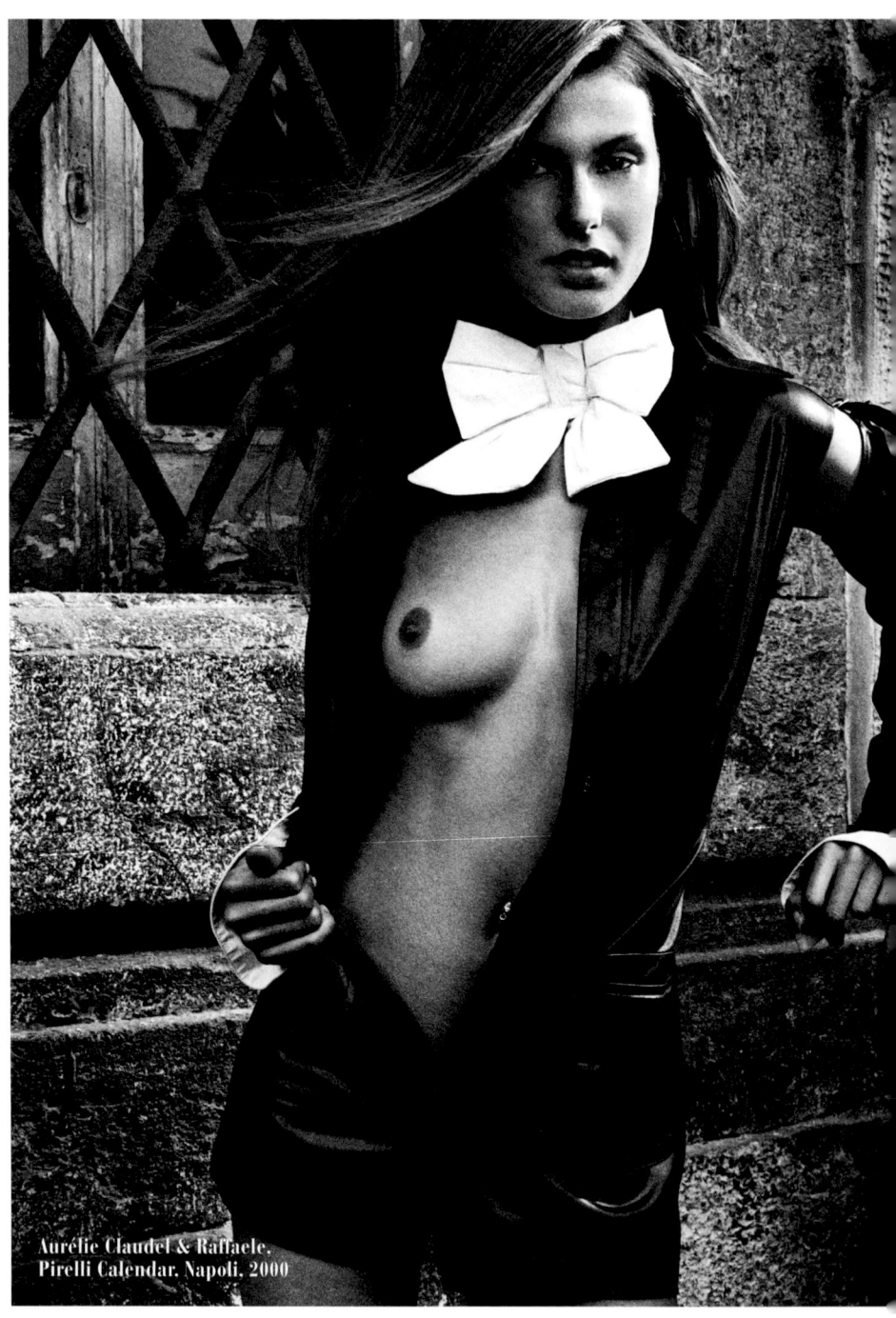

Aurélie Claudel & Raffaele,
Pirelli Calendar, Napoli, 2000

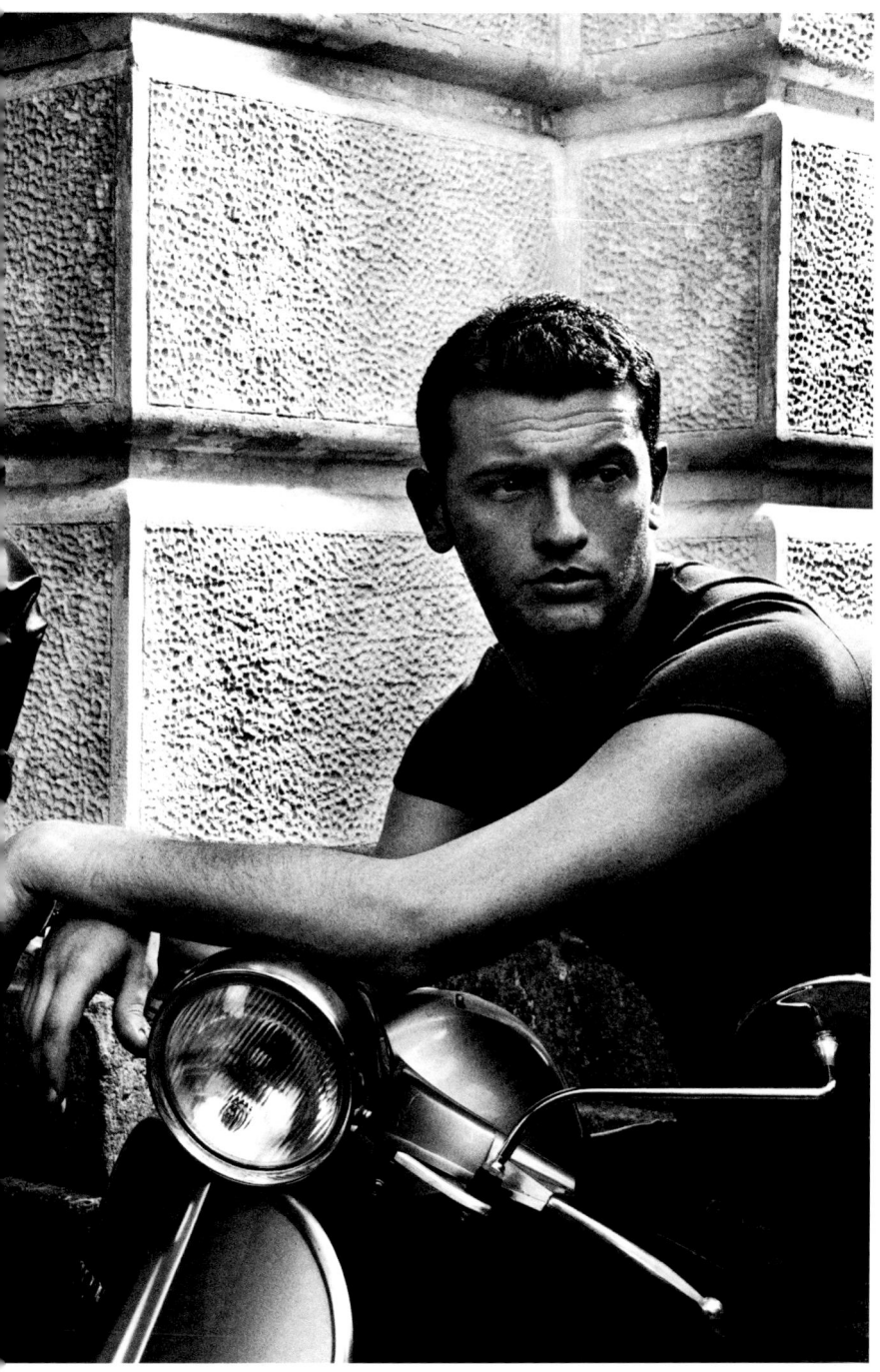

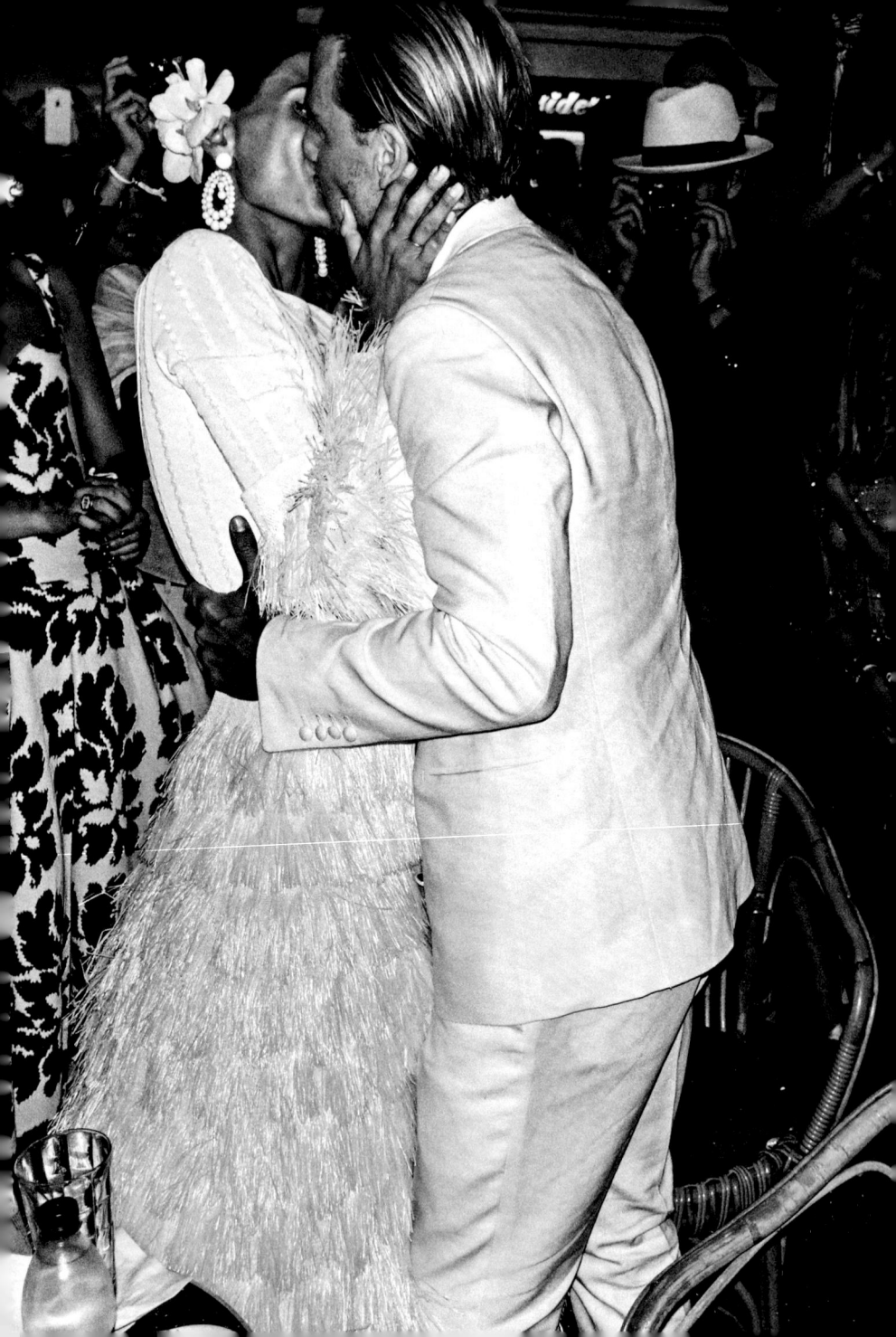

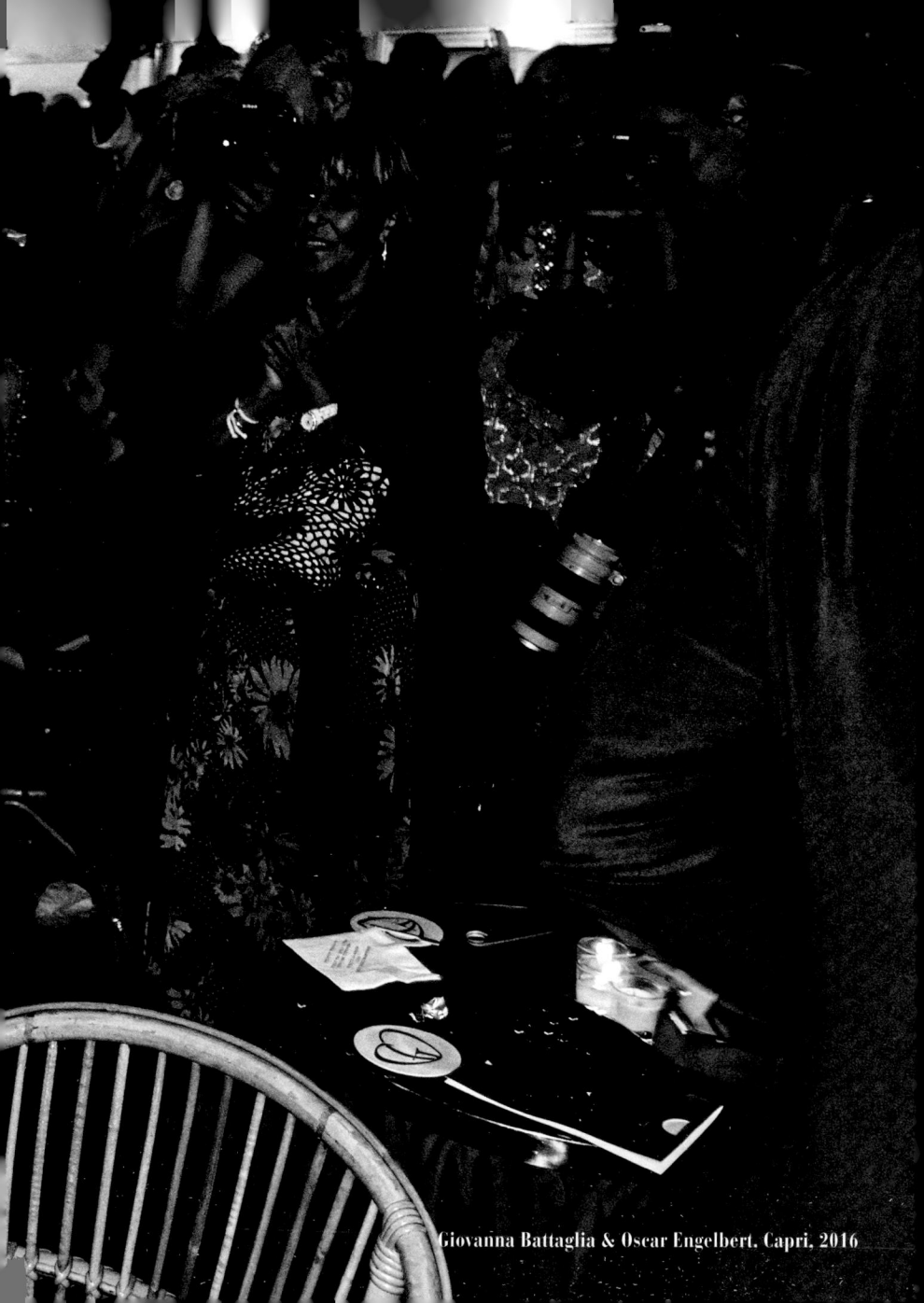

Giovanna Battaglia & Oscar Engelbert, Capri, 2016

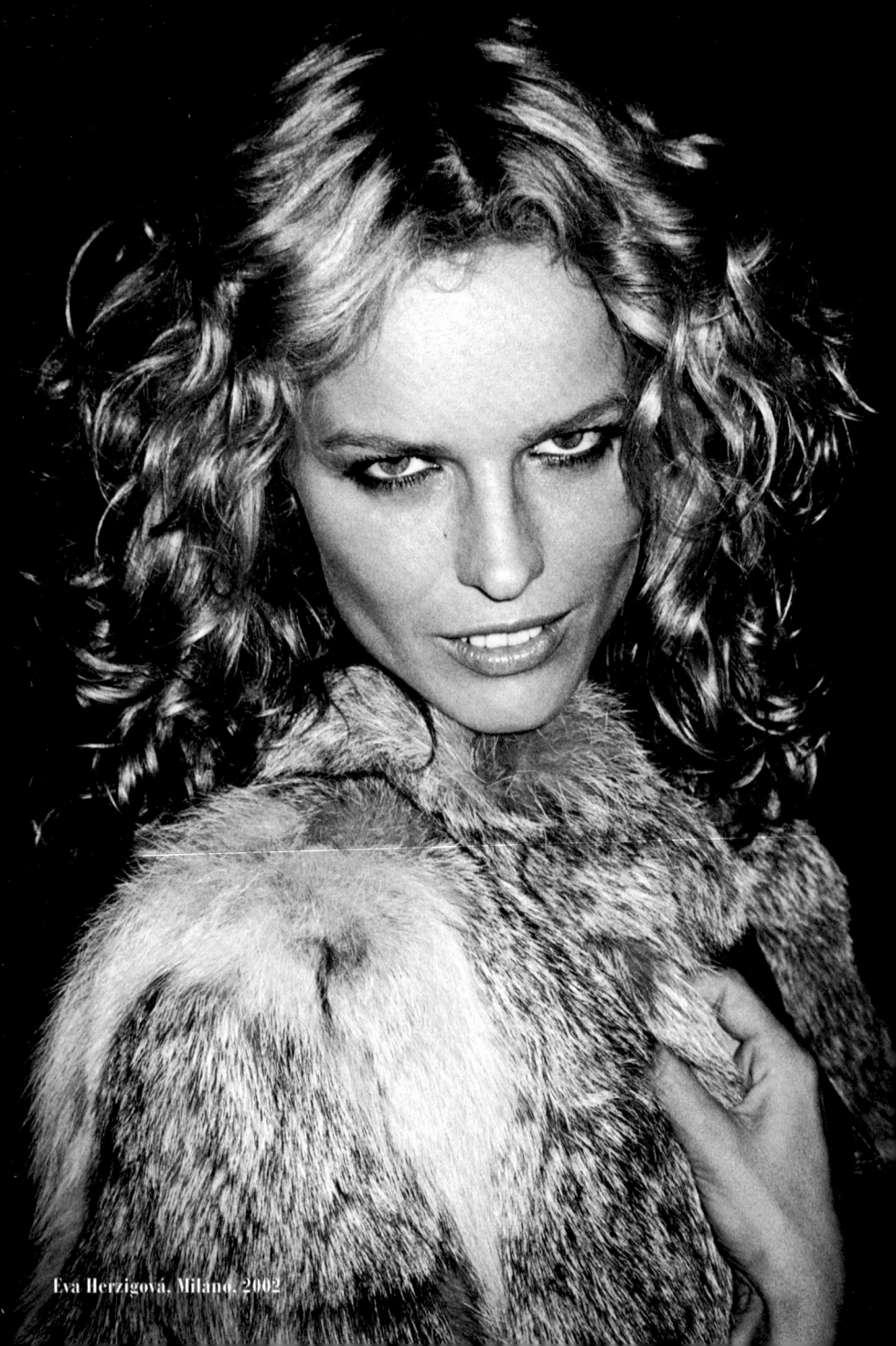

Eva Herzigová, Milano, 2002

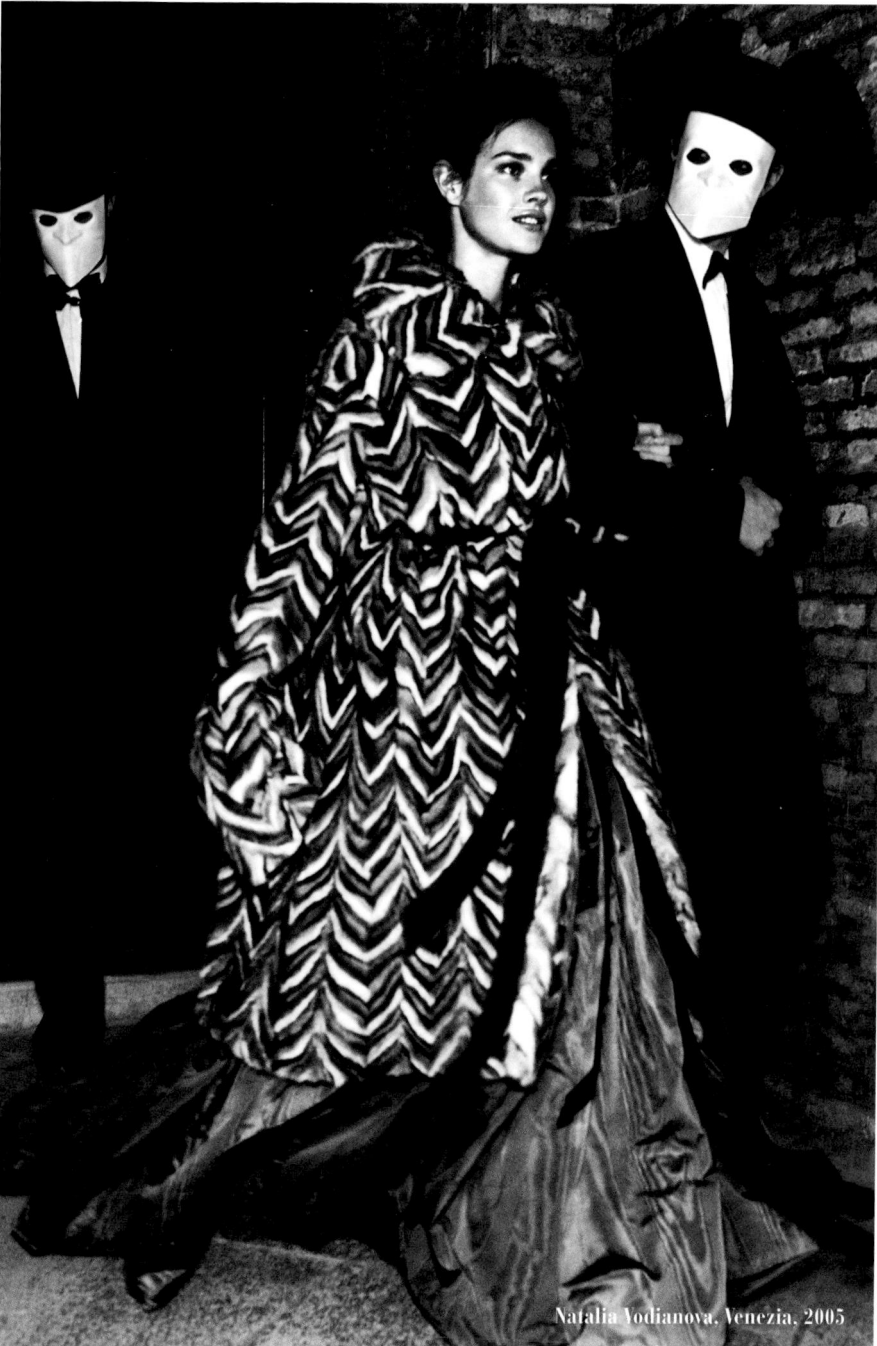

Natalia Vodianova, Venezia, 2005

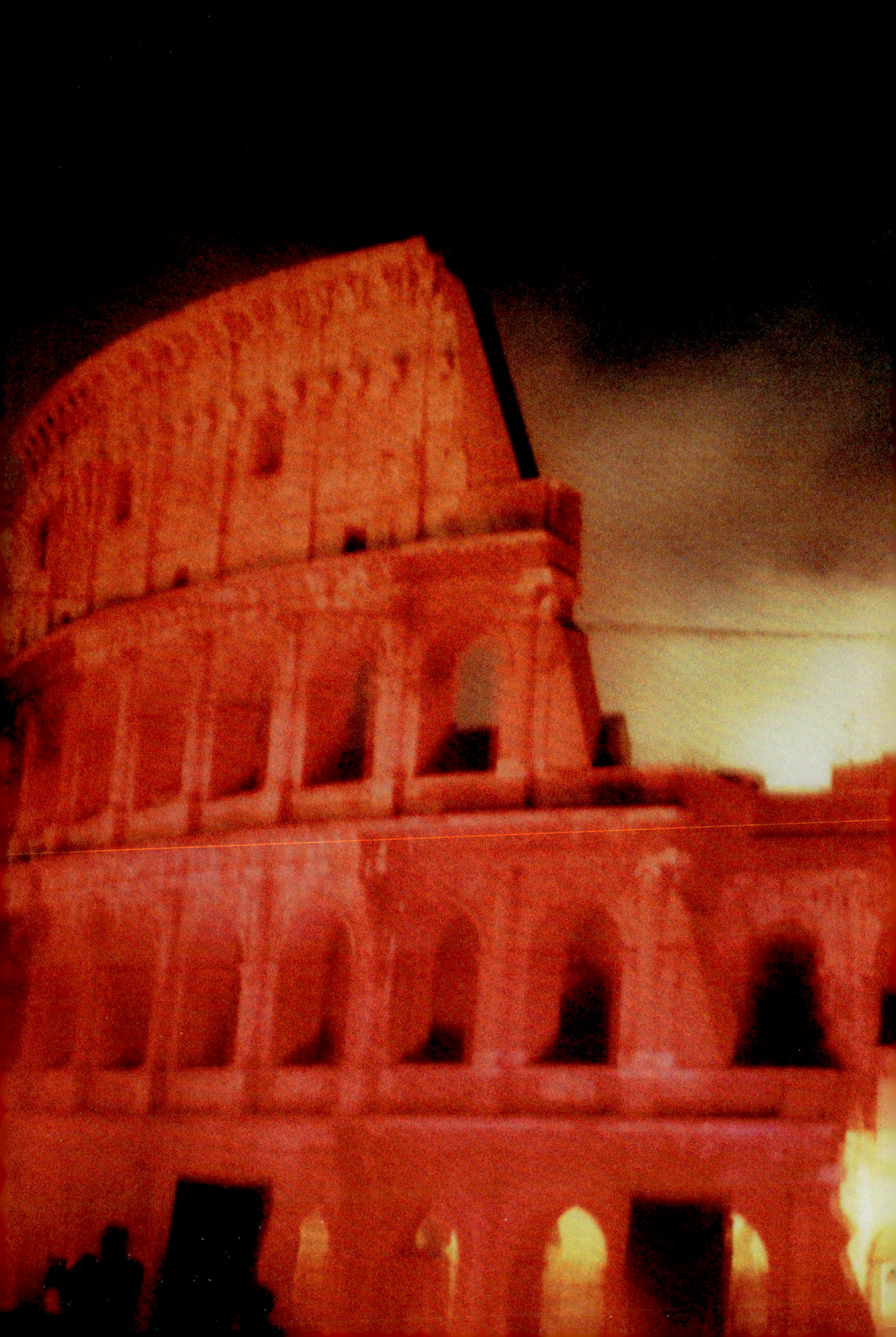

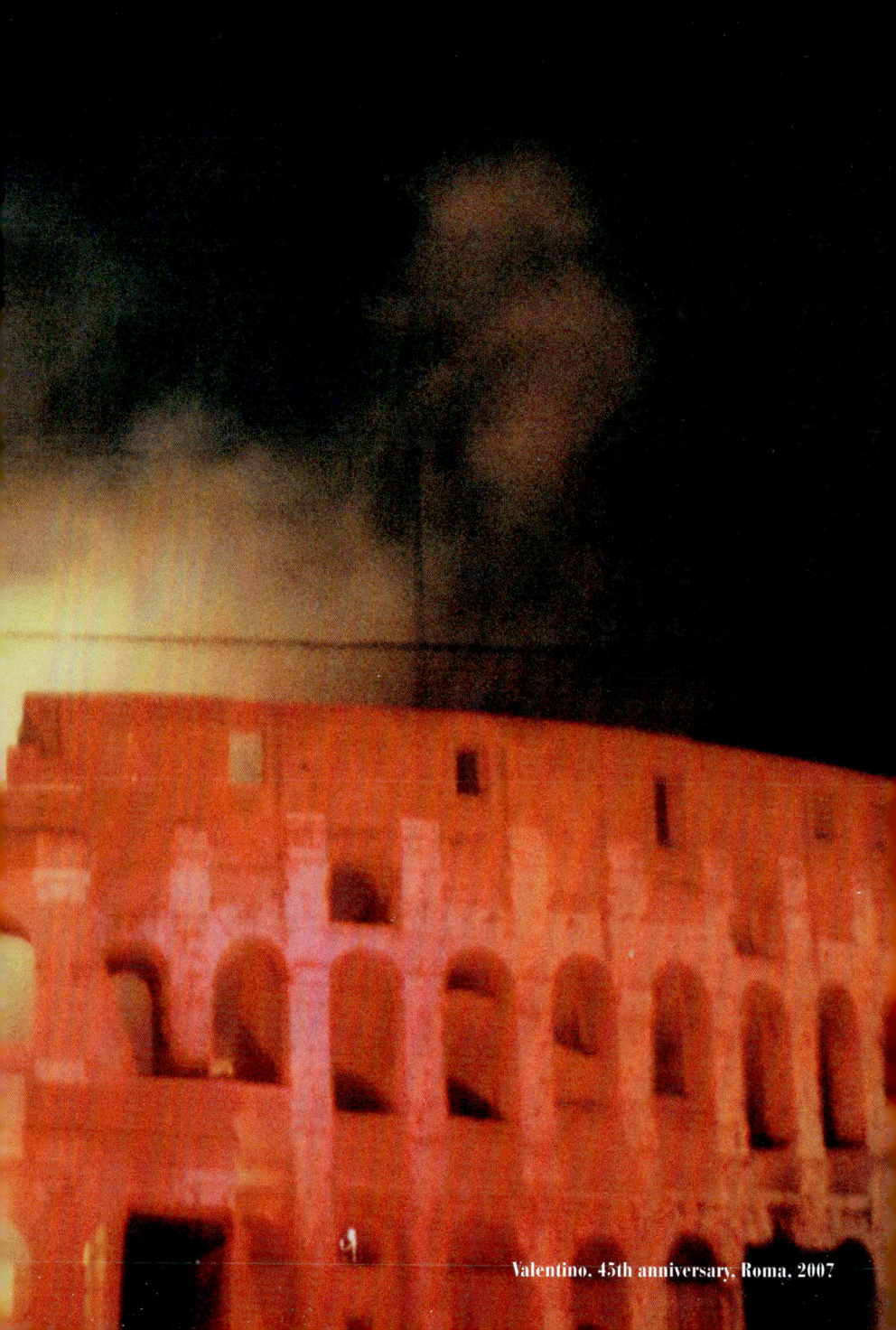

Valentino, 45th anniversary, Roma, 2007

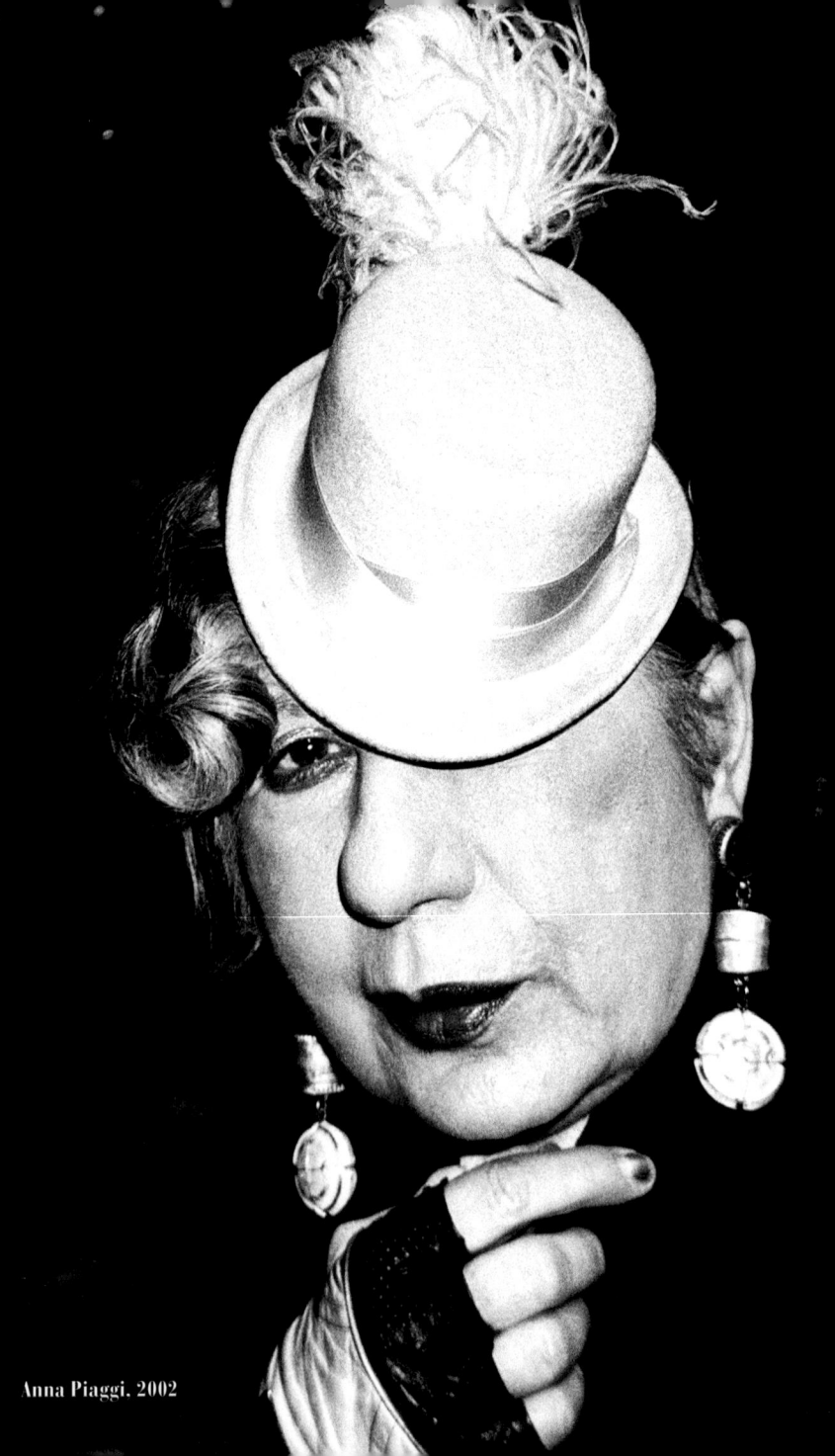

Anna Piaggi. 2002

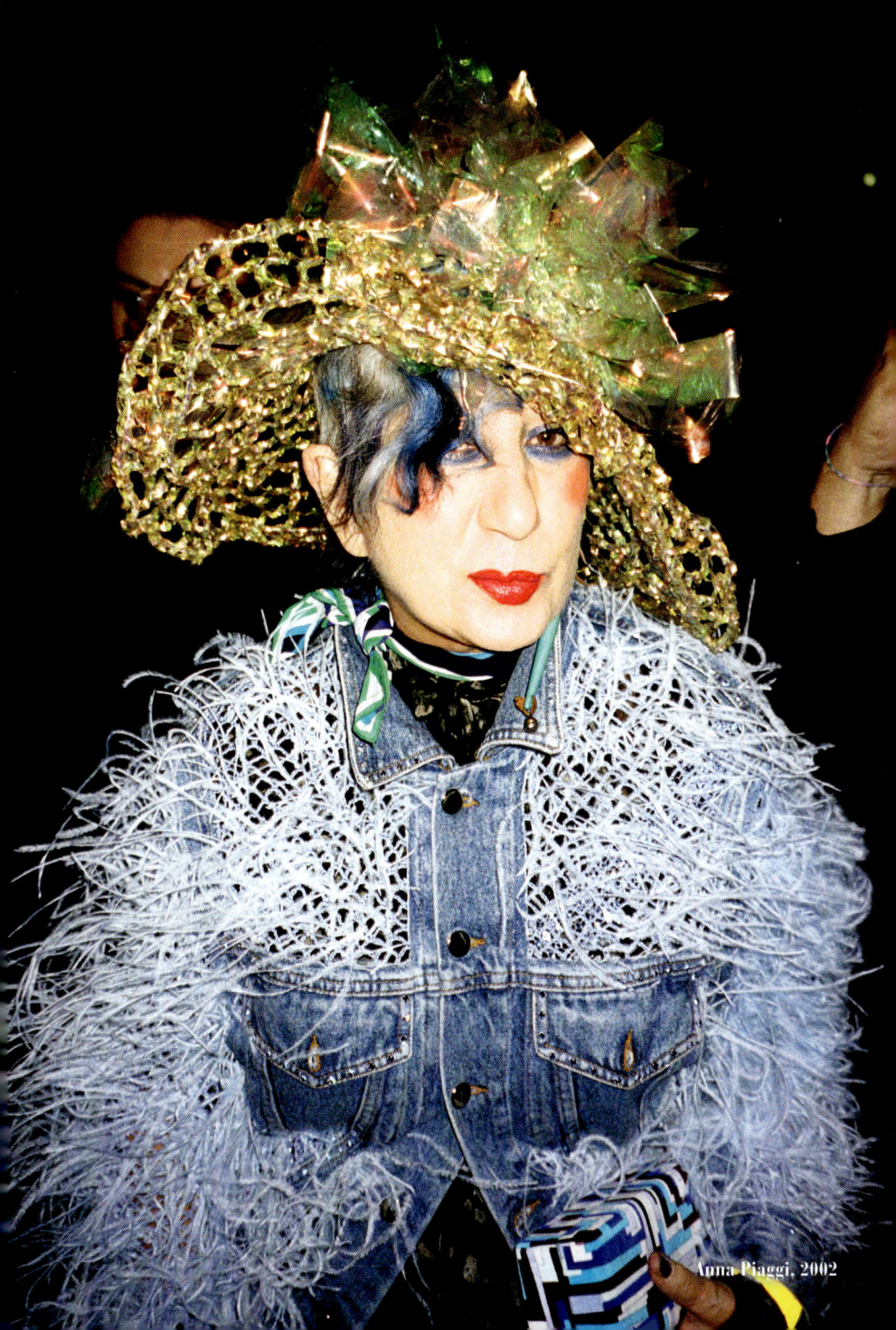

Anna Piaggi, 2002

AT
SEA

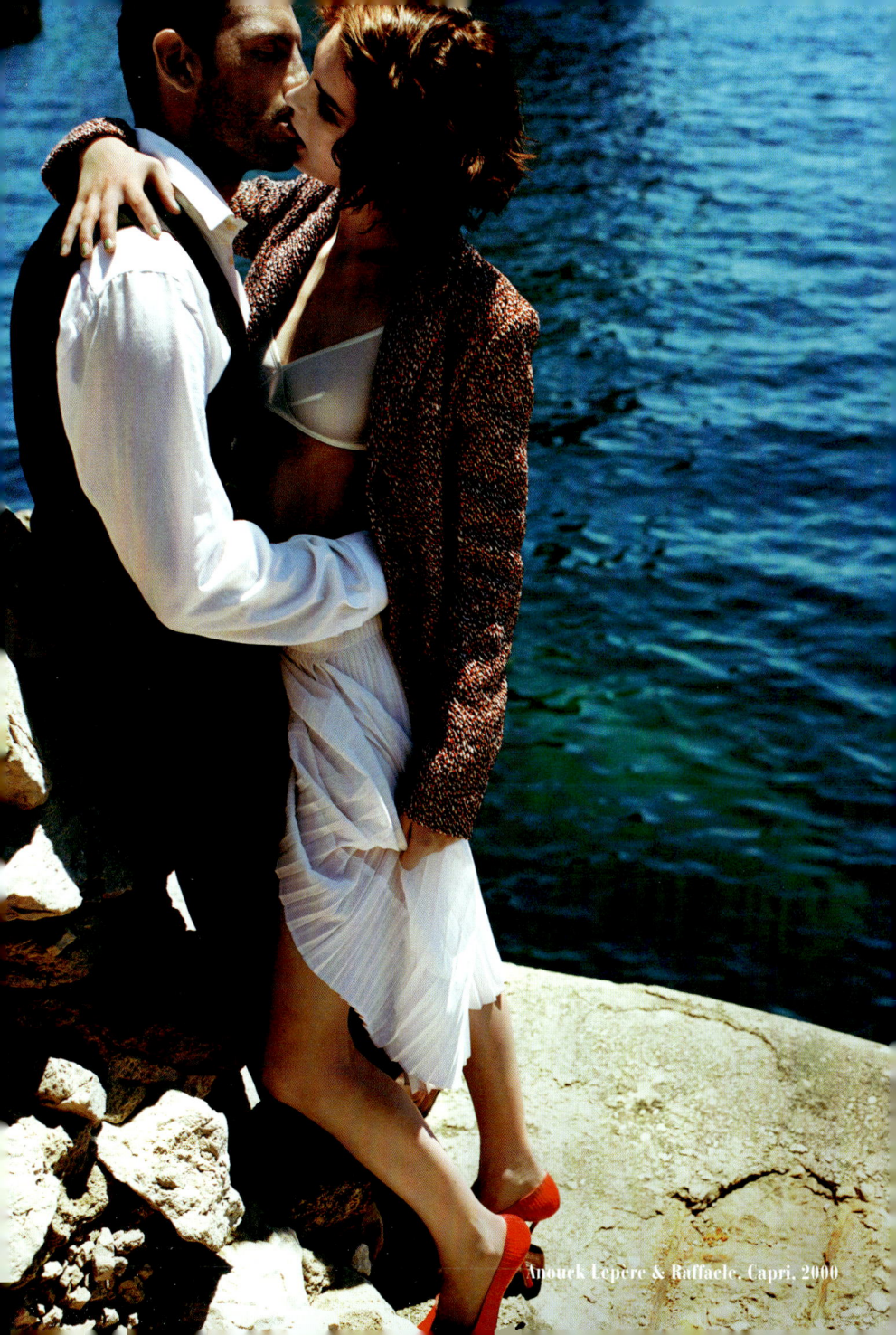

Anouck Lepère & Raffaele, Capri, 2000

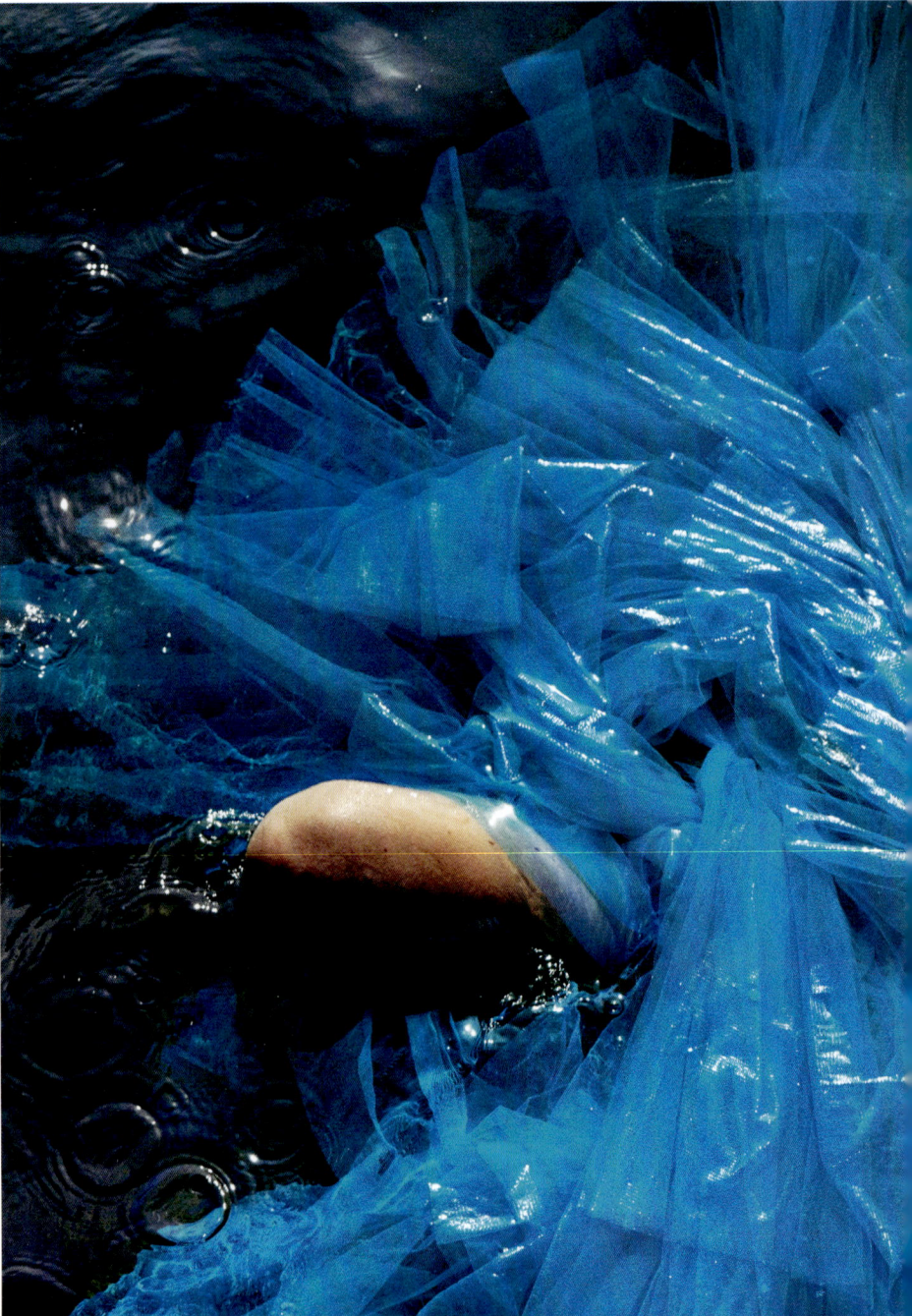

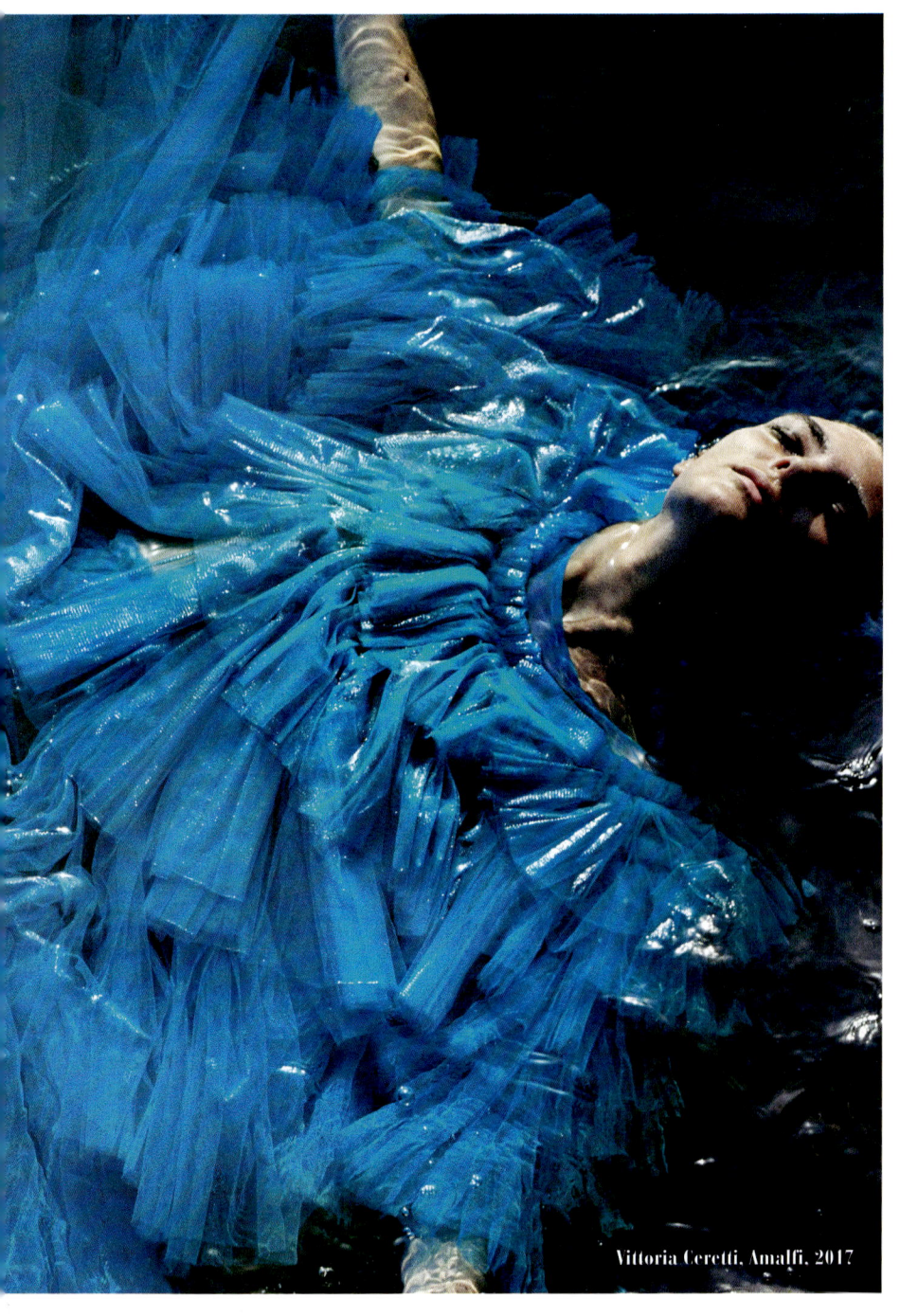

Vittoria Ceretti, Amalfi, 2017

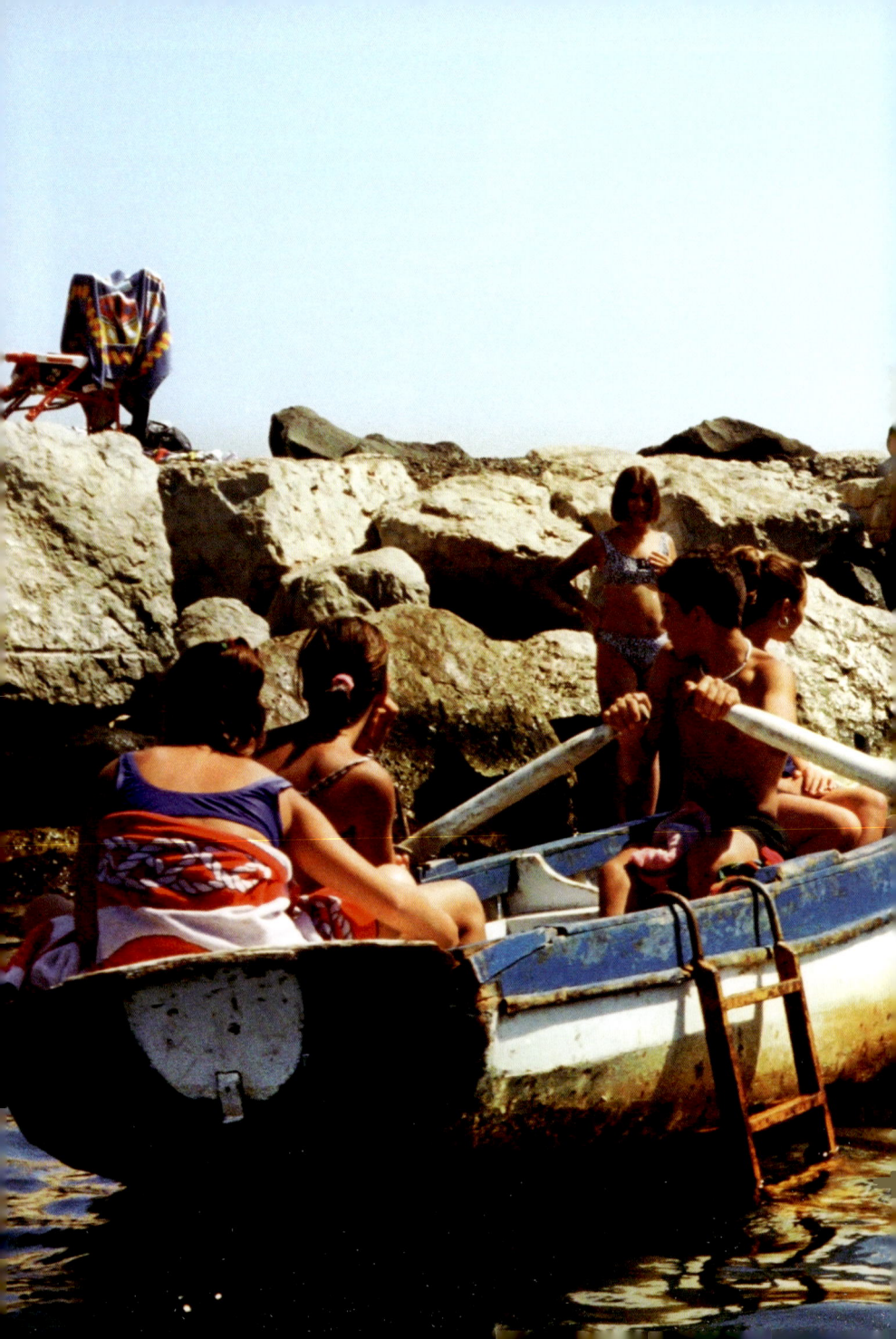

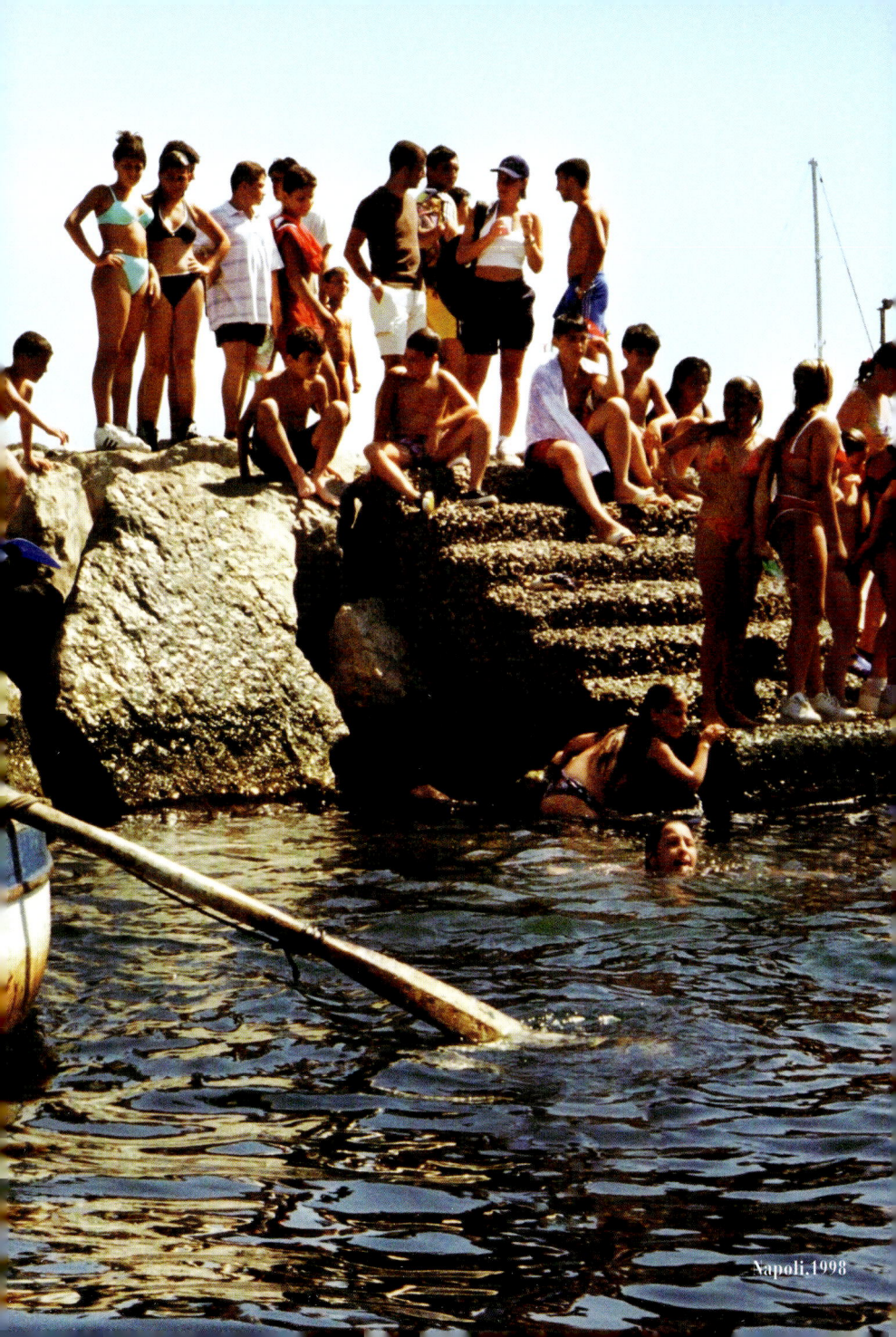

Napoli,1998

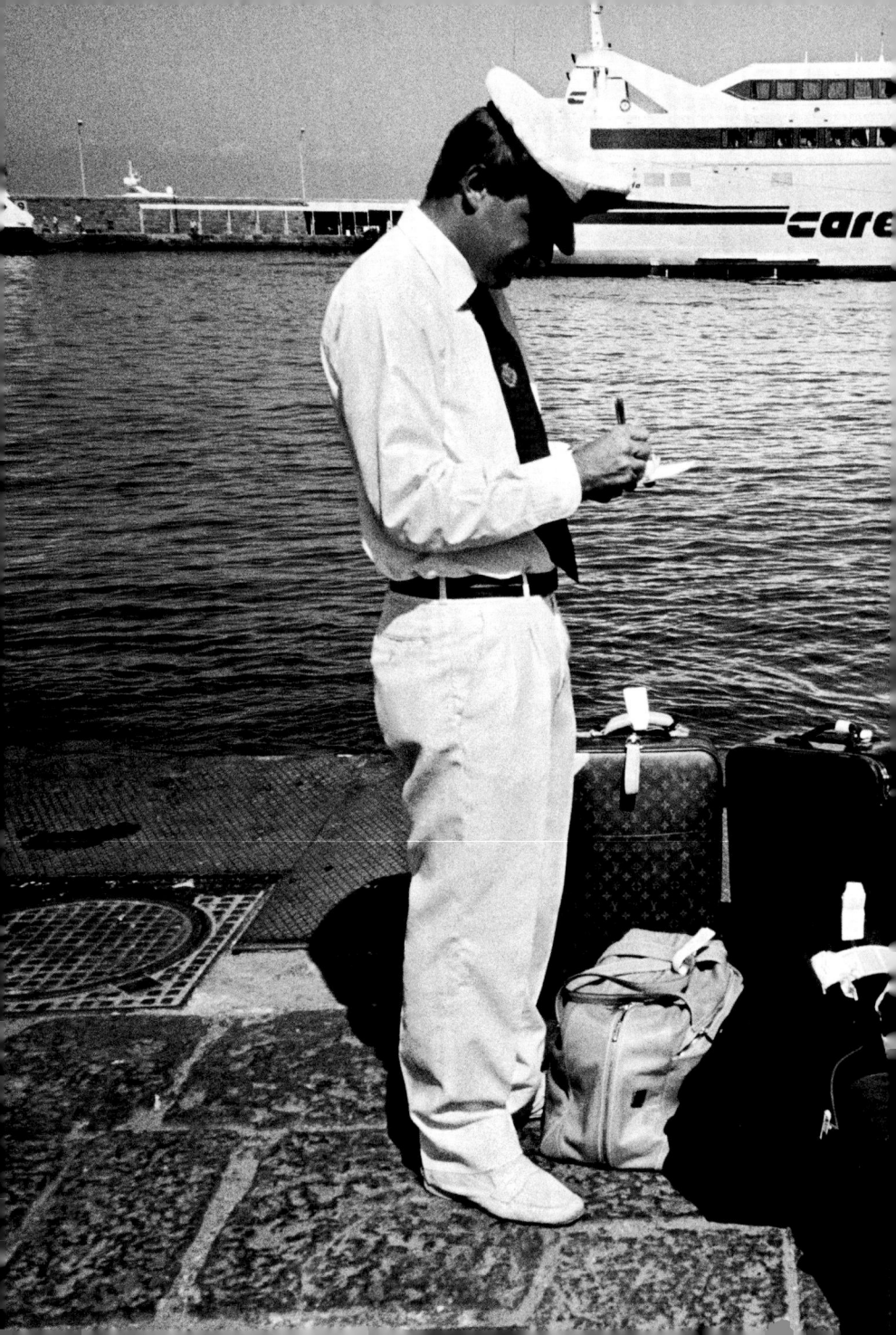

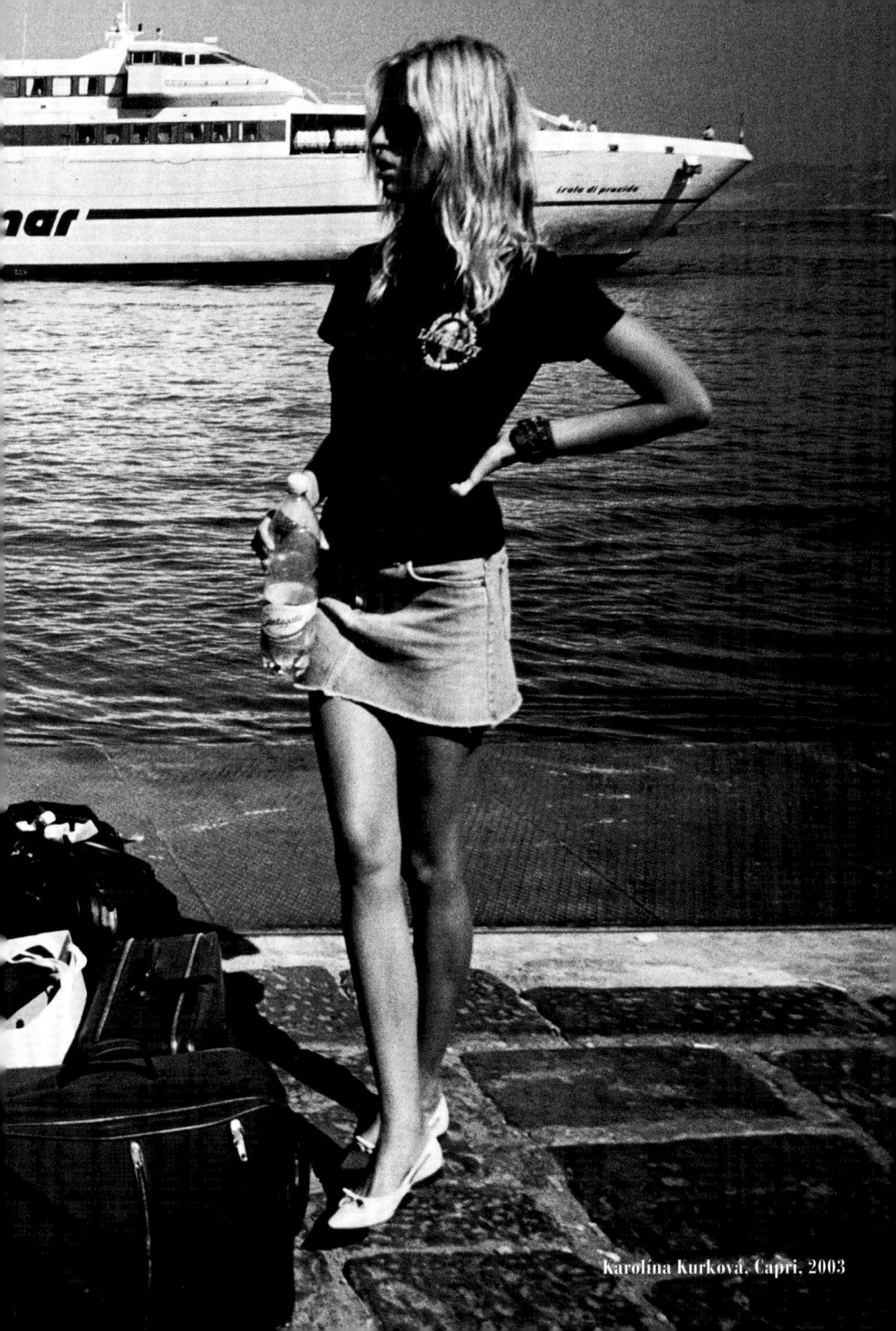

Karolina Kurková. Capri. 2003

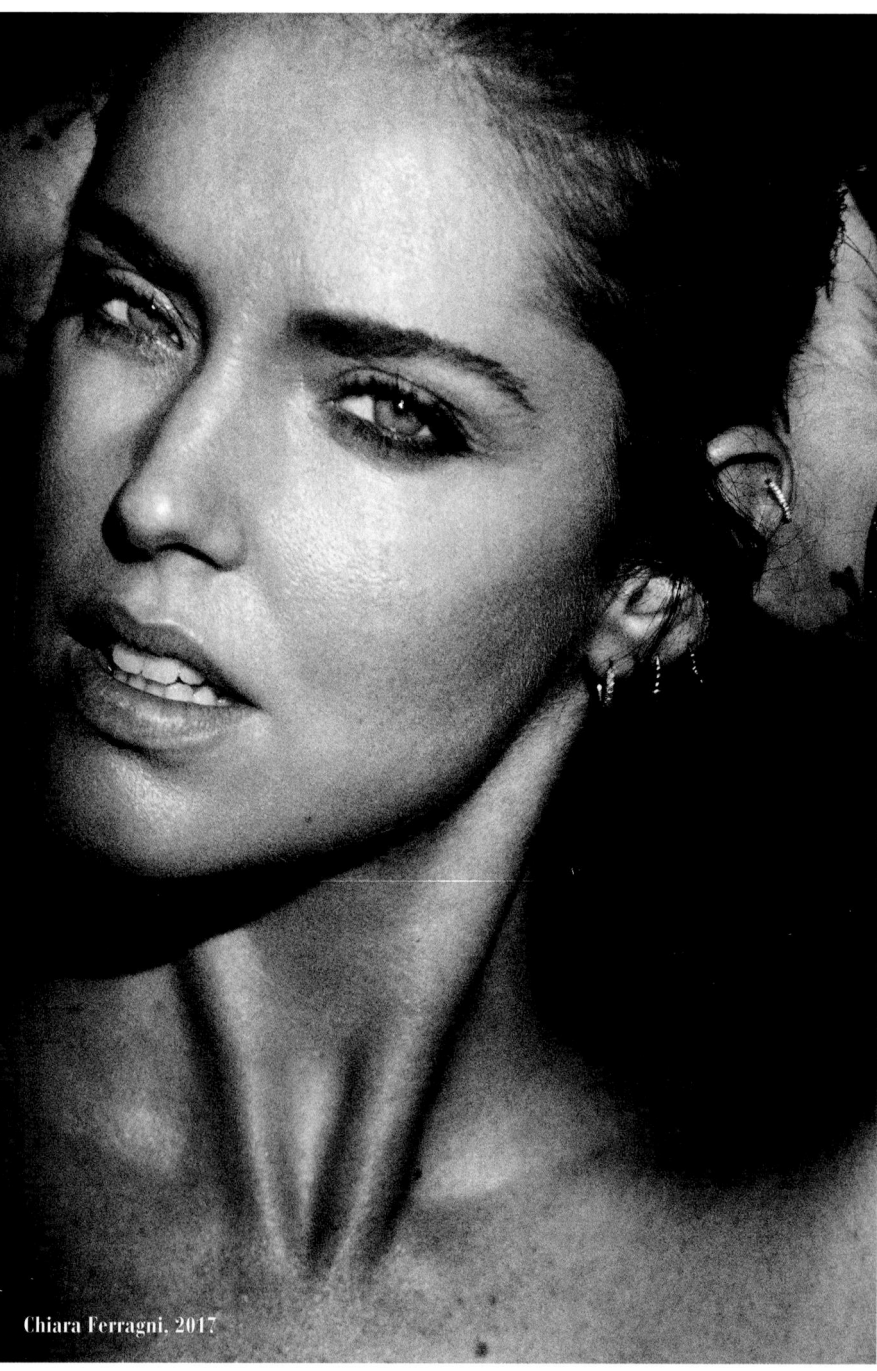

Chiara Ferragni, 2017

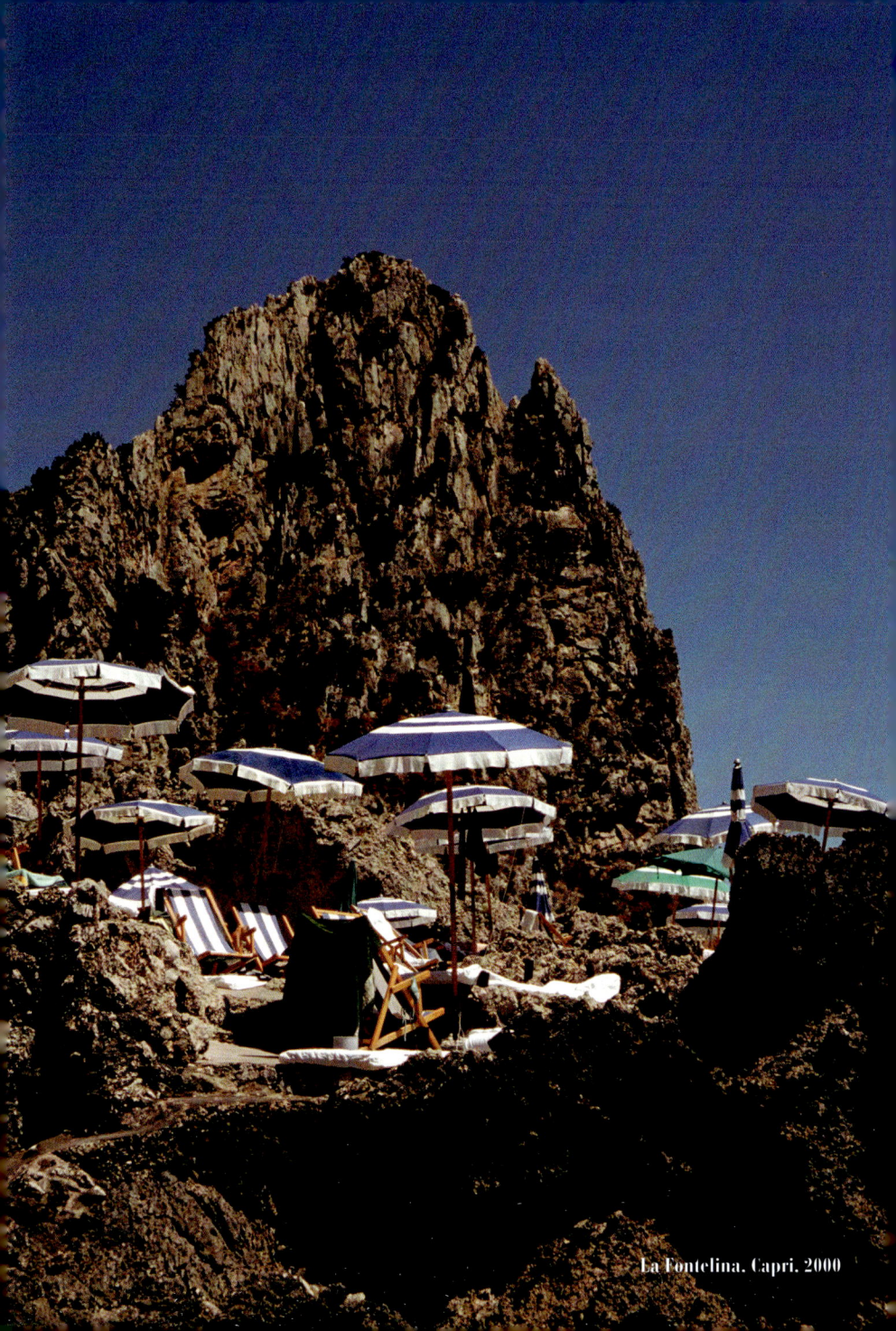

La Fontelina. Capri. 2000

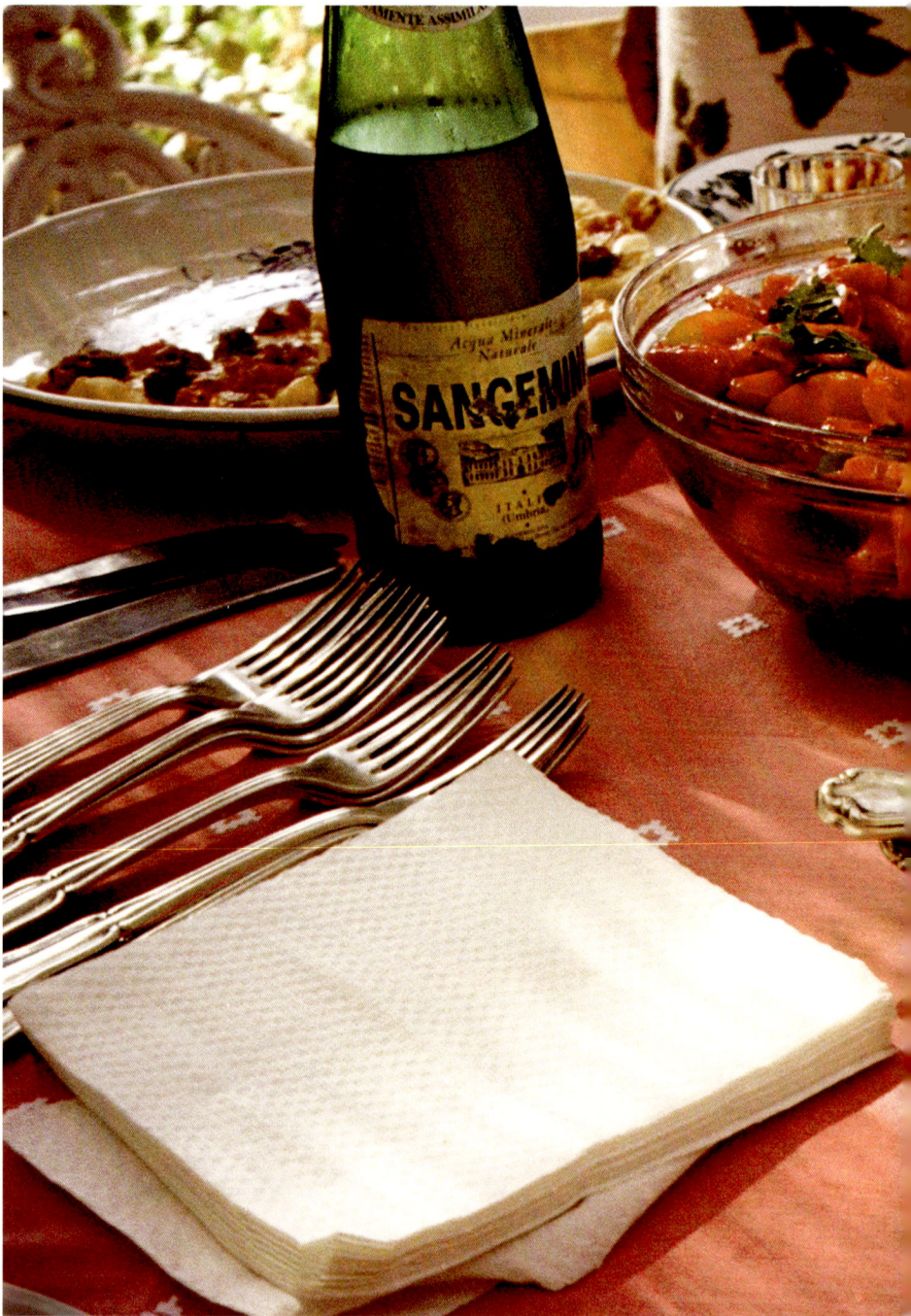

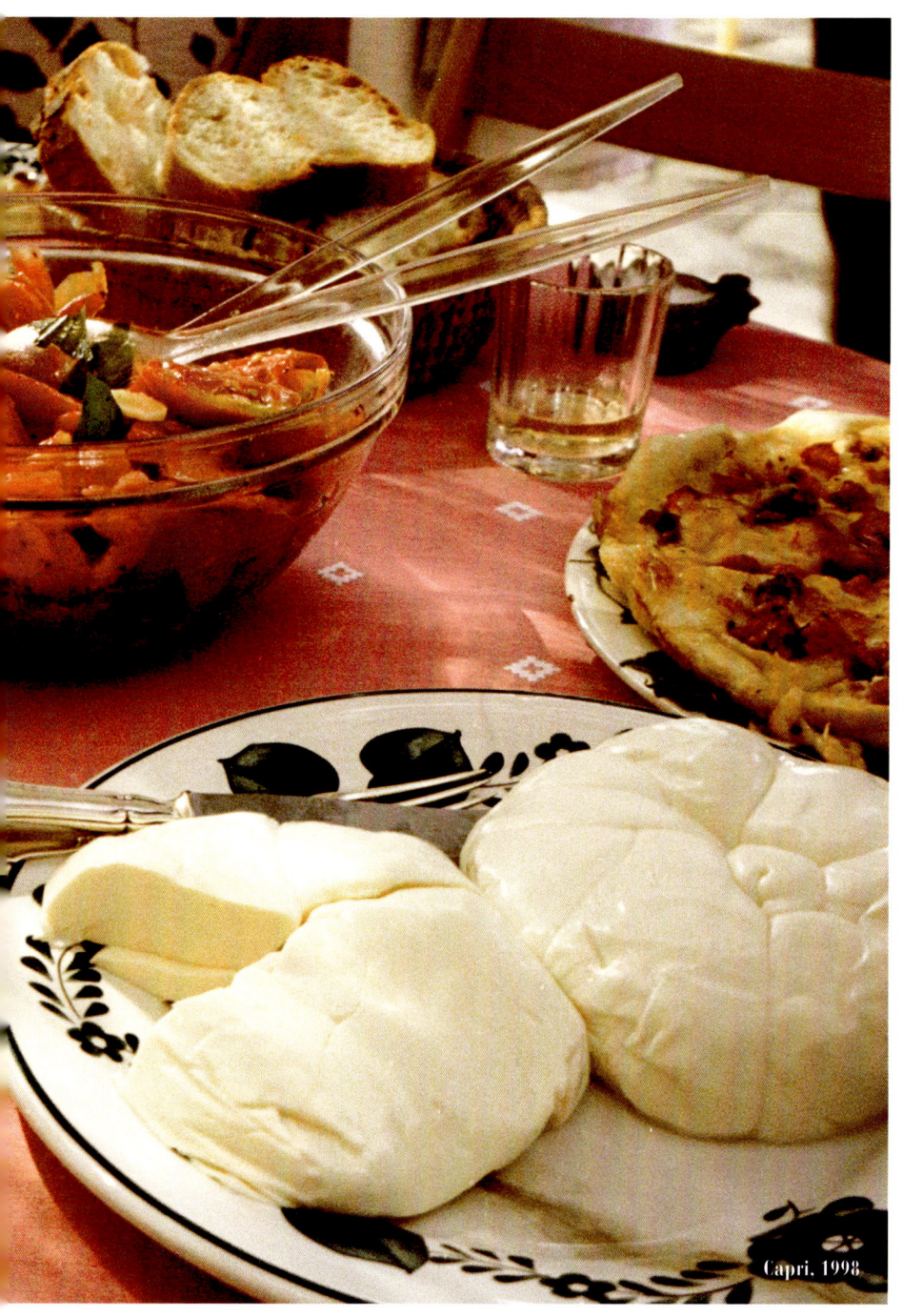

Capri. 1998

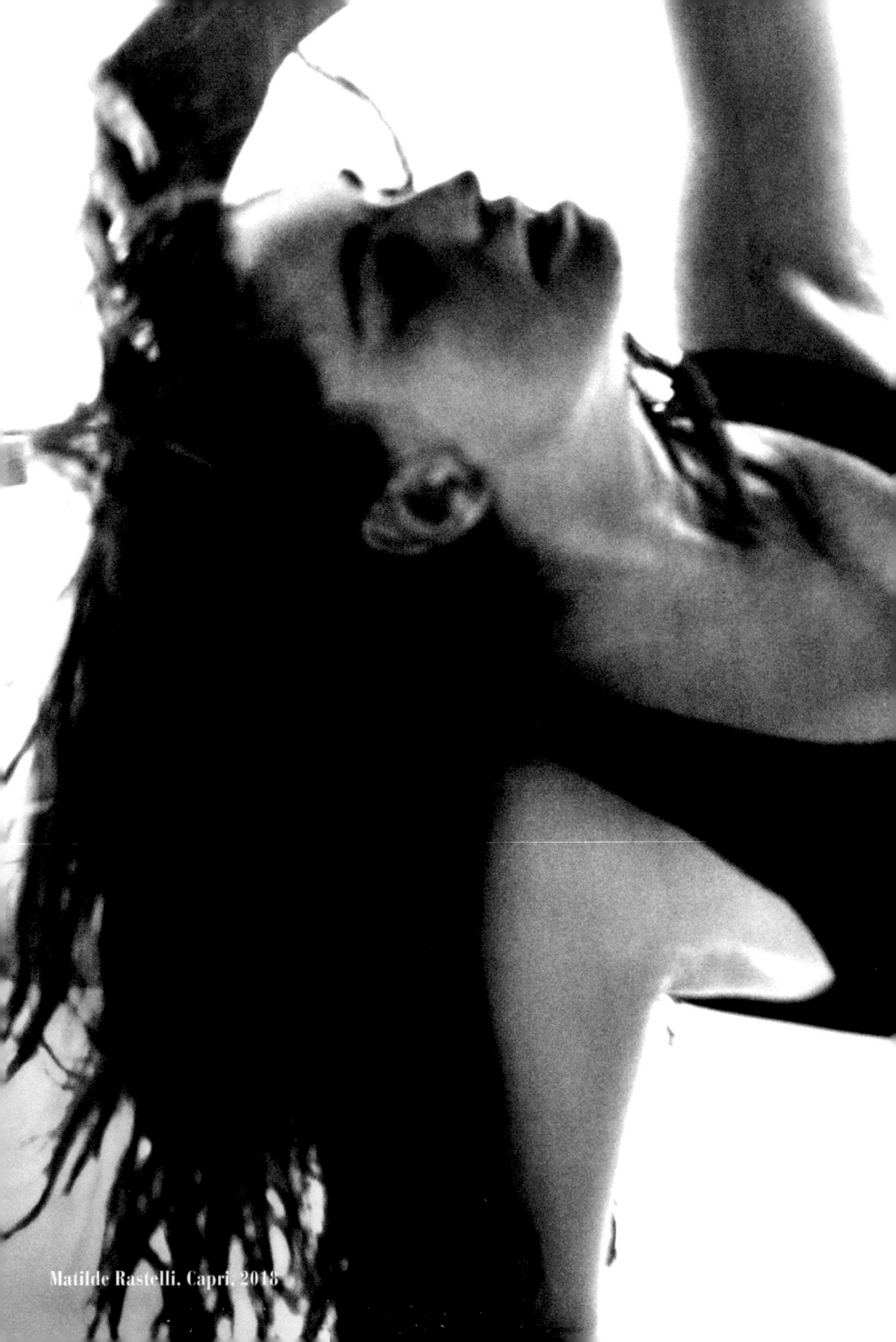

Matilde Rastelli, Capri, 2013

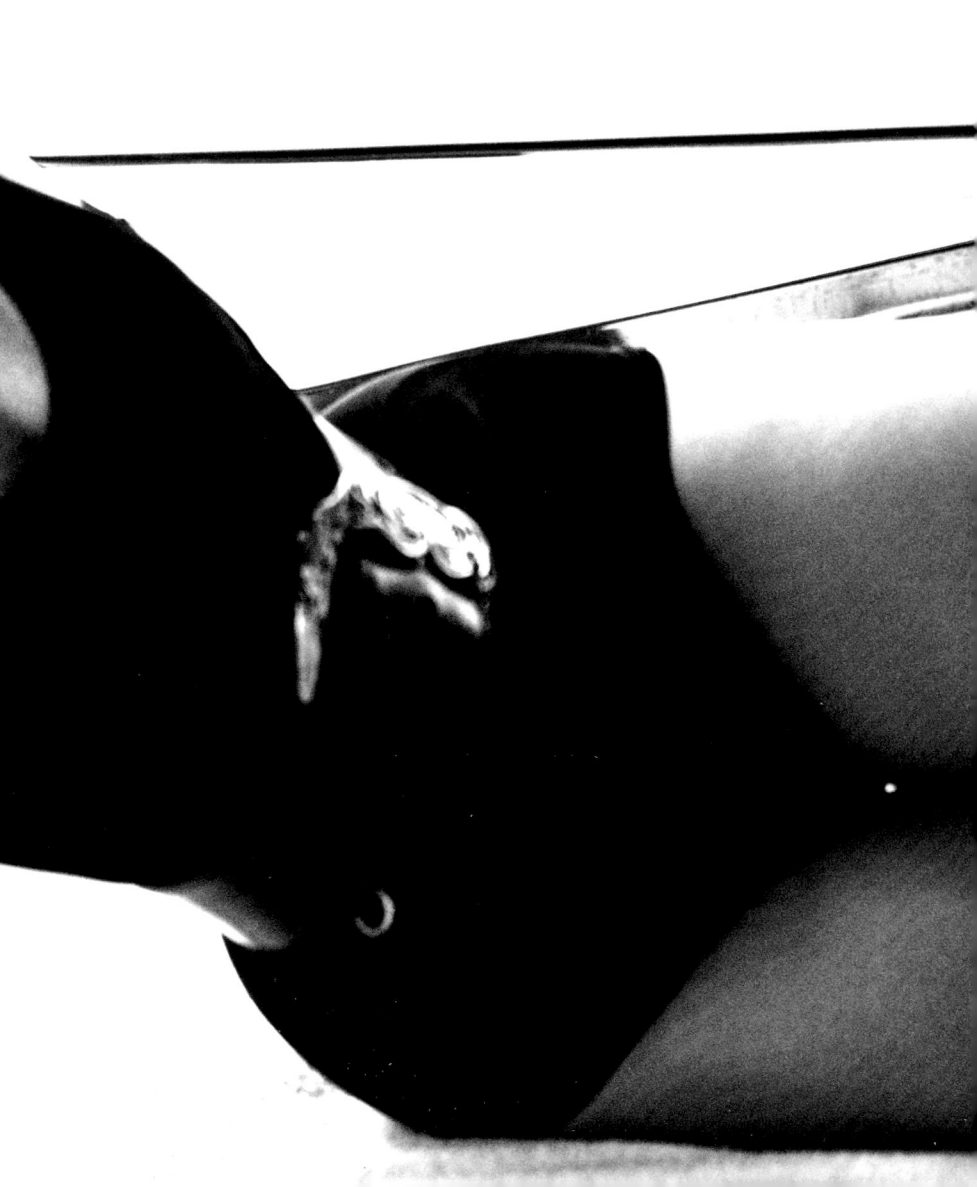

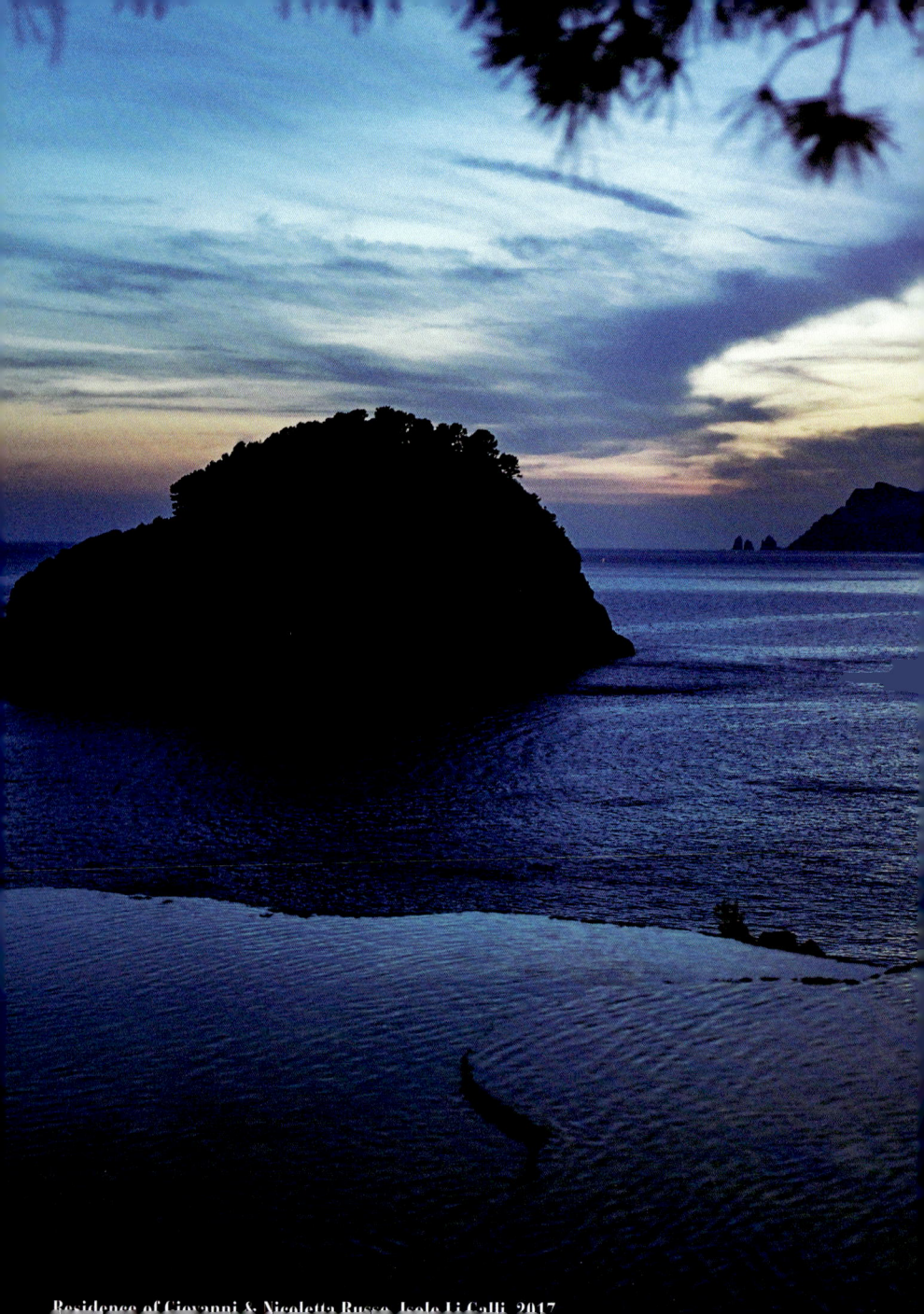

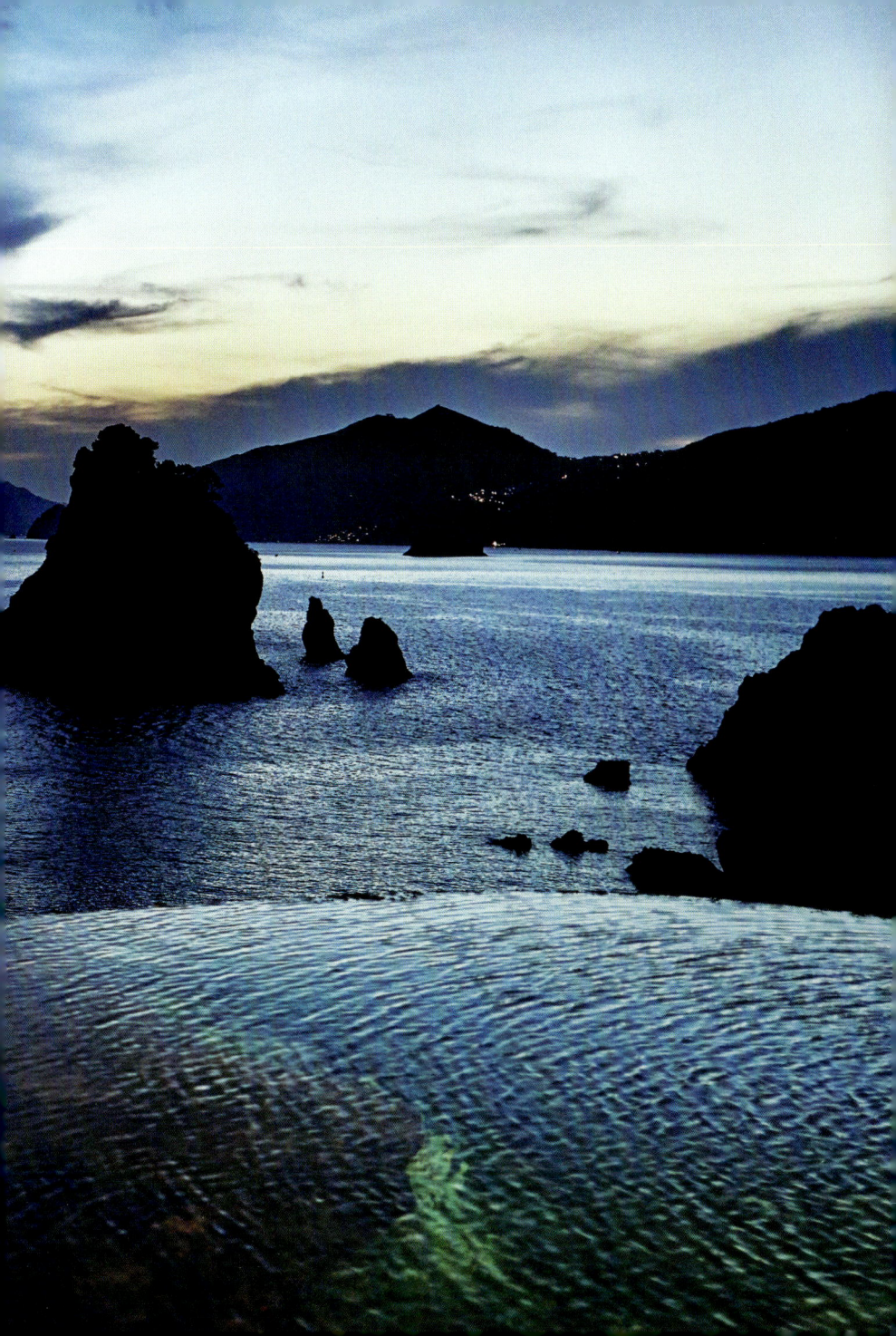

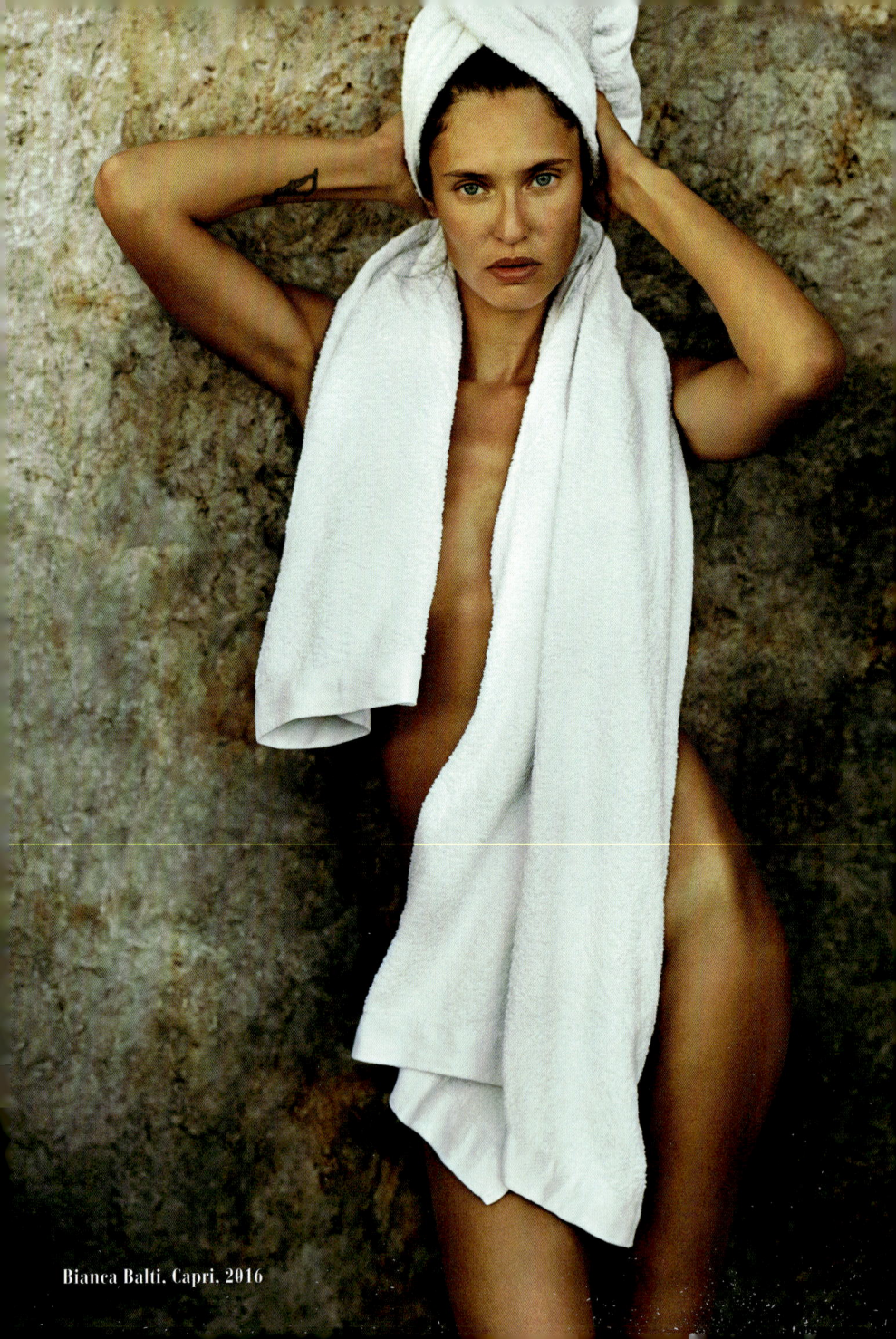

Bianca Balti. Capri, 2016

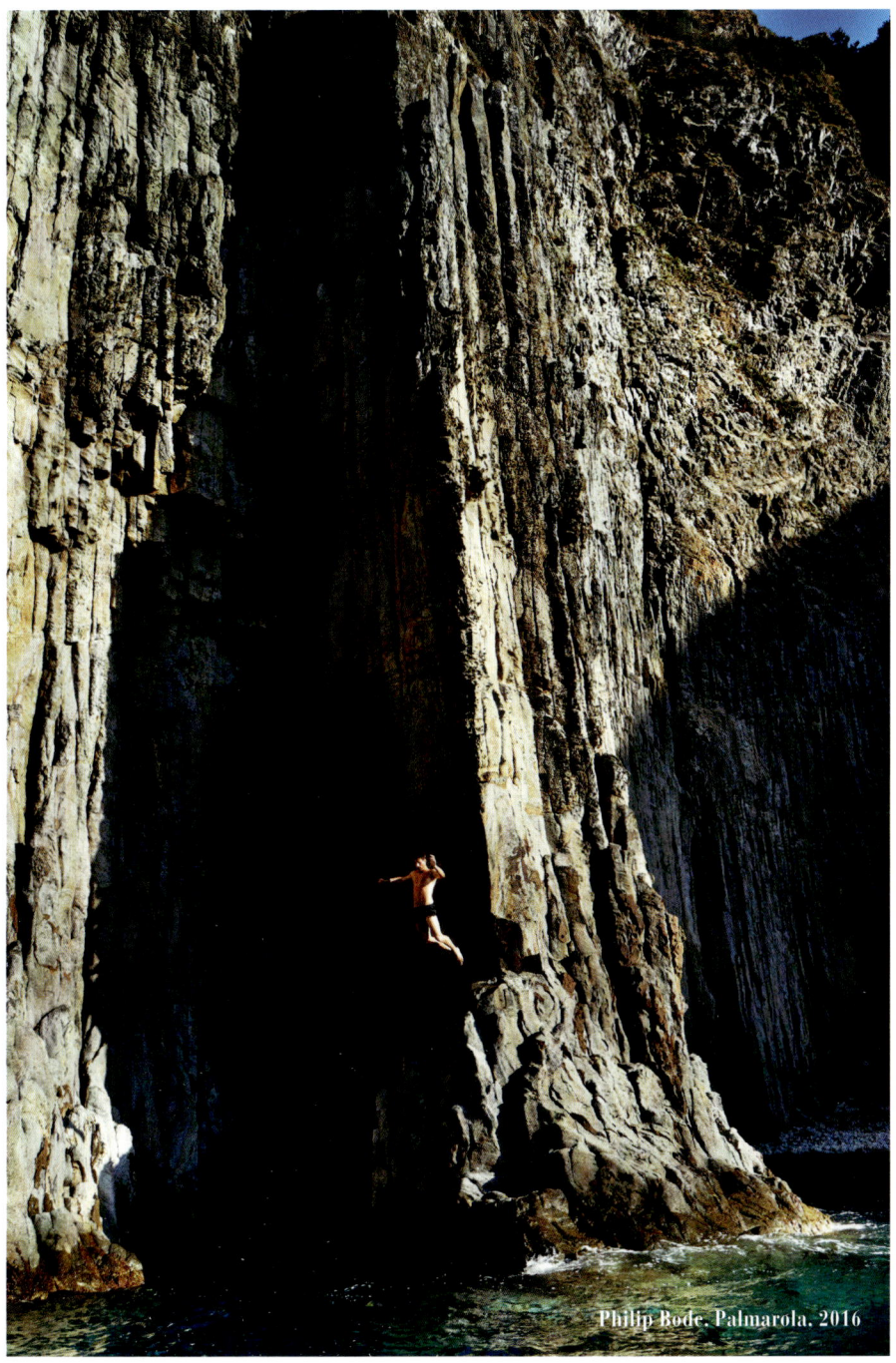

Philip Bode, Palmarola, 2016

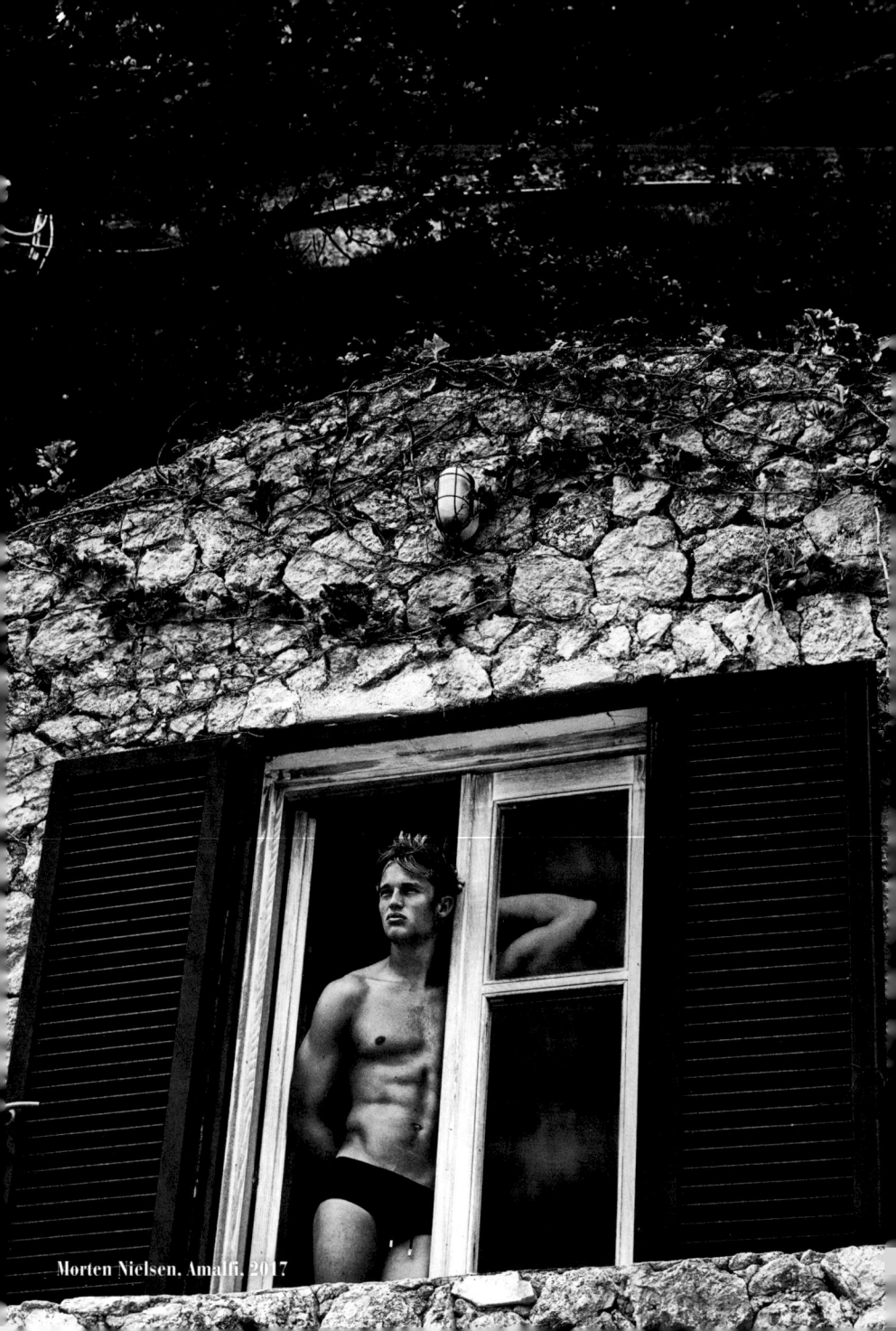

Morten Nielsen, Amalfi, 2017

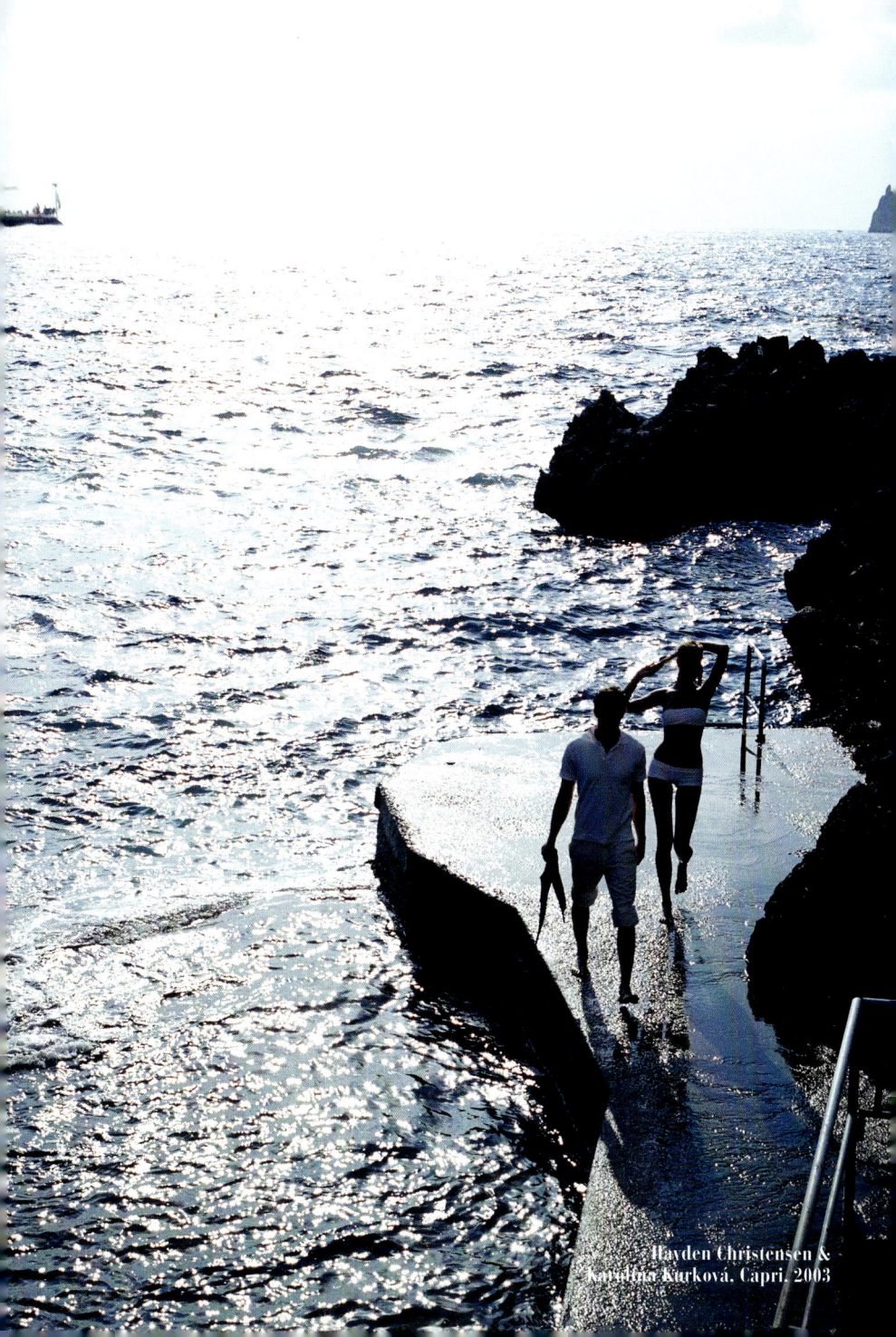

Hayden Christensen &
Karolina Kurkova, Capri, 2003

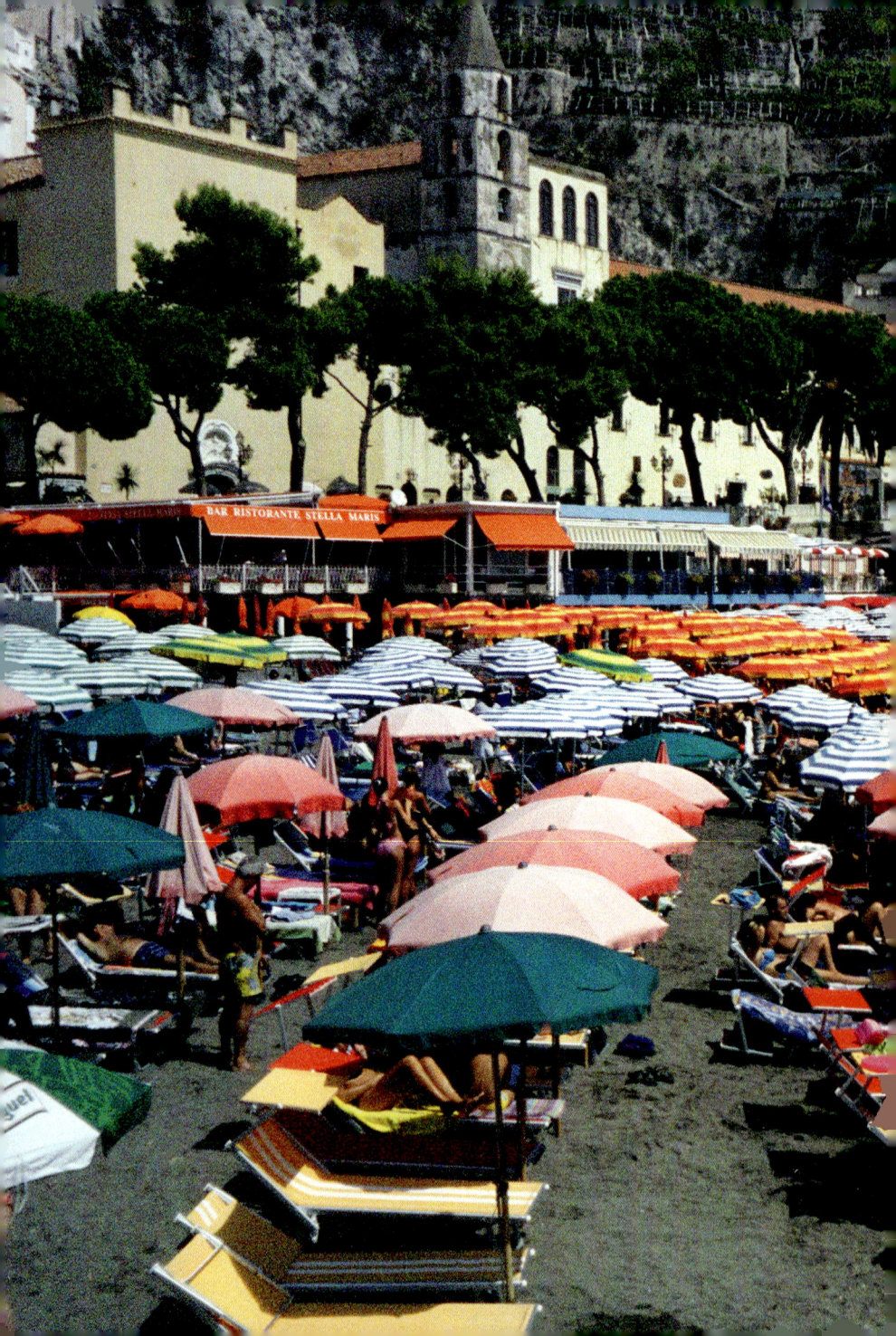

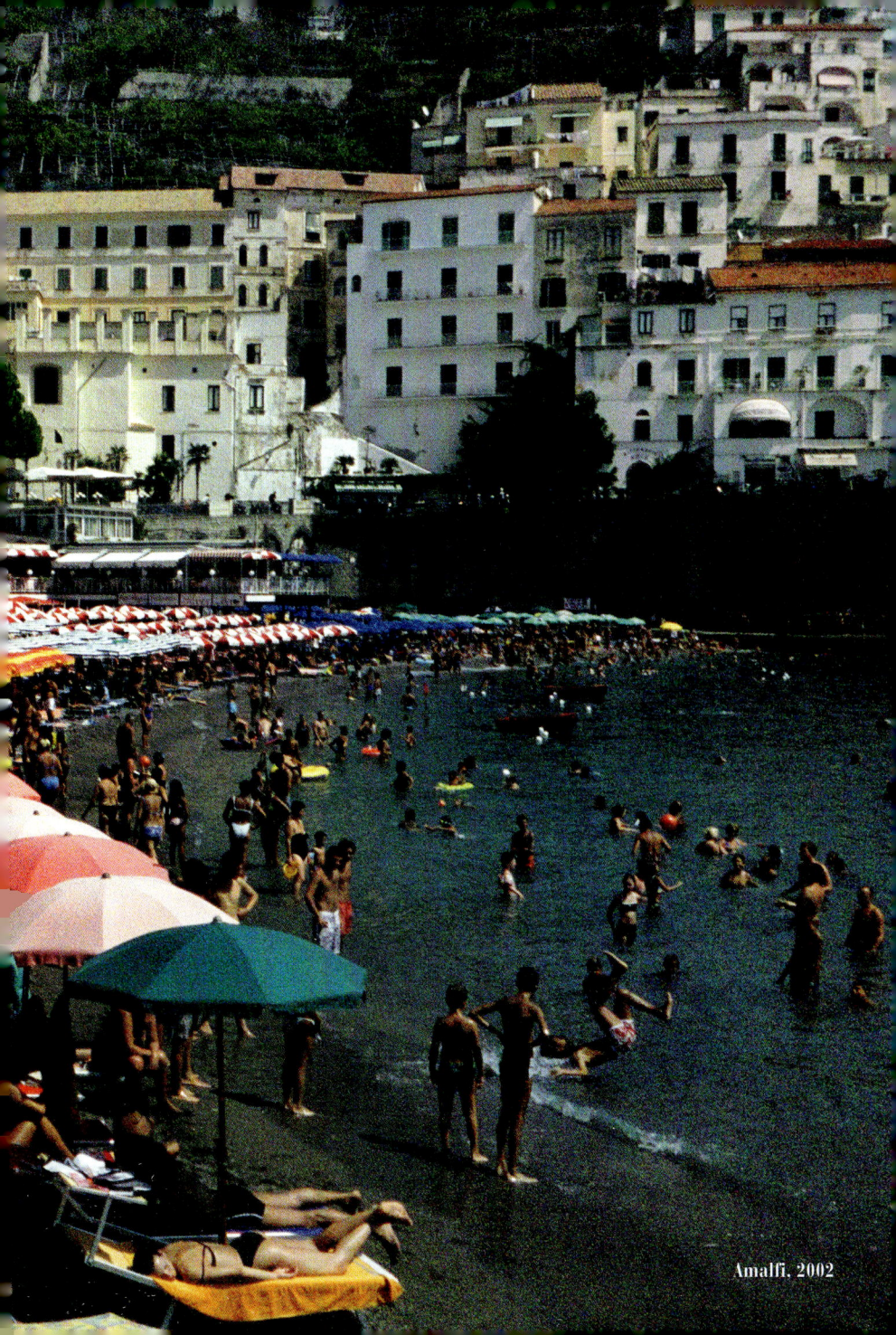

Amalfi, 2002

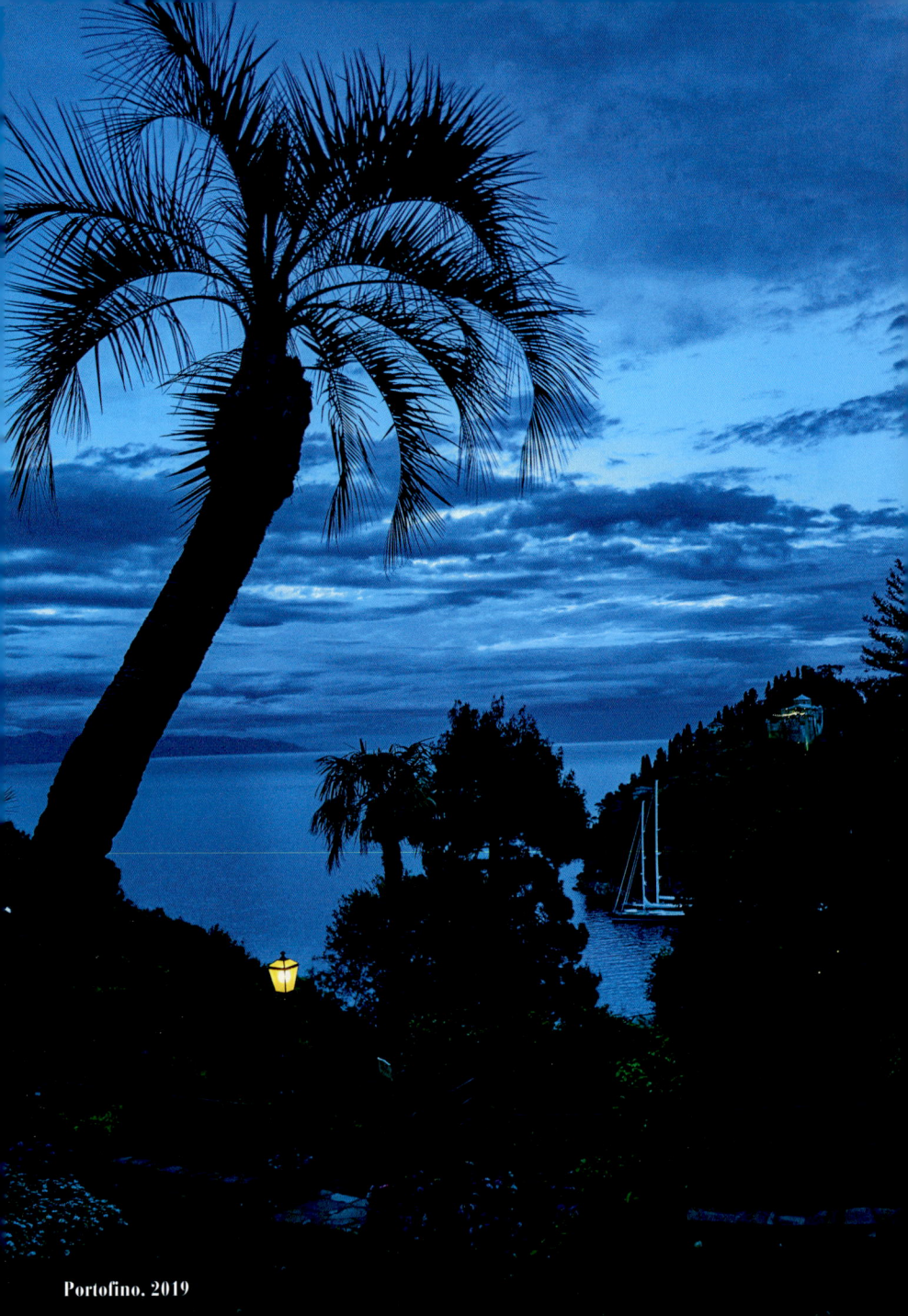

Portofino. 2019

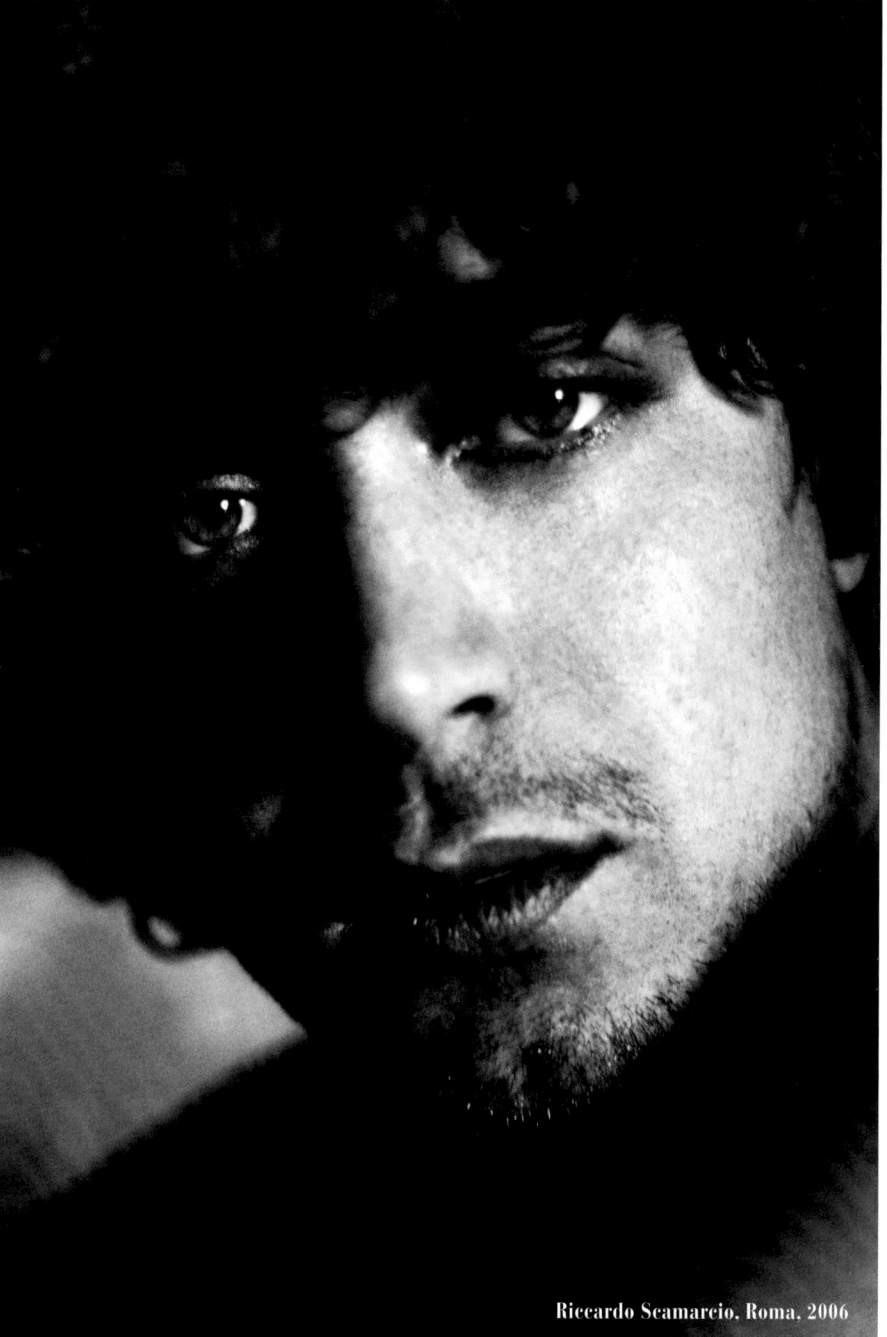

Riccardo Scamarcio, Roma, 2006

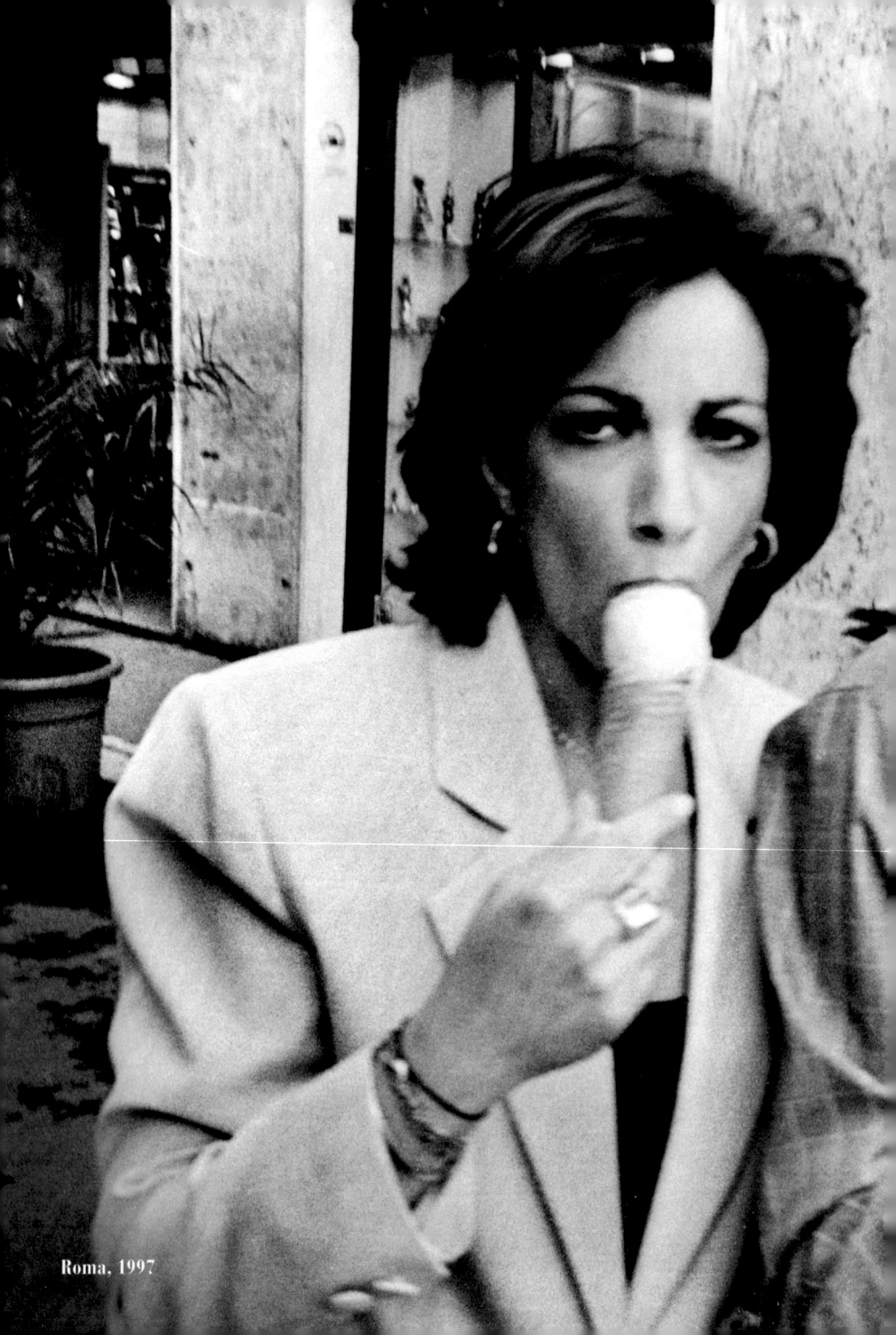

Roma, 1997

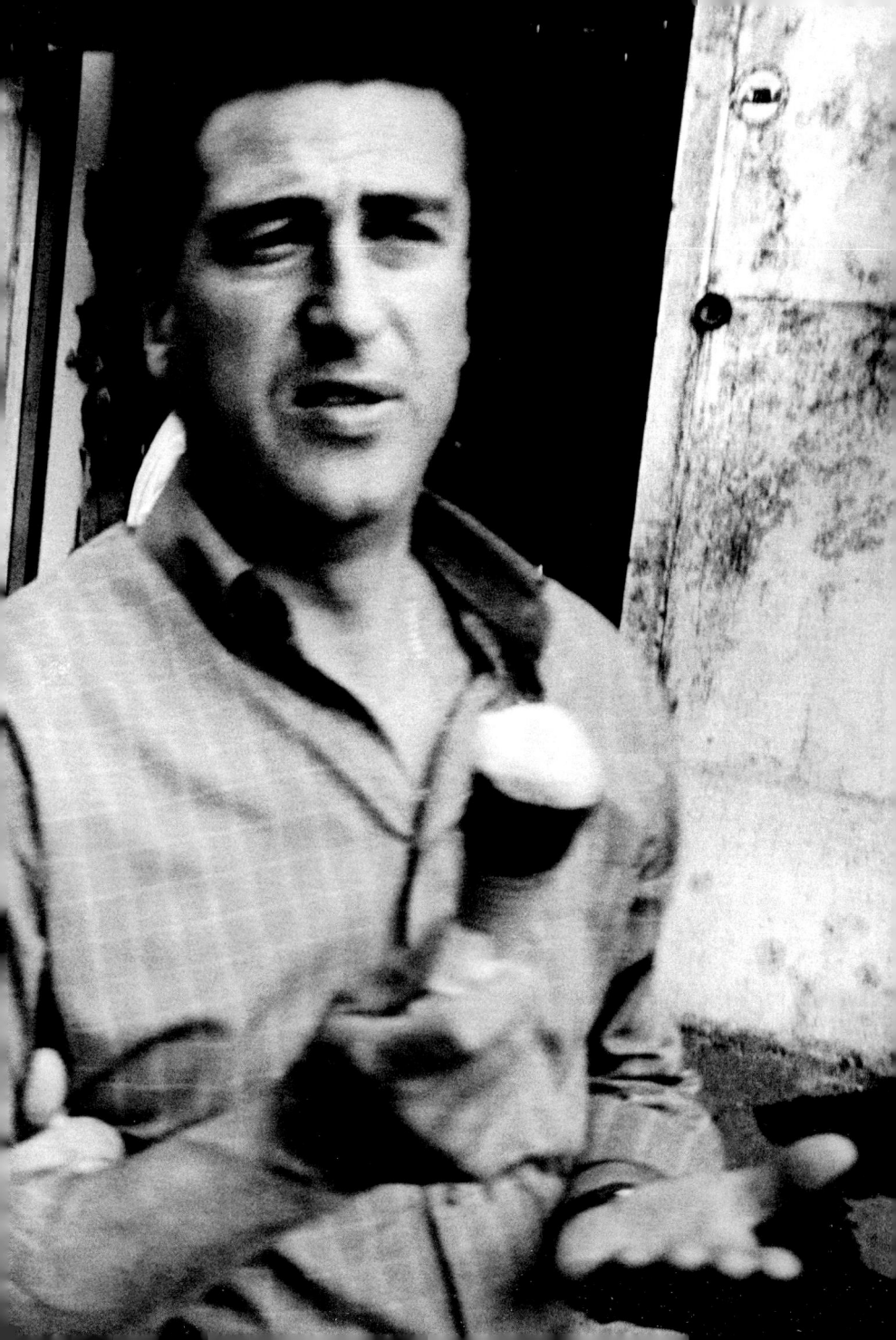

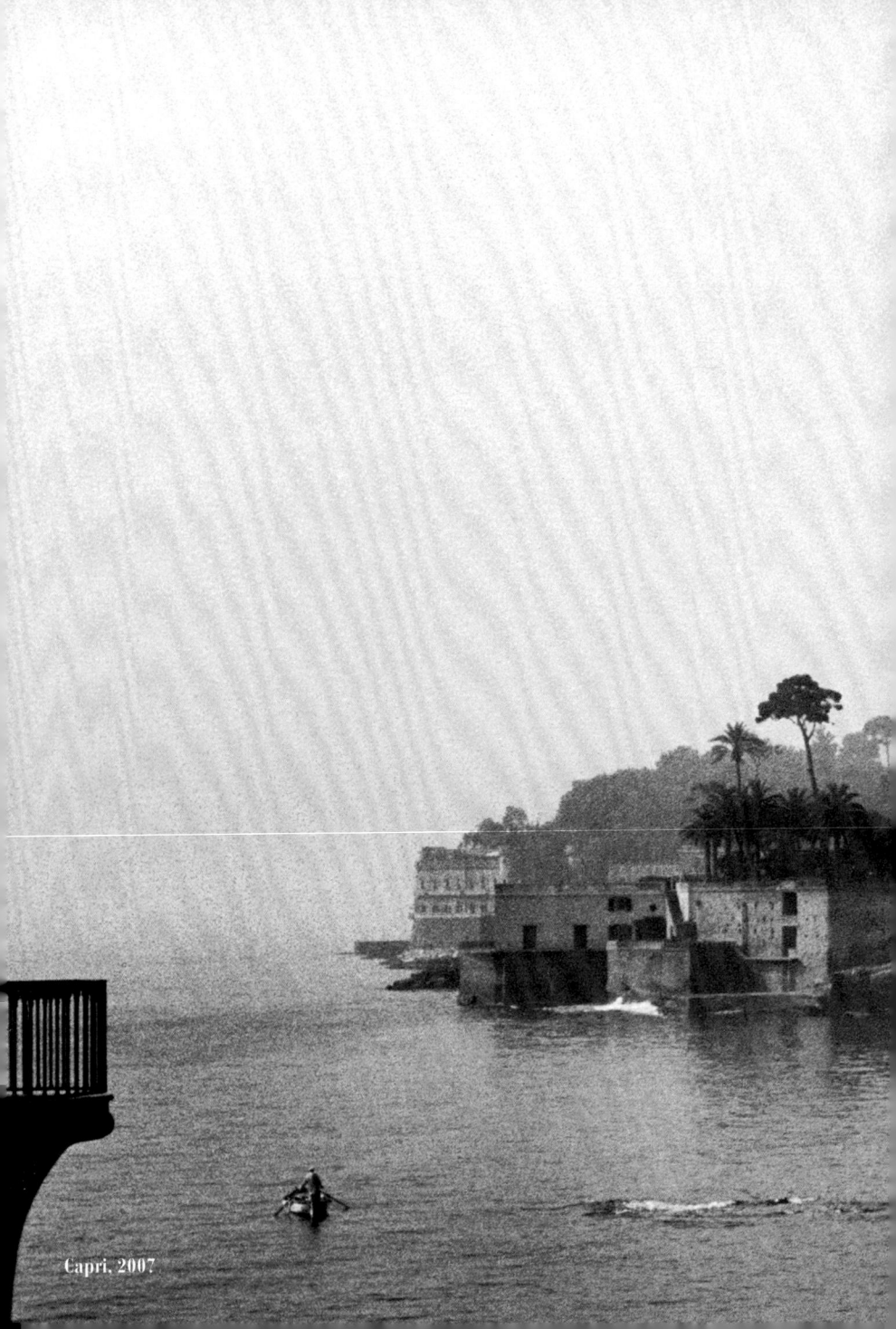

Capri, 2007

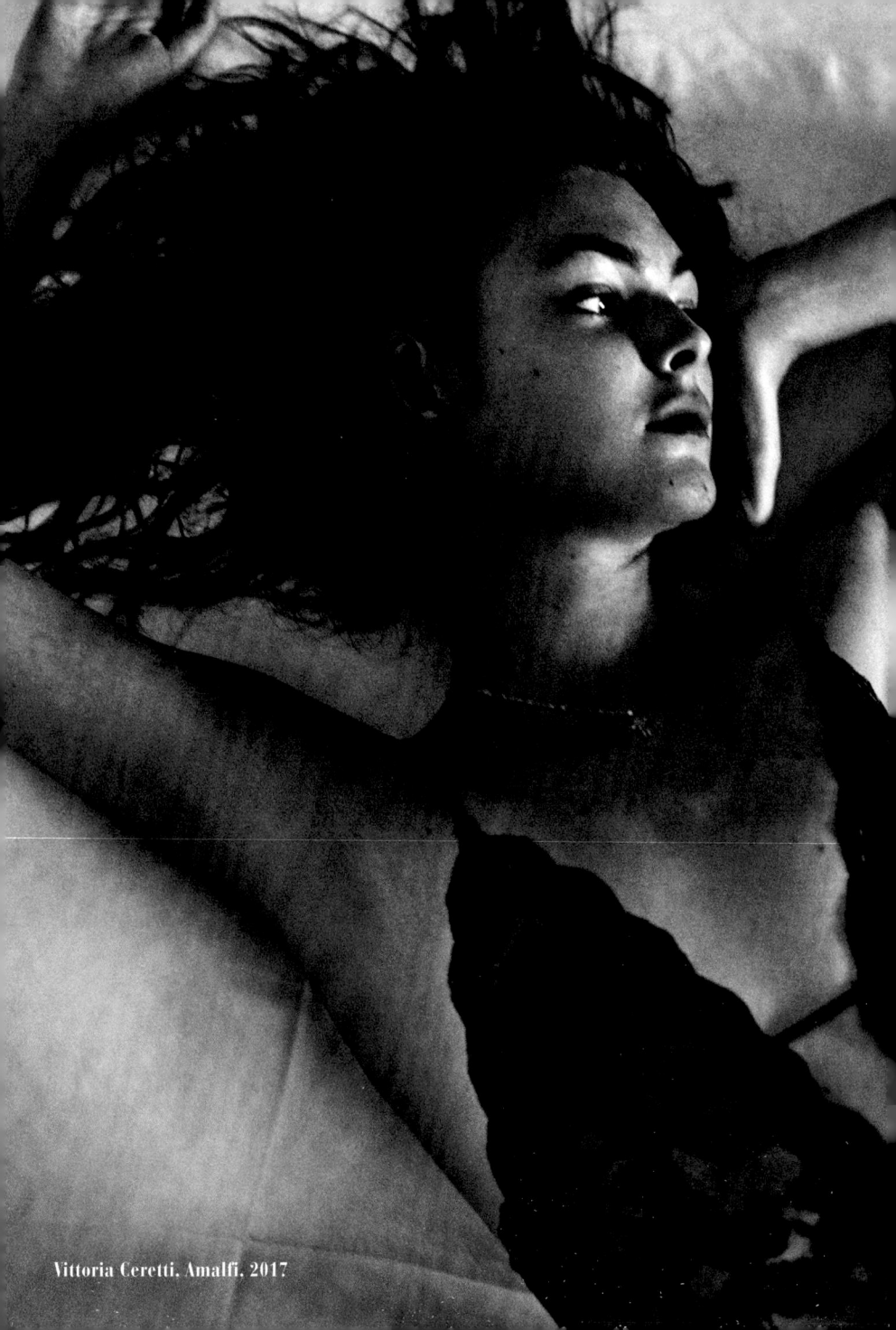

Vittoria Ceretti, Amalfi, 2017

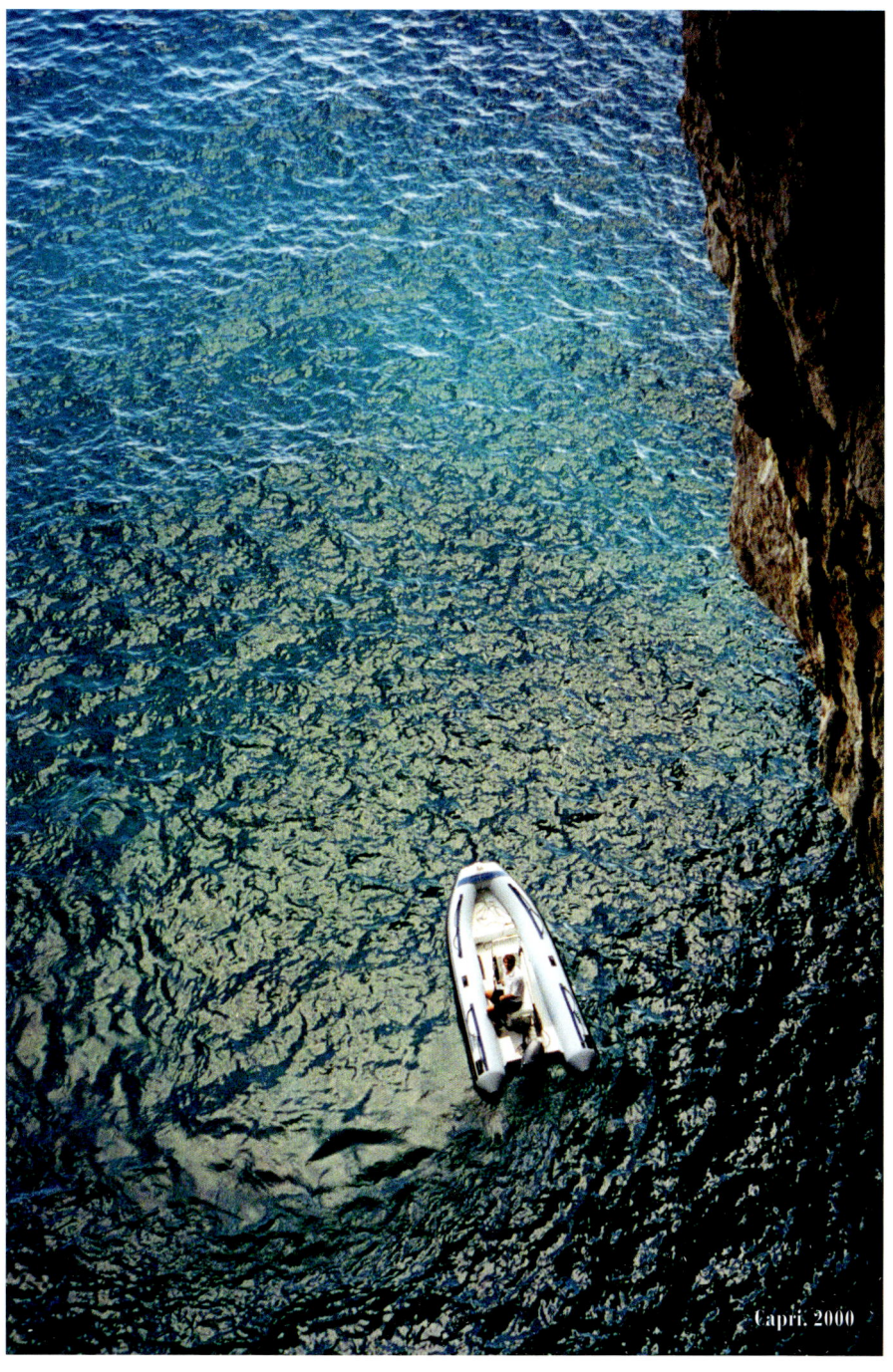

Capri. 2000

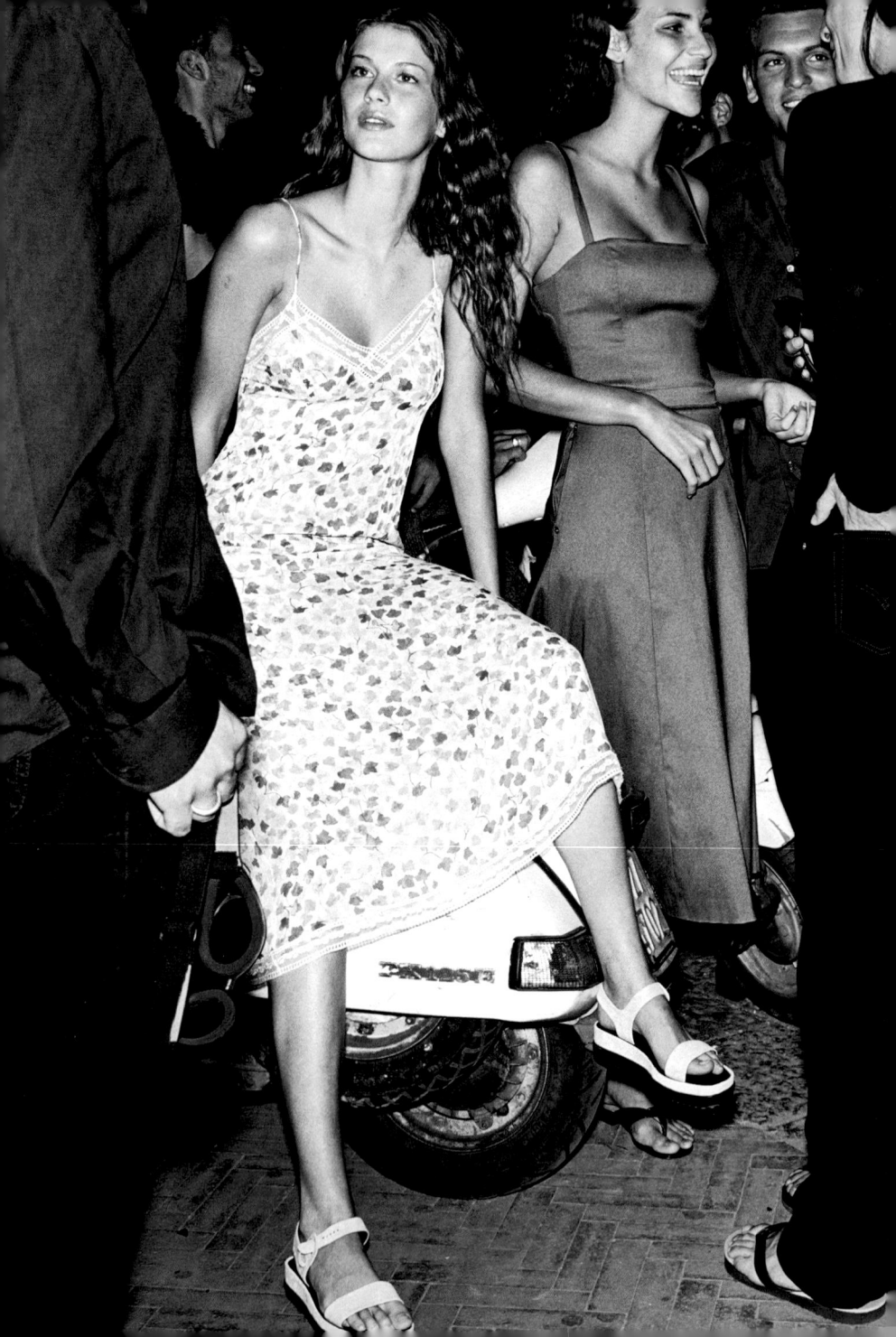

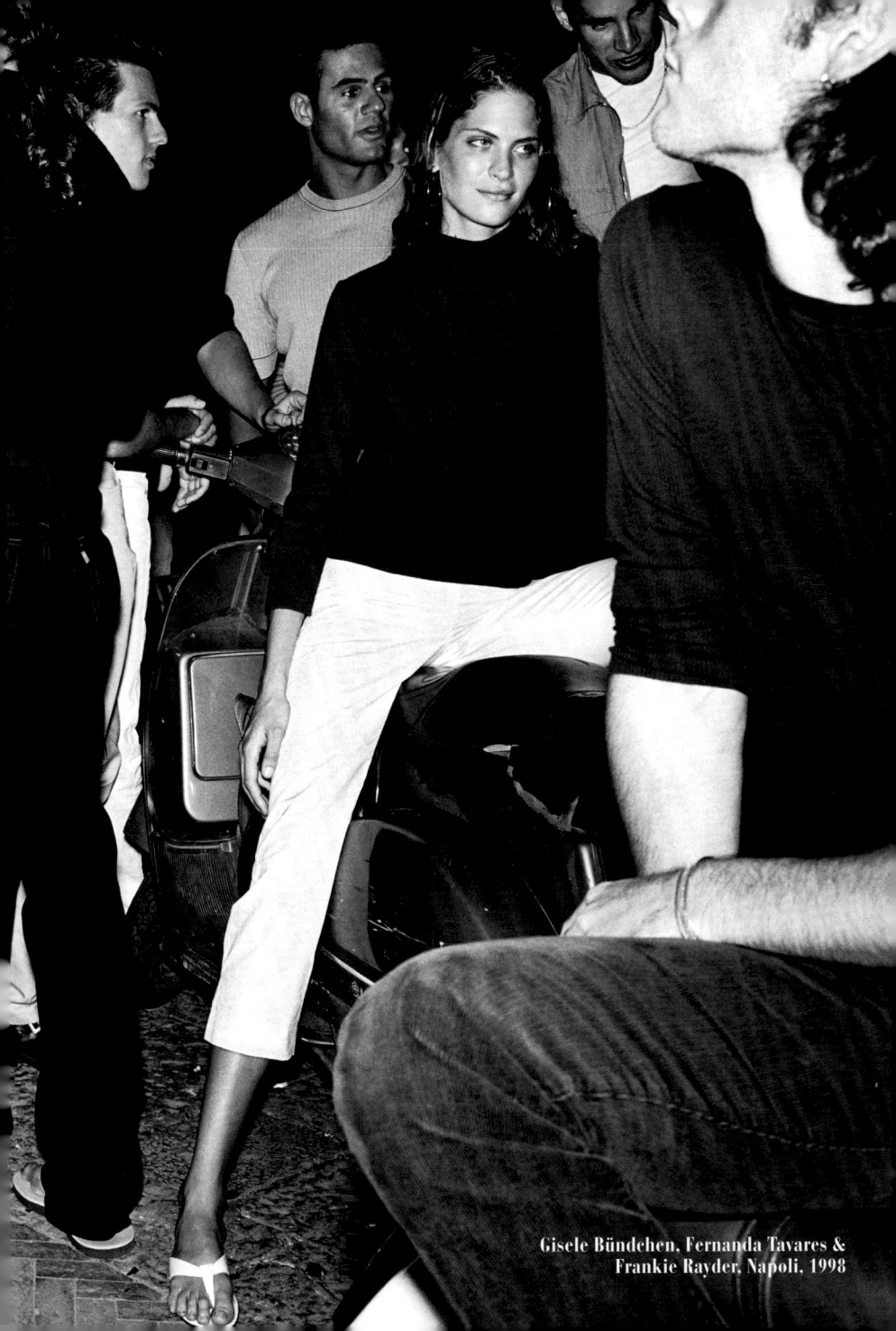

Gisele Bündchen, Fernanda Tavares &
Frankie Rayder, Napoli, 1998

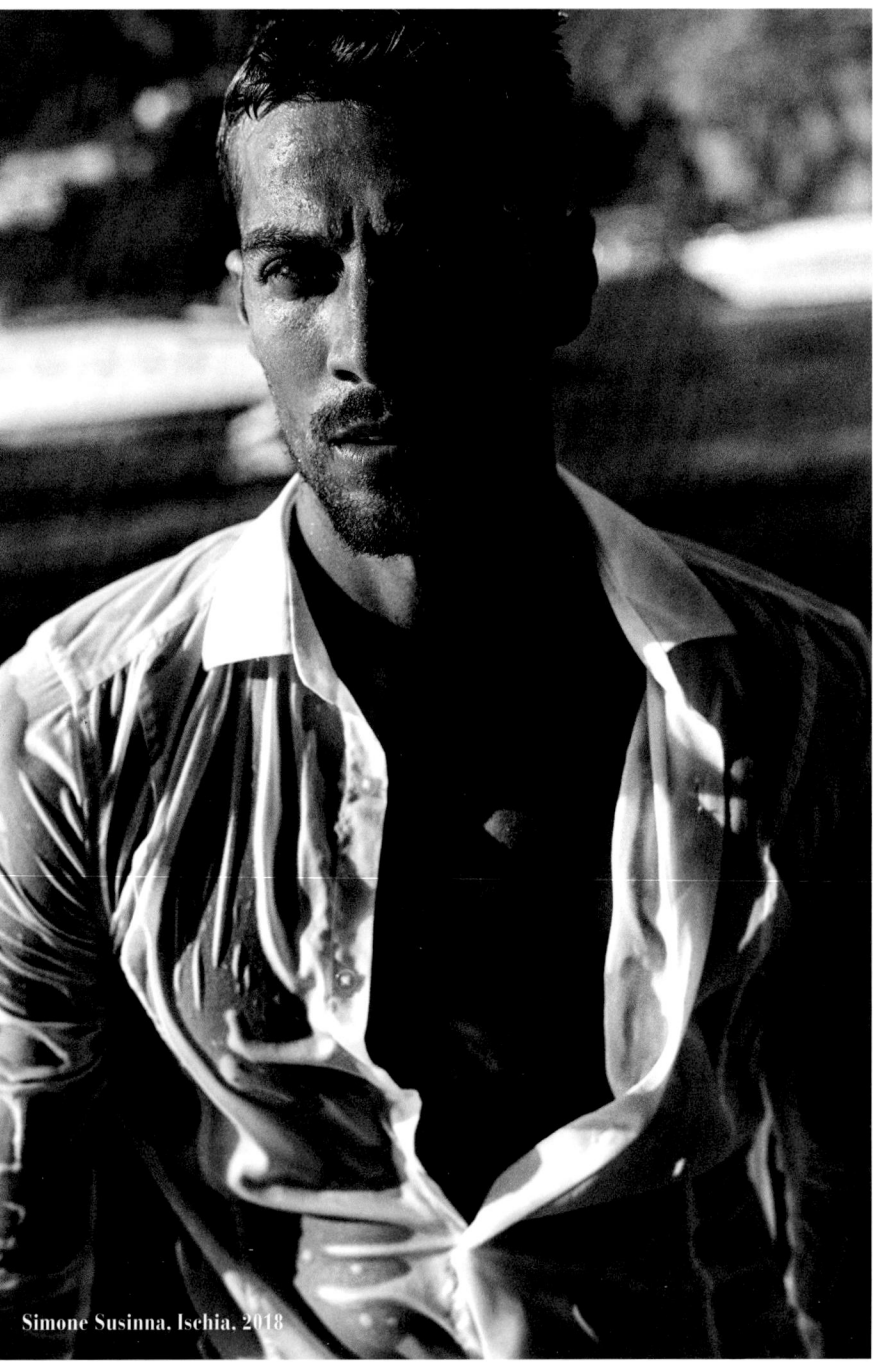

Simone Susinna, Ischia, 2018

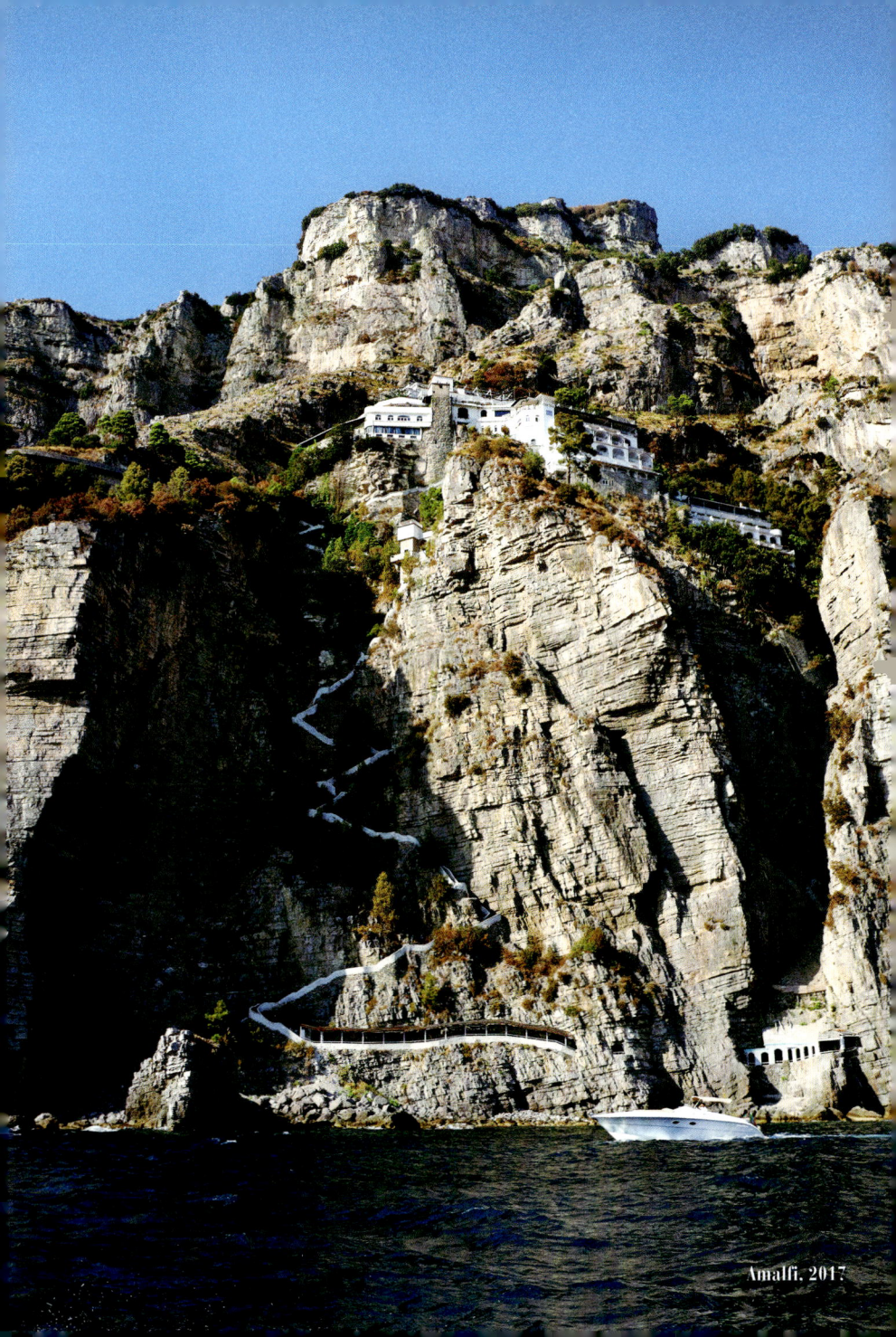

Amalfi, 2017

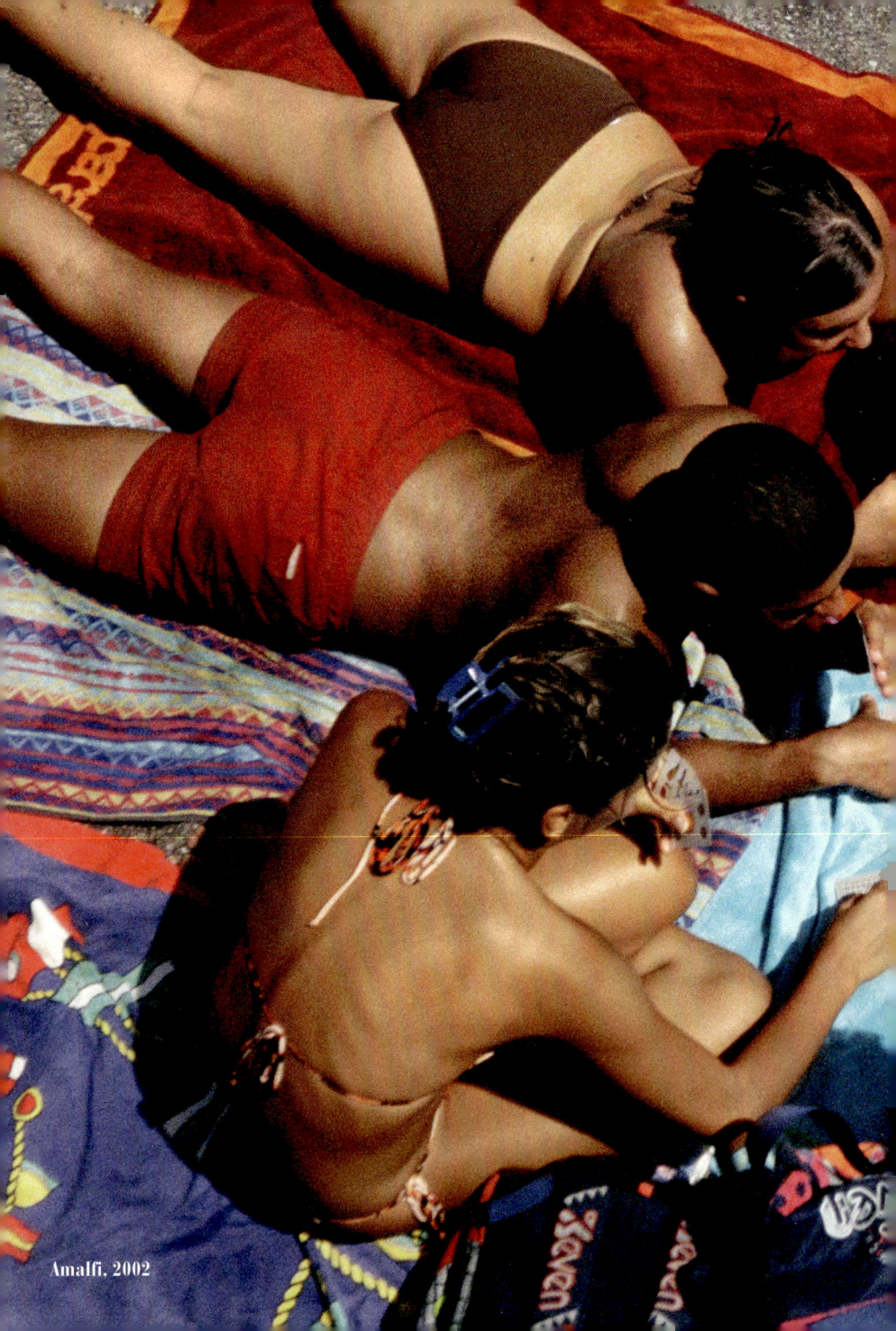

Amalfi, 2002

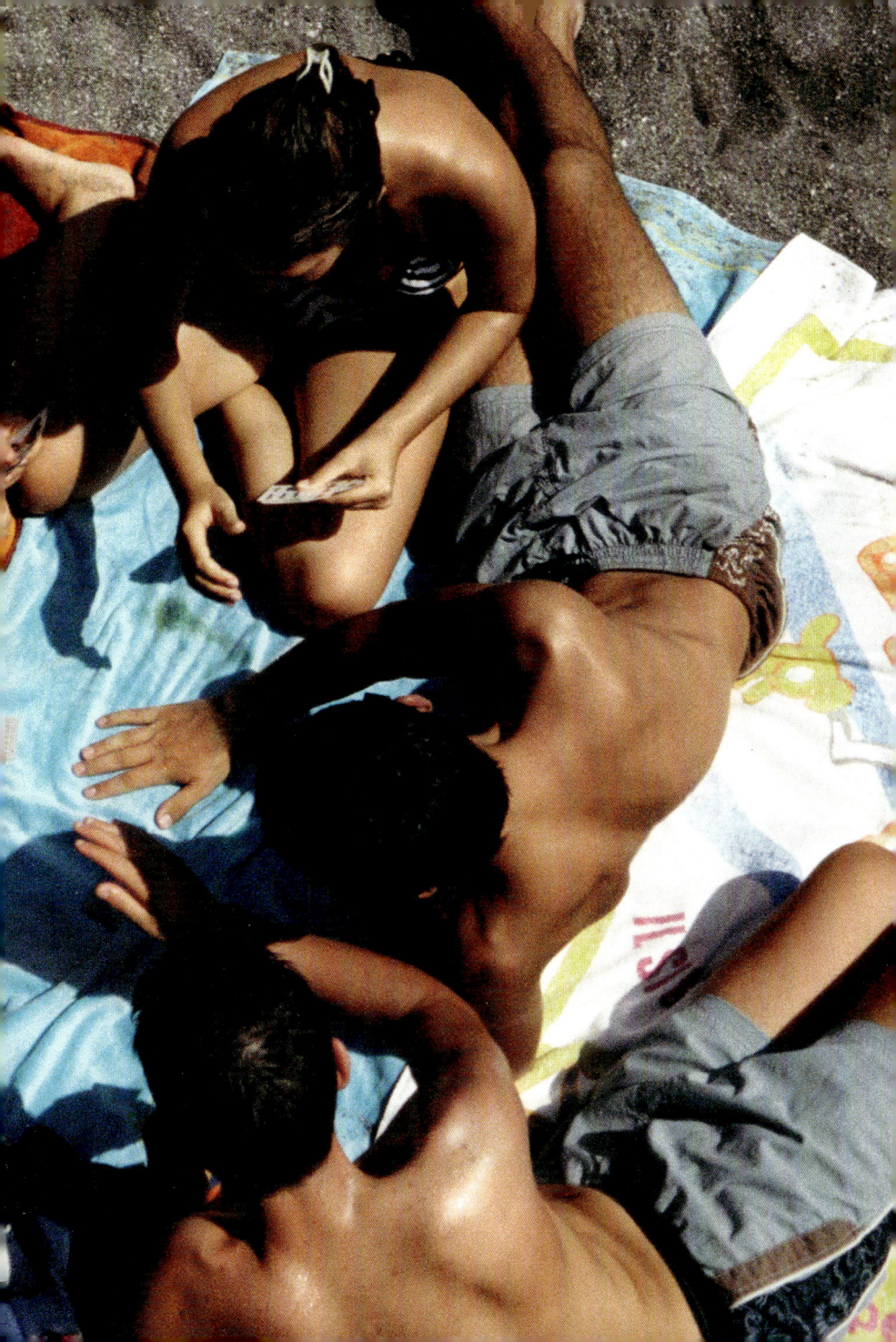

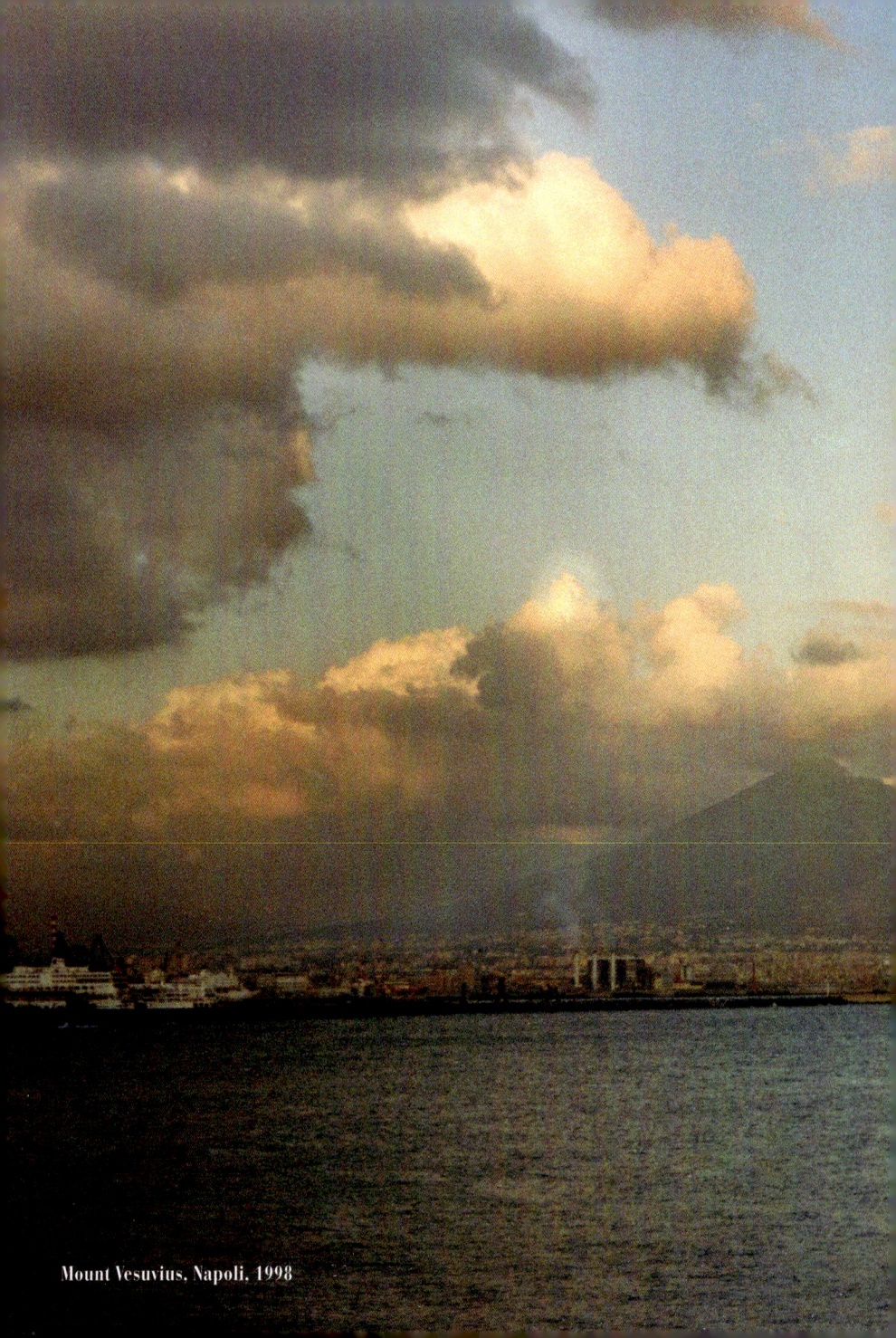

Mount Vesuvius, Napoli, 1998

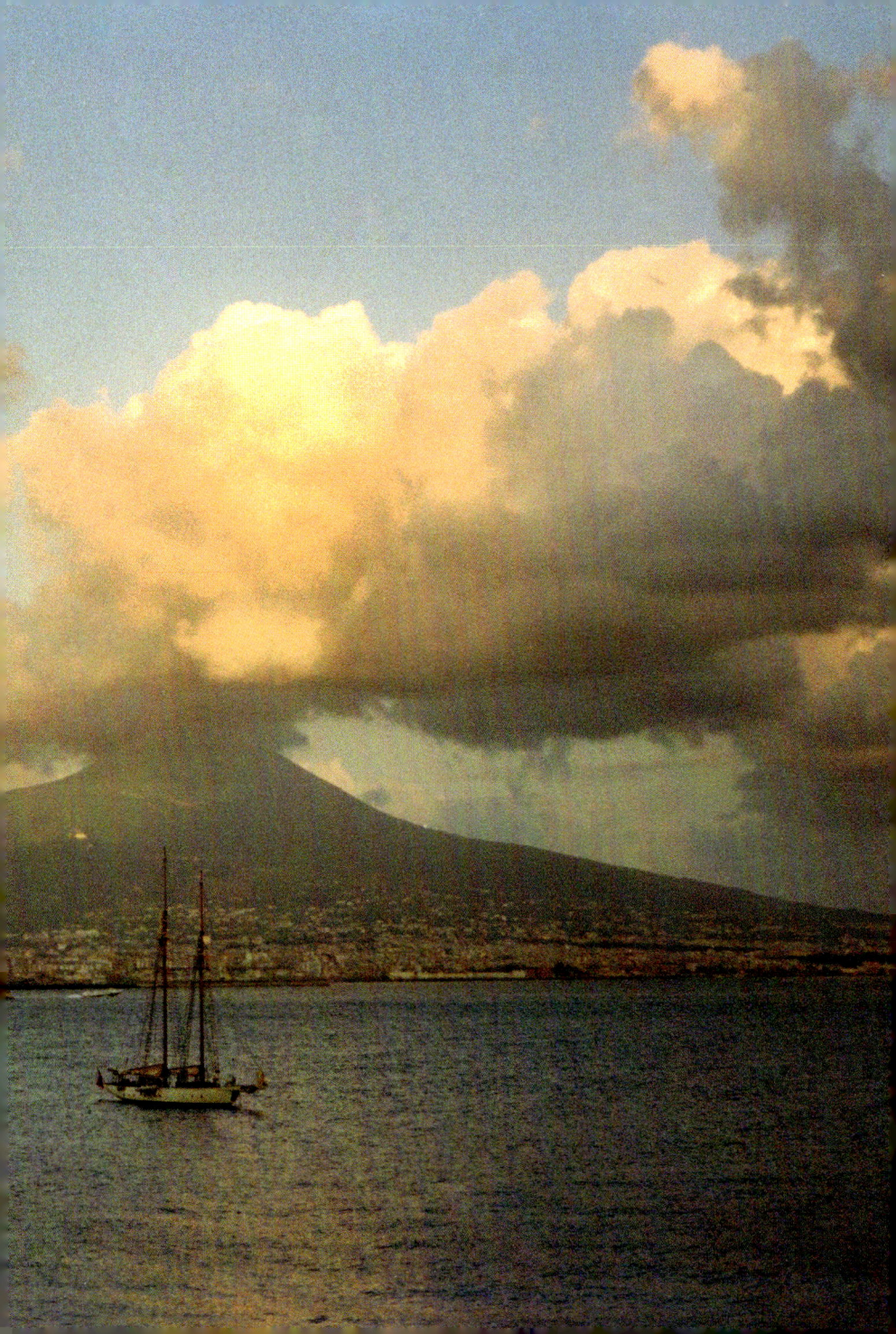

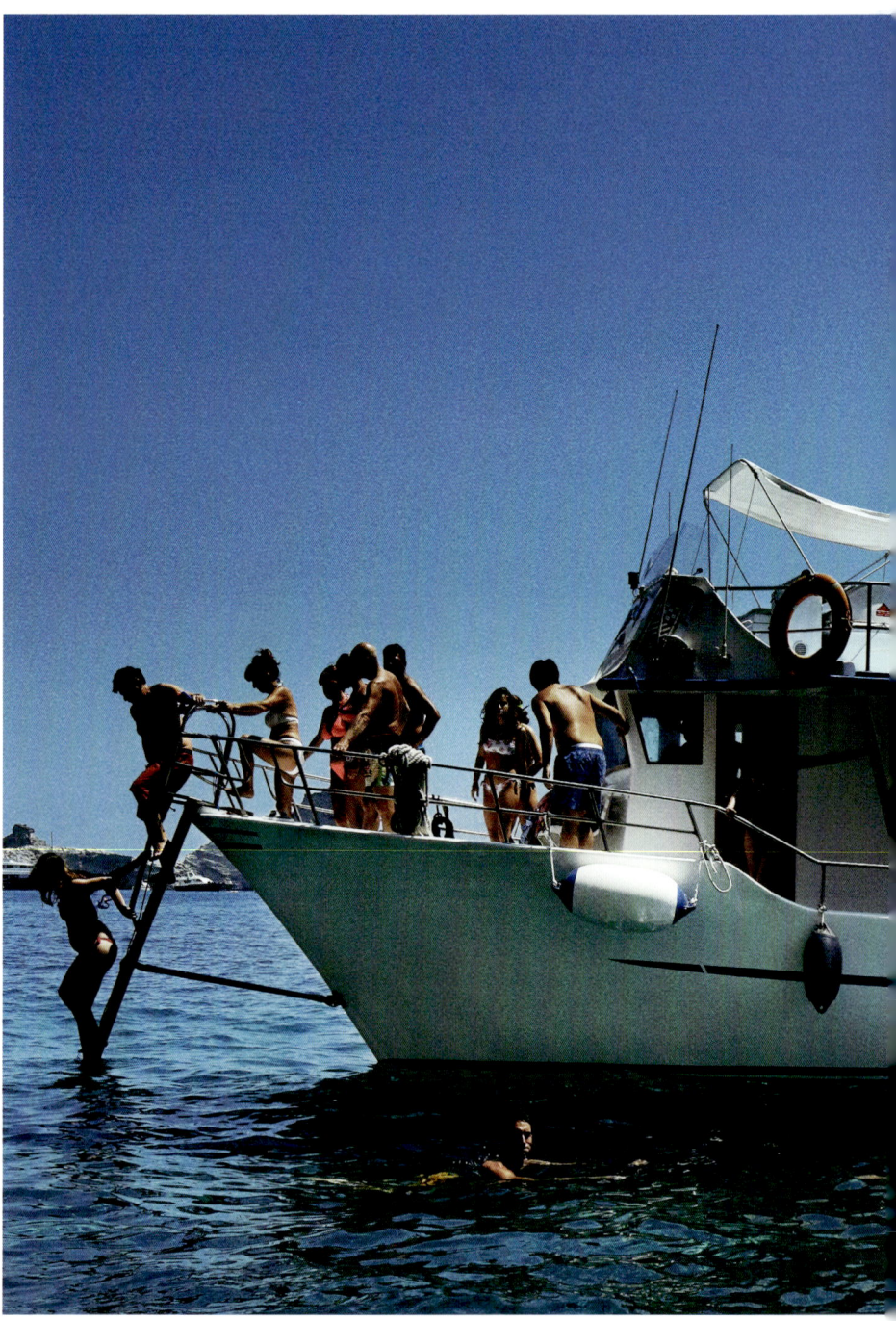

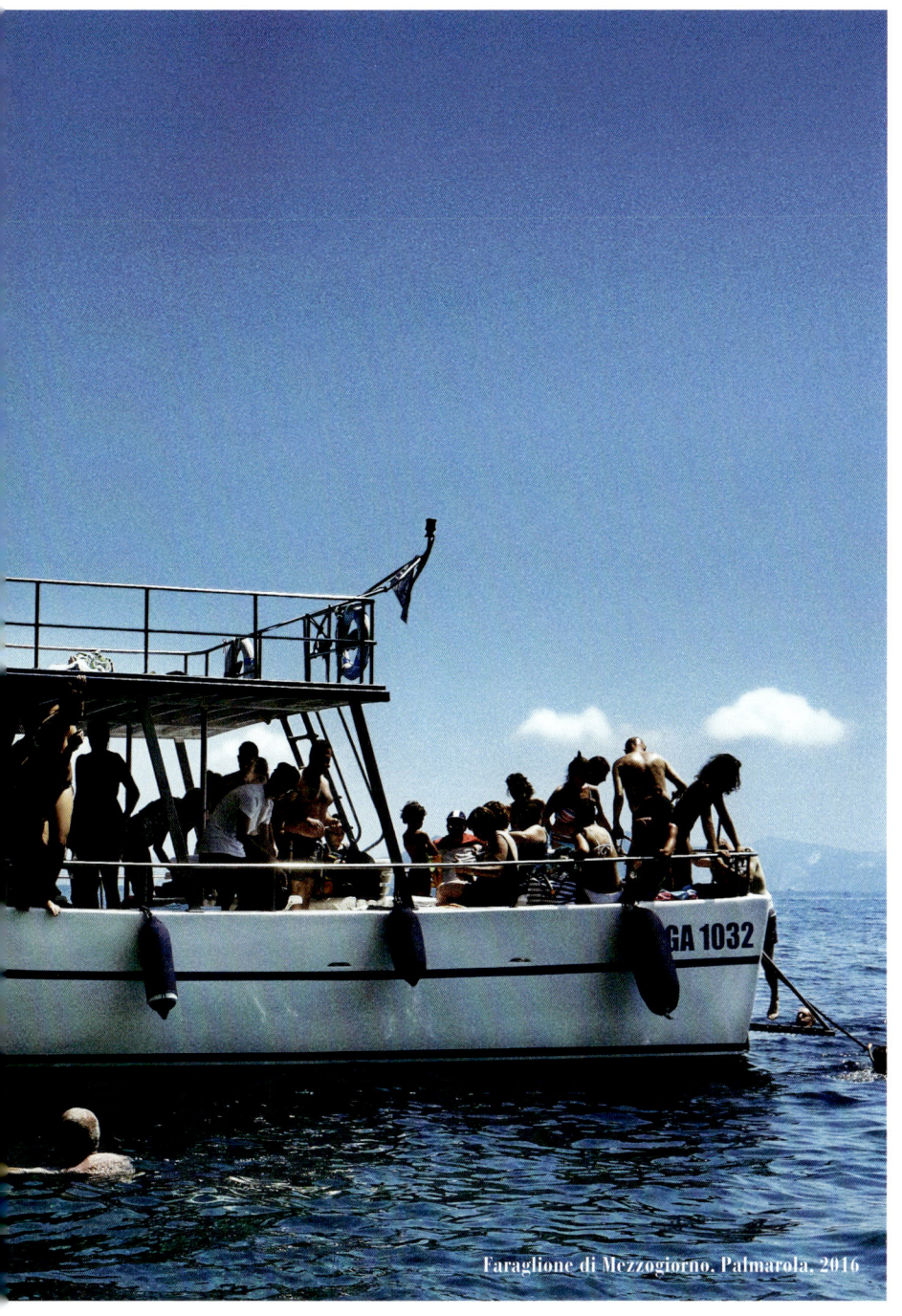

Faraglione di Mezzogiorno, Palmarola, 2016

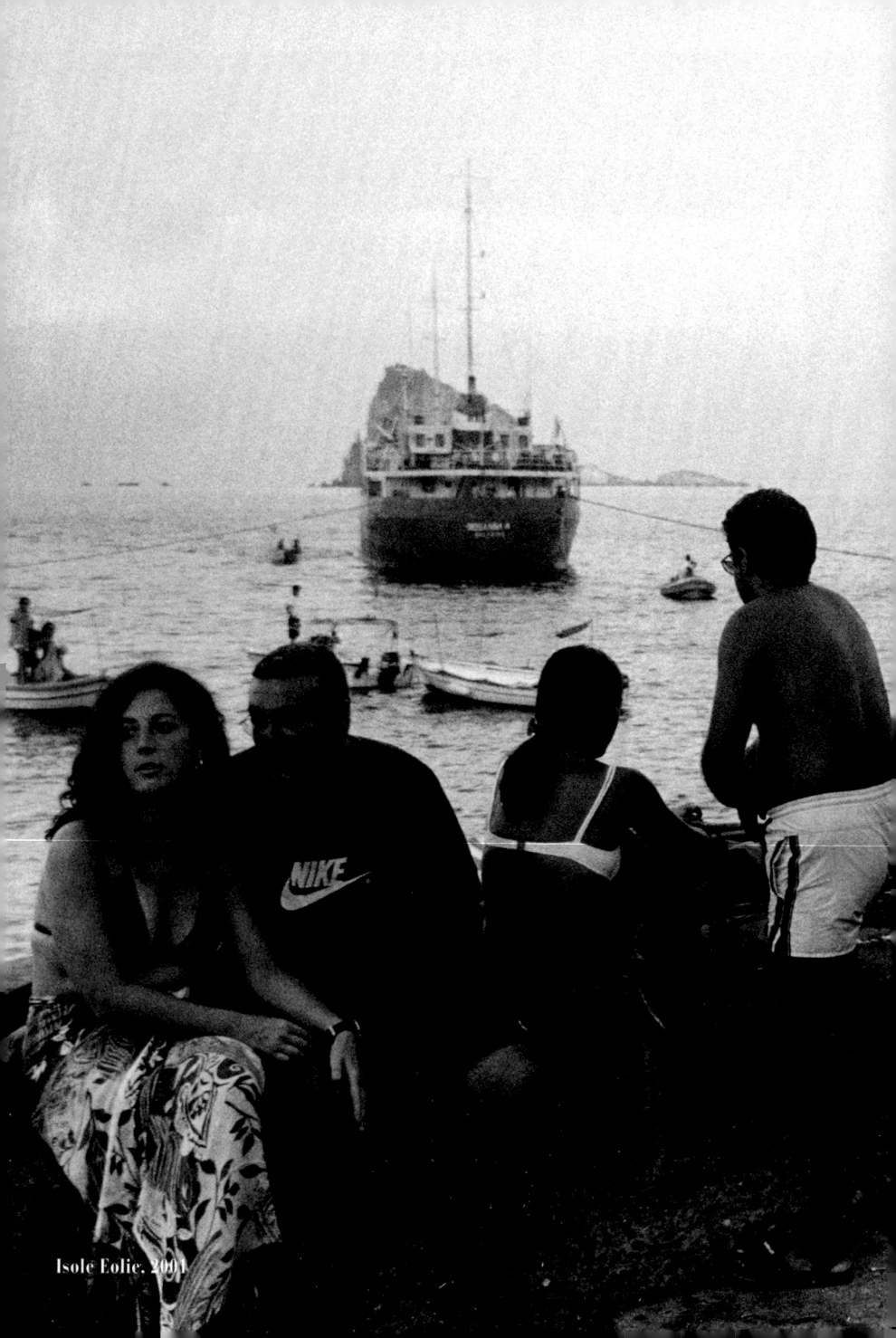

Isole Eolie, 2001

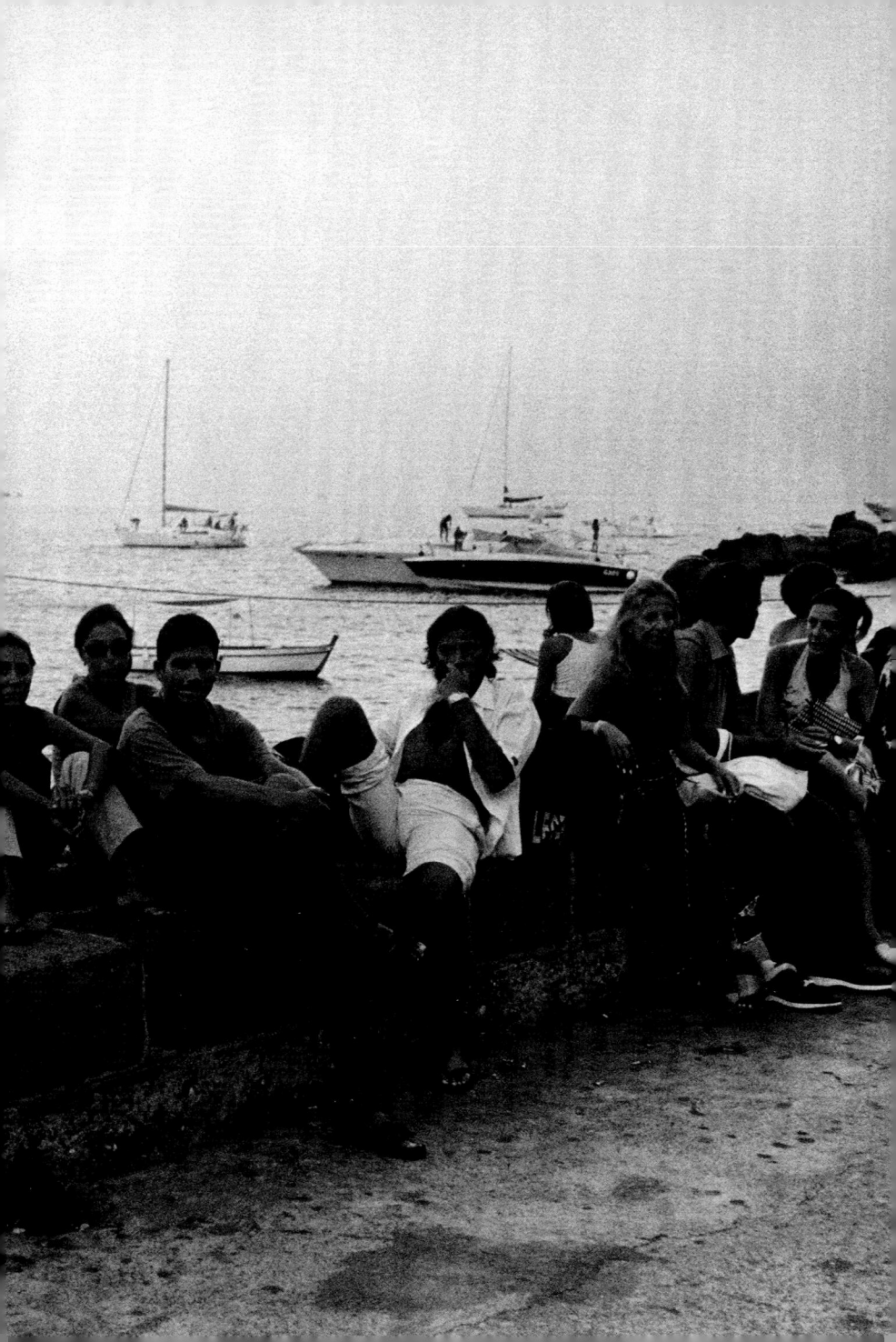

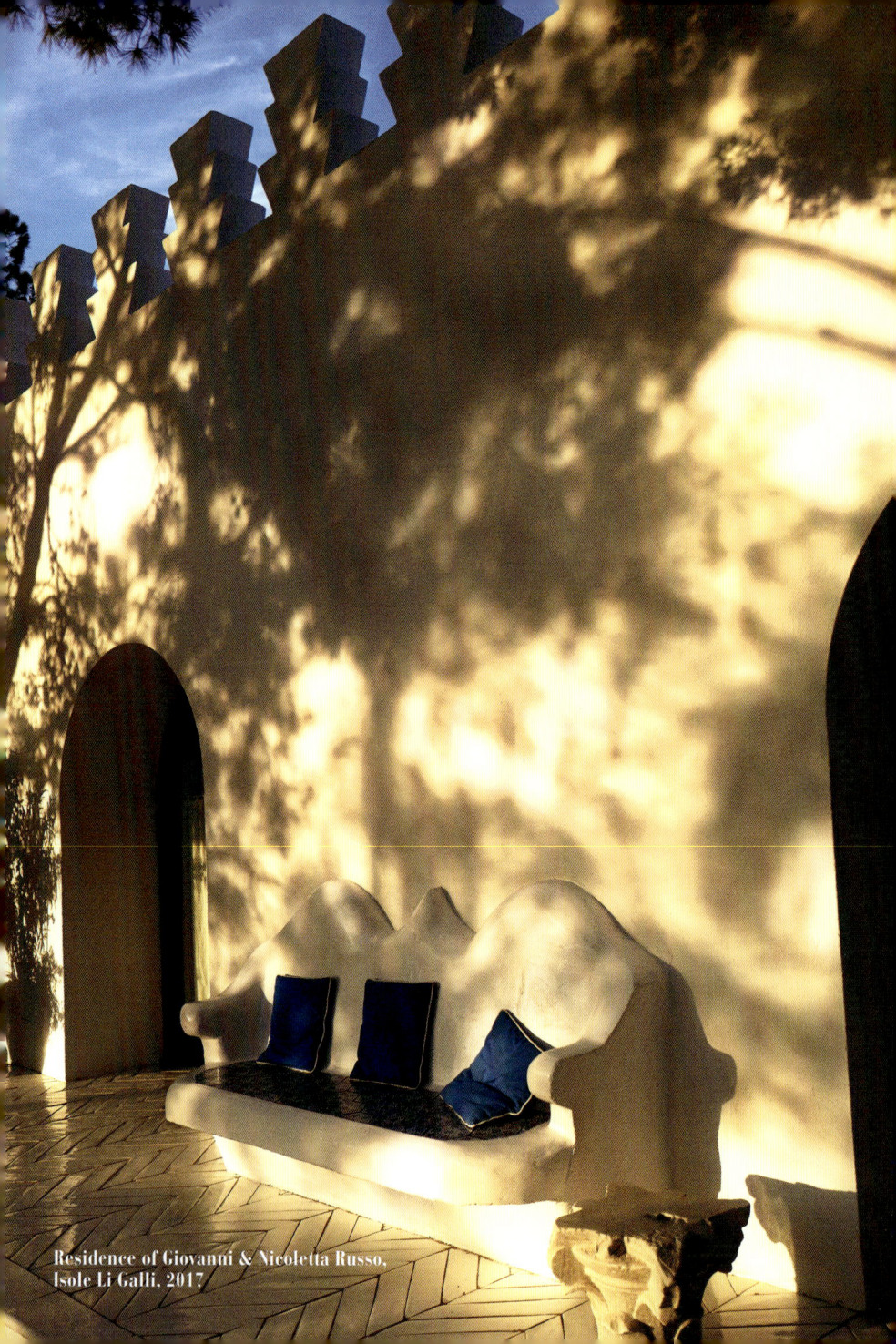

Residence of Giovanni & Nicoletta Russo,
Isole Li Galli, 2017

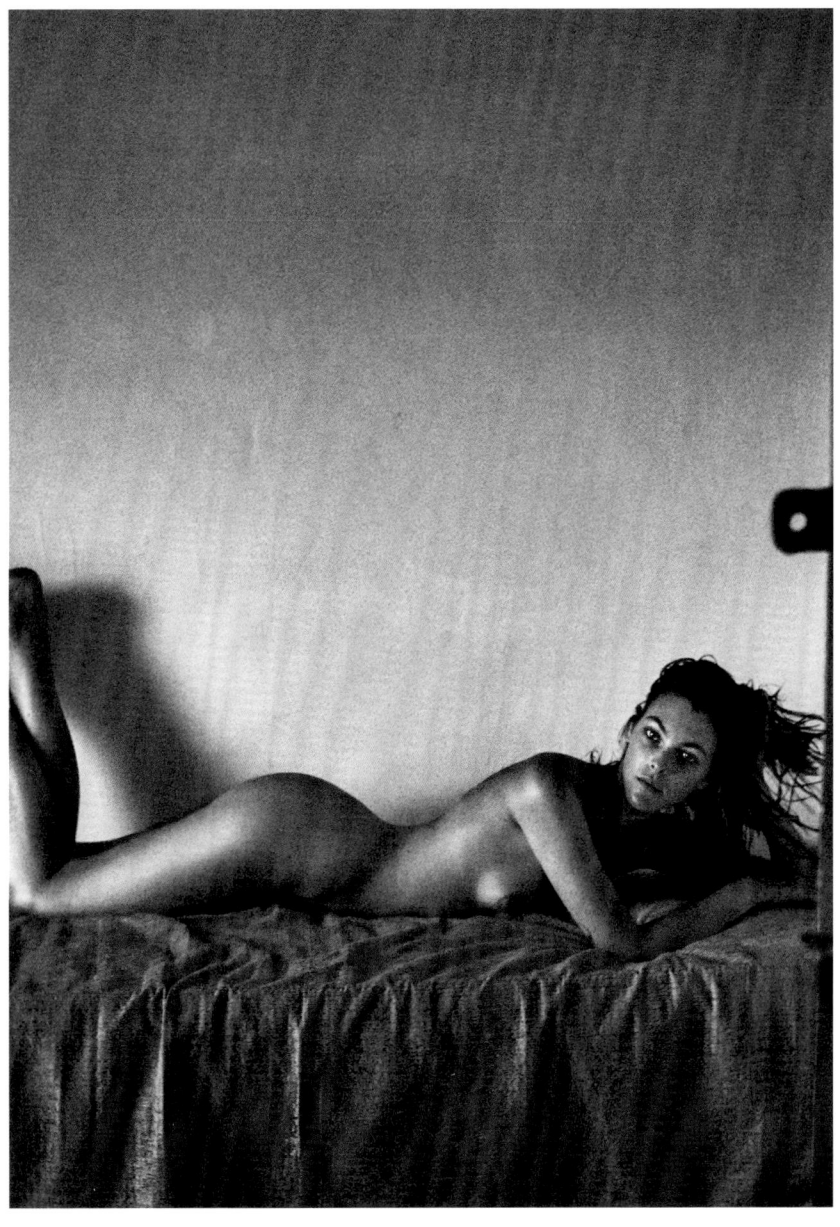

Vittoria Ceretti, Amalfi, 2017

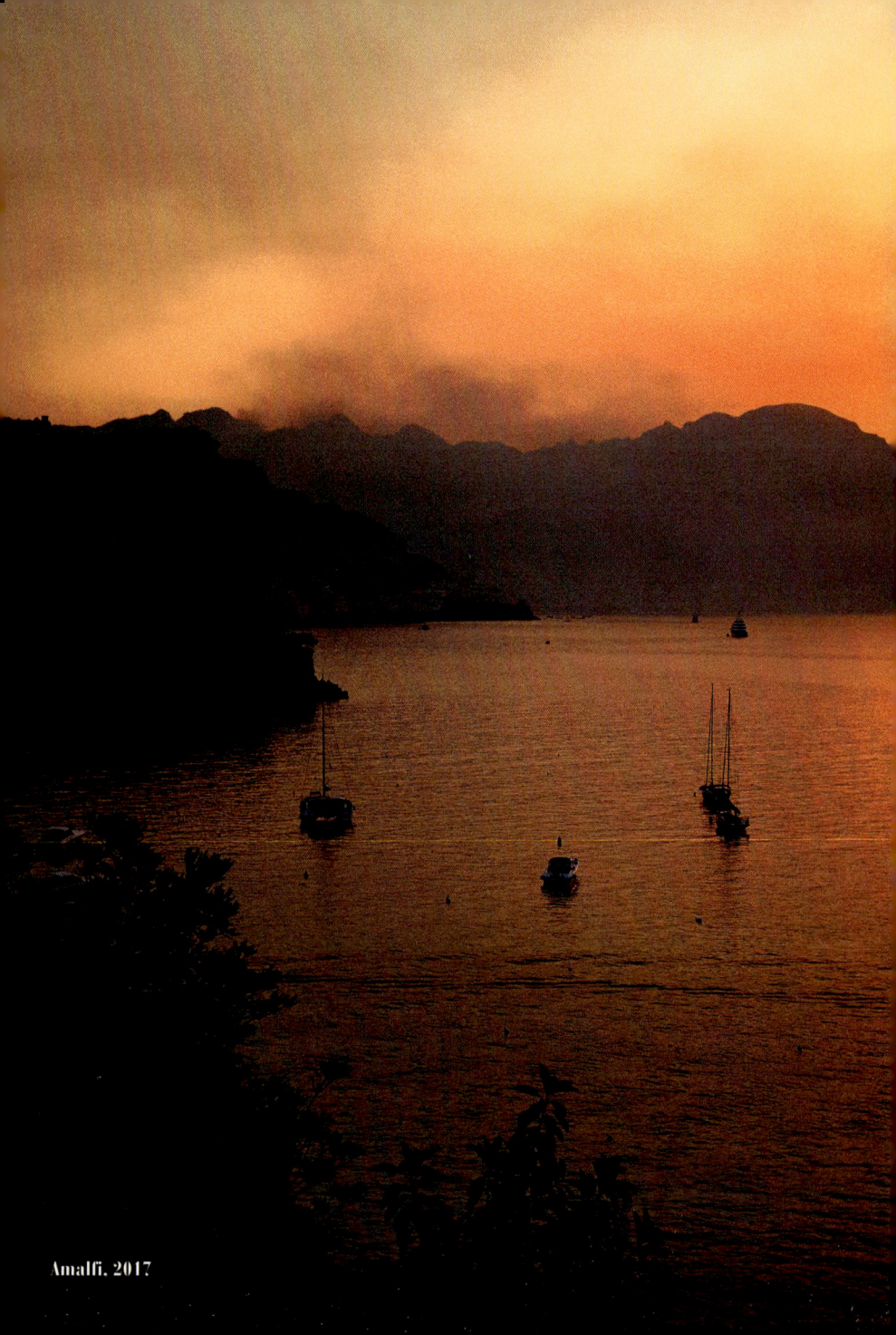

Amalfi. 2017

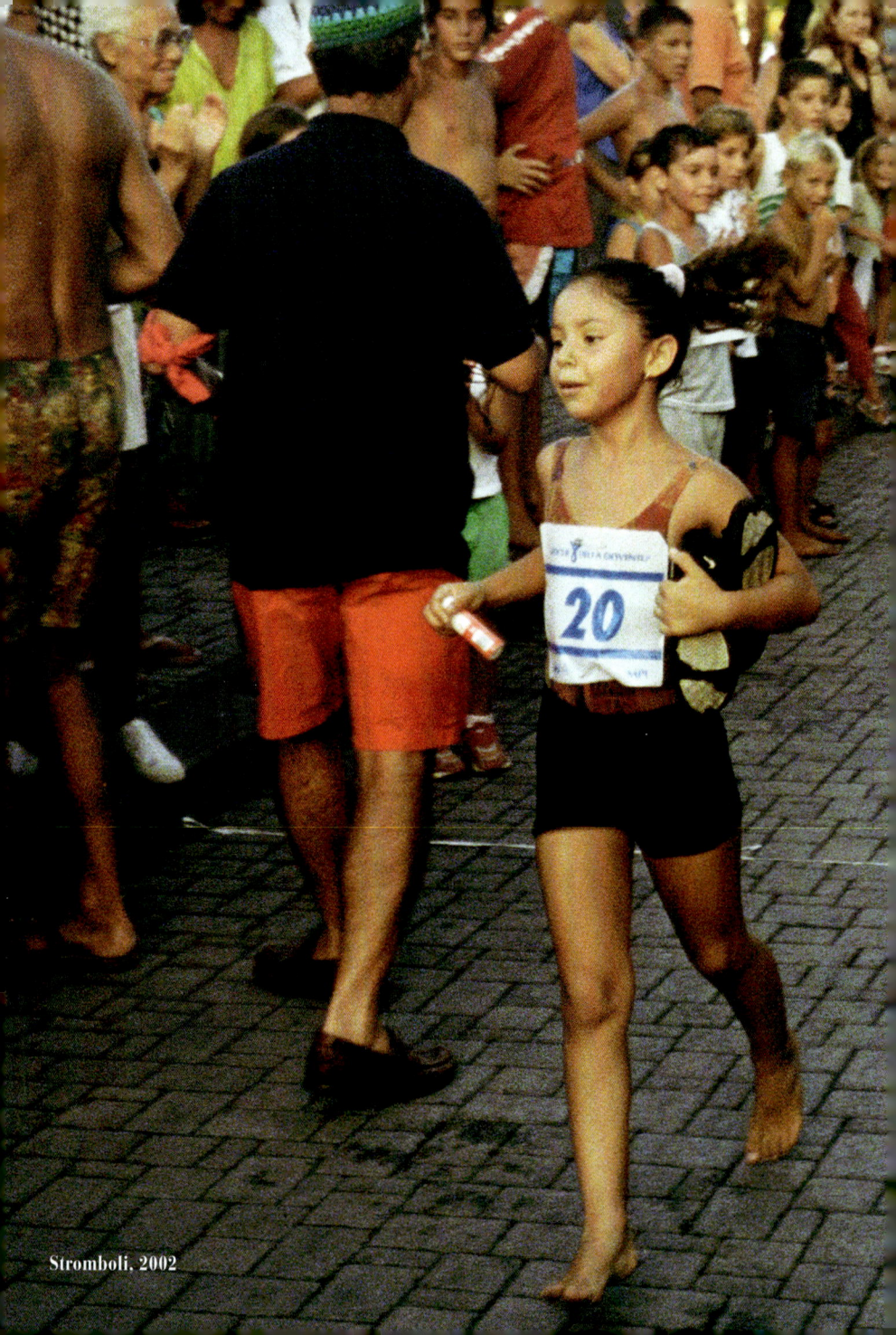

Stromboli, 2002

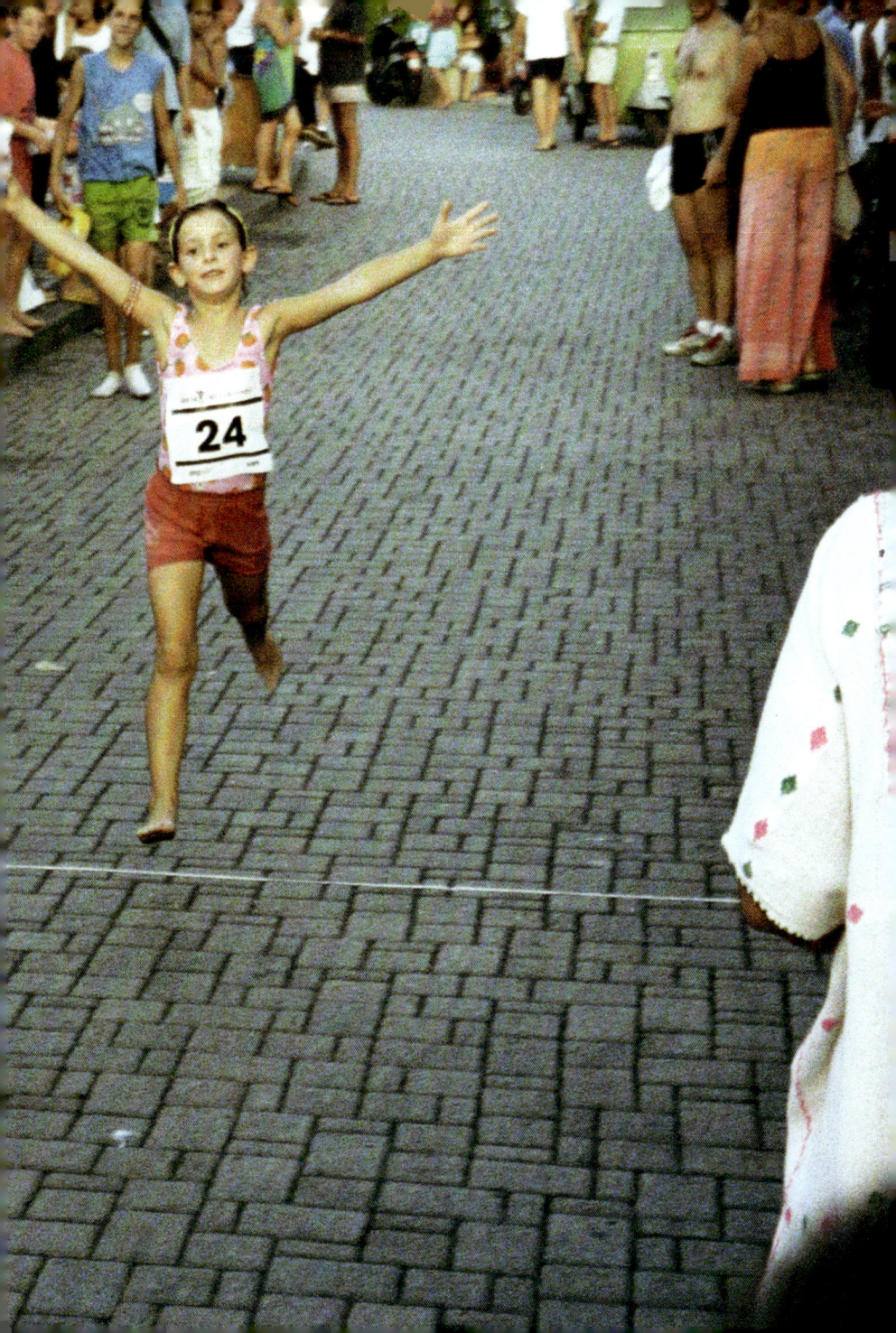

GRAZIE!

Jan Olesen

Emanuele Anselmi, Anastasia Barbieri, Alessandro Belgiojoso, Philip Bode,
Sciascia Gambaccini, Riccardo Lanza, Emanuele Mascioni, Generoso di Meo,
Antonio Monfreda, Benedikt Taschen, Antonieta Testino, Giovanni Testino.

Stefano Accorsi, Emmanuelle Alt, Giovanni Gaetani dell'Aquila d'Aragona, Pietro, Marella and
Giacomo Gaetani dell'Aquila d'Aragona, Pablo Ardizzone, Giorgio Armani, Contessa Bianca Savoia di
Savoia Aosta Arrivabene, Conte Giberto Arrivabene Valenti Gonzaga, Vera, Mafalda, Maddalena and
Viola Arrivabene, Nadja Auermann, Bianca Balti, Fabien Baron, Giovanna Battaglia Engelbert,
Antonio Baucina, Luisa Beccaria, Betty Bee, Monica Bellucci, Luchino, Lucilla, Lucrezia, Ludovico and
Luna Bonaccorsi, Lucio Bonaccorsi di Reburdone, Alessandra Borghese, Mariacarla Boscono,
Ben Bowers, Benedetta Brachetti Peretti, Bianca Brandolini, Gisele Bündchen, Naomi Campbell,
Francesco Carrozzini, Beatrice Borromeo Casiraghi, Pierre Casiraghi, Vittoria Ceretti,
Lucinda Chambers, Hayden Christensen, Andrew M. Giuda, Aurélie Claudel, George Clooney,
Grace Coddington, Louis Dellafaille, Domenico Dolce, Nadège Dubospertus, Sascha Eiblmayr,
Ginevra Elkann, Oscar Engelbert, Ernesto Esposito, Marisela Federici, Chiara Ferragni,
Emanuele Fiore, Federico Floriani, Vanna Fois, Stefano Gabbana, Sciascia Gambaccini, David Gandy,
Valentino Garavani, Val Garland, Björn Frederic Gerling, Yasmeen Ghauri, Pasquale Giacca,
Odile Gilbert, Luca, Eugenio, Ludovico and Lucilla Gnecchi Ruscone, Tonne Goodman, Gigi Hadid,
Marpessa Hennink, Eva Herzigová, Paris Hilton, Christiaan Houtenbos, Patrick Kinmonth,
Pedro Koechlin, Birgit Kos, Karolína Kurková, Marcus Kurz, Lady Gaga, Salim Langatta,
Giovanni Dario Laudicina, Anouck Lepère, Marc López, Sophia Loren, Elle Macpherson, Madonna,
Didier Malige, Keith Mallos, Stéphane Marais, Edoardo Marchiori, Italo and Tommaso Marzotto,
Emanuele Mascioni, Giacomo Leone Massimo-Brancaccio, Sam McKnight, Kristen McMenamy,
Suzy Menkes, Aaron de Mey, Sienna Miller, Flavio Misciattelli, Angela Missoni, Margherita Missoni,
Nicola Monari, Kay Montano, Luigi Murenu, Ottavio Nieddu, Morten Nielsen, Tom Pecheux,
Peter Philips, Anna Piaggi, Famiglia Piromallo Capece Piscicelli di Montebello dei Duchi di Capracotta,
Patty Pravo, Gawain Rainey, Matilde Rastelli, Umberto Raucci, Frankie Rayder, Jean-Louis Remilleux,
Julia Roberts, Carine Roitfeld, Isabella Rossellini, Anna Dello Russo, Giovanni Russo, Nicoletta Russo,
Carlo Santamaria, Andrea Santarelli, Riccardo Scamarcio, Claudia Schiffer, Akki Shirakawa,
Alexandra Shulman, Franca Sozzani, Charlotte Stockdale, Simone Susinna, His Excellency Monsignor
Francesco Pio Tamburrino, Nicola Tartaglione, Marlene Taschen, Fernanda Tavares, Carla Testino,
Elena Testino, Giuliana Testino, Gloria, Princess of Thurn and Taxis, Charlotte Tilbury,
Marco Di Vaio, Amber Valletta, Donatella Versace, Gianni Versace, Francesco Vezzoli,
Edita Vilkevičiūtė, Natalia Vodianova, Alex Waltl, Alex White, Anna Wintour.

Belmond Hotel Splendido, Comune di Cagliari, Calendario Pirelli, Comune di Siena,
Contrada della Torre, Edmiston Boats, Napoli, Fondazione Gianfranco Ferré,
Galleria Nazionale d'Arte Moderna, Roma, Hotel d'Inghilterra, Hotel de Bauer, Hotel de Russie,
Hotel Excelsior, Hotel Il Pellicano, Ministero per i Beni e le Attività Culturali –
Museo Archeologico Nazionale di Napoli, Palazzo Gritti, Teatro Massimo Comunale, Siracusa.